English Prose and Criticism in the Nineteenth Century

AMERICAN LITERATURE, ENGLISH LITERATURE, AND WORLD LITERATURES IN ENGLISH: AN INFORMATION GUIDE SERIES

Series Editor: Theodore Grieder, Curator, Division of Special Collections, Fales Library, New York University, New York, New York

Associate Editor: Duane DeVries, Associate Professor, Polytechnic Institute of New York, Brooklyn, New York

Other books on English literature in this series:

AUTHOR NEWSLETTERS AND JOURNALS—*Edited by Margaret Patterson**

ENGLISH DRAMA TO 1660 (EXCLUDING SHAKESPEARE)—*Edited by Frieda Elaine Penninger*

ENGLISH DRAMA, 1660-1800—*Edited by Frederick M. Link*

ENGLISH DRAMA AND THEATRE, 1800-1900—*Edited by L.W. Conolly and J.P. Wearing*

ENGLISH DRAMA, 1900-1950—*Edited by E.H. Mikhail*

ENGLISH FICTION, 1660-1800—*Edited by Jerry C. Beasley*

ENGLISH FICTION, 1800-1850—*Edited by Duane DeVries**

ENGLISH NOVEL, 1851-1900—*Edited by Robert Schweik and Albert Dunn**

CONTEMPORARY FICTION IN AMERICA AND ENGLAND, 1950-1970—*Edited by Alfred F. Rosa and Paul A. Echholz*

OLD AND MIDDLE ENGLISH POETRY TO 1500—*Edited by Walter H. Beale*

VICTORIAN POETRY, 1835-1900—*Edited by Ronald E. Freeman**

ENGLISH PROSE, PROSE FICTION, AND CRITICISM TO 1660—*Edited by S.K. Heninger, Jr.*

ENGLISH PROSE AND CRITICISM, 1660-1800—*Edited by John J. Shawcross**

ENGLISH PROSE AND CRITICISM, 1900-1950—*Edited by Christopher C. Brown and William B. Thesing**

ENGLISH LITERARY JOURNAL TO 1900—*Edited by Robert B. White, Jr.*

ENGLISH LITERARY JOURNAL, 1900-1950—*Edited by Michael N. Stanton**

*in preparation

The above series is part of the
GALE INFORMATION GUIDE LIBRARY

The Library consists of a number of separate series of guides covering major areas in the social sciences, humanities, and current affairs.

General Editor: Paul Wasserman, Professor and former Dean, School of Library and Information Services, University of Maryland

Managing Editor: Denise Allard Adzigian, Gale Research Company

English Prose and Criticism in the Nineteenth Century

A GUIDE TO INFORMATION SOURCES

Volume 18 in the American Literature, English Literature, and World Literatures in English Information Guide Series

Harris W. Wilson

Department of English
University of Illinois
Urbana

Diane Long Hoeveler

Department of English
University of Louisville
Louisville, Kentucky

Gale Research Company
Book Tower, Detroit, Michigan 48226

Library of Congress Cataloging in Publication Data

Wilson, Harris Ward, 1919-
    English prose and criticism in the nineteenth century.

    (American literature, English literature, and world literatures in English; v. 18)
    Bibliography: p. 437
    Includes index.
    1. English prose literature—19th century—Bibliography.
I. Hoeveler, Diane Long, joint author. II. Title.
Z2014.P795W54   [PR771]   016.08   73-17500
ISBN 0-8103-1235-2

Copyright © 1979 by
Harris W. Wilson and Diane Long Hoeveler

No part of this book may be reproduced in any form without permission in writing from the publisher, except by a reviewer who wishes to quote brief passages or entries in connection with a review written for inclusion in a magazine or newspaper. Manufactured in the United States of America.

VITAE

Harris W. Wilson is a professor of late Victorian and early twentieth-century English literature at the University of Illinois, where he received his Ph.D. in 1953. He has written articles on Henry James, H.G. Wells, and various aspects of the teaching of composition. He has edited ARNOLD BENNETT AND H.G. WELLS: A RECORD OF A PERSONAL AND LITERARY FRIENDSHIP (1960), and is currently working on a study of Wells and the Fabians.

Diane Long Hoeveler received her Ph.D. in English in 1976 from the University of Illinois. She has taught at Alverno College, the University of Illinois, and the University of Wisconsin-Milwaukee, and has published articles on Charlotte Brontë, Richard Wright, and Arthur Miller. She is currently an assistant professor of English at the University of Louisville.

CONTENTS

Acknowledgments ix

Introduction xi

Table of Abbreviations xiii

1. Basic Surveys and Reference Works 1
   A. Bibliographies 1
   B. Literary Histories and Anthologies 6

2. Background 13
   A. Literary 13
   B. Cultural 24

3. Individual Authors 35

   Critical, Philosophical, Polemical
   Matthew Arnold (1822-88) 39
   Walter Bagehot (1826-77) 64
   Jeremy Bentham (1748-1832) 73
   Samuel Butler (1835-1902) 80
   Thomas Carlyle (1795-1881) 88
   William Cobbett (1763-1835) 108
   Samuel Taylor Coleridge (1772-1834) 114
   Thomas De Quincey (1785-1859) 139
   William Godwin (1756-1836) 147
   William Hazlitt (1778-1830) 154
   Leigh Hunt (1784-1859) 163
   Charles Lamb (1775-1834) 171
   Walter Savage Landor (1775-1864) 180
   John Stuart Mill (1806-73) 186
   William Morris (1834-96) 205
   Leslie Stephen (1832-1904) 216
   Robert Louis Stevenson (1850-94) 221

   Aesthetic
   Walter Horatio Pater (1839-94) 233
   John Ruskin (1819-1900) 245

Contents

Historical
James Anthony Froude (1818-94) 261
Thomas Babington Macaulay (1800-1859) 264

Journalistic
Francis Jeffrey (1773-1850) 275
Sydney Smith (1771-1845) 279
John Wilson ["Christopher North"] (1785-1854) 283

Religious
Richard Hurrell Froude (1803-36) 289
John Keble (1792-1866) 291
John Henry Newman (1801-90) 294
Edward Bouverie Pusey (1800-1882) 316
William Wilberforce (1759-1833) 318

Scientific
Charles Darwin (1809-82) 323
Thomas Henry Huxley (1825-95) 335
Herbert Spencer (1820-1903) 342

Travel
George Borrow (1803-81) 349
Richard Burton (1821-90) 354

4. Nineteenth-Century Periodicals: Guides and Studies 359

Author Index 369

Title Index 386

Subject Index 413

ACKNOWLEDGMENTS

The coauthors wish to acknowledge specifically the patient assistance of Sonia Carringer, David Hoeveler, Sister André Kroupa, and the staffs of the Interlibrary Loan services of both Alverno College and the University of Wisconsin-Milwaukee, as well as the careful editorial assistance of Professors Theodore Grieder and Duane DeVries.

INTRODUCTION

This information guide, a compilation of primary and secondary materials on major nineteenth-century writers of prose and criticism, is intended as an aid to researchers and students working in the field. The first section of this book consists of basic surveys and reference works:

    A. Bibliographies: including general bibliographies such as the MODERN LANGUAGE ASSOCIATION INTERNATIONAL and the NEW CAMBRIDGE BIBLIOGRAPHY OF ENGLISH LITERATURE and others more directly devoted to nineteenth-century studies.

    B. Literary Histories and Anthologies: including those works that provide a general historical background indispensable to an understanding of the nineteenth century, as well as anthologies containing primary writings by nineteenth-century writers of prose and criticism.

The second section deals with background:

    A. Literary: including major studies in romantic and Victorian literature. Most of these works treat more than one author and are concerned with trends in literary history. There are a few references to individual authors in collections of essays, so the reader should consult the index for additional entries on individual authors.

    B. Cultural: including social, economic, religious, political, and intellectual histories that describe the complex cultural milieu in which the literature under consideration was written.

The third, and largest section of this guide is concerned with thirty-four individual authors, about whom the following information is given:

    1. Principal Prose Works: listed according to the date of their first English publication. Such genres as poetry or drama, which are considered in other Gale guides, are excluded.

    2. Collected Works: including standard, definitive collections, as well as anthologies exclusively devoted to a particular author.

Introduction

These are listed alphabetically by title.

3. Letters: including both collections of letters in book format and critical studies in journals that present previously unpublished correspondence. These are listed alphabetically under authors of critical studies and titles of letters collected in book format.

4. Biographies: listed alphabetically by biographer.

5. Critical Studies: listed alphabetically by author, these studies are necessarily selective. They have been chosen on two principles: first, the focus is on prose writings exclusive of other literary genres; therefore, critical studies on the poetry of Coleridge are not included except as they are relevant to an understanding of his prose. Second, the emphasis is on recent critical studies--published since 1960 and supplementing already extant bibliographies--with some attention, however, to earlier major studies that may be considered indispensable to an understanding of a writer's work.

6. Bibliographies: including, when available, the standard, definitive bibliography of an author's work and useful bibliographical essays and checklists. These are listed alphabetically by author or editor.

It should be pointed out that the selection of secondary titles in this book is in itself a critical function. The emphasis on recent publications carries this guide into the present; selected resources and annotations aim at representing in one volume materials essential for both general and specific work in the prose of the period.

TABLE OF ABBREVIATIONS

ABR	AMERICAN BENEDICTINE REVIEW
AHR	AMERICAN HISTORICAL REVIEW
AL	AMERICAN LITERATURE
AM	ATLANTIC MONTHLY
AN	ACTA NEOPHILOLOGIA
APQ	AMERICAN PHILOSOPHICAL QUARTERLY
AQ	AMERICAN QUARTERLY
AR	ANTIGONISH REVIEW
AS	AMERICAN SCHOLAR
ATQ	AMERICAN TRANSCENDENTAL QUARTERLY
AUMLA	JOURNAL OF THE AUSTRALASIAN UNIVERSITIES LANGUAGE AND LITERATURE ASSOCIATION
AWR	ANGLO-WELSH REVIEW
BAASB	BRITISH ASSOCIATION FOR AMERICAN STUDIES BULLETIN
BB	BULLETIN OF BIBLIOGRAPHY
BC	BOOK COLLECTOR
BHM	BULLETIN OF THE HISTORY OF MEDICINE
BI	BOOKS AT IOWA
BJA	BRITISH JOURNAL OF AESTHETICS
BJRL	BULLETIN OF THE JOHN RYLANDS LIBRARY
BN	BLAKE NEWSLETTER
BNYPL	BULLETIN OF THE NEW YORK PUBLIC LIBRARY
BR	BUCKNELL REVIEW
BSE	BRNO STUDIES IN ENGLISH

Abbreviations

BSUF	BALL STATE UNIVERSITY FORUM
BYUS	BRIGHAM YOUNG UNIVERSITY STUDIES
CAJ	CAMBRIDGE JOURNAL
CBEL	CAMBRIDGE BIBLIOGRAPHY OF ENGLISH LITERATURE
CCC	COLLEGE COMPOSITION AND COMMUNICATION
CE	COLLEGE ENGLISH
CG	COLLOQUIA GERMANICA
CH	CHURCH HISTORY
CHQ	CHURCH QUARTERLY
CHR	CATHOLIC HISTORICAL REVIEW
CJ	CLASSICAL JOURNAL
CL	COMPARATIVE LITERATURE
CLAJ	COLLEGE LANGUAGE ASSOCIATION JOURNAL
CLB	CHARLES LAMB BULLETIN
ClioW	CLIO (University of Wisconsin)
CLJ	CORNELL LIBRARY JOURNAL
CLS	COMPARATIVE LITERATURE STUDIES
COR	CONTEMPORARY REVIEW
CQ	CAMBRIDGE QUARTERLY
CQR	CHURCH QUARTERLY REVIEW
CR	CENTENNIAL REVIEW
CRQ	CRITICAL QUARTERLY
DA	DISSERTATION ABSTRACTS
DAI	DISSERTATION ABSTRACTS INTERNATIONAL
DOR	DOWNSIDE REVIEW
DR	DALHOUSIE REVIEW
DSN	DICKENS STUDIES NEWSLETTER
DUR	DUBLIN REVIEW
EA	ETUDES ANGLAISES
E&S	ESSAYS AND STUDIES BY MEMBERS OF THE ENGLISH ASSOCIATION
ECS	EIGHTEENTH-CENTURY STUDIES
EDH	ESSAYS BY DIVERS HANDS
EFT	ENGLISH FICTION IN TRANSITION; superseded by ELT

Abbreviations

EHR	ENGLISH HISTORICAL REVIEW
EIC	ESSAYS IN CRITICISM
EJ	ECONOMIC JOURNAL
ELH	ENGLISH LITERARY HISTORY
ELN	ENGLISH LANGUAGE NOTES
ELT	ENGLISH LITERATURE IN TRANSITION
EM	ENGLISH MISCELLANY
ES	ENGLISH STUDIES
ESA	ENGLISH STUDIES IN AFRICA
ESQ	EMERSON SOCIETY QUARTERLY
EUQ	EMORY UNIVERSITY QUARTERLY
FF	FOLKLORE FORUM
FH	FORUM HOUSTON
FR	FORTNIGHTLY REVIEW
FSUS	FLORIDA STATE UNIVERSITY STUDIES
GL&L	GERMAN LIFE AND LETTERS
HAB	HUMANITIES ASSOCIATION BULLETIN
HIJ	HISTORICAL JOURNAL
HINL	HISTORY OF IDEAS NEWSLETTER
HLB	HARVARD LIBRARY BULLETIN
HLQ	HUNTINGTON LIBRARY QUARTERLY
HMPEC	HISTORICAL MAGAZINE OF THE PROTESTANT EPISCOPAL CHURCH
HR	HUDSON REVIEW
HSL	HARTFORD STUDIES IN LITERATURE
HT	HISTORY TODAY
HTR	HARVARD THEOLOGICAL REVIEW
IJES	INDIAN JOURNAL OF ENGLISH STUDIES
IQ	ILLINOIS QUARTERLY
ISE	IBADAN STUDIES IN ENGLISH
J	JOURNAL
JAAC	JOURNAL OF AESTHETICS AND ART CRITICISM
JBS	JOURNAL OF BRITISH STUDIES
JC	JOURNAL OF COMMUNICATION

Abbreviations

JEGP	JOURNAL OF ENGLISH AND GERMAN PHILOLOGY
JEH	JOURNAL OF ECCLESIASTICAL HISTORY
JGE	JOURNAL OF GENERAL EDUCATION
JGLS	JOURNAL OF THE GYPSY LORE SOCIETY
JHI	JOURNAL OF THE HISTORY OF IDEAS
JHP	JOURNAL OF THE HISTORY OF PHILOSOPHY
JJQ	JAMES JOYCE QUARTERLY
JNH	JOURNAL OF NEGRO HISTORY
JP	JOURNAL OF POLITICS
JQ	JOURNALISM QUARTERLY
JR	JOURNAL OF RELIGION
JRUL	JOURNAL OF RUTGERS UNIVERSITY LIBRARY
JSSR	JOURNAL OF THE SCIENTIFIC STUDY OF RELIGION
JWMS	JOURNAL OF THE WILLIAM MORRIS SOCIETY
KJ	KIPLING JOURNAL
KR	KENYON REVIEW
KSJ	KEATS-SHELLEY JOURNAL
KSMB	KEATS-SHELLEY MEMORIAL BULLETIN
L&I	LITERATURE AND IDEOLOGY
L&P	LITERATURE AND PSYCHOLOGY
L&S	LANGUAGE AND STYLE
LC	LITERARY CRITERION
LCUT	LIBRARY CHRONICLE OF THE UNIVERSITY OF TEXAS
LHB	LOCK HAVEN BULLETIN
LHR	LOCK HAVEN REVIEW
MA	MODERN AGE
MCNR	MACNEESE REVIEW
MFS	MODERN FICTION STUDIES
MIA	MICHIGAN ACADEMICIAN
MIQ	MISSISSIPPI QUARTERLY
MLA	MODERN LANGUAGE ASSOCIATION
MLN	MODERN LANGUAGE NOTES
MLQ	MODERN LANGUAGE QUARTERLY
MLR	MODERN LANGUAGE REVIEW

Abbreviations

MNL	MILL NEWSLETTER
MP	MODERN PHILOLOGY
MQ	MUSICAL QUARTERLY
MS	MONASTIC STUDIES
MSE	MASSACHUSETTS STUDIES IN ENGLISH
N&Q	NOTES AND QUERIES
NC	NINETEENTH CENTURY
NCBEL	NEW CAMBRIDGE BIBLIOGRAPHY OF ENGLISH LITERATURE
NCF	NINETEENTH-CENTURY FICTION
NDQ	NORTH DAKOTA QUARTERLY
NEO	NEOPHILOLOGUS
NLB	NEWBERRY LIBRARY BULLETIN
NLH	NEW LITERATURE HISTORY
NM	NEUPHILOGISCHE MITTEILUNGEN
NS	DIE NEUEREN SPRACHEN
NSC	NEW SCHOLASTICISM
NST	NEW STATESMAN
NYRB	NEW YORK REVIEW OF BOOKS
NYTBR	NEW YORK TIMES BOOK REVIEW
OL	ORBIS LITTERARUM
PAAS	PROCEEDINGS OF THE AMERICAN ANTIQUARIAN SOCIETY
PAPS	PROCEEDINGS OF THE AMERICAN PHILOSOPHICAL SOCIETY
PBA	PROCEEDINGS OF THE BRITISH ACADEMY
PBSA	PAPERS OF THE BIBLIOGRAPHICAL SOCIETY OF AMERICA
PEGS	PUBLICATIONS OF THE ENGLISH GOETHE SOCIETY
PERSON	PERSONALIST
PHR	PHILOSOPHICAL REVIEW
PLL	PAPERS ON LANGUAGE AND LITERATURE
PMLA	PUBLICATIONS OF THE MODERN LANGUAGE ASSOCIATION
PPR	PHILOSOPHY AND PHENOMENOLOGICAL RESEARCH
PQ	PHILOLOGICAL QUARTERLY
PR	PSYCHOANALYTIC REVIEW
PS	POLITICAL STUDIES
PSQ	POLITICAL SCIENCE QUARTERLY

Abbreviations

Q	QUARTERLY
QJS	QUARTERLY JOURNAL OF SPEECH
QNL	QUARTERLY NEWSLETTER
QQ	QUEEN'S QUARTERLY
QR	QUARTERLY REVIEW
R	REVIEW
REL	REVIEW OF ENGLISH LITERATURE
REN	RENASCENCE
RES	REVIEW OF ENGLISH STUDIES
RLC	REVUE DE LITTERATURE COMPAREE
RMS	RENAISSANCE & MODERN STUDIES
RP	REVIEW OF POLITICS
RRL	REVUE ROUMAINE DE LINGUISTIQUE
RS	RELIGIOUS STUDIES
RUO	REVUE DE L'UNIVERSITIE D'OTTAWA
RUS	RICE UNIVERSITY STUDIES
SAB	SOUTH ATLANTIC BULLETIN
SAQ	SOUTH ATLANTIC QUARTERLY
SAR	SATURDAY REVIEW
SB	STUDIES IN BIBLIOGRAPHY
SBHT	STUDIES IN BURKE AND HIS TIME
SCB	SOUTH CENTRAL BULLETIN
SCUL	SOUNDINGS: COLLECTIONS OF THE UNIVERSITY LIBRARY, UNIVERSITY OF CALIFORNIA, SANTA BARBARA
SE	STUDIES IN ENGLISH
SEL	STUDIES IN ENGLISH LITERATURE, 1500-1900
SGG	STUDIA GERMANICA GANDENSIA
SHJB	SHAKESPEARE JAHRBUCH
SHN	SHAKESPEARE NEWSLETTER
SHR	SOUTHERN HUMANITIES REVIEW
SHS	SHAKESPEARE SURVEY
SIR	STUDIES IN ROMANTICISM
SLI	STUDIES IN THE LITERARY IMAGINATION
SM	SPEECH MONOGRAPHS

Abbreviations

SNL	SATIRE NEWSLETTER
SNNTS	STUDIES IN THE NOVEL (North Texas State)
SOQ	SOUTHERN QUARTERLY
SOR	SOUTHERN REVIEW
SORA	SOUTHERN REVIEW: AUSTRALIAN JOURNAL OF LITERARY STUDIES
SP	STUDIES IN PHILOLOGY
SQ	SHAKESPEARE QUARTERLY
SR	SEWANEE REVIEW
SS	SCANDINAVIAN STUDIES
SSF	STUDIES IN SHORT FICTION
SSJ	SOUTHERN SPEECH JOURNAL
SSL	STUDIES IN SCOTTISH LITERATURE
SV&EC	STUDIES IN VOLTAIRE AND THE EIGHTEENTH CENTURY
TC	TWENTIETH CENTURY
TCBS	TRANSACTIONS OF THE CAMBRIDGE BIBLIOGRAPHICAL SOCIETY
TKR	TAMKANG REVIEW SOCIETY
TLS	TIMES LITERARY SUPPLEMENT
TQ	TEXAS QUARTERLY
TS	THEOLOGICAL STUDIES
TSE	TULANE STUDIES IN ENGLISH
TSLL	TEXAS STUDIES IN LITERATURE AND LANGUAGE
TWA	TRANSACTIONS OF THE WISCONSIN ACADEMY OF SCIENCES, ARTS, AND LETTERS
UDR	UNIVERSITY OF DAYTON REVIEW
UMSE	UNIVERSITY OF MISSISSIPPI STUDIES IN ENGLISH
UR	UNIVERSITY REVIEW
USE	UNISA STUDIES IN ENGLISH
UTQ	UNIVERSITY OF TORONTO QUARTERLY
UTSE	UNIVERSITY OF TEXAS STUDIES IN ENGLISH
VN	VICTORIAN NEWSLETTER
VP	VICTORIAN POETRY
VPN	VICTORIAN PERIODICALS NEWSLETTER
VQR	VIRGINIA QUARTERLY REVIEW
VS	VICTORIAN STUDIES

Abbreviations

WAR	WASCANA REVIEW
WC	WORDSWORTH CIRCLE
WHR	WESTERN HUMANITIES REVIEW
WPQ	WESTERN POLITICAL QUARTERLY
WR	WISEMAN REVIEW
WS	WESTERN SPEECH
WVUPP	WEST VIRGINIA UNIVERSITY PHILOLOGICAL PAPERS
XUS	XAVIER UNIVERSITY STUDIES
YES	YEARBOOK OF ENGLISH STUDIES
YFS	YALE FRENCH STUDIES
YR	YALE REVIEW
ZAA	ZEITSCHRIFT FUR ANGLISTIK UND AMERIKANISTIK

1. BASIC SURVEYS AND REFERENCE WORKS

A. BIBLIOGRAPHIES

Altholz, Josef Lewis, ed. VICTORIAN ENGLAND, 1837-1901. Cambridge: Conference on British Studies for the University Press, 1970.

An extremely useful bibliography that groups material under such topics as "Social History," "Religious History," and "Intellectual History."

Altick, Richard D., and William R. Matthews, eds. GUIDE TO DOCTORAL DISSERTATIONS IN VICTORIAN LITERATURE, 1886-1958. Urbana: University of Illinois Press, 1960.

Dissertations are grouped under such headings as "Themes and Intellectual Influences," "Literary Criticism," and "Individual Authors."

ANNUAL BIBLIOGRAPHY OF ENGLISH LANGUAGE AND LITERATURE. Cambridge, Mass.: Modern Humanities Research Association, 1920-- .

Includes bibliographical listings according to author, but contains no critical commentary.

Bateson, Frederick W. A GUIDE TO ENGLISH LITERATURE. 2nd ed. Chicago: Aldine Publishing Co., 1968.

Contains bibliographical information on general literary history and criticism, as well as sections on romantic and Victorian literature.

Bateson, Frederick W., et al., eds. THE CAMBRIDGE BIBLIOGRAPHY OF ENGLISH LITERATURE. 4 vols. Cambridge: At the University Press, 1940; supplement, 1957.

Volume 3 contains extensive bibliographical information on authors writing between 1800 and 1900. Has been largely superseded by Watson (NCBEL, vol. 3), below. However, should be retained for nonliterary sections and Commonwealth literatures dropped from NCBEL.

Basic Surveys and Reference Works

Batho, Edith C., et al., eds. "Summary of Periodical Literature." RES, 1925-- . Annual.

> Batho began this listing of articles published in English journals. It has been expanded to include articles published in major American journals.

Besterman, Theodore, ed. LITERATURE ENGLISH AND AMERICAN: A BIBLIOGRAPHY OF BIBLIOGRAPHIES. 4th ed. Lowets, N.J.: Rowman and Littlefield, 1971.

BIBLIOGRAPHIES OF STUDIES IN VICTORIAN LITERATURE FOR THE TEN YEARS 1955-1964. Ed. Robert C. Slack. Urbana: University of Illinois Press, 1967.

> These three bibliographies present their listings year by year under individual authors; some critical annotations. The years 1965-74 are in preparation by Ronald Freeman.

BIBLIOGRAPHIES OF STUDIES IN VICTORIAN LITERATURE FOR THE TEN YEARS 1945-1954. Ed. Austin Wright. Urbana: University of Illinois Press, 1956.

BIBLIOGRAPHIES OF STUDIES IN VICTORIAN LITERATURE FOR THE THIRTEEN YEARS 1932-1944. Ed. William D. Templeman. Urbana: University of Illinois Press, 1945.

Bostetter, Edward E. "The New Romantic Criticism." SR, 69 (1961), 490-500.

> Discusses eight major studies of romanticism published during the 1950s.

Buckley, Jerome, ed. VICTORIAN POETS AND PROSE WRITERS. 2nd ed. Goldentree Bibliographies. New York: Appleton-Century-Crofts, 1977.

> A valuable bibliography which, besides containing a section on poets, presents a useful introduction to the prose writers.

CBEL. See Bateson, above.

Crane, Ronald S., et al., eds. ENGLISH LITERATURE 1660-1800. A BIBLIOGRAPHY OF MODERN STUDIES COMPILED FOR THE PHILOLOGICAL QUARTERLY. 6 vols. Princeton, N.J.: Princeton University Press, 1950-72.

> Contains bibliography of 1925-69 on major eighteenth-century figures like Bentham, Cobbett, and Godwin.

"Current Bibliography." KSJ, 1952-- . Annual.

> A comprehensive, international bibliography of the romantic poets

and the romantic era, arranged by individual author, with cross-indexing and annotations.

DeLaura, David J., ed. VICTORIAN PROSE: A GUIDE TO RESEARCH. New York: MLA, 1973.

>The most thorough and valuable collection of bibliographical essays on this topic. Besides an introductory chapter, "General Materials," that discusses bibliographical material, there are individual chapters on the major figures: Carlyle, Arnold, Newman, Ruskin, Mill, Macaulay, and Pater. Four chapters are devoted to "The Critics," "The Unbelievers," "The Oxford Movement," and "Victorian Churches."

Ehrsam, Theodore G., and Robert H. Deily, eds. BIBLIOGRAPHIES OF TWELVE VICTORIAN AUTHORS. New York: Wilson, 1936; rpt. New York: Octagon, 1968.

>Contains bibliographical listings for Arnold, Morris, and Stevenson.

Elkins, A.C., and L.J. Forstner, eds. THE ROMANTIC MOVEMENT BIBLIOGRAPHY, 1936-1970. 7 vols. Ann Arbor, Mich.: Pierian Press, 1973.

>A master cumulation of the romanticism bibliography previously published in ELH, PQ, and ELN.

ENGLISH LANGUAGE NOTES (ELN). 1963-- . Quarterly.

>Publishes the annual romanticism bibliography, "The Romantic Movement," below.

Fogle, Richard H., ed. ROMANTIC POETS AND PROSE WRITERS. Goldentree Bibliographies. New York: Appleton-Century-Crofts, 1966.

>This work groups entries by general topics, such as "Literary and Aesthetic Foregrounds" and "Background," as well as by major writers.

Fredeman, William E. PRE-RAPHAELITISM: A BIBLIOCRITICAL STUDY. Cambridge, Mass.: Harvard University Press, 1965.

>A useful compilation of materials relevant to all aspects of the subject--bibliographies, permanent collections, biographies, and catalogs. Includes a bibliographical essay on Morris and discussions of Ruskin and Pater.

Green, David B., ed. KEATS, SHELLEY, BYRON, HUNT AND THEIR CIRCLES: A BIBLIOGRAPHY: JULY 1, 1950-JUNE 30, 1962. Lincoln: University of Nebraska Press, 1965.

>Collects the bibliographical material from KSJ, 1-12. Also con-

Basic Surveys and Reference Works

tains an index to the first twelve volumes of KSJ; see "Current Bibliography," KSJ, above.

GUIDE TO THE YEAR'S WORK IN VICTORIAN POETRY AND PROSE. Morgantown: West Virginia University, 1974-- . Annual.

Publication intended to supplement DeLaura, above; coverage from 1967 with bibliographical surveys focusing on individual authors and schools.

Harrold, Charles F. "Recent Trends in Victorian Studies: 1932-1939." SP, 37 (1940), 667-97.

An early discussion of the state of Victorian scholarship. Harrold reviews studies and exhorts critics to be more aware of the relation between literature and the religious, social, and philosophical concerns of the age.

Houtchens, Carolyn W., and Lawrence H. Houtchens, eds. ENGLISH ROMANTIC POETS AND ESSAYISTS. 2nd ed. New York: MLA, 1966.

A valuable collection of bibliographical essays on Hazlitt, Hunt, Lamb, Landor, De Quincey, and Carlyle.

Howard-Hill, Trevor H., ed. BIBLIOGRAPHY OF BRITISH LITERARY BIBLIOGRAPHIES. Oxford: Clarendon Press, 1969.

A collection that lists comprehensive bibliographies and author, period, and genre bibliographies written in English and published in the English-speaking Commonwealth and the United States after 1890.

Kennedy, Arthur G., and Donald B. Sands, eds. A CONCISE BIBLIOGRAPHY FOR STUDENTS OF ENGLISH. 5th ed. Stanford, Calif.: Stanford University Press, 1972.

Contains a section on comprehensive bibliographies, as well as a section on nineteenth-century bibliographies.

Lauterbach, Edward S., and W. Eugene Davis, eds. THE TRANSITIONAL AGE: BRITISH LITERATURE 1880-1920. Troy, N.Y.: Whitston, 1973.

Contains bibliographies of prose and prose fiction, and of such authors as Stevenson and Butler.

Leary, Lewis, ed. CONTEMPORARY LITERARARY SCHOLARSHIP. New York: Appleton-Century-Crofts, 1958.

This collection includes a bibliography of "The Victorian Period" by Lionel Stevenson and of "The Romantic Movement" by Richard H. Fogle.

Basic Surveys and Reference Works

McNamee, Laurence F., ed. DISSERTATIONS IN ENGLISH AND AMERICAN LITERATURE: THESES ACCEPTED BY AMERICAN, BRITISH, AND GERMAN UNIVERSITIES, 1865-1964. New York: Bowker, 1968-74. Supplement, 1964-68.

> Includes over 5,000 dissertations abstracts listed under individual authors and topics. Note: Altick and Matthews, above, contains European dissertations not in McNamee.

Madden, Lionel, ed. HOW TO FIND OUT ABOUT THE VICTORIAN PERIOD: A GUIDE TO SOURCES OF INFORMATION. Oxford: Pergamon, 1970.

> An extremely useful guide to the background materials on the period. Includes chapters on "Victorian Periodicals," "The Christian Church," and "English Literature."

MLA ABSTRACTS OF ARTICLES IN SCHOLARLY JOURNALS. New York: MLA, 1970-76.

MLA INTERNATIONAL BIBLIOGRAPHY OF BOOKS AND ARTICLES ON THE MODERN LANGUAGES AND LITERATURES. New York: MLA, 1921-- . Annual.

> The largest of the annual bibliographies. Until 1969, this appeared as a June feature of PMLA; it became an independent publication in 1970.

NCBEL. See Watson, below.

Patterson, Margaret, ed. LITERARY RESEARCH GUIDE. Detroit: Gale, 1976.

> This excellent recent work should be consulted as well for other period-genre resources.

"Recent Studies in Nineteenth-Century English Literature." SEL, 1961-- . Annual.

> This bibliographical essay appears in the autumn issue every year, written by such scholars as Richard H. Fogle, Morse B. Peckham, and G. Robert Stange.

"The Romantic Movement: A Selective and Critical Bibliography." ELH, 1937-48; PQ, 1949-62; ELN, 1863-- . Annual.

> A useful bibliography that includes critical commentary on books and significant articles. See Elkins and Forstner, above, which ELN continues.

Sawin, Lewis, et al., eds. ABSTRACTS OF ENGLISH STUDIES. 1958-- . Monthly.

> Summaries of periodical literature.

Basic Surveys and Reference Works

Slack, Robert C. See BIBLIOGRAPHIES OF STUDIES IN VICTORIAN LITERATURE FOR TEN YEARS 1955-1964, above.

Templeman, William D. See BIBLIOGRAPHIES OF STUDIES IN VICTORIAN LITERATURE FOR THE THIRTEEN YEARS 1932-1944, above.

"Victorian Bibliography." VICTORIAN STUDIES. 1958-- . Annual.

    Contains the bibliographical listing previously published by MP, 1933-57. Also see BIBLIOGRAPHIES OF STUDIES IN VICTORIAN LITERATURE, above.

VICTORIAN NEWSLETTER. New York: MLA English X Group, 1952-- . Semiannual.

    Publishes a quarterly bibliography.

Watson, George, ed. THE CONCISE CAMBRIDGE BIBLIOGRAPHY OF ENGLISH LITERATURE, 600-1950. 2nd ed. Cambridge: At the University Press, 1965.

    Contains useful information on general introductory materials, as well as listings of first editions by major nineteenth-century writers.

_____. THE NEW CAMBRIDGE BIBLIOGRAPHY OF ENGLISH LITERATURE. Vol. 3 (1800-1900). Cambridge: At the University Press, 1969.

    NCBEL contains much of the information from the 1940 CBEL and the 1957 supplement, and brings the listings of new materials through 1967. Volume 3 is the largest single-volume resource for nineteenth-century English literature and, after CBEL, has the most changes and additions. See preface to volume 3 for scope and exclusions in coverage from CBEL.

Wright, Austin. See BIBLIOGRAPHIES OF STUDIES IN VICTORIAN LITERATURE FOR TEN YEARS 1945-1954, above.

THE YEAR'S WORK IN ENGLISH STUDIES. London: Oxford University Press, 1919-- .

    This bibliography concentrates on studies published in England. Before 1960 listed only titles, but since then has annotated important works.

B. LITERARY HISTORIES AND ANTHOLOGIES

Abrams, Meyer H., et al., eds. THE NORTON ANTHOLOGY OF ENGLISH LITERATURE. 2 vols. 3rd ed. New York: Norton, 1974.

Basic Surveys and Reference Works

Abrams edited the "Romantic Period" and George Ford the "Victorian Period."

Allott, Kenneth, and Miriam Allott, eds. VICTORIAN PROSE, 1830-1880. Harmondsworth, Engl.: Penguin, 1956.

> Allott's introduction discusses the "Romantic" elements in Victorian prose.

Batho, Edith C., and Bonamy Dobrée, eds. THE VICTORIANS AND AFTER, 1830-1914. London: Cresset Press, 1958; rpt. 1962.

> A literary history containing chapters on "The Background: 1830-1914" and a survey of the economic background by Guy Chapman. Also includes a 220-page bibliography divided by genres.

Baugh, Albert C., et al., eds. A LITERARY HISTORY OF ENGLAND. 2nd ed. New York: Appleton-Century-Crofts, 1967.

> Generally considered the most compendious 1-volume history of English literature. "The Nineteenth Century and After, 1789-1939" is written by Samuel C. Chew and Richard D. Altick.

Beers, Henry A. A HISTORY OF ENGLISH ROMANTICISM IN THE NINETEENTH CENTURY. New York: Holt, 1901.

> Includes chapters on "Coleridge, Bowles, and the Pope Controversy," "Keats, Leigh Hunt, and the Dante Revival," and "Diffused Romanticism in the Literature of the Nineteenth Century."

Bowyer, John W., and John L. Brooks, eds. THE VICTORIAN AGE: PROSE, POETRY, AND DRAMA. New York: Appleton-Century-Crofts, 1954.

> This anthology attempts "to represent the Victorian literature in its magnitude and variety against the social, historical, and intellectual background of the period."

Buckler, William [E.], ed. PROSE OF THE VICTORIAN PERIOD. Boston: Houghton Mifflin, 1958.

> A useful period anthology with an introduction that reflects more recent approaches (at date of publication) to the study of Victorian prose.

Chadwick, Owen, ed. THE MIND OF THE OXFORD MOVEMENT. Stanford, Calif.: Stanford University Press, 1960.

> Chadwick's collection contains chapters on "Newman and Faith," "Keble," and "Pusey and the Language of Mysticism." Writings by the Tractarians are arranged under the general headings of "Authority of the Church," "Faith," and "Sanctification."

Basic Surveys and Reference Works

Churchill, Reginald. ENGLISH LITERATURE OF THE NINETEENTH CENTURY. Freeport, N.Y.: Books for Libraries Press, 1951; rpt. 1970.

> Contains chapters on romantic prose, the Oxford Movement, and science and culture.

Cook, John D., and Lionel Stevenson. ENGLISH LITERATURE OF THE VICTORIAN PERIOD. New York: Appleton-Century-Crofts, 1949.

> Discusses the political and social background of the Victorian age and analyzes the major prose writers: Arnold, Butler, Carlyle, Mill, Macaulay, Ruskin, and Pater.

Craig, Hardin, ed. A HISTORY OF ENGLISH LITERATURE. New York: Oxford University Press, 1950.

> Includes a survey of the nineteenth century by Joseph Beach.

Daiches, David. A CRITICAL HISTORY OF ENGLISH LITERATURE. 2 vols. New York: Ronald Press, 1960.

> Daiches claims that his history is "intended less as a work of reference than as a work of description, explanation, and critical interpretation." Volume 2 contains chapters on "Familiar, Critical, and Miscellaneous Prose of the Early and Middle Nineteenth Century" and "Victorian Prose: Newman to Morris."

Elton, Oliver. A SURVEY OF ENGLISH LITERATURE: 1780-1880. 4 vols. New York: Macmillan, 1920.

> Elton is generally considered the most dependable, comprehensive, and accurate English literary historian for this period, and his SURVEY has been reissued frequently.

Fairweather, Eugene R., ed. THE OXFORD MOVEMENT. New York: Oxford University Press, 1964.

> A large collection of writings by the major figures in the movement--Newman, Keble, Pusey, and Robert Wilberforce. Also contains a useful bibliography.

Ford, Boris, ed. THE PELICAN GUIDE TO ENGLISH LITERATURE. 7 vols. Baltimore: Pelican, 1963.

> Each volume contains essays that set the literature into the social background. Volume 5, "From Blake to Byron," and volume 6, "From Dickens to Hardy," contain several valuable essays on the Victorian period and full bibliographies.

Haight, Gordon S., ed. THE PORTABLE VICTORIAN READER. New York: Viking Press, 1972.

Basic Surveys and Reference Works

A selection of excerpts from major Victorian writers arranged by theme. Suitable for undergraduate classroom use.

Harrold, Charles F., and William D. Templeman, eds. ENGLISH PROSE OF THE VICTORIAN ERA. New York: Oxford University Press, 1938.

This anthology is the largest, containing lengthy selections from Carlyle, Macaulay, Mill, Newman, Froude, Arnold, Ruskin, and Pater. It also contains an excellent, though somewhat dated, introduction that examines "The Triumph of the Middle Class Spirit" and analyzes the various characteristics of the period, 1832-1901. For each author, there is a biography, bibliography, and critical commentary.

Hoffman, Daniel, and Samuel Hynes, eds. ENGLISH LITERARY CRITICISM: ROMANTIC AND VICTORIAN. Goldentree Books. London: Owen, 1963.

This collection contains essays by Hazlitt, Mill, Ruskin, Arnold, and Pater.

Jones, Howard Mumford, and I. Bernard Cohen, eds. SCIENCE BEFORE DARWIN: A NINETEENTH-CENTURY ANTHOLOGY. London: Deutsch, 1963.

The American edition was published as a TREASURY OF SCIENTIFIC PROSE (Boston: Little, Brown, 1963).

Kauvar, Gerald [B.], and G. Sorenson, eds. THE VICTORIAN MIND. New York: Putnam's, 1969.

A wide range of selections by the major prose writers, grouped under the headings "Education," "Social Welfare," "Religion," "Science," and "Art."

Kermode, John Frank, and John Hollander, eds. THE OXFORD ANTHOLOGY OF ENGLISH LITERATURE. 2 vols. New York: Oxford University Press, 1973.

The sections on romantic and Victorian prose were edited by Harold Bloom and Lionel Trilling. This collection may supersede the NORTON ANTHOLOGY (see Abrams, above) for classroom use.

Legouis, Emile, and Louis Cazamian. A HISTORY OF ENGLISH LITERATURE. Trans. Helen Douglas Irvine. 2 vols. Rev. ed. London: Dent, 1971.

A classic, pioneering work. Volume 2 deals with the nineteenth century.

Levine, George [L.], ed. THE EMERGENCE OF VICTORIAN CONSCIOUSNESS: THE SPIRIT OF THE AGE. New York: Free Press, 1967.

Levine groups Victorian writings under the headings "The March of

Basic Surveys and Reference Works

Mind," "Society and Reform," "Religion," and "Art and Literature." His introduction notes that the selections illustrate "the enormous expansion of self-consciousness that was leading to the first serious and sustained analyses of industrial society and its malaises."

Moody, William V., and Robert M. Lovett, eds. A HISTORY OF ENGLISH LITERATURE. 8th ed. by Fred B. Millett. New York: Scribner's, 1964.

Includes four chapters surveying various aspects of the nineteenth century.

Nabholtz, John R., ed. PROSE OF THE BRITISH ROMANTIC MOVEMENT. New York: Macmillan, 1974.

The most recent and complete collection of prose writings. Includes selections by Coleridge, Lamb, Landor, Hazlitt, Hunt, De Quincey, Jeffrey, and Wilson.

Pollard, Arthur, ed. THE VICTORIANS. London: Barrie & Jenkins, 1970.

A collection of essays including "Victorian Thought" by A.O.J. Cockshut and "Arnold (and Clough)" by Kenneth Allott.

Preyer, Robert O., ed. VICTORIAN LITERATURE: SELECTED ESSAYS. New York: Harper and Row, 1966.

A useful collection containing essays on Macaulay, Newman, Bagehot, and Arnold.

Roe, Frederick W[illiam], ed. NINETEENTH-CENTURY ENGLISH PROSE: EARLY ESSAYISTS. New York: Harcourt, 1923; rpt. Freeport, N.Y.: Books for Libraries Press, 1971.

A collection of essays by Lamb, Hazlitt, Hunt, De Quincey, and Macaulay.

_____. VICTORIAN PROSE. New York: Ronald Press, 1947.

Contains selections from the major Victorians arranged chronologically. Includes a bibliography, notes, and introduction.

Routh, H.V. TOWARDS THE TWENTIETH CENTURY: ESSAYS IN THE SPIRITUAL HISTORY OF THE NINETEENTH CENTURY. New York: Macmillan, 1937.

Routh claims that the true spirit of Victorianism was "spiritual isolation, not intellectual fellowship." He discusses Newman, Froude, Carlyle, Arnold, and Mill.

Basic Surveys and Reference Works

Saintsbury, George. A HISTORY OF ENGLISH CRITICISM. Edinburgh: Blackwood, 1922.

    Chapters 7 and 8 trace the development of critical theories from Coleridge through Pater.

――――. A HISTORY OF ENGLISH PROSE RHYTHM. New York and London: Macmillan, 1912; rpt. Bloomington: Indiana University Press, 1965.

    Examines the prose style of the major writers in three chapters on the nineteenth century.

――――. A HISTORY OF NINETEENTH-CENTURY LITERATURE, 1780-1895. New York and London: Macmillan, 1896.

    This history includes chapters on "The Development of Periodicals," "The Historians of the Century," "Philosophy and Theology," and "Criticism in Art and Letters."

Taine, Hippolyte. A HISTORY OF ENGLISH LITERATURE. Trans. H. Van Laun. 2 vols. New York: Holt, 1900.

    With Legouis and Cazamian, above, Taine's study ranks as a distinguished and perceptive survey of English literature from a continental point of view.

Tennyson, George B., and Donald J. Gray, eds. VICTORIAN LITERATURE: PROSE. New York: Macmillan, 1976.

    An anthology with very broad coverage. The introduction emphasizes the "literary" and "artistic dimensions of nonfiction prose."

Walker, Hugh. THE LITERATURE OF THE VICTORIAN ERA. Cambridge: At the University Press, 1910.

    Rather dated, but does contain worthwhile sections on "Theology and Philosophy," "History and Biography," and "Literary and Aesthetic Criticism."

Ward, Adolphus W., and Alfred R. Waller, eds. THE CAMBRIDGE HISTORY OF ENGLISH LITERATURE. 15 vols. Cambridge: At the University Press, 1907-27.

    Volumes 12-14 (1914-16) cover the nineteenth century.

Wilson, F.P., and Bonamy Dobrée, eds. OXFORD HISTORY OF ENGLISH LITERATURE. 10 vols. Oxford: Clarendon Press, 1945-63.

    This history contains two very useful volumes on the early nineteenth century: W.L. Renwick, ENGLISH LITERATURE, 1789-1815 (1963); and Ian Jack, ENGLISH LITERATURE, 1815-1832 (1963).

Basic Surveys and Reference Works

Wimsatt, William K., and Cleanth Brooks. LITERARY CRITICISM: A SHORT HISTORY. New York: Knopf, 1957.

> Contains several chapters pertinent to the nineteenth century: "Imagination: Wordsworth and Coleridge," "The Arnoldian Prophecy," and "The Real and the Social: Art as Propaganda."

Woodring, Carl R., ed. PROSE OF THE ROMANTIC PERIOD. Boston: Houghton Mifflin, 1961.

> A selection of writings by Lamb, Landor, Hazlitt, Hunt, and De Quincey.

Wright, Raymond, ed. PROSE OF THE ROMANTIC PERIOD, 1780-1830. Harmondsworth, Engl.: Penguin, 1956.

> Contains an excellent introduction that analyzes the period's shift from poetry to prose.

2. BACKGROUND

A. LITERARY

Abrams, Meyer H. THE MILK OF PARADISE: THE EFFECT OF OPIUM VISIONS ON THE WORKS OF DE QUINCEY, CRABBE, FRANCIS THOMPSON, AND COLERIDGE. Cambridge, Mass.: Harvard University Press, 1934.

_____. THE MIRROR AND THE LAMP: ROMANTIC THEORY AND THE CRITICAL TRADITION. New York: Oxford University Press, 1953.

> The most influential work on romantic criticism, providing the fundamental terminology for discussions of romantic aestheticism.

_____. NATURAL SUPERNATURALISM: TRADITION AND REVOLUTION IN ROMANTIC LITERATURE. New York: Norton, 1971.

> A complex work that discusses attempts made by the romantics to restore traditional beliefs.

Anderson, Warren D., and T.D. Clareson, eds. VICTORIAN ESSAYS: A SYMPOSIUM. Kent, Ohio: Kent State University Press, 1965.

> Contains "Symbols of Eternity: The Victorian Escape from Time" by Jerome Buckley, as well as essays on Arnold.

Baker, Joseph E., ed. THE REINTERPRETATION OF VICTORIAN LITERATURE. Princeton, N.J.: Princeton University Press, 1950.

> Emphasizes prose writers and contains articles by Charles F. Harrold, "The Oxford Movement: A Reconsideration," and Emery Neff, "Social Background and Social Thought."

Ball, Patricia M. THE CENTRAL SELF: A STUDY IN ROMANTIC AND VICTORIAN IMAGINATION. London: Athlone Press, 1968.

> Discusses "Sincerity" as a literary criterion in Arnold. Also considers Coleridge and "The Romantics as Dramatists."

Background

_____. THE SCIENCE OF ASPECTS: THE CHANGING ROLE OF FACT IN THE WORK OF COLERIDGE, RUSKIN, AND HOPKINS. New York: Oxford University Press, 1971.

According to Ball, Coleridge's text as a theorist is that "Body is but a striving to become mind." Ruskin, however, fought for the "dignity of the object [and] transferred the Romantic respect for the mystery of identity to a different centre."

Bernbaum, Ernest. GUIDE THROUGH THE ROMANTIC MOVEMENT. Rev. ed. New York: Ronald Press, 1949.

First published in 1930 as volume 1 of the author's ANTHOLOGY OF ROMANTICISM (New York: Nelson, 1929-38). Somewhat dated, but contains criticism and bibliography of Coleridge, Lamb, Hazlitt, Hunt, De Quincey, and Carlyle.

Brownell, William C. VICTORIAN PROSE MASTERS. New York: Scribner's, 1909.

Contains essays on Carlyle, Arnold, and Ruskin.

Bruns, Gerald L. "The Formal Nature of Victorian Thinking." PMLA, 90 (1975), 904-18.

Discusses how Carlyle, Arnold, and Ruskin use history as "a formal property of thought." This, according to Bruns, is the characteristic pattern of Victorian writings: "their sense of the historicity of things derived their meanings from the world of processes and events."

Buckley, Jerome. "The Revolt from 'Rationalism' in the Seventies and Some of Its Literary Consequences." BOOKER MEMORIAL STUDIES: EIGHT ESSAYS ON VICTORIAN LITERATURE IN MEMORY OF JOHN MANNING BOOKER. Ed. Hill Shine. Chapel Hill: University of North Carolina Press, 1950.

Buckley maintains that the "Religion of Humanity" in the later nineteenth century was the result of "scientific rationalism."

_____. THE TRIUMPH OF TIME: A STUDY OF THE VICTORIAN CONCEPTS OF TIME, HISTORY, PROGRESS, AND DECADENCE. Cambridge, Mass.: Harvard University Press, 1966.

Buckley examines four levels of time--past, present, future, and eternity--as they are treated by the major Victorian writers.

_____. THE VICTORIAN TEMPER: A STUDY IN LITERARY CULTURE. Cambridge, Mass.: Harvard University Press, 1951; rpt. New York: Vintage, 1964.

Concentrates on the influence of Carlyle, Kingsley, and Ruskin on the taste of the age.

Background

Chandler, Alice. A DREAM OF ORDER: THE MEDIEVAL IDEAL IN NINE-TEENTH-CENTURY ENGLISH LITERATURE. Lincoln: University of Nebraska Press, 1970.

Chandler's thesis is that the Victorians adopted the medieval ideal because it represented for them an ordered and organically vital world view.

Charlesworth, Barbara. DARK PASSAGES: THE DECADENT CONSCIOUSNESS IN VICTORIAN LITERATURE Madison: University of Wisconsin Press, 1965.

Includes discussions of Rossetti, Pater, Beardsley, and Lionel Johnson.

Chesterton, George K. THE VICTORIAN AGE IN LITERATURE. Notre Dame, Ind.: University of Notre Dame Press, 1962.

Somewhat capricious, but still a classic literary study of the period.

Cockshut, A.O.J. THE UNBELIEVERS: ENGLISH AGNOSTIC THOUGHT, 1840-1890. London: Collins, 1964.

Discusses Arnold, Butler, Huxley, Mill, Spencer, and Stephen; contains general chapters on "The Attack on Religion," "Alternative Religions," and "Evolution and Ethics."

Cruse, Amy. THE VICTORIANS AND THEIR READING. Boston: Houghton Mifflin, 1936.

Cruse analyzes the intellectual life of the Victorians; also includes critical evaluations of nineteenth-century English literature.

Culler, A. Dwight. "Method in the Study of Victorian Prose." VN, 9 (1956), 1-4.

Culler pleads for an analysis of Victorian prose based on a broad understanding of the religious beliefs and social conditions of the age. See also Holloway, below.

Daiches, David. SOME LATE VICTORIAN ATTITUDES. London: Deutsch, 1969.

Emphasizes the anxiety and pessimism prevalent in late nineteenth-century writings.

DeLaura, David J. HEBREW AND HELLENE IN VICTORIAN ENGLAND: NEWMAN, ARNOLD, AND PATER. Austin: University of Texas Press, 1969.

An important study that discusses the intellectual and religious background of the period. Emphasizes the "religionizing" of culture.

Background

THE EIGHTEEN-EIGHTIES. Ed. Walter De La Mare. Cambridge: At the University Press, 1930.

    This collection of essays, by the Fellows of the Royal Society of Literature, discusses various aspects of the literary milieu of the decade. Contains "The Place of Pater" by T.S. Eliot and "The Sibyl and the Sphinx: Newman and Manning" by Father Martindale.

THE EIGHTEEN-SEVENTIES. Ed. Harley Granville-Barker. Cambridge: At the University Press, 1929.

    Contains "Critics and Criticism in the 'Seventies" by Frederick S. Boas.

THE EIGHTEEN-SIXTIES. Ed. John Drinkwater. Cambridge: At the University Press, 1932.

    Contains "Historians in the 'Sixties" by Frederick S. Boas and "Science in the 'Sixties" by Sir Oliver Lodge.

Frye, Northrop. "The Problem of Spiritual Authority in the Nineteenth Century." ESSAYS IN ENGLISH LITERATURE FROM THE RENAISSANCE TO THE VICTORIAN AGE. Eds. Millar MacLure and F.W. Watt. Toronto: University of Toronto Press, 1964.

    Focuses on the use of educational theories as substitute forms of temporal authority in Arnold, Butler, Carlyle, Mill, and Newman.

_____, ed. ROMANTICISM RECONSIDERED: SELECTED PAPERS FROM THE ENGLISH INSTITUTE. New York: Columbia University Press, 1966.

    Includes essays on the theory of romanticism by Northrop Frye, Meyer H. Abrams, René Wellek, and Lionel Trilling.

Fulweiler, Howard W. "Tractarians and Philistines: THE TRACTS FOR THE TIMES versus Middle-Class Values." HMPEC, 31 (1962): 36-53.

    Fulweiler discusses the Tractarian movement as a reaction against prevailing middle-class secularism.

Gaunt, William. THE AESTHETIC ADVENTURE. London: Cape, 1945.

    Discusses Ruskin and the latter part of the nineteenth century from the viewpoint of "the strong moral tone of the arts" as compared with French aestheticism.

_____. THE PRE-RAPHAELITE TRAGEDY. New York: Harcourt, Brace, 1942.

    Discusses Morris and Ruskin, among others, as questers "in pursuit

Background

of an ideal." Later published as THE PRE-RAPHAELITE DREAM, New York: Schocken Books, 1966.

Gooch, George P. HISTORY AND HISTORIANS IN THE NINETEENTH CENTURY. 2nd ed. London: Longmans, Green, 1920.

A somewhat dated study of the historiography of the period, emphasizing Macaulay and Carlyle as the only historians of the early nineteenth century still being read.

Gross, John. THE RISE AND FALL OF THE MAN OF LETTERS: ENGLISH LITERARY LIFE SINCE 1800. London: Weidenfeld and Nicolson, 1969.

Gross discusses "the role of literature in public life, and the social context of criticism." He focuses on Arnold, Carlyle, and the Grub street writers.

Hartman, Geoffrey [H.]. "Romanticism and 'Anti-Self-Consciousness.'" CR,6 (1962), 553-65.

Hartman emphasizes the necessary disjunction between nature and consciousness.

Holland, Norman. "Prose and Minds: A Psychoanalytic Approach to Non-Fiction." THE ART OF VICTORIAN PROSE. Eds. George L. Levine and William A. Madden. New York: Oxford University Press, 1968.

Holland analyzes the figurative language in the prose of Mill, Carlyle, Newman, and Arnold in an attempt to probe their unconscious minds.

Holloway, John. THE VICTORIAN SAGE. London: Macmillan, 1953.

Holloway's study of Arnold, Carlyle, Hardy, and Newman inspired a controversy about method in the study of prose writers (see Culler, above). Holloway analyzes Victorian writings from a New Critical viewpoint, that is, apart from their social context.

Hough, Graham. IMAGE AND EXPERIENCE: STUDIES IN A LITERARY REVOLUTION. London: Duckworth, 1960.

Includes an informative discussion of Ruskin's aesthetic theory: "Ruskin and Roger Fry: Two Aesthetic Theories."

_____. THE LAST ROMANTICS. London: Duckworth, 1949; rpt. New York: Barnes and Noble, 1961.

Hough's thesis is that the major preoccupation of the later nineteenth century was to find a connection between art and religious experience. Deals with Ruskin, Morris, Pater, and the Pre-Raphaelites.

Background

Hyman, Stanley E. THE TANGLED BANK: DARWIN, MARX, FRAZER, AND FREUD AS IMAGINATIVE WRITERS. New York: Atheneum, 1962.

    Hyman states that his work is "literary criticism" that treats his subjects' works "as though they were poems." His thesis is that "the power and influence of their ideas is due in some substantial part to their ability as imaginative writers."

Jackson, Holbrook. DREAMERS OF DREAMS: THE RISE AND FALL OF NINE-TEENTH-CENTURY IDEALISM. New York: Farrar, Straus, 1949.

    Discusses Carlyle, Ruskin, and Morris as "pessimists" who "look upon the Industrial Revolution and the doctrine of laissez-faire as a calamity."

_____. THE EIGHTEEN-NINETIES: A REVIEW OF ARTS AND IDEAS AT THE CLOSE OF THE NINETEENTH CENTURY. New York: Knopf, 1927.

    A collection of essays by Jackson focusing on the influence of Ruskin and the Pre-Raphaelites on the fin-de-siècle mentality.

Kissane, James. "Victorian Mythology." VS, 6 (1962), 5-28.

    Deals with Ruskin's and Pater's uses of myth. Kissane claims that, for them, myth was humanistic and aesthetic, flexible and organic, and therefore could never be outmoded.

Kroeber, Karl, ed. BACKGROUND TO ENGLISH ROMANTIC LITERATURE. San Francisco: Chandler, 1968.

    A collection of essays and a selective annotated bibliography. Contains "The Literary Periodicals" by Walter Graham, "Orthodoxy and Its Challenges" by D.C. Somerville, and "Intellectual Currents" by Elie Halévy.

Kumar, Shiv K., ed. BRITISH VICTORIAN LITERATURE: RECENT REVALUATIONS. New York: New York University Press, 1969.

    Contains Jerome Buckley's "Victorianism," as well as essays by various hands on the prose of Arnold, Carlyle, Newman, Pater, and Ruskin.

Langbaum, Robert. THE VICTORIAN AGE: ESSAYS IN HISTORY AND IN SOCIAL AND LITERARY CRITICISM. Greenwich, Conn.: Fawcett, 1967.

    An interesting collection of essays by G.M. Young, G. Kitson Clark, Noel Annan, and Raymond Williams grouped under the heading, "The Historical View."

Levine, George L. THE BOUNDARIES OF FICTION: CARLYLE, MACAULAY, NEWMAN. Princeton, N.J.: Princeton University Press, 1968.

Background

Levine discusses Carlyle and Newman and concludes that for both "the discovery of self in the world becomes the discovery of God." Levine claims that, for Macaulay, literature was a "retreat from life rather than an extension of it."

Levine, George L., and William A. Madden, eds. THE ART OF VICTORIAN PROSE. New York: Oxford University Press, 1968.

Probably the most useful collection of essays on this topic. Includes valuable studies of Arnold, Carlyle, Darwin, Macaulay, Mill, Pater, and Ruskin, as well as essays on prose style and genres. Annotations of specific articles are included in this guide.

Lovejoy, Arthur O. ESSAYS IN THE HISTORY OF IDEAS. Baltimore: Johns Hopkins University Press, 1948.

Contains several valuable essays, including "Coleridge and Kant's Two Worlds" and "On the Discriminations of Romanticism." The latter essay concludes that romanticism has come to mean so many things that "it means nothing."

_____. THE REASON, THE UNDERSTANDING AND TIME. Baltimore: Johns Hopkins University Press, 1961.

A reaffirmation of Lovejoy's denial of romantic unity, see above. Also see Peckham and Wellek, below.

Madden, William [A.]. "The Divided Tradition of English Criticism." PMLA, 83 (1958), 69-80.

Discusses the split between the Victorians' concept of duty and their love of aestheticism.

_____. "The Victorian Sensibility." VS, 7 (1963), 69-97.

An important essay that attempts "to chart in broad outline the major shifts in English sensibility as these are reflected in the work of some of the major Victorian writers." Discusses Arnold, Carlyle, Mill, Newman, Pater, and Morris.

Massingham, Harold J., and Hugh Massingham, eds. THE GREAT VICTORIANS. London: Nicholson and Watson, 1932.

Includes portraits of Arnold, Butler, Carlyle, Darwin, Huxley, Macaulay, Mill, Morris, and Newman.

Merritt, Travis R. "Taste, Opinion, and Theory in the Rise of Victorian Prose Stylism." THE ART OF VICTORIAN PROSE. Eds. George L. Levine and William A. Madden. New York: Oxford University, 1968.

Background

Merritt explores the rise of what he calls the late-Victorian cult of prose style.

Miles, Josephine. STYLE AND PROPORTION: THE LANGUAGE OF PROSE AND POETRY. Boston: Little, Brown, 1967.

Includes a chapter on "Style in British Prose" that deals with the major nineteenth-century figures.

Miller, J. Hillis. THE DISAPPEARANCE OF GOD: FIVE NINETEENTH-CENTURY WRITERS. Cambridge, Mass.: Harvard University Press, 1963.

Miller's thesis is that "literature is the act whereby mind takes possession of space, time, nature, or other mind." He treats De Quincey and Arnold from a theological perspective.

More, Paul Elmer. THE DRIFT OF ROMANTICISM: SHELBURNE ESSAYS, EIGHTH SERIES. Boston: Houghton Mifflin, 1913.

The conservative New Humanist indicts romantic naturalism and pleads for a philosophy of humanistic dualism.

Morris, John N. VERSIONS OF THE SELF: STUDIES IN ENGLISH AUTOBIOGRAPHY FROM JOHN BUNYAN TO JOHN STUART MILL. New York: Basic Books, 1966.

Includes a discussion of Mill's AUTOBIOGRAPHY as literary art.

Murry, John Middleton. "English Prose in the Nineteenth Century." In his DISCOVERIES. London: Cape, 1924.

An early essay which is more appreciative than critical.

Neff, Emery E. CARLYLE AND MILL: AN INTRODUCTION TO VICTORIAN THOUGHT. 2nd rev. ed. New York: Octagon, 1964.

Neff sees the two as "representative men" who reveal the political, economic, religious, and literary sympathies of their day.

_____. THE POETRY OF HISTORY: THE CONTRIBUTION OF LITERATURE AND LITERARY SCHOLARSHIP TO THE WRITING OF HISTORY SINCE VOLTAIRE. New York: Columbia University Press, 1947.

Ohmann, Richard. "A Linguistic Appraisal of Victorian Style." THE ART OF VICTORIAN PROSE. Eds. George L. Levine and William A. Madden. New York: Oxford University Press, 1968.

Ohmann claims that critics cannot write about a specific "Victorian" style because there is little consistency among the writers of the period.

Background

Peckham, Morse. BEYOND THE TRAGIC VISION: THE QUEST FOR IDENTITY IN THE NINETEENTH CENTURY. New York: Braziller, 1962.

Peckham's study contains chapters on Ruskin, Carlyle, and Darwin, among others. He considers his study "the cultural history of the nineteenth century in Europe and America."

_____. "Toward a Theory of Romanticism." PMLA, 64 (1951), 5-23.

Peckham criticizes Lovejoy's theory of romanticism, above, and Wellek's, below, to assert that romantic values are "change, imperfection, growth, diversity, the creative imagination, the unconscious."

_____. "Toward a Theory of Romanticism: A Reconsideration." SIR, 1 (1961), 1-8.

Peckham revises his earlier essay, above, by emphasizing the influence of the Enlightenment on romantic values.

_____. THE TRIUMPH OF ROMANTICISM: COLLECTED ESSAYS. Columbia: University of South Carolina Press, 1970.

A collection of Peckham's essays on romanticism, as well as "Can 'Victorian' Have a Useful Meaning?" and "Darwinism and Darwinisticism."

_____. VICTORIAN REVOLUTIONARIES: SPECULATIONS ON SOME HEROES OF A CULTURE CRISIS. New York: Braziller, 1970.

Peckham's study examines "cultural transcendence" and asserts that "the culture crisis of the nineteenth century was the greatest not merely in European history, but in human history."

_____, ed. ROMANTICISM: THE CULTURE OF THE NINETEENTH CENTURY. New York: Braziller, 1965.

Peckham's introduction distinguishes the "four stages of Romanticism: Analogism, Transcendentalism, Objectism, and Stylism."

Peters, Robert L., ed. VICTORIANS ON LITERATURE AND ART. New York: Appleton-Century-Crofts, 1961.

A useful collection that reprints contemporary critical prose on "the problem of the artist, his struggle to evolve a satisfying system of aesthetics and to define his role in society."

Praz, Mario. THE ROMANTIC AGONY. 2nd ed. Trans. Angus Davidson. New York: Oxford University Press, 1951.

A classic work that attempts to analyze the romantic mentality through its obsession with suffering and sadomasochism.

Background

Robertson, John M. A HISTORY OF FREETHOUGHT IN THE NINETEENTH CENTURY. Edinburgh: Blackwood, 1907.

Robertson states that his study is "a compendious history of the mutual and social reactions of critical freethought, science, and religion, as indicated in books and movements, doctrines, changes of theological thought, creed and temper."

_____. MODERN HUMANISTS. New York: 1891; rpt. New York: Kennikat Press, 1968.

Includes chapters on Carlyle, Ruskin, Arnold, Mill, and Spencer.

Saintsbury, George. ESSAYS IN ENGLISH LITERATURE, 1780-1860. 3rd ed. London: Rivington, 1896.

Shrewd, well-informed appreciations of about twenty relatively minor figures, including Borrow, Sydney Smith, Jeffrey, and John Wilson.

_____. THE LATER NINETEENTH CENTURY. Edinburgh: Blackwood, 1907.

Of interest as a perceptive, contemporary commentary.

Schilling, Bernard N. HUMAN DIGNITY AND THE GREAT VICTORIANS. New York: Columbia University Press, 1946.

Concentrates on Coleridge, Carlyle, Arnold, Morris, and Ruskin as spokesmen against the "degradation of human dignity." According to Schilling, these writers should be considered "less as social reformers than as important followers of the great spiritual leaders of mankind."

Stange, George Robert. "Art Criticism as a Prose Genre." THE ART OF VICTORIAN PROSE. Eds. George L. Levine and William A. Madden. New York: Oxford University Press, 1968.

Stange discusses the attempts made by Ruskin and Pater to break down the traditional distinctions between poety and prose.

Stephen, Leslie. STUDIES OF A BIOGRAPHER. 4 vols. London: Duckworth, 1898-1902.

Contains sketches of Arnold, Ruskin, Godwin, Bagehot, Huxley, Froude, and Stevenson.

Sussman, Herbert L. VICTORIANS AND THE MACHINE: THE LITERARY RESPONSE TO TECHNOLOGY. Cambridge, Mass.: Harvard University Press, 1968.

Discusses the contradictory attitudes held by the Victorians toward

Background

technology. Carlyle, Butler, and Morris, according to Sussman, thought the contradictions destroyed emotional life.

Sutherland, James R. ON ENGLISH PROSE. Toronto: University of Toronto Press, 1957.

> Sutherland traces the history of English prose and includes a chapter on "The Nineteenth Century and After," which deals with Jeffrey, Arnold, and Carlyle.

Thompson, Francis. LITERARY CRITICISMS. Ed. Terence L. Connolly. New York: Dutton, 1948.

> Includes Thompson's essays on Arnold, Carlyle, Landor, Morris, Ruskin, and "Leslie Stephen's Biographies."

Tillotson, Geoffrey. CRITICISM AND THE NINETEENTH CENTURY. London: Athlone Press, 1951.

> Includes essays on Arnold, Newman, and Pater, as well as two chapters on nineteenth-century criticism as a genre.

Tillotson, Geoffrey, and Kathleen Tillotson. MID-VICTORIAN STUDIES. London: Athlone Press, 1965.

> Includes essays on Arnold, Carlyle, and Newman. Also contains the articles "The Victorian Frame of Mind" and "Writers and Readers in 1851."

Walker, Hugh. THE LITERATURE OF THE VICTORIAN ERA. Cambridge: At the University Press, 1910.

> A rather dated general survey of the period.

Wellek, René. A HISTORY OF MODERN CRITICISM, 1750-1950. 5 vols. New Haven, Conn.: Yale University Press, 1955-65.

> Volume 2 is entitled "The Romantic Age" and volume 3 is "The Age of Transition."

_____. "The Term 'Romantic' and Its Derivations." CL, 1 (1949), 1-23.

> Wellek attacks Lovejoy's theory of romanticism, above, and claims that "the major Romantic movements form a unity of theories, philosophies, and styles." Also see Peckham, above.

_____. "The Unity of European Romanticism." CL, 1 (1949), 147-72.

> Wellek asserts that European romanticism is unified through its use of the imagination, nature, symbol, and myth.

Background

Willey, Basil. MORE NINETEENTH-CENTURY STUDIES: A GROUP OF HONEST DOUBTERS. London: Chatto and Windus, 1956.

    Willey discusses Froude, F.W. Newman, John Morley, and others.

_____. NINETEENTH-CENTURY STUDIES: COLERIDGE TO MATTHEW ARNOLD. London: Chatto and Windus, 1949.

    Discusses Arnold, Coleridge, Carlyle, and Newman and holds that these writers are unified in their similar spiritual struggles.

Williams, Stanley T. STUDIES IN VICTORIAN LITERATURE. New York: Dutton, 1923.

    Deals with the literary criticism of Carlyle, Arnold, Newman, and Clough.

Wright, Austin, ed. VICTORIAN LITERATURE: MODERN ESSAYS IN CRITICISM. New York: Oxford University Press, 1961.

    Contains several useful essays, including "Victorianism" by Jerome Buckley, and essays on Arnold by Walter J. Bate, F.L. Lucas, and T.S. Eliot. Also contains essays on Carlyle, Huxley, Macaulay, Newman, Pater, and Ruskin.

B. CULTURAL

Altholz, Josef L[ewis]. THE CHURCHES IN THE NINETEENTH CENTURY. Indianapolis: Bobbs-Merrill, 1967.

    Altholz states that his study is both "general and concise" and is organized for "comprehensiveness, European emphasis, and historical relevance."

Altick, Richard D. VICTORIAN PEOPLE AND IDEAS: A COMPANION FOR THE MODERN READER OF VICTORIAN LITERATURE. New York: Norton, 1973.

    A valuable study that details the intellectual background in such chapters as "The Evangelical Temper," "Religious Movements and Crises," "Democracy, Industry, and Culture," and "The Nature of Art and Its Place in Society."

Appleman, Philip, et al., eds. 1859: ENTERING AN AGE OF CRISIS. Bloomington: Indiana University Press, 1959.

    A collection of essays that deal with the major intellectual controversies of the era. Specific articles are annotated in this guide.

Ashton, Thomas S. THE INDUSTRIAL REVOLUTION, 1760-1830. New York:

Background

Oxford University Press, 1970.
A general survey that was first published in 1948.

Aspinall, Arthur. POLITICS AND THE PRESS, 1780-1850. London: Home and Van Thal, 1949.
Generally considered the best treatment of the subject.

Beer, Max. A HISTORY OF BRITISH SOCIALISM. 2 vols. London: Allen and Unwin, 1953.
Beer's study is considered the most complete account of the development of Socialist thought in Great Britain.

Benn, Alfred W. A HISTORY OF ENGLISH RATIONALISM IN THE NINETEENTH CENTURY. 2 vols. London: Longmans, Green, 1906; rpt. New York: Russell and Russell, 1962.
Benn's detailed study contains chapters on Coleridge's religious beliefs, Bentham's legal and educational theory, Newman's religious affinities with Keble and Pusey, and Carlyle and Mill's "rationalism."

Booth, Charles, et al. LIFE AND LABOUR OF THE PEOPLE OF LONDON. 3rd rev. ed. London and New York: Macmillan, 1902; rpt. New York: AMS Press, 1970.

Briggs, Asa. VICTORIAN CITIES. London: Odhams, 1963.
Includes a general survey of "City and Society: Victorian Attitudes," as well as studies of Manchester, Leeds, Birmingham, and London.

_____. VICTORIAN PEOPLE: A REASSESSMENT OF PERSONS AND THEMES, 1851-1867. Chicago: University of Chicago Press, 1955; rpt. 1970.
A useful collection of essays including "The Crystal Palace and the Men of 1851" and "Trollope, Bagehot, and the English Constitution."

Briggs, John, and Ian Sellers, eds. VICTORIAN NONCONFORMITY. London: Arnold, 1973.
Includes chapters that explore Nonconformity in relation to the individual, the Church, society, culture, and the State.

Brinton, Crane. ENGLISH POLITICAL THOUGHT IN THE NINETEENTH CENTURY. 2nd ed. Cambridge: At the University Press, 1949; rpt. New York: Harper and Row, 1962.

Background

A valuable survey of the political theories of Cobbett, Coleridge, Mill, Newman, Carlyle, Bagehot, and Spencer.

Brown, Alan W. THE METAPHYSICAL SOCIETY: VICTORIAN MINDS IN CRISIS. New York: Columbia University Press, 1947.

Brown discusses a group of Victorians who sought spiritual reassurance during the intellectual debate of the 1870s.

Bryant, Sir Arthur. THE YEARS OF ENDURANCE, 1873-1902. New York: Harper's, 1942.

_____. THE YEARS OF VICTORY, 1802-1812. London: Collins, 1944.

Bryant's book offers a vivid and picturesque account of the Napoleonic Wars.

Burn, William L. THE AGE OF EQUIPOISE: A STUDY OF THE MID-VICTORIAN GENERATION. New York: Norton, 1964.

Analyzes the "social theory of the day" and "the disciplinary forces, legal and social, which helped to give to that age the notable degree of cohesiveness which it possessed."

Bury, John B. THE IDEA OF PROGRESS: AN INQUIRY INTO ITS ORIGINS AND GROWTH. New York: Dover Publications, 1955.

The standard work on a critical nineteenth-century concept.

Chadwick, Owen. THE VICTORIAN CHURCH. New York: Oxford University Press, 1966.

A valuable treatment of the entire subject, but especially useful on the Oxford Movement and Whig attempts to reform the Church.

Chapman, Raymond [W.]. FAITH AND REVOLT. London: Weidenfeld and Nicolson, 1970.

Studies the relation between literature and the Oxford Movement, which is seen as a reactionary quest for authority and a protest against state interference in church affairs.

_____. THE VICTORIAN DEBATE: ENGLISH LITERATURE AND SOCIETY. New York: Basic Books, 1968.

Discusses Carlyle and Arnold, and the relation of the artist to society.

Church, Richard W. THE OXFORD MOVEMENT: TWELVE YEARS, 1833-1845. New York: Macmillan, 1891; rpt. Chicago: University of Chicago Press, 1970.

Background

The major study of Oxford in the 1830s, with chapters on Keble, R.H. Froude, Pusey, and the TRACTS themselves.

Clark, G. Kitson. THE MAKING OF VICTORIAN ENGLAND. Cambridge, Mass.: Harvard University Press, 1962.

    A valuable history with sections on "The Religion of the People," "The Nobility and Gentry--Old Style," and "The New Politics and the New Gentry."

Clark, Sir Kenneth M. THE GOTHIC REVIVAL: AN ESSAY IN THE HISTORY OF TASTE. 3rd ed. New York: Holt, Rinehart and Winston, 1962.

    The definitive work on this subject.

Cockshut, A.O.J., ed. RELIGIOUS CONTROVERSIES OF THE NINETEENTH CENTURY: SELECTED DOCUMENTS. Lincoln: University of Nebraska Press, 1966.

    Includes selections written by Coleridge, Newman, and William Wilberforce.

Cole, George D.H. A SHORT HISTORY OF THE BRITISH WORKING CLASS, 1789-1947. Rev. ed. London: Allen and Unwin, 1948.

    Cole describes his study as a general survey of the political, industrial, and cooperative aspects of the labor revolution.

Court, W.H.B. A CONCISE ECONOMIC HISTORY OF BRITAIN FROM 1750 TO RECENT TIMES. Cambridge: At the University Press, 1954.

    One of the best examinations of the industrial revolution.

Darvall, Frank O. POPULAR DISTURBANCES AND PUBLIC ORDER IN REGENCY ENGLAND. London: Oxford University Press, 1934.

    Interesting interpretation of a turbulent period, containing an account of the Luddite and other disorders in England during 1811-17.

Davidson, William L. POLITICAL THOUGHT IN ENGLAND: THE UTILITARIANS FROM BENTHAM TO MILL. London: Williams and Norgate, 1915.

    A concise examination of one of the most important philosophical currents in nineteenth-century England.

Dawson, Christopher. THE SPIRIT OF THE OXFORD MOVEMENT. London: Sheed and Ward, 1933.

    Compares the Tractarians with Comte, Feuerbach, Renan, and Strauss.

Background

Faber, Geoffrey. OXFORD APOSTLES: A CHARACTER STUDY. London: Faber and Faber, 1933.

> Provides a Freudian interpretation of Newman, Keble, R.H. Froude, and Pusey.

Gillispie, Charles C. GENESIS AND GEOLOGY: A STUDY IN THE RELATIONS OF SCIENTIFIC THOUGHT, NATURAL THEOLOGY, AND SOCIAL OPINION IN GREAT BRITAIN, 1790-1850. Cambridge, Mass.: Harvard University Press, 1951; rpt. New York: Harper's, 1959.

> This study discusses pre-Darwinian theories of evolution and their relationship to theology.

Halévy, Elie. A HISTORY OF THE ENGLISH PEOPLE IN THE NINETEENTH CENTURY. 2nd rev. ed. Trans. E.I. Watkins and D.A. Baker. 6 vols. London: Benn, 1949-52.

> The most monumental and detailed history of nineteenth-century England. It has had immeasurable influence on all later historians of the period.

Hammond, J.L., and Barbara Hammond. THE TOWN LABOURER, 1760-1832: THE NEW CIVILIZATION. 4th ed. London: Gollancz, 1937.

──────. THE VILLAGE LABOURER: A STUDY IN THE GOVERNMENT OF ENGLAND BEFORE THE REFORM BILL. 4th ed. London: Longmans, Green, 1936.

Harris, Ronald W. ROMANTICISM AND THE SOCIAL ORDER, 1780-1830. New York: Barnes and Noble, 1969.

> Includes chapters on Godwin as the "Philosopher of Anarchism" and Coleridge as the "Philosopher of Conservatism."

Hearnshaw, Fossey J., ed. THE SOCIAL AND POLITICAL IDEAS OF SOME REPRESENTATIVE THINKERS OF THE VICTORIAN AGE. New York: Barnes and Noble, 1930.

> A useful collection of essays, including "Introductory: The Victorian Age, 1837-1901" by George P. Gooch, "Thomas Carlyle" by Robert S. Downer, and "Matthew Arnold and the Educationists" by J. Dover Wilson.

Himmelfarb, Gertrude. VICTORIAN MINDS. New York: Knopf, 1968.

> Himmelfarb focuses on Bentham, J.S. Mill, Stephen, Bagehot, and J.A. Froude. Chapters also on "The Victorian Angst" and "Varieties of Social Darwinism."

Houghton, Walter E. THE VICTORIAN FRAME OF MIND, 1830-1870. New

Haven, Conn.: Yale University Press, 1957.

An excellent introduction to Victorian thought, with sections on "The Commercial Spirit," "The Worship of Force," "Hero Worship," "Love," and "Hypocrisy."

Irvine, William. APES, ANGELS, AND VICTORIANS: DARWIN, HUXLEY, AND EVOLUTION. New York: McGraw-Hill; London: Weidenfeld and Nicolson, 1955.

A composite biography that focuses on the scientific milieu of the later nineteenth century.

Klingender, Francis D. ART AND INDUSTRIAL REVOLUTION. London: Carrington, 1947.

An attempt to show the influence of the industrial age on the art of the century. Chapters on "The Sublime and the Picturesque," "The Railway Age," and "New-Fangled Men."

Knoepflmacher, Ulrich C. RELIGIOUS HUMANISM AND THE VICTORIAN NOVEL. Princeton, N.J.: Princeton University Press, 1965.

This study discusses the Victorian attempts to reconcile classicism and Christianity.

Knox, Bishop E.A. THE TRACTARIAN MOVEMENT. London: Putnam's, 1933.

Knox compares the Oxford Movement with the tradition of Evangelicalism, seeing the former as "a phase of the religious revival in Western Europe."

Lefebvre, Georges. THE FRENCH REVOLUTION. Trans. Elizabeth Moss Evanson, John Hall Stewart, and James Friguglietti. 2 vols. London: Routledge and Kegan Paul, 1962-64.

Traces the Revolution from its origins to 1799 and discusses its tremendous influence on English life and literature.

Levine, Richard A., ed. BACKGROUNDS TO VICTORIAN LITERATURE. San Francisco: Chandler, 1967.

An excellent collection of modern interpretive essays including Noel Annan's "Science, Religion, and the Critical Mind."

Lippincott, Benjamin E. VICTORIAN CRITICS OF DEMOCRACY. London: Oxford University Press, 1938.

Lippincott's thesis is that Carlyle and Ruskin both opposed democracy for the same reason Plato did--a belief that democracy led to disorder.

Marcus, Steven. ENGELS, MANCHESTER, AND THE WORKING CLASS.

Background

New York: Random House, 1974.

Marcus uses Engels' THE CONDITION OF THE WORKING CLASS IN ENGLAND IN 1844 to evaluate Engels' social criticism and literary ability.

──────. THE OTHER VICTORIANS. New York: Basic Books, 1966.

Deals with examples of and attitudes toward pornography in the Victorian period.

Mayhew, Henry. LONDON LABOUR AND THE LONDON POOR. 4 vols. London: Griffin, Bohn, 1861-62; rpt. New York: Dover Publications, 1968.

A basic resource for studying the kinds of poverty among Victorian London's laboring poor (and its criminal types as well). Demonstrates the economic and social conditions tackled by the various Victorian reform movements.

Merz, John T. A HISTORY OF EUROPEAN THOUGHT IN THE NINETEENTH CENTURY. 4 vols. Edinburgh: Blackwood, 1896-1914.

Metz, Rudolf. A HUNDRED YEARS OF BRITISH PHILOSOPHY. Trans. J.W. Harvey, T.E. Jessop, and Henry Sturt. Ed. J[ohn] H. Muirhead. London: Allen and Unwin, 1938.

Moorman, John R. A HISTORY OF THE CHURCH IN ENGLAND. London: Black, 1953.

Parrott, T.M., and Robert B. Martin, eds. COMPANION TO VICTORIAN LITERATURE. New York: Scribner's, 1955.

Includes essays on the political, social, and literary background of the period, as well as on Arnold, Carlyle, Huxley, Mill, Morris, Newman, and Ruskin.

Pilcher, Donald. THE REGENCY STYLE, 1800-1830. London: Batsford, 1947.

Contains over 150 illustrations.

Razzell, P.E., and R.W. Wainwright, eds. THE VICTORIAN WORKING CLASS: SELECTIONS FROM THE MORNING CHRONICLE. London: Cass, 1974.

The newspaper excerpts reveal the "social structure of England during the Industrial Revolution."

Reardon, Bernard M.[G.]. RELIGIOUS THOUGHT IN THE NINETEENTH CENTURY. Cambridge: At the University Press, 1966.

Background

A valuable survey of religious writers on the Continent and in England. Part 2 focuses on Coleridge, F.D. Maurice, Newman, Mill, and Arnold.

Reed, John R. OLD SCHOOL TIES: THE PUBLIC SCHOOLS IN BRITISH LITERATURE. Syracuse, N.Y.: Syracuse University Press, 1964.

Schneewind, Jerome. BACKGROUNDS OF ENGLISH VICTORIAN LITERATURE. New York: Random House, 1970.

Schneewind writes as a professional philosopher about the political, social, and religious developments during 1828-1906.

Seton-Watson, R.W. BRITAIN IN EUROPE, 1789-1914: A SURVEY OF FOREIGN POLICY. Cambridge: At the University Press, 1937.

Generally considered the best examination of this topic.

Singer, Charles, et al., eds. A HISTORY OF TECHNOLOGY. 5 vols. Oxford: Clarendon Press, 1954-58.

A definitive treatment of the subject.

Somerville, D.C. ENGLISH THOUGHT IN THE NINETEENTH CENTURY. 4th ed. London: Methuen, 1940.

A stimulating analysis of the major intellectual developments during the century.

Sorley, William R. A HISTORY OF BRITISH PHILOSOPHY TO 1900. Rev. ed. Cambridge: At the University Press, 1965.

Steegman, John. THE CONSORT OF TASTE. London: Sidgwick and Jackson, 1950; rpt. as VICTORIAN TASTE, Cambridge, Mass.: MIT Press, 1971.

The revised edition includes chapters on art and architectural critics, Ruskin, the Pre-Raphaelite Brotherhood, and the development of the "New Connoisseurship" in the 1850s.

Stephenson, Anthony. "The Development and Immutability of Christian Doctrine." TS, 29 (1958), 481-532.

Deals with the religious climate of nineteenth-century England.

Thompson, Edward P. THE MAKING OF THE ENGLISH WORKING CLASS. New York: Pantheon Books, 1963; rpt. New York: Gollancz, 1966.

Generally considered the authoritative investigation of this subject. Includes a chapter on Cobbett.

Background

Traill, Henry D., ed. SOCIAL ENGLAND, A RECORD OF THE PROGRESS IN RELIGION, LAWS, LEARNING, ARTS, INDUSTRY, COMMERCE, SCIENCE, LITERATURE, AND MANNERS. 6 vols. London: Cassell, 1894-98.

>Volume 6 is FROM THE BATTLE OF WATERLOO TO THE GENERAL ELECTION OF 1885 (1898).

Trevelyan, George O. BRITISH HISTORY IN THE NINETEENTH CENTURY AND AFTER. 2nd ed. London: Longmans, Green, 1946.

>See also White, below.

_____. ILLUSTRATED ENGLISH SOCIAL HISTORY. 4 vols. London: Longmans, Green, 1952.

>Both of Trevelyan's books are classics, although somewhat dated. Volume 4 of the ILLUSTRATED ENGLISH SOCIAL HISTORY deals with the nineteenth century.

Tulloch, John. MOVEMENTS OF RELIGIOUS THOUGHT IN BRITAIN DURING THE NINETEENTH CENTURY. New York: Scribner's, 1885; rpt. Leicester, Engl.: Leicester University Press, 1971.

>Tulloch's study is still valuable as a general survey of the age.

Turner, Frank Miller. BETWEEN SCIENCE AND RELIGION: THE REACTION TO SCIENTIFIC NATURALISM IN LATE VICTORIAN ENGLAND. New Haven, Conn.: Yale University Press, 1974.

>A major work that analyzes Butler as a believer in subjective faith rather than reason as the guide for man's actions.

Vidler, Alec R. THE CHURCH IN AN AGE OF REVOLUTION: 1789 TO THE PRESENT DAY. Baltimore: Penguin, 1962.

Ward, William R. RELIGION AND SOCIETY IN ENGLAND, 1790-1850. London: Batsford, 1972.

>Ward's study traces the impact of political changes on the established religions.

Watson, J. Steven. THE REIGN OF GEORGE III, 1760-1815. London: Oxford University Press, 1963.

>A general survey of the age.

Wearmouth, Robert F. SOME WORKING CLASS MOVEMENTS OF THE NINETEENTH CENTURY. London: Epworth Press, 1948.

White, Reginald J. WATERLOO TO PETERLOO. London: Heinemann, 1957.

Background

White's study is a valuable supplement to Trevelyan's BRITISH HISTORY, above.

Whitley, William T. ART IN ENGLAND: 1800-1820. Cambridge: At the University Press, 1928.

_____. ART IN ENGLAND: 1821-1837. Cambridge: At the University Press, 1930.

Willey, Basil. CHRISTIANITY PAST AND PRESENT. Cambridge: At the University Press, 1952.

> A brief survey of the development of Christian beliefs. Sections on the nineteenth century include discussions of the de-Christianization of humanism, and of Huxley and Stephen as "honest doubters."

_____. THE EIGHTEENTH-CENTURY BACKGROUND: STUDIES ON THE IDEA OF NATURE IN THE PERIOD. Boston: Beacon Press, 1966.

> Discusses "natural" science, religion, and law, as well as "nature in literary theory." Also includes a section on Godwin and the early romantics.

Williams, Raymond. CULTURE AND SOCIETY, 1780-1950. 2nd ed. New York: Anchor Books, 1959.

> A valuable survey of the idea of culture--"our responses in thought and feeling to the changes in English society since the late eighteenth century." The introduction defines key words of the nineteenth century--"industry," "democracy," "class," "art," and "culture." Includes discussions of Bentham, Cobbett, Coleridge, Mill, Carlyle, Newman, Arnold, Ruskin, and Morris.

Wood, Anthony. NINETEENTH-CENTURY BRITAIN. London: Longmans, Green, 1960.

Woodward, Sir E. Llewellyn. THE AGE OF REFORM, 1815-1870. London: Oxford University Press, 1962.

> A thorough history of the era with a portrait of England in 1815 and chapters on "Religion and the Churches," "English Literature and the Development of Ideas," and "Movements in the Sciences and Arts."

Young, George M., ed. EARLY VICTORIAN ENGLAND, 1830-1865. 2 vols. London: Oxford University Press, 1934.

> Contains several interesting essays on periodicals, travel, education,

Background

and religion. The final essay, "Portrait of an Age," is a valuable summary of the entire period. Young expanded this essay into a book-length study, below.

_____. VICTORIAN ENGLAND: PORTRAIT OF AN AGE. 2nd ed. London: Oxford University Press, 1963.

Generally considered a classic, though it is complex. Historical, social, political, literary, religious, and artistic topics are discussed. Also contains a year-by-year chronological table of important events.

3. INDIVIDUAL AUTHORS

As the table of contents indicates, writers listed in this section are arranged by the major subjects of their prose. For every author the order of entries is:

PRINCIPAL PROSE WORKS (arranged chronologically)

COLLECTED WORKS (arranged alphabetically by title; includes selected recent collections)

LETTERS (arranged alphabetically by author of critical studies; includes representations of letters) or by titles of books of selections or collections of letters

BIOGRAPHIES (arranged alphabetically by author)

CRITICAL STUDIES (arranged alphabetically by author and selected with emphasis on studies published after 1960, although important works before this date are also included)

BIBLIOGRAPHIES, including checklists and bibliographical essays (arranged alphabetically by author or editor)

CRITICAL, PHILOSOPHICAL, POLEMICAL

MATTHEW ARNOLD (1822-88)

PRINCIPAL PROSE WORKS

ENGLAND AND THE ITALIAN QUESTION, 1859.

ON TRANSLATING HOMER. THREE LECTURES GIVEN AT OXFORD, 1861.

HEINRICH HEINE, 1863.

ESSAYS IN CRITICISM, 1865; 1869; 1875.

ON THE STUDY OF CELTIC LITERATURE, 1867.

SCHOOLS AND UNIVERSITIES ON THE CONTINENT, 1868.

CULTURE AND ANARCHY: AN ESSAY IN POLITICAL AND SOCIAL CRITICISM, 1869.

ST. PAUL AND PROTESTANTISM; WITH AN INTRODUCTION ON PURITANISM AND THE CHURCH OF ENGLAND, 1870.

FRIENDSHIP'S GARLAND: BEING THE CONVERSATIONS, LETTERS, AND OPINIONS OF THE LATE ARMINIUS, BARON VON THUNDER-TEN-TRONCKH, 1871.

LITERATURE AND DOGMA. AN ESSAY TOWARDS A BETTER APPREHENSION OF THE BIBLE, 1873.

GOD AND THE BIBLE: A REVIEW OF OBJECTIONS TO LITERATURE AND DOGMA, 1875.

LAST ESSAYS ON CHURCH AND RELIGION, 1877.

Matthew Arnold

MIXED ESSAYS, 1879.

IRISH ESSAYS AND OTHERS, 1882.

EMERSON, 1884.

DISCOURSES IN AMERICA, 1885.

CIVILIZATION IN THE UNITED STATES: FIRST AND LAST IMPRESSIONS OF AMERICA, 1888.

COLLECTED WORKS

THE COMPLETE PROSE WORKS OF MATTHEW ARNOLD. Ed. R[obert] H. Super. 10 vols. Ann Arbor: University of Michigan Press, 1960-74.
> The authoritative edition of the prose works. Volume 1: ON THE CLASSICAL TRADITION, 1960; volume 2: DEMOCRATIC EDUCATION, 1962; volume 3: LECTURES AND ESSAYS IN CRITICISM, 1962; volume 4: SCHOOLS AND UNIVERSITIES ON THE CONTINENT, 1964; volume 5: CULTURE AND ANARCHY, 1965; volume 6: DISSENT AND DOGMA, 1968; volume 7: GOD AND THE BIBLE, 1970; volume 8: ESSAYS RELIGIOUS AND MIXED, 1972; volume 9: ENGLISH LITERATURE AND IRISH POLITICS, 1973; volume 10: PHILISTINISM IN ENGLAND AND AMERICA, 1974.

ESSAYS IN CRITICISM, FIRST SERIES; A CRITICAL EDITION. Ed. Sister T.M. Hoctor. Chicago: University of Chicago Press, 1968.

ESSAYS, LETTERS, AND REVIEWS BY MATTHEW ARNOLD. Ed. Fraser Neiman. Cambridge, Mass.: Harvard University Press, 1960.

ESSAYS ON ENGLISH LITERATURE. Ed. F[rederick] W. Bateson. London: McBride 1938; rpt. London: University of London Press, 1965.

FIVE UNCOLLECTED ESSAYS OF MATTHEW ARNOLD. Ed. Kenneth Allott. Liverpool, Engl.: University Press of Liverpool, 1953.

MATTHEW ARNOLD: SELECTED PROSE. Ed. P.J. Keating. London: Penguin, 1971.

A MATTHEW ARNOLD PROSE SELECTION. Ed. John D. Jump. London: Macmillan, 1965.

Matthew Arnold

THE NOTEBOOKS OF MATTHEW ARNOLD. Eds. H.F. Lowry et al. London: Oxford University Press, 1952.

PASSAGES FROM THE PROSE WRITINGS OF MATTHEW ARNOLD SELECTED BY THE AUTHOR. Ed. William E. Buckler. New York: New York University Press, 1963.

POETRY AND CRITICISM OF MATTHEW ARNOLD. Ed. A. Dwight Culler. Boston: Houghton Mifflin, 1961.

THE PORTABLE MATTHEW ARNOLD. Ed. Lionel Trilling. New York: Viking, 1949.

THE WORKS OF MATTHEW ARNOLD. 15 vols. London: Macmillan, 1903-04; rpt. New York: AMS Press, 1970.

LETTERS

Armytage, Walter H.G. "Matthew Arnold and T.H. Huxley: Some New Letters: 1870-1880." RES, 4 (1953), 346-53.

Baylen, Joseph O. "Matthew Arnold and the PALL MALL GAZETTE: Some Unpublished Letters, 1884-1887." SAQ, 68 (1969), 543-55.

Brooks, Roger L. "Letters of Matthew Arnold: A Supplementary Checklist." SP, 63 (1966), 93-98.

_____. "Matthew Arnold and His Contemporaries: A Checklist of Unpublished and Published Letters." SP, 56 (1959), 647-53.

_____. "Matthew Arnold's Correspondence." MP, 59 (1962), 273-75.

LETTERS OF MATTHEW ARNOLD, 1848-1888. Ed. George W.E. Russell. 2 vols. New York: Macmillan, 1895.
> The standard edition, but lacks an index and has few annotations. Must be supplemented heavily by later publications of letters. For commentary see Peterson, under "Critical Studies," p. 56.

LETTERS OF MATTHEW ARNOLD TO ARTHUR HENRY CLOUGH. Ed. H[oward] F. Lowry. London: Oxford University Press, 1932.
> A valuable collection that reveals the development of Arnold's poetic theories.

Rea, E.E. "Matthew Arnold on Education: Unpublished Letters to Harriet Martineau." YES, 2 (1972), 181-91.

> Reprints unpublished letters that discuss Arnold's views on "providing the best education for the rapidly expanding middle classes."

Williamson, Eugene. "Matthew Arnold's Letters to George Stacey Gibson." VN, 31 (1967), 40-42.

> Reprints Arnold's letters to the botanist.

BIOGRAPHIES

Chambers, Edmund K. MATTHEW ARNOLD: A STUDY. Oxford: Clarendon Press, 1947; rpt. New York: Russell and Russell, 1964.

> Includes chapters on "The Professor" and "The Philosopher;" however, use with caution. This work has been criticized for containing factual errors.

Paul, Herbert W. MATTHEW ARNOLD. London: Macmillan, 1902.

> Includes chapters on ESSAYS IN CRITICISM and discussions of Arnold's philosophy, theology, and politics. An early and admiring study that praises Arnold as "our English Goethe."

Russell, George W.E. MATTHEW ARNOLD. New York: Scribner's, 1904; rpt. New York: Haskell House, 1970.

> An admiring biography that praises Arnold's prose, for "in all questions affecting national character and tendency, his insight was penetrating, his point of view perfectly original."

Trilling, Lionel. MATTHEW ARNOLD. 3rd ed. New York: Meridian Books, 1955.

> Arnold wanted no biography to be written of him. None really has. The most valuable approach is Trilling's study, which, according to the author, "may be thought of as a biography of Arnold's mind."

CRITICAL STUDIES

Alaya, Flavia M. "Arnold and Renan on the Popular Uses of History." JHI, 28 (1967), 551-74.

> Discusses the two writers' similarities as popularizers of intellectual and cultural history.

Alexander, Edward. MATTHEW ARNOLD AND JOHN STUART MILL. New York: Columbia University Press; London: Routledge and Kegan Paul, 1965.

    Alexander states he wants "to show the confluence of humanism and liberalism by comparing the chief representatives of the two traditions in Victorian England."

_____. MATTHEW ARNOLD, JOHN RUSKIN AND THE MODERN TEMPER. Columbus: Ohio State University Press, 1973.

    Discusses the war both writers waged with society about the artist's role as social critic.

_____. "Roles of the Victorian Critic: Matthew Arnold and John Ruskin." LITERARY CRITICISM AND HISTORICAL UNDERSTANDING: SELECTED PAPERS FROM THE ENGLISH INSTITUTE. Ed. Philip Damon. New York: Columbia University Press, 1967.

    "Arnold's career as a critic was shaped in part by his desire to subordinate his personality to the task of persuasion." Discusses Ruskin's social criticism only as it differs with Arnold's.

Allott, Kenneth. "Conditional Immortality: Matthew Arnold and Goethe." N&Q, 19 (1972), 253.

_____. MATTHEW ARNOLD. London: Longmans, Green, 1955.

    A brief study that discusses Arnold as a "great critic" who "commits himself unambiguously and in an 'unprofessional' language [to] the relationship between his literary opinions and his views on the 'great questions' of life and society."

_____. "Matthew Arnold and Mary Claude." N&Q, 17 (1969), 209-11.

_____. "Matthew Arnold's Reading Lists in Three Early Diaries." VS, 2 (1959), 254-66.

    Uses the six early reading lists to show the "striking continuity" between the young poet of the 1840s and the author of the ESSAYS IN CRITICISM.

Anderson, Warren D. MATTHEW ARNOLD AND THE CLASSICAL TRADITION. Ann Arbor: University of Michigan Press, 1971.

    Written by a classicist, this work explores the elements of Stoicism and Epicureanism in Arnold's work.

Bachem-Alent, Rose. "Arnold's and Renan's View of Perfection." RLC, 41 (1967), 228-37.

Arnold was not influenced by Renan, but instead found in the French writer "a mirror of his own thought."

_____. "A Comparison of Two Moralists: Arnold and Scherer." RLC, 43 (1969), 344-52.

A comparative study that concludes there are "astonishing intellectual and spiritual parallels between the two writers."

Bantock, Geoffrey H. "Matthew Arnold, H.M.I." SCRUTINY, 18 (1951), 32-44.

Emphasizes Arnold's importance as an educator.

Blount, Paul G. "Matthew Arnold on Wordsworth." SLI, 1 (1967), 3-11.

Comments on "Arnold's views on Wordsworth, not so much to arrive at a better understanding of Wordsworth, but to examine Arnold as poet and as critic."

Bromwich, Rachel. ARNOLD AND CELTIC LITERATURE: A RETROSPECT, 1865-1965. Oxford: Clarendon Press, 1965.

Discusses "the importance both of Arnold's direct, and of his indirect contribution towards the development of Celtic studies."

Brooks, Roger L. "Matthew Arnold and the LONDON REVIEW." PMLA, 76 (1961), 622-23.

Uses Arnold's unpublished diaries to identify and discuss an Arnold essay published anonymously in the LONDON REVIEW.

_____. "Matthew Arnold's 'Joseph de Maistre on Russia.'" HLQ, 30 (1967), 185-88.

Brown, Edward K. MATTHEW ARNOLD: A STUDY IN CONFLICT. Chicago: University of Chicago Press, 1948.

Brown intends to "illuminate Arnold's writings by tracing the history of a lifelong conflict within his personality."

_____. STUDIES IN THE TEXT OF MATTHEW ARNOLD'S PROSE WORKS. Paris: Andre, 1935.

Brown attempts to explore Arnold's "personality, thought, and art by a study of his revisions," primarily those of CULTURE AND ANARCHY.

Buckler, William E. MATTHEW ARNOLD'S BOOKS: TOWARD A PUBLISHING DIARY. Geneva: Droz, 1958.

Analyzes Arnold's correspondence with his publishers to detail Arnold's business transactions and the public reception of his works.

_____. "Studies in Three Arnold Problems." PMLA, 73 (1958), 260-69.

"Adds some new information and a new speculation or two about the evolution and text of Arnold's major effort at social criticism, CULTURE AND ANARCHY."

Buckley, Vincent. POETRY AND MORALITY: STUDIES ON THE CRITICISM OF MATTHEW ARNOLD, T.S. ELIOT, AND F.R. LEAVIS. London: Chatto and Windus, 1959.

Includes two chapters on Arnold which conclude that he is "a didactic critic" and "a moralist of a quasi-religious kind" who sees "the poet as a priest of the religion of elevated naturalism."

Burgum, Edwin B. "The Humanism of Matthew Arnold." SYMPOSIUM, 2 (1931), 85-112.

Burgum concludes that Arnold's "great success was due to his being thoroughly at one with his generation in fundamentals while he was obviously superior in being able to reason a little better."

Bush, Douglas. MATTHEW ARNOLD: A SURVEY OF HIS POETRY AND PROSE. New York: Macmillan, 1971.

A valuable survey that utilizes recent scholarship.

Butts, Denis. "Newman's Influence on Matthew Arnold's Theory of Poetry." N&Q, 5 (1958), 255-56.

Butts claims that Newman's influence on Arnold reveals Arnold was more in sympathy with Christianity than is often recognized.

Buyniak, Victor O. "Leo Tolstoy and Matthew Arnold." WAR, 3 (1968), 63-71.

"In his continuous search for answers to questions in the field of art, philosophy, and religion Arnold greatly resembled Tolstoy."

Carnall, Geoffrey. "Matthew Arnold's 'Great Critical Effort.'" EIC, 8 (1958), 256-68.

Carnall states that "it is not always realised how very commonplace Arnold's social criticism is," particularly in the sixth chapter of CULTURE AND ANARCHY.

Cherry, Douglas. "The Two Cultures of Matthew Arnold and T.H. Huxley." WAR, 1 (1966), 53-61.

Matthew Arnold

Discusses the inadequacy of Arnold's "Literature and Science" as
a defense of the study of literature.

Cockshut, A.O.J. "Matthew Arnold: Conservative Revolutionary." In his
THE UNBELIEVERS: ENGLISH AGNOSTIC THOUGHT, 1840-1890. New York:
New York University Press, 1966.

Arnold "undertook the immense task of transforming the religious
consciousness of mankind" by accepting "the whole Christian system as if it were a work of art."

Connell, William F. THE EDUCATIONAL THOUGHT AND INFLUENCE OF
MATTHEW ARNOLD. London: Routledge and Kegan Paul, 1950.

Connell places Arnold in the development of nineteenth-century
English educational theory and explores his impact on later educators.

Corner, Martin. "Steadily and Whole: Arnold's Early Understanding of Poetry, 1845-49." ISE, 1 (1969), 7-25.

Claims that, in his earliest statements, Arnold saw poetry "as a
work of art and not as a vehicle for either a moral or an intellectual criticism of life." The "deficiencies in Arnold's understanding of poetry relate to the role which he gives to language
in the process of creation."

_____. "Text and Context in Arnold's ESSAYS IN CRITICISM." NEO, 57
(1973), 188-97.

"In most of his earlier essays Arnold establishes his critical context
explicitly and extensively before beginning any discussion of text,
whereas in the later essays he generally starts to discuss the writing
straight away, and establishes the critical context incidentally,
point by point, as the discussion advances."

Coulling, Sidney M.B. "The Background of 'The Function of Criticism at the
Present Time.'" PQ, 42 (1963), 36-54.

Coulling traces the evolution of Arnold's critical and cultural
theories and maintains that various disappointments motivated Arnold's later view of perfection, "Culture."

_____. "The Evolution of CULTURE AND ANARCHY." SP, 40 (1963), 637-68.

Coulling emphasizes the continuity of Arnold's thought, but criticizes CULTURE AND ANARCHY for its immersion in topical concerns.

_____. MATTHEW ARNOLD AND HIS CRITICS. Athens: Ohio University
Press, 1974.

This study centers on the "polemical encounters" between Arnold
and the contemporary reviewers. Coulling focuses on Arnold's attempts to answer his critics' charges in his later works.

———. "Matthew Arnold's 1853 Preface: Its Origin and Aftermath." VS, 7
(1964), 233-63.

A comprehensive analysis of the contemporary critical milieu in
which Arnold wrote.

———. "Renan's Influence on Arnold's Literary and Social Criticism." FSUS,
5 (1952), 95-112.

States "Renan's influence on Arnold's critical writings has been
greatly exaggerated and that these writings do not, in fact, offer
evidence of significant influence by Renan."

———. "Swinburne and Arnold." PQ, 49 (1970), 211-33.

Traces the literary relationship and concludes that Arnold's comment
on Swinburne as a "pseudo-Shelley" caused bitterness in Swinburne.
See Meyers, below.

Cox, R[eginald] G. "Victorian Criticism of Poetry: The Minority Tradition."
SCRUTINY, 18 (1951), 2-17.

Cox shows that Arnold's unfavorable view of the romantics was
anticipated by reviewers writing for BLACKWOOD'S, FRASER'S,
and the QUARTERLY.

Culler, A. Dwight. "No Arnold Could Ever Write a Novel." VN, 29 (1966),
1-5.

Article claims that ESSAYS IN CRITICISM recounts Arnold's intellectual quest--his wandering from the forsaken romantic and Christian traditions to his ideal of culture.

Day, Paul W. MATTHEW ARNOLD AND THE PHILOSOPHY OF VICO.
Auckland, New Zealand: West, 1964.

"The aim of this paper is to show that Arnold's observation of the
past was not a vague yearning for escape, but the manifestation
of a habit of thought which provided him with a framework."
This framework was "ultimately derived" from Giambattista Vico.

DeLaura, David J. "Arnold and Carlyle." PMLA, 79 (1964), 104-29.

An important essay in which DeLaura explores Arnold's "persistent
ambivalence toward Carlyle," which was caused by Arnold's
need to conceal Carlyle's influence on his writing. For a different view, see Wilkinson, below.

Matthew Arnold

_____. "Arnold and Hazlitt." ELN, 9 (1972), 277-83.

Arnold was influenced by Hazlitt in at least two ways: "Hazlitt's presentation of Coleridge" was the basis for Arnold's depiction of Coleridge, while Arnold's portrait of Oxford is indebted to Hazlitt's "Pictures at Oxford and Blenheim."

_____. "Arnold, Clough, Dr. Arnold, and 'Thyrsis.'" VP, 7 (1969), 191-202.

Examines an unpublished letter from Arnold to his mother that reveals that Arnold "did not know certain essential facts about Clough's development until 1865."

_____. "A Background for Arnold's 'Shakespeare.'" NINETEENTH-CENTURY LITERARY PERSPECTIVES. Eds. Clyde de L. Ryals et al. Durham, N.C.: Duke University Press, 1974.

Explores the "attitudes held by Arnold's contemporaries and his Romantic predecessors" about Shakespeare as a poet who effaced the self from his works.

_____. "Matthew Arnold and John Henry Newman: The 'Oxford Sentiment' and the Religion of the Future." TSLL, 6 (1965), 571-602.

Stresses Arnold's great debt to Newman's critical writings.

_____. "What, Then, Does Matthew Arnold Mean?" MP, 66 (1969), 345-55.

An essay review of William Madden's MATTHEW ARNOLD, below, which asks the question, "Why should Arnold's poetry and criticism continue to engage this generation?"

_____. "The 'Wordsworth' of Pater and Arnold: 'The Supreme Artistic View of Life.'" SEL, 6 (1966), 651-67.

Discusses Arnold's condemnation of Pater's formalism and aestheticism.

_____, ed. MATTHEW ARNOLD: A COLLECTION OF CRITICAL ESSAYS. Englewood Cliffs, N.J.: Prentice-Hall, 1973.

A useful collection, including essays by T.S. Eliot, Hillis Miller, Dwight Culler, and A.O.J. Cockshut.

Donovan, Robert A. "The Method of Arnold's ESSAYS IN CRITICISM." PMLA, 71 (1956), 922-31.

Attempts to discover a "simple, clear-cut thesis" in the ESSAYS, which seem like a "hodgepodge, a collection of odds and ends."

Matthew Arnold

Eells, John S., Jr. THE TOUCHSTONES OF MATTHEW ARNOLD. New York: Bookman, 1955.

    A study of Arnold's "touchstone" theory of criticism; asks if "a new link may be established between Arnold's criticism and his poetry." Eells concludes that Arnold's method "reveals serious difficulties and limitations in the touchstone theory."

Eliot, T.S. "Arnold and Pater." In his SELECTED ESSAYS. 3rd ed. London: Faber and Faber, 1951.

    Explores Pater's indebtedness to Arnold and claims that Pater's "art for art's sake" was an "offspring of Arnold's culture."

----------. "Matthew Arnold." In his THE USE OF POETRY AND THE USE OF CRITICISM. London: Faber and Faber, 1933.

    Eliot attacks Arnold by stating: "To ask poetry that it give religious and philosophical satisfaction while deprecating philosophy and dogmatic religion, is of course to embrace the shadow of a shade."

Engelberg, Edward. "James and Arnold: Conscience and Consciousness in Victorian 'Künstlerroman.'" CRITICISM, 10 (1968), 93-114.

    Article suggests the complexity of James's reaction to major theories in Arnold.

Farrell, John P. "Homeward Bound: Arnold's Late Criticism." VS, 17 (1974), 187-206.

    Arnold's "late literary criticism seems at once more flexible and more controlled, more searching and yet more assured than the work which initially earned him his reputation. There is also, in his late criticism, a softening of tensions. . . . It is, therefore, difficult to find a context for the late criticism."

----------. "Matthew Arnold and the Middle Ages: The Uses of the Past." VS, 13 (1970), 319-38.

    Farrell claims that Arnold was able to control the fluctuations in his thought through his uses of the past for reference points.

----------. "Matthew Arnold's Tragic Vision." PMLA, 85 (1970), 107-17.

    Arnold defined tragedy as man's victimization by the historical order, not a supernatural one.

Faverty, Frederic E. MATTHEW ARNOLD, THE ETHNOLOGIST. Evanston, Ill.: Northwestern University Press, 1951; rpt. New York: AMS Press, 1968.

    Includes an examination of Arnold's writings on Celtic literature and racial theories. Arnold "desires not to divide races or nations, but to bring them together."

Feltes, N[orman] N. "Matthew Arnold and the Modern Spirit: A Reassessment." UTQ, 32 (1962), 27-36.

> Feltes claims that Arnold's criticism is not consistent, but rather that "his work is divided into two fairly distinct periods, periods characterized by two distinct attitudes towards what Arnold thought of as 'the modern spirit.'"

Fuller, Roy. "Philistines and Jacobins." SR, 77 (1969), 692-706.

> Fuller discusses Arnold's concept of culture as an antidote to prevailing currents of anarchism and irrationality.

Goldberg, James F. "'Culture' and 'Anarchy' and the Present Time." KR, 31 (1969), 127.

> Applies Arnold's critical views to the contemporary scene and observes that "no essay of the last hundred years has been more influential in formulating the values of liberal humanism."

Goode, John. "1848 and the Strange Disease of Modern Love." LITERATURE AND POLITICS IN THE NINETEENTH CENTURY. Ed. John Lucas. New York: Barnes and Noble, 1971.

> Goode sets Arnold (and secondarily Mill and Bagehot) into their political milieu and claims that they all display "the despair, hysteria or mystification which appears in so much of the literature of the mid-Victorian period."

Goodstein, Jack D. "Poetry, Religion, and Fact: Matthew Arnold." COSTERUS, 1 (1972), 115-22.

> Discusses Arnold's "The Study of Poetry" for its "over-emphasis on the moral aspects of poetry, his overall confusion of poetry and religion."

Gordon, Jan B. "Hebraism, Hellenism, and THE PICTURE OF DORIAN GRAY." VN, 33 (1968), 36-38.

> An interesting article which explores Arnold's influence on Wilde.

Gottfried, Leon. MATTHEW ARNOLD AND THE ROMANTICS. Lincoln: University of Nebraska Press, 1963.

> Gottfried states that Arnold experienced a "deep split between his inherited conditioning toward Romanticism as the only available 'great tradition' at once modern and English, and his belief that it was a tradition inadequate to the needs of the modern world."

Gregor, Ian. "The Critic and the Age: Some Observations on the Social Criticism of Matthew Arnold and T.S. Eliot." DUR, 227 (1953), 394-404.

    Gregor claims that Arnold's criticism contains a sense of human potential while Eliot's is deficient in recommending social melioration.

Haney, James E. "The Scholarly Edition: Professor Robert H. Super's Preparation of THE COMPLETE PROSE WORKS OF MATTHEW ARNOLD." RESEARCH NEWS, 19 (1969), 3-6.

    See THE COMPLETE PROSE WORKS, p. 40.

Harding, F.J.W. MATTHEW ARNOLD: THE CRITIC AND FRANCE. Geneva: Droz, 1964.

    Harding asserts that Arnold used French writers to provide guidance for his own directions, and celebrated France as a model of humanistic culture.

Harris, Alan. "Matthew Arnold: The 'Unknown Years.'" NC, 118 (1933), 498-509.

    Discusses Arnold's friendship with Clough as revealed in the letters. Also conjectures about his relationships with various women, particularly "Marguerite."

Harris, Wendell V. "Arnold, Pater, Wilde, and the Object as in Themselves They See It." SEL, 11 (1971), 733-47.

    "Arnold had not faced the question of how the artist or critic can get beyond or behind immediate individual impressions."

Haworth, Helen E. "Arnold's Keats." RUO, 41 (1971), 245-52.

    Discusses Arnold's negative views of Keats's letters and poetry.

Hipple, Walter J. "Matthew Arnold, Dialectician." UTQ, 32 (1962), 1-26.

    Hipple claims that Arnold's "teaching is coherent and grounded on first principles" while his thought is "whole, coherent, consistent, stable."

Holloway, John. "Matthew Arnold and the Modern Dilemma." In his THE CHARTED MIRROR. New York: Horizon, 1960.

    Holloway discusses Arnold as Eliot's precursor in poetic theory.

Honan, Park. "A Note on Matthew Arnold in Love." VN, 39 (1971), 11-15.

    Honan summarizes the evidence for identifying Mary Claude as Arnold's inspiration for Marguerite.

Matthew Arnold

Houghton, Walter [E.]. "Victorian Anti-Intellectualism." JHI, 13 (1952), 291-313.

> Discusses Arnold's condemnation of the philistines in CULTURE AND ANARCHY.

Hunt, Everett Lee. "Matthew Arnold: The Critic as Rhetorician." QJS, 20 (1934), 483-507.

> Hunt analyzes Arnold's claim of disinterestedness and instead sees a note of persuasion in his criticism.

James, David [G.]. MATTHEW ARNOLD AND THE DECLINE OF ENGLISH ROMANTICISM. Oxford: Clarendon Press, 1961.

> James discusses Arnold's personal and critical temperament and "illustrates the decline of Romanticism in England by reviewing Arnold's critical works."

Jamison, William A. ARNOLD AND THE ROMANTICS. Copenhagen: Rosenkilde and Baggar, 1958.

> Jamison discusses both Arnold's reliance on Coleridge's critical theories and his extensive comments on the romantics in ESSAYS IN CRITICISM.

Jump, John D. "Matthew Arnold." FROM DICKENS TO HARDY. Ed. Boris Ford. Baltimore: Penguin, 1958.

> Discusses Arnold's prose as an "exemplification of the value to the community of the flexible, non-specialist, critical intelligence."

_____. MATTHEW ARNOLD. London: Longmans, Green, 1955.

> Considers Arnold as man, poet, and critic, and concludes that although "Arnold's poetry appears narrow in theme," his prose is "impressive in its clear sense of things as they are."

_____. "Matthew Arnold and the SATURDAY REVIEW." RES, 22 (1946), 322-24.

> Discusses the SATURDAY REVIEW's decreasing hostility toward Arnold.

_____. "Matthew Arnold and THE SPECTATOR." RES, 25 (1959), 61-64.

> Discusses critical exchanges between Arnold and the SPECTATOR that reveal "how Arnold's classical doctrines struck a representative cultured contemporary."

_____. "Weekly Reviewing in the Eighteen-Sixties." RES, 3 (1952), 244-62.

Places Arnold's work in the literary journalism of the decade.

Knickerbocker, William S. "Matthew Arnold at Oxford." SR, 35 (1927), 399-418.

Traces the "natural history" of the relationship between Thomas and Matthew Arnold, and concludes that it caused "Arnold's complete change in the subject-matter of his writing after 1867."

Kogan, Pauline. "The Bourgeois Line on Culture and Anarchy in Matthew Arnold and T.S. Eliot." L&I, 8 (1971), 1-14.

"That Arnold's culture-mongering reduces itself to support for bourgeois dictatorship is apparent throughout CULTURE AND ANARCHY." Marxist critical approach.

Krieger, Murray. "The Critical Legacy of Matthew Arnold: Or the Strange Brotherhood of T.S. Eliot, I.A. Richards, and Northrop Frye." SOR, 5 (1969), 457-74.

Krieger claims that Arnold's 1853 preface to his POEMS was crucial to Eliot's doctrine of the objective correlative and unified sensibility.

Leavis, Frank R. "Arnold as Critic." SCRUTINY, 7 (1938), 319-32.

One of the staple essays in the Arnold critical canon. Leavis defines Arnold's continuing importance and refutes Eliot's criticisms.

Lee, Robert A. "James Baldwin and Matthew Arnold: Thoughts on 'Relevance.'" CLAJ, 14 (1971), 324-30.

LeRoy, Gaylord C. "Ambivalence in Matthew Arnold's Prose Criticism." CE, 13 (1952), 432-38.

LeRoy discusses Arnold's ambivalence toward the modern world as the cause of a personal and psychic dilemma.

Lowry, Howard F. MATTHEW ARNOLD AND THE MODERN SPIRIT. Princeton, N.J.: Princeton University Press, 1941.

Drawing on his experience in editing Arnold's correspondence with Clough, Lowry anayzes the development of Arnold's poetic theories.

Lubell, Albert J. "Matthew Arnold: Between Two Worlds." MLQ, 22 (1961), 248-63.

Lubell analyzes the 1845-47 notebooks as a composite of naturalism and idealism.

Matthew Arnold

Lucas, John. "Dickens and Arnold." RMS, 16 (1971), 86-111.

> Lucas considers Dickens a greater critic of Victorian society: "his kind of radical greatness makes Arnold look minor in comparison."

McCarthy, Patrick J. ARNOLD AND THE THREE CLASSES. New York: Columbia University Press, 1964.

> McCarthy discusses Arnold's three classes--"Barbarians," "Philistines," and "Populace"--as literary constructs created for social criticism.

―――. "Reading Victorian Prose: Arnold's 'Culture and Its Enemies.'" UTQ, 40 (1971), 119-35.

> McCarthy argues that Arnold's prose tries to bridge the oppositions in nineteenth-century society by attempting to inhabit the "real and ideal, artistic and practical, temporal and eternal" realms.

Madden, William [A.]. MATTHEW ARNOLD: A STUDY OF THE AESTHETIC TEMPERAMENT IN VICTORIAN ENGLAND. Bloomington: Indiana University Press, 1967.

> Madden's study stresses the pervasiveness of aestheticism in Arnold's personality and works. See DeLaura, "What, Then, Does Matthew Arnold Mean?," p. 48.

Mahan, Charles. "Matthew Arnold's Concept of History." STUDIES IN THE HUMANITIES, 1 (1969-70), 19-30.

> "One of the important aspects of Arnold's contributions to English letters is his concept of alternating epochs of creative synthesis and critical analysis in history."

Major, John Campbell. "Matthew Arnold and Attic Prose Style." PMLA, 59 (1944), 1086-1103.

> An important summary of Arnold's theory and practice of prose style.

Mathewson, George. "Matthew Arnold's 'Ineffectual Angel.'" KSMB, 21 (1970), 3-6.

> Contrasts Arnold's attitude toward Shelley with his opinion of Goethe as "the effectual incarnation of the modern spirit."

Meyers, Terry L. "Swinburne's Later Opinion of Arnold." ELN, 10 (1972), 118-22.

> Disagrees with Coulling, p. 47, and states that Swinburne's final opinion of Arnold was not one of bitterness but of "narrow appreciation."

Moyer, Charles R. "The Idea of History in Thomas and Matthew Arnold." MP, 67 (1969), 160-67.

> Asserts that "the historical nature of Arnold's thinking is everywhere apparent in his works" and is indebted to his father's theories.

Murry, John Middleton. "Matthew Arnold and His Ideals." In his LOOKING BEFORE AND AFTER. London: Sheppard Press, 1948.

> Discusses Arnold's attempt "to restate the fundamentals of Christianity in a form which might serve as the basis of the new universal society."

Neiman, Fraser. MATTHEW ARNOLD. New York: Twayne, 1968.

> A reliable and scholarly introduction to the many aspects of Arnold's career.

──────. "The 'Zeitgeist' of Matthew Arnold." PMLA, 72 (1957), 977-96.

> Analyzes the "metaphysical suggestions" and "demonic force" that Arnold attributed to the term "Zeitgeist."

Newton, J.M. "Some Notes on Religion, Irreligion, and Matthew Arnold." CQ, 4 (1969), 115-24.

> Newton attempts to evaluate Arnold's poetic and religious ideas and their interrelation.

Noland, Richard Wells. "The Uses of Imaginative Reason." HSL, 2 (1970), 75-84.

> An essay review of six major recent studies of Arnold that concludes Arnold's importance lies in his "modernity."

Ohmann, Richard. "Methods in the Study of Victorian Style." VN, 27 (1965), 1-4.

> Ohmann concentrates on Arnold's prose as an example.

Orrick, James Bentley. "Matthew Arnold and Goethe." PEGS, 4 (1928), 5-54.

> An early study of Arnold's complex perception of Goethe as transmitted by Carlyle.

Osbourn, R.V. "The British Quarterly Review." RES, 1 (1950), 147-52.

> Examines Arnold's relationship with the periodical, concluding that his social criticism was "at variance with his own precept of reasonableness."

Matthew Arnold

Peterson, William S. "G.W.E. Russell and the Editing of Matthew Arnold's Letters." VN, 37 (1970), 27-29.

    Utilizes unpublished letters between Mrs. Arnold and Russell to conclude that the Arnold family is to blame for the defects in the standard edition of the letters.

Prickett, Stephen. ROMANTICISM AND RELIGION: THE TRADITION OF COLERIDGE AND WORDSWORTH IN THE VICTORIAN CHURCH. Cambridge: At the University Press, 1976.

    Includes an essay on "Demythologizing and Myth-Making: Arnold versus MacDonald" that contrasts Arnold's religious views as reflected in LITERATURE AND DOGMA to MacDonald's PHANTASIES.

Raleigh, John Henry. MATTHEW ARNOLD AND AMERICAN CULTURE. Berkeley and Los Angeles: University of California Press, 1957.

    Among other topics, Raleigh discusses the importance of Arnold to the New Humanists.

Reeves, Paschal. "'Neither Saint Nor Sophist-Led': Matthew Arnold's Christology." MIQ, 16 (1963), 57-66.

    Reeves summarizes Arnold's rejection of key Christological beliefs.

Ricks, Christopher. "Arnold Once More." VS, 11 (1968), 539-45.

    By reviewing the study by Madden, above, Ricks analyzes contradiction between Arnold's theory of poetry, and its treatment by the critics.

Robbins, William. THE ETHICAL IDEALISM OF MATTHEW ARNOLD: A STUDY OF THE NATURE AND SOURCES OF HIS MORAL AND RELIGIOUS IDEAS. London: Heinemann, 1959.

    Robbins discusses Arnold's treatment of the "human problem" and his proferred solution--to live by "that happy fusion of powers he calls 'the imaginative reason.'"

Roberts, John K. "English Writers and Welsh Railways." AWR, 39 (1968), 136-38.

    Discusses Arnold, Borrow, and Ruskin.

Robson, John [M.]. "Mill and Arnold: Liberty and Culture--Friends or Enemies." HAB, 12 (1961), 20-32.

    Compares and contrasts their attitudes toward authority.

Ronson, R.H. "The Death of Matthew Arnold." TLS, 10 October 1968, p. 1159.

See also TLS, 17 October 1968, p. 1185; 24 October 1968, p. 1210; 31 October 1968, p. 1233.

Ryals, Clyde de L. "The Two Desires: The Ambivalence Towards Action in Arnold." LHB, 1 (1960), 58-68.

"It would seem that the basis of these conflicts in Arnold was an ambivalent attitude towards action, a desire to escape from the life of action into a world of make-believe where no action was required."

San Juan, Epifanio. "Matthew Arnold and the Poetics of Unbelief." HTR, 57 (1964), 97-118.

San Juan connects Arnold's religious writings to his later literary position by claiming that literature became his means of imposing a spiritual structure on human experience.

Schickel, Richard. "Speaking of Books: Matthew Arnold's Times, Our Times." NYTBR, 11 October 1970, pp. 2, 48.

Schumaker, Wayne. "Matthew Arnold's Humanism: Literature as a Criticism of Life." SEL, 2 (1962), 385-402.

Schumaker attempts to synthesize Arnold's views on literary classicism.

Scott, P.G. "The Michigan Edition of Matthew Arnold." N&Q, 19 (1972), 248-50.

See THE COMPLETE PROSE WORKS, p. 40.

Sharples, Edward. "The Holistic Principle in Arnold." ENGLISH, 19 (1970), 49-53.

Sharples' thesis is that Arnold's organizing vision of life is based on the complete man with a society, art, and Christian religion that accept the factual realm.

Sheppard, R. "Two Liberals: A Comparison of the Humanism of Matthew Arnold and Wilhelm von Humboldt." GL&L, 24 (1971), 219-34.

Sherman, Stuart P. MATTHEW ARNOLD: HOW TO KNOW HIM. Indianapolis: Bobbs-Merrill, 1919.

A New Humanist appraisal of Arnold by an admiring critic. Sherman presents Arnold as a cultural standard-bearer for the post-World War I world.

Matthew Arnold

Simpson, J. "Five Notes on Matthew Arnold and Goethe." N&Q, 19 (1972), 50-52.

> Lists and discusses echoes of Goethe in Arnold's poems and letters.

Starzyk, Lawrence. "Arnold and Carlyle." CRITICISM, 12 (1970), 281-300.

> Explores "Carlyle's influence on the development of Arnold's aesthetic theory in two major areas: Arnold's dialectical orientation and his view of the moral or religious function of art."

Steele, Peter. "Newman and Arnold: Cadences of Belief." TWENTIETH CENTURY, AN AUSTRALIAN QUARTERLY, 24 (1969), 170-78.

> Contrasts their religious temperaments: "For Arnold, the notion of linking the supernatural and the scenic would have been perverse."

Straumann, Heinrich. "Matthew Arnold and the Continental Idea." THE ENGLISH MIND: STUDIES IN THE ENGLISH MORALISTS PRESENTED TO BASIL WILLEY. Eds. H[ugh] S. Davies and George Watson. Cambridge: At the University Press, 1964.

> Discusses Arnold's SCHOOLS AND UNIVERSITIES ON THE CONTINENT (1868), because "it shows Arnold as a remarkably precise observer and careful interpreter."

Sundell, Michael G. "Arnold's Dramatic Meditations." VN, 32 (1967), 1-5.

> Arnold "believed that for men reality and truth are flexible and uncertain. He saw this as a central fact of life."

Super, Robert H. "American Piracies of Matthew Arnold." AL, 38 (1966), 123-25.

_____. "Arnold's Notebooks and Arnold Bibliography." MP, 56 (1959), 268-69.

> Comments on the use of Arnold's personal account books as a guide to the discovery of four new additions to the Arnold bibliography.

_____. "Documents in the Matthew Arnold-Saint-Beuve Relationship." MP, 60 (1963), 206-10.

> Lists a chronology of letters between the two writers and contends that Arnold regarded Saint-Beuve as valuable in establishing Arnold's European reputation.

_____. "The Dust of the Past." RUS, 55 (1969), 91-99.

> Super discusses books he has needed to edit Arnold's works and defends historical scholarship.

_____. THE TIME-SPIRIT OF MATTHEW ARNOLD. Ann Arbor: University of Michigan Press, 1970.

> Includes three lectures on Arnold.

_____. "Vivacity and the Philistines." SEL, 6 (1967), 629-37.

For Arnold as periodical writer, "the enemy was dullness, the remedy was wit: 'vivacity' may be the only effective weapon for defeating gravity."

Thorpe, Michael. MATTHEW ARNOLD. London: Evans, 1969.

A perceptive study geared to a younger audience.

Tillotson, Geoffrey. "Arnold and Pater: Critics Historical, Aesthetic, and Unlabelled." In his CRITICISM AND THE NINETEENTH CENTURY. London: Athlone Press, 1951.

Criticizes both writers' concern with "the object as in itself it really is," and concludes that "Pater was not much more of an historian than Arnold was."

_____. "Arnold the Lecturer and Journalist." In his MID-VICTORIAN STUDIES. Atlantic Highlands, N.J.: Humanities Press, 1965.

Claims that "journalism is certainly in the bones of all the prose literature of Arnold, which was both decorous and mercantile, both a thing to remember and a tract for the times."

_____. "Matthew Arnold: The Critic and the Advocate." In his CRITICISM AND THE NINETEENTH CENTURY. London: Athlone Press, 1951.

"As soon as Arnold left 'mere' literary criticism for this larger field [of life], he ceased to be disinterested though he did not cease to claim to be disinterested."

_____. "Matthew Arnold and Eighteenth-Century Poetry." In his CRITICISM AND THE NINETEENTH CENTURY. London: Athlone Press, 1951.

Accuses Arnold of being particularly weak as an historian and critic of past periods. Also discusses Arnold's criticism of Addison, Swift, and Pope.

_____. "Matthew Arnold In Our Time." In his MID-VICTORIAN STUDIES. Atlantic Highlands, N.J.: Humanities Press, 1965.

"There are defects in Arnold's prose, and great ones, but they are scarcely defects of technique. What was wrong with his prose was owing to lack of knowledge and grasp."

_____. "Matthew Arnold's Prose: Theory and Practice." THE ART OF VICTORIAN PROSE. Eds. George L. Levine and William A. Madden. New York: Oxford University Press, 1968.

Arnold valued "regularity, uniformity, precision, balance" in prose

Matthew Arnold

style, but his tactlessness and pretentiousness led to rhetorical blunders.

Tillotson, Kathleen. "Matthew Arnold and Carlyle." PBA, 42 (1956), 133-53.

Examines "the complexity of Arnold's response" to Carlyle, "Arnold's acceptance and his rebellion": "There is often an affinity with Carlyle's ideas, both in Arnold's literary and social criticism."

Timko, Michael. "Corydon Had a Rival." VN, 19 (1961), 5-11.

Claims that Clough was the major influence in Arnold's shift from aestheticism to moralism.

Townsend, Francis G. "The Third Installment of Arnold's Literature and Dogma." MP, 50 (1953), 195-200.

Explores the theory that Arnold's third installment was written but rejected by the CORNHILL.

Townsend, Robert C. "Matthew Arnold, H.M.I., on the Study of Poetry." CE, 30 (1968), 212-30.

Townsend discusses Arnold's annual school reports and their resemblance to the touchstone method.

Ullman, Samson O.A. "A 'New' Version of Arnold's Essay on Wordsworth." N&Q, 2 (1955), 543-44.

Vogeler, Martha S. "Matthew Arnold and Frederic Harrison: The Prophet of Culture and the Prophet of Positivism." SEL, 2 (1962), 441-62.

Examines Arnold's depiction of Harrison in CULTURE AND ANARCHY, and concludes that, although the two writers had similar aims, "CULTURE AND ANARCHY is not an unsuitable vehicle for the perpetuation of Harrison's name."

Walcott, Fred G. THE ORIGINS OF CULTURE AND ANARCHY: MATTHEW ARNOLD AND POPULAR EDUCATION IN ENGLAND. Toronto: University of Toronto Press, 1970.

Walcott discusses the many parallels between Arnold's educational concerns and his social views.

Watson, George. "Arnold and the Victorian Mind." REL, 8 (1967), 33-45.

Watson argues that Arnold's essays were "remote from any concern with accuracy or fair-mindedness" and that he was therefore an inaccurate critic of Victorian society and culture.

———. "Matthew Arnold." In his THE LITERARY CRITICS. Baltimore: Johns Hopkins University Press, 1962.

> Discusses Arnold's literary criticism as "measuring the distance between his ambition as a poet and his performance." Watson calls Arnold "the great gainsayer of English criticism, the most insistent and professional of noncomformists."

Wilkinson, D.R.M. "Carlyle, Arnold, and Literary Justice." PMLA, 86 (1971), 225-35.

> Criticizes DeLaura's "Arnold and Carlyle," above. Claims that "every effort is made to expose the weaknesses, the deceitfulness (conscious and unconscious) and the complacency of Arnold."

Williams, T.L. "Matthew Arnold and 'The Times.'" N&Q, 16 (1969), 211-12.

> Williams claims that letter 12 of FRIENDSHIP'S GARLAND is a satire of the "Times."

Williamson, Eugene. THE LIBERALISM OF THOMAS ARNOLD: A STUDY OF HIS RELIGIOUS AND POLITICAL WRITINGS. University: University of Alabama Press, 1964.

> Contains interesting material on the similar attitudes towards Biblical criticism, church, and state held by father and son.

———. "Matthew Arnold and the Archbishops." MLQ, 24 (1963), 245-52.

> "Despite his reputation among the orthodox for 'patronizing Jesus Christ for cash,' Arnold was a close friend of three well-known Anglican archbishops."

———. "Matthew Arnold's 'Eternal Not Ourselves. . . .'" MLN, 75 (1960), 309-12.

> Analyzes Arnold's rejection of anthropomorphism and the concept of divine immanence.

———. "Words from Westminster Abbey: Matthew Arnold and Arthur Stanley." SEL, 11 (1971), 749-61.

> Discusses the relationship between these men.

Wright, Charles D. ARNOLD'S RESPONSE TO GERMAN CULTURE. Ann Arbor: University of Michigan Press, 1964.

———. "How Matthew Arnold Altered 'Goethe on Poetry.'" VP, 5 (1967), 57-61.

Thesis is that Arnold differed with Goethe about whether the basis of poetry was intellectual or inspirational.

―――. "Matthew Arnold on Heine as 'Continuator of Goethe.'" SP, 65 (1968), 693-701.

Examines Arnold's assertion that Heine was "the continuator of Goethe," and concludes that "it is mostly wrong and only limitedly and inadvertently correct."

BIBLIOGRAPHIES

See also Super's bibliographical article under "Critical Studies," above.

Davis, Arthur Kyle. MATTHEW ARNOLD'S LETTERS: A DESCRIPTIVE CHECKLIST. Charlottesville: University Press of Virginia, 1968.

Includes the history of the publication of Arnold's letter to date and provides lists of letters chronologically and by the names of correspondents.

DeLaura, David J. "Matthew Arnold." In his VICTORIAN PROSE: A GUIDE TO RESEARCH. New York: MLA, 1973.

A valuable and critically annotated bibliographical essay.

Ehrsam, Theodore G., and Robert H. Deily, eds. BIBLIOGRAPHIES OF TWELVE VICTORIAN AUTHORS. New York: Wilson, 1936; rpt. New York: Octagon, 1968.

Lists reviews of Arnold's books and much critical commentary up to 1932.

Faverty, Frederic E. "Matthew Arnold." In his THE VICTORIAN POETS. 2nd ed. Cambridge, Mass.: Harvard University Press, 1968.

Although it concentrates on Arnold as a poet, this useful bibliographical essay discusses all important scholarship through 1968.

Mainwaring, Marion. "Notes Toward a Matthew Arnold Bibliography." MP, 49 (1952), 189-94.

Points out the deficiencies in Smart's bibliography, below, and adds new items.

Neiman, Fraser. "Some Newly Attributed Contributions of Matthew Arnold to the PALL MALL GAZETTE." MP, 55 (1957), 84-92.

Discovers five new articles written by Arnold.

Smart, Thomas Burnett. BIBLIOGRAPHY OF MATTHEW ARNOLD. London: Davy, 1892; rpt. London: Franklin, 1968.

    Remains the standard bibliography of Arnold's works. It includes a "synoptical index" to the various editions of Arnold's works and also lists "Criticisms and Reviews of Arnold's Writings."

Tollers, Vincent L., ed. A BIBLIOGRAPHY OF MATTHEW ARNOLD, 1932-1970. University Park: Pennsylvania State University Press, 1974.

    Toller's bibliography provides a complete listing of articles on Arnold since the Ehrsam bibliography, above. He also lists all reprinted editions of Arnold's writings and arranges secondary critical studies according to topics such as "Arnold and the Romantics," "Arnold and Education," "Arnold and Religion and Philosophy."

WALTER BAGEHOT (1826-77)

PRINCIPAL PROSE WORKS

ESTIMATES OF SOME ENGLISHMEN AND SCOTCHMEN. REPRINTED FROM THE NATIONAL REVIEW, 1858.

PARLIAMENTARY REFORM: AN ESSAY REPRINTED WITH CONSIDERABLE ADDITIONS, FROM THE NATIONAL REVIEW, 1859.

THE HISTORY OF THE UNREFORMED PARLIAMENT AND ITS LESSONS: AN ESSAY REPRINTED FROM THE NATIONAL REVIEW, 1860.

MEMOIR OF THE RIGHT HONORABLE JOHN WILSON. REPRINTED FROM THE ECONOMIST, 1861.

COUNT YOUR ENEMIES AND ECONOMISE YOUR EXPENDITURE, 1862.

THE ENGLISH CONSTITUTION. REPRINTED FROM THE FORTNIGHTLY REVIEW, 1867.

A PRACTICAL PLAN FOR ASSIMILATING THE ENGLISH AND AMERICAN MONEY. REPRINTED FROM THE ECONOMIST WITH ADDITIONS, 1869.

PHYSICS AND POLITICS, OR THOUGHTS ON THE APPLICATION OF THE PRINCIPLES OF NATURAL SELECTION AND INHERITANCE TO POLITICAL SOCIETY, 1872.

LOMBARD STREET. A DESCRIPTION OF THE MONEY MARKET, 1873.

SOME ARTICLES ON THE DEPRECIATION OF SILVER AND ON TOPICS CONNECTED WITH IT. REPRINTED FROM THE ECONOMIST, 1877.

LITERARY STUDIES. Ed. R.H. Hutton. 2 vols. 1879.

    Includes Bagehot's ESTIMATIONS IN CRITICISM, in which he discusses Coleridge, Cowper, Shelley, Macaulay, Dickens, and Gibbon.

ESSAYS ON PARLIAMENTARY REFORM, 1883.

THE POSTULATES OF ENGLISH POLITICAL ECONOMY, 1885.

COLLECTED WORKS

BAGEHOT'S HISTORICAL ESSAYS. Ed. Norman St. John-Stevas. New York: New York University Press, 1966.

BAGEHOT'S LITERARY STUDIES. Ed. Ernest Rhys. London: Dent, 1911.

BIOGRAPHICAL STUDIES BY THE LATE WALTER BAGEHOT. Ed. Richard H. Hutton. London: 1881; rpt. New York: AMS Press, 1970.

    Hutton was a close friend of Bagehot and the first editor of his works. This edition includes Bagehot's portraits of Peel, Brougham, Pitt, Gladstone, Bolingbroke, Adam Smith, and Disraeli.

THE COLLECTED WORKS OF WALTER BAGEHOT. Ed. Norman St. John-Stevas. Projected 9 vols. Cambridge, Mass.: Harvard University Press, 1965-- .

    The standard edition. Volumes 1 and 2; LITERARY ESSAYS; volumes 3 and 4: HISTORICAL ESSAYS; volumes 5 and 6: POLITICAL ESSAYS; volumes 7 and 8: ECONOMIC ESSAYS; volume 9: LETTERS AND MISCELLANY. See St. John-Stevas, "On Editing Bagehot," p. 70.

ECONOMIC STUDIES BY THE LATE WALTER BAGEHOT. Ed. R.H. Hutton. London: Longmans, Green, 1880.

    Contains Bagehot's studies of Adam Smith, Malthus, and Ricardo.

LITERARY STUDIES BY THE LATE WALTER BAGEHOT. Ed. R.H. Hutton. 2 vols. London: Longmans, Green, 1879.

    Volume 1 contains Hutton's "Preliminary Memoir" and Bagehot's studies of Coleridge, Shelley, Shakespeare, Milton, and Cowper. Volume 2 contains essays on Gibbon, Sterne, Thackeray, Scott, Clough, and Wordsworth.

THE WORKS AND LIFE OF WALTER BAGEHOT. Ed. Mrs. Russell Barrington.

Walter Bagehot

10 vols. London: Longmans, Green, 1915.

    Volume 10 contains the LIFE by Barrington and two memoirs by Hutton. Volumes 1-9 contain the works. Full index in volume 9.

THE WORKS OF WALTER BAGEHOT WITH MEMOIRS BY R.H. HUTTON. Ed. Forrest Morgan. 5 vols. Hartford, Conn.: Traveler's Insurance Co., 1891.

    Volume 1: Memoirs by Hutton and LITERARY STUDIES; volume 2: LITERARY STUDIES, RELIGIOUS AND METAPHYSICAL ESSAYS, and LETTERS ON THE FRENCH COUP D'ETAT; volume 3: BIOGRAPHICAL STUDIES; volume 4: THE ENGLISH CONSTITUTION and PHYSICS AND POLITICS; volume 5: LOMBARD STREET and ECONOMIC STUDIES.

LETTERS

See also THE COLLECTED WORKS, ed. St. John-Stevas, above.

THE LOVE-LETTERS OF WALTER BAGEHOT AND ELIZA WILSON WRITTEN FROM 10 NOVEMBER 1857 TO 23 APRIL 1858. Ed. Mrs. Russell Barrington. London: Faber and Faber, 1933.

    Letters are in chronological order, preceded by a brief introduction and preface.

BIOGRAPHIES

Barrington, Mrs. Russell. LIFE OF WALTER BAGEHOT. London: Longmans, Green, 1914.

    Includes chapters on THE ECONOMIST, PHYSICS AND POLITICS, and LOMBARD STREET. Prints "Tributes from Contemporaries" and several letters. Mrs. Barrington was Bagehot's sister-in-law. Her biography is interesting as a family portrait, but inexpert as a study of his position in the world at large.

Buchan, Alastair. THE SPARE CHANCELLOR: THE LIFE OF WALTER BAGEHOT. London: Chatto and Windus, 1959.

    The major biography that deals with the political and economic aspects of Bagehot's work, rather than with his literary studies.

Irvine, William. WALTER BAGEHOT. London: Longmans, Green, 1939; rpt. Hamden, Conn.: Archon Books, 1970.

    A critical biography that emphasizes Bagehot's literary and intellectual nature. Contains six chapters on his theory and practice as a writer and presents Bagehot as a "broad, many-sided, moderate man of the world."

St. John-Stevas, Norman. WALTER BAGEHOT: A STUDY OF HIS LIFE AND THOUGHT, TOGETHER WITH A SELECTION FROM HIS POLITICAL WRITINGS. London: Eyre and Spottiswoode, 1959.

An introductory biography that surveys Bagehot's life, stressing his role as "banker, economist, political thinker, and commentator."

CRITICAL STUDIES

Ames, Robert J. "Walter Bagehot: A Study in Religious Compromise." DA, 12 (1952), 419-20.

Concludes that Bagehot found a middle course "between the extremes of Puritanism and Paganism, Hebraism and Hellenism, to arrive at a philosophy of experience and a love of this world as a necessary condition for a knowledge and love of the next world."

Barzun, Jacques. "Bagehot: or the Human Comedy." In his ENERGIES OF ART. New York: Harper's, 1956.

"Bagehot unfortunately was versatile. The result is that his varied achievements never had time to become established as a coherent whole."

_____. "The Critic as Statesman." AM, 178 (1946), 128-32.

Claims that Bagehot is "so great as a political thinker and a literary critic that he deserves the title of genius in either kind."

Birrell, Augustine. COLLECTED ESSAYS AND ADDRESSES. 2 vols. London: Dent, 1907.

Volume 2 contains an analysis of Bagehot's literary writings.

Briggs, Asa. "Trollope, Bagehot and the English Constitution." CAJ, 5 (1952), 327-38.

Briggs claims that both writers represented the same superficially secure and comfortable England.

Brinton, Crane. ENGLISH POLITICAL THOUGHT IN THE NINETEENTH CENTURY. 2nd ed. Cambridge: At the University Press, 1949; rpt. New York: Harper and Row, 1962.

A general survey which deals with Bagehot to some extent.

Buchan, Alastair. "Walter Bagehot." HT, 4 (1954), 764-70.

Presents Bagehot as "the antithesis of the grand Victorian man of letters" and "a fine blend of the Cavalier and puritan strain in the English temperament."

Walter Bagehot

Burgess, Anthony. "Bagehot on Books." SPECTATOR, 7 January 1966, p. 15.

Cameron, James M. "Men and Ideas: Walter Bagehot." ENCOUNTER, 3 (1954), 61-66.

> Discusses Bagehot's political writings and concludes that "the value of his writings lies in their perception of the concrete tasks and specific limits of men engaged in the art of politics."

Chapman, Raymond W. "The Text of Bagehot's CONSTITUTION." PQ, 31 (1952), 446-47.

> Analyzes the 1867 edition paragraph-by-paragraph and compares it to the 1928 version edited by Lord Balfour.

Crossman, R.H.S. "Machine Politics: Walter Bagehot (II)." ENCOUNTER, 20 (1963), 42-55.

> Analyzes THE ENGLISH CONSTITUTION by asking "whether Bagehot was a reliable observer of his own times." Answers affirmatively and claims that Bagehot discovered "the secret of British politics."

_____. "Walter Bagehot." ENCOUNTER, 20 (1963), 17-26.

> Crossman asks about the CONSTITUTION, "What is the secret of this remarkable longevity, this timeless quality, in a book dashed off as a serial?"

Driver, Cecil. H. "Bagehot and the Social Psychologists." THE SOCIAL AND POLITICAL IDEAS OF SOME REPRESENTATIVE THINKERS OF THE VICTORIAN AGE. Ed. Fossey J.C. Hearnshaw. London: Harrap, 1933.

> Attempts to sketch "the development of some of the leading ideas pertaining to social psychology in England prior to the appearance of Bagehot's PHYSICS AND POLITICS" in order to put Bagehot's work in historical context.

ECONOMIST, 1843-1943: A CENTENARY VOLUME. Oxford: Oxford University Press, 1943.

> This collection includes "Walter Bagehot" by Francis W. Hirst and "Bagehot and the Trade Cycle" by W.W. Rostow.

Fairlie, Henry. "Walter Bagehot, or, The Political Journalist as Entertainer." ENCOUNTER, 36 (1971), 30-41.

> "Bagehot raised common sense to a principle, almost to a system, by which men and nations should govern themselves and their affairs. But common sense cannot bear such a weight and, in the process, what is commonsensical becomes nonsensical."

Fetter, Frank W. "A Historical Confusion in Bagehot's LOMBARD STREET."
ECONOMICA, 34 (1967), 80-83.

> Fetter points out that Bagehot "attributed to the [economic] panic weeks of December, 1825, events which happened nearly three months later," thus producing some historical confusion.

Greenberg, Robert A. "Mill on Bagehot and Reform." N&Q, 5 (1958), 83-84.

> Greenberg suggests Bagehot as a possible source for Mill's views on reform.

Halsted, John Burt. "Walter Bagehot on Toleration." JHI, 19 (1958), 119-28.

> Analyzes "On the Metaphysical Basis of Toleration" for its basic liberalism and free expression.

Himmelfarb, Gertrude. "The Politics of Democracy: The English Reform Act of 1867." JBS, 6 (1966), 97-138.

> Himmelfarb draws on the theories of Bagehot and Mill to discuss the course of the Act's passage in the face of public antipathy.

Holloway, John. "Walter Bagehot and the Divided Present." LISTENER, 75 (1966), 610-11.

> Reviews St. John-Stevas' edition of Bagehot's literary essays, above, and concludes that "Bagehot's literary criticism does not quite stand on a par with his economic or more especially his political work."

Kohn, Hans. REFLECTIONS ON MODERN HISTORY: THE HISTORIAN AND HUMAN RESPONSIBILITY. Princeton, N.J.: Van Nostrand, 1963.

> Contains a secion on "Walter Bagehot, Victorian" that reviews Bagehot's life and writings and asserts that "the concept of animated moderation is the central ideal of Bagehot's thought. In it he reveals himself as a true Aristotelian."

McKenzie, Robert. "Bagehot and the Rule of Mere Numbers." LISTENER, 62 (1959), 870-72.

> McKenzie discusses Bagehot's articulate liberal distrust of "mass democracy."

Marriott, Sir. J.A.R. "Walter Bagehot." FR, 119 (1926), 263-72.

> Praises Bagehot's political writings: "He was the first to familiarize the reformed and enlarged electorate with the operation of the machine entrusted to their hands."

Walter Bagehot

Paden, William D. "Swinburne, the SPECTATOR in 1862, and Walter Bagehot."
SIX STUDIES IN NINETEENTH-CENTURY ENGLISH LITERATURE AND THOUGHT.
Eds. Harold Orel and George J. Worth. Lawrence: University of Kansas Press,
1962.

> Attempts to prove that Bagehot reviewed Swinburne's contributions
> to the SPECTATOR in which he presented a "moral reason for read-
> ing immoral books."

Pearson, J.G. "The Acute Realism of Walter Bagehot." LISTENER, 53 (1955),
419-20.

> Pearson observes that Bagehot wasn't cynical or brutal, but rather
> "something far deeper and far subtler . . . an acute realist."

_____. "The Aristocratic View of Statesmanship." NEW REPUBLIC, 18 April
1955, pp. 18-20.

> Pearson presents a critique of PHYSICS AND POLITICS.

Read, Herbert [Sir]. SENSE OF GLORY. Cambridge: At the University Press,
1929.

> In a section on Bagehot, states that he was the best critic of his
> time, after Arnold.

Rudman, Harry W. "Walter Bagehot--'The Greatest Victorian'?" HINL, 5
(1960), 75-77.

> Reviews St. John-Stevas' biography, above, and disagrees with
> Young, below: "Bagehot was not the greatest Victorian because
> he viewed society solely from the coign of vantage and from the
> vested interests of those at the top of the human pyramid."

St. John-Stevas, Norman. "Bagehot on Tennyson." TLS, 26 April 1963,
p. 314.

> This essay features a letter confirming Tener's assertion, below,
> that a review of Tennyson's IDYLLS in the NATIONAL REVIEW for
> October 1859 was written by Bagehot.

_____. "On Editing Bagehot." ECONOMIST, 8 January 1966, p. 106.

_____. "Walter Bagehot." EDH, 36 (1970), 133-46.

> Considers Bagehot as a literary critic.

_____. WALTER BAGEHOT. London: Longmans, Green, 1963.

> Emphasizes Bagehot's "duomania" in his writings: a passion for

polarities that resulted from a split in Bagehot's character between the man of the world and the "dark" mystic.

———. "Walter Bagehot as a Writer." WR, 237 (1963), 38-65.

An examination of Bagehot's life and major writings, concluding that Bagehot was a great critic, although "his criticism is so highly idiosyncratic, so personal, he has founded no school."

Sisson, Charles H. THE CASE OF WALTER BAGEHOT. London: Faber and Faber, 1972.

Sisson presents an almost totally negative view of Bagehot, condemning him for his "banker-like mind and interest in Anglo-Saxondom."

Smith, Adrian. "Walter Bagehot." DUR, 240 (1966), 48-60.

Examines Bagehot's importance in understanding the mid-Victorian period. Sees Bagehot as "an authority on the mores of upper-class belief and behaviour with a unique measure of involvement and detachment which explains his durability as a writer."

Stanford, Derek. "Bagehot and the Monarchy." MA, 3 (1959), 33-39.

Analyzes Bagehot's "minimal defense" of the monarchy in THE ENGLISH CONSTITUTION.

Stang, Richard. THE THEORY OF THE NOVEL IN ENGLAND: 1850-1870. London: Routledge and Kegan Paul, 1959.

Using contemporary periodicals, Stang emphasizes the important role Bagehot played in developing specific criteria for writing about the novel as a genre in its own right.

Stephen, Leslie. STUDIES OF A BIOGRAPHER. Vol. 3. London: Duckworth, 1902.

Presents a competent survey of Bagehot's literary pieces.

Sullivan, Harry R. WALTER BAGEHOT. New York: Twayne, 1975.

"It is the purpose of this study to present Bagehot as the Victorian par excellence: more specifically, as one who in manner, expression, and thought represents the more excellent accomplishment of Victorianism at its apex." Includes chapters on Bagehot's estimates of poets, prose writers, and science, society, and religion. Includes a helpful bibliography.

Tener, Robert H. "Bagehot and Tennyson." TLS, 12 August 1959, p. 483.

See St. John-Stevas, above.

Walter Bagehot

_____. "Bagehot, Jeffrey, and Renan." TLS, 11 August 1961, p. 515.

Tener, Robert H., and Norman St. John-Stevas. "Bagehot and Bailey." TLS, 8 February 1963, p. 93.

> Discusses a hitherto unnoticed review by Bagehot of FESTUS.

Wain, John. "An Introduction to Bagehot." REL, 1 (1960), 66-72.

> Wain suggests that Bagehot's usefulness today lies in his ability to reason from ordinary observation.

"Walter Bagehot." TLS, 28 January 1926, pp. 49-50.

> A stimulating, brief account of Bagehot's criticism claiming that Bagehot believed "the materials for the creative faculty must be provided by the receptive faculty." The article concludes that this belief caused Bagehot to put great emphasis on "experiencing nature."

Webster, David H. "The Critical Writings of Walter Bagehot." SUMMARIES OF DOCTORAL DISSERTATIONS. University of Wisconsin, 1938, pp. 294-96.

Young, George M. "The Case for Walter Bagehot." SPECTATOR, 159 (1937), 9-10.

> Praises Bagehot's "breadth and vigour of mind," "the perfect management of all his energies and all his resources," and his "genial and ironic delight."

_____. "The Greatest Victorian." SPECTATOR, 158 (1937), 1137-38.

> Young claims that Bagehot was the "greatest" Victorian in the sense of being the most typical of his age. See replies in the SPECTATOR, 25 June 1937, p. 1190; 2 July 1937, p. 18. Also see Rudman, above.

_____. "Victorian Psychology." TLS, 25 January 1936, p. 75.

JEREMY BENTHAM (1748-1832)

PRINCIPAL PROSE WORKS

A FRAGMENT ON GOVERNMENT, 1776.

AN INTRODUCTION TO THE PRINCIPLES OF MORALS AND LEGISLATION, 1789.

A PLEA FOR THE CONSTITUTION, 1803.

BOOK OF FALLACIES. Ed. P. Bingham. 1824.

THE RATIONALE OF EVIDENCE. Ed. John Stuart Mill. 5 vols. 1827.

DEONTOLOGY OR SCIENCE OF MORALITY. Ed. J[ohn] Bowring. 2 vols. 1834.

COLLECTED WORKS

A BENTHAM READER. Ed. Mary [P.] Mack. New York: Pegasus, 1969.

THE COLLECTED WORKS OF JEREMY BENTHAM. Ed. James [H.] Burns and H.L.A. Hart. Projected 10 vols. London: Athlone Press, 1968-- .

> Volume 1: CORRESPONDENCE; volume 2, AN INTRODUCTION TO THE PRINCIPLES OF MORALS AND LEGISLATION; volume 3: PENOLOGY AND CRIMINAL LAW; volume 4: CIVIL LAW; volume 5: CONSTITUTIONAL LAW; volume 6: POLITICAL WRITINGS; volume 7: JUDICIAL PROCEDURES; volume 8: ECONOMICS AND SOCIETY; volume 9: PHILOSOPHY AND EDUCATION; volume 10: RELIGION AND THE CHURCH. Only the CORRESPONDENCE has been published so far. See Burns under "Critical Studies," below, for commentary on this edition.

Jeremy Bentham

HANDBOOK OF POLITICAL FALLACIES. Ed. H.A. Larrabee. Baltimore: Johns Hopkins University Press, 1952.

JEREMY BENTHAM'S ECONOMIC WRITINGS. Ed. W[illiam] Stark. 3 vols. London: Allen and Unwin, 1952-54.

THE WORKS OF JEREMY BENTHAM. Ed. John Bowring. 11 vols. Edinburgh: W. Tait, 1838-43; rpt. New York: Russell and Russell, 1962.

> This edition has been superseded by Burns and Hart's definitive edition. Bowring's edition, however, contains a LIFE in volumes 10 and 11.

LETTERS

Allentuck, Marcia. "Jeremy Bentham: An Unpublished Letter." ELN, 6 (1969), 185-86.

THE CORRESPONDENCE OF JEREMY BENTHAM. Eds. Timothy L. Sprigge and Ian R. Christie. 3 vols. London: Athlone Press, 1968-71.

> Volume 1 contains correspondence for 1752-76; volume 2: 1777-80; volume 3: 1781-88.

BIOGRAPHIES

Atkinson, C.M. JEREMY BENTHAM. London: Methuen, 1905; rpt. Greenwich, Conn.: Greenwood Press, 1970.

> This is the only full-scale treatment of Bentham's life written between Bowring, THE WORKS OF BENTHAM, vols. 10 and 11, and Mack, below.

Mack, Mary P. JEREMY BENTHAM: AN ODYSSEY OF IDEAS. New York: Columbia University Press, 1962.

> A biography which concentrates on Bentham's intellectual development. The best and most thorough work on the subject.

CRITICAL STUDIES

Albee, Ernest. A HISTORY OF ENGLISH UTILITARIANISM. London: Allen and Unwin, 1901; rpt. New York: Macmillan, 1957.

> Places Bentham within the tradition.

August, Eugene R. "Mill as Sage: The Essay on Bentham." PMLA, 89 (1974), 142-53.

Examines Mill's essay and asserts that Mill "employed many of the techniques of the literary artist" in his portrait of Bentham.

Baumgardt, David. BENTHAM AND THE ETHICS OF TODAY. Princeton, N.J.: Princeton University Press, 1952.

A full-scale study of Bentham's ethics as reflected in his published and unpublished writings. Attempts to show "their connections with pre-Benthamite thought, and to comment in detail on their importance for contemporary systematic ethics."

_____. "Bentham's Censorial Method." JHI, 6 (1945), 456-67.

Cites an unpublished manuscript at University College, London, to discuss "the radical character of Bentham's ethics."

Brockriede, Wayne E. "Bentham's Criticism of Rhetoric and Rhetoricians." QJS, 41 (1955), 377-82.

Analyzes Bentham's condemnation of "narrow" rhetoric, which he considered shallow and deceptive.

_____. "Bentham's Philosophy of Rhetoric." SM, 23 (1956), 235-46.

Discusses Bentham's concept of "original" rhetoric, which he defined as "the art of using language for the purpose of achieving the greatest happiness for the greatest number of people."

Burns, James H. "The Bentham Project." EDITING TEXTS OF THE ROMANTIC PERIOD. Ed. John D. Baird. Toronto: Hakkert, 1972.

See THE COLLECTED WORKS, p. 73.

_____. "Jeremy Bentham." TLS, 11 January 1968, p. 45.

Discusses the problems in preparing the definitive edition of the works of Bentham.

_____. JEREMY BENTHAM AND UNIVERSITY COLLEGE. London: Athlone Press, 1962.

Everett, C[harles] W. THE EDUCATION OF BENTHAM. New York: Columbia University Press, 1931.

Emphasizes early influences on Bentham.

_____. JEREMY BENTHAM. London: Weidenfeld & Nicolson, 1966.

A general survey of Bentham's life and writings set into the contemporary historical context.

Goldberg, Michael. "From Bentham to Carlyle: Dickens' Political Development." JHI, 33 (1972), 61-76.

> Examines Bentham's early influence on Dickens.

Goldsworth, Amnon. "The Meaning of Bentham's Greatest Happiness Principle." JHP, 7 (1969), 315-21.

> Defends Bentham's phrase from the criticisms of other commentators by stating: "What Bentham meant by his greatest happiness principle is not the production of the greatest happiness of the greatest number, but simply the production of the greatest happiness."

Grave, S.A. "Some Eighteenth-Century Attempts to Use the Notion of Happiness." STUDIES IN THE EIGHTEENTH CENTURY: PAPERS PRESENTED AT THE DAVID NICKOL SMITH MEMORIAL SEMINAR, CANBERRA, 1966. Canberra: Australian National University Press, 1968.

Halévy, Elie. THE GROWTH OF PHILOSOPHIC RADICALISM. Trans. Mary Morris. New York: Kelley; London: Faber and Gwyer, 1949.

> Contains a chapter on the "Youth of Bentham, 1776-1789," as well as sections on the evolution of Utilitarian doctrine.

Hart, H.L.A. "Bentham." PBA, 48 (1963), 297-320.

> A critique of Bentham's philosophical theories that concludes Bentham "has become almost exclusively a text for the debate of a few questions regarded of prime importance in the teaching of moral philosophy."

Himmelfarb, Gertrude. "On Reading Bentham Seriously." SBHT, 14 (1972), 179-86.

> Contrasts Bentham to Burke and claims that "the whole of Bentham's thought is, from the vantage of the Burkean, an absurdity--and not a playful and trivial absurdity but a deliberate, calculated, and consequential one."

Korshin, Paul J. "Dr. Johnson and Jeremy Bentham: An Unnoticed Relationship." MP, 70 (1972), 38-45.

> Examines Bowring's account of the Johnson-Bentham friendship as it appears in THE WORKS OF JEREMY BENTHAM, p. 74.

Letwin, Shirley R. "Men and Ideas: Bentham." ENCOUNTER, 23 (1958), 55-62.

Assesses Bentham's reputation and his legal and political writings, concluding that "it is this reluctance to give his contrivances spiritual significance that marks him as an eighteenth-century Englishman."

──────. THE PURSUIT OF CERTAINTY: DAVID HUME, JEREMY BENTHAM, JOHN STUART MILL, BEATRICE WEBB. New York: Columbia University Press, 1965.

Lomer, Gerhard R. "Jeremy Bentham." QQ, 67 (1960), 28-40.

A biographical sketch that concludes with a discussion of Bentham's essay "Auto-Icon; or Further Uses of the Dead to the Living."

Lyons, David. IN THE INTERESTS OF THE GOVERNED. Oxford: Clarendon Press, 1973.

A study of Bentham's utilitarianism and his legal theory.

──────. "Rights, Claimants, and Beneficiaries." APQ, 6 (1969), 173-85.

Includes a discussion of Bentham's legal theory.

Manning, David J. THE MIND OF JEREMY BENTHAM. New York: Barnes and Noble, 1968.

A survey of Bentham's thought, including chapters on his political, economic, educational, and legal theories. Manning concludes that Bentham's reputation ought to be based on "the ground that he has the materials, if not the making, of a post-Hobbesian philosophy of state."

Mill, John Stuart. MILL ON BENTHAM AND COLERIDGE. Ed. F[rank] R. Leavis. London: Chatto and Windus, 1950.

A classic essay that sees Bentham as antihistorical and contemptuous of the romantic interest in the past, as contrasted with Coleridge's German historical spirit.

Ogden, C.K. BENTHAM'S THEORY OF FICTION. London: Littlefield, 1959.

Ogden's thesis is that Bentham's importance lies in his grappling with "the primary technique of linguistic psychology" and "the problem of fictional entities" in psychology, law, ethics, language, and logic.

Parekh, Bhikhie, ed. JEREMY BENTHAM: TEN CRITICAL ESSAYS. London: Cass, 1974.

A useful collection of essays on various aspects of Bentham's thought, including "Bentham on Sovereignty" by H.L.A. Hart, "Bentham's

Jeremy Bentham

Critique of Political Fallacies" by J.H. Burns, and "Bentham's Justification of the Principle of Utility" by himself.

Park, Roy. "Hazlitt and Bentham." JHI, 30 (1969), 369-84.

> Park asks "whether in fact Hazlitt's criticism of Bentham is important." He proceeds to contrast the two writers' theories of utilitarianism and states that, for Bentham, "the right act is the act which promotes the good, which is in turn construed as happiness."

Preyer, Robert O. BENTHAM, COLERIDGE, AND THE SCIENCE OF HISTORY. Bochum-Langendreer, West Germany: Poppinhaus, 1958.

> Surveys prevailing historical theories in England and Germany in the first part of the nineteenth century. Also discusses "the ways in which the Anglican and idealist versions of history were fused into a 'Germano-Coleridgean' school which influenced Bentham's utilitarian assimilation of Continental historical thought."

Robbins, Lionel. BENTHAM IN THE TWENTIETH CENTURY. London: Athlone Press, 1965.

> Discusses Bentham in relation "to the problems of this century"--legal theory and constitutional and administrative structures.

Robson, John M. "John Stuart Mill and Jeremy Bentham, with Some Observations on James Mill." ESSAYS IN ENGLISH LITERATURE FROM THE RENAISSANCE TO THE VICTORIAN AGE PRESENTED TO A.S.P. WOODHOUSE. Eds. Millar MacLure and F.W. Watt. Toronto: University of Toronto Press, 1964.

> Explores Bentham's influence on James and J.S. Mill, as well as J.S. Mill's later assessment of Bentham in his essay, above.

Rodman, Barbee-Sue. "Bentham and the Paradox of Penal Reform." JHI, 29 (1968), 197-210.

> Analyzes the contradictions in Bentham's thought as "they provide a key to understanding the tensions of eighteenth-century penal thought and the failures experienced by nineteenth-century penal practice."

Shackleton, Robert. "The Greatest Happiness of the Greatest Number: The History of Bentham's Phrase." SVEC, 90 (1972), 1461-82.

> Traces the history of the phrase, but emphasizes that Bentham's use of the formula was "a great event in Bentham's intellectual development."

Stark, William. "Bentham as an Economist." EJ, 51 (1941), 56-79; rpt. EJ, 56 (1946), 583-608.

Steintrager, James. "Morality and Belief: The Origin and Purpose of Bentham's Writings on Religion." MNL, 6 (1971), 3-15.

    Analyzes Bentham's religious writings "as influences on Mill and other nineteenth-century thinkers." Concludes that Bentham's views on religion are considerably more complex than other scholars have recognized.

Stephen, Leslie. THE ENGLISH UTILITARIANS. 3 vols. London: Duckworth, 1900; rpt. New York: Smith, 1950.

    A standard work which discusses contemporary political, industrial, social, and philosophical background and has two chapters on Bentham: "Bentham's Life" and "Bentham's Doctrine."

Wallis, Graham. "Bentham as Political Inventor." COR, 129 (1926), 308-19.

    Wallis discusses Bentham's constitutional and economic contributions to his age.

_____. "Jeremy Bentham." PSQ, 38 (1923), 45-56.

    Wallis reviews Bentham's life with an emphasis on the evolution of his political theories.

BIBLIOGRAPHIES

Halévy, Elie. THE GROWTH OF PHILOSOPHIC RADICALISM. Trans. Mary Morris. New York: Kelly; London: Faber & Gwyer, 1949.

    Contains a useful bibliography compiled by Charles W. Everett.

Milne, A[lexander] T., ed. CATALOGUE OF THE MANUSCRIPTS OF JEREMY BENTHAM IN THE LIBRARY OF UNIVERSITY COLLEGE, LONDON. 2nd ed. London: Athlone Press, 1962.

Muirhead, Arnold M. A BENTHAM COLLECTION. London: Library 5th Series, 1946.

SAMUEL BUTLER (1835-1902)

PRINCIPAL PROSE WORKS

A FIRST YEAR IN CANTERBURY SETTLEMENT, 1863.

THE EVIDENCE FOR THE RESURRECTION OF JESUS CHRIST, 1865.

EREWHON, 1872.

THE FAIR HAVEN, 1873.

LIFE AND HABIT, 1878.

EVOLUTION, OLD AND NEW, 1879.

UNCONSCIOUS MEMORY, 1880.

ALPS AND SANCTUARIES, 1882.

LUCK, OR CUNNING AS THE MAIN MEANS OF ORGANIC MODIFICATION, 1887.

ON THE TRAPENESE ORIGIN OF THE ODYSSEY, 1893.

THE AUTHORESS OF THE ODYSSEY, 1897.

EREWHON REVISITED, 1901.

THE WAY OF ALL FLESH. Ed. R.A. Streatfeild. 1903.

ESSAYS ON LIFE, ART AND SCIENCE. Ed. R.A. Streatfeild, 1904.

GOD THE KNOWN AND GOD THE UNKNOWN. Ed. R.A. Streatfeild. 1909.

ERNEST PONTIFEX OR THE WAY OF ALL FLESH. Ed. Daniel F. Howard, 1964.
This edition indicates changes and deletions made by Streatfeild in his 1904 edition.

COLLECTED WORKS

BUTLERIANA. Ed. A.T. Bartholomew. London: Nonesuch, 1932.

BUTLER'S NOTEBOOKS. Eds. Geoffrey Keynes and Brian Hill. London: Cape, 1951.

THE ESSENTIAL BUTLER. Ed. G[eorge] D.H. Cole. London: Cape, 1950.

FURTHER EXTRACTS FROM THE NOTE-BOOKS. Ed. A.T. Bartholomew. London: Cape, 1934.

THE NOTEBOOKS OF SAMUEL BUTLER. Ed. H[enry] F. Jones. New York: Dutton, 1912.

SELECTED ESSAYS. Ed. H[enry] F. Jones. New York: Cape, 1929.

SELECTIONS FROM THE NOTE-BOOKS OF SAMUEL BUTLER. Ed. A.T. Bartholomew. London: Cape, 1930.

THE SHREWSBURY EDITION OF THE WORKS. Eds. H[enry] F. Jones and A.T. Bartholomew. 20 vols. London: Cape, 1923-26.
The definitive edition of the complete works.

LETTERS

CORRESPONDENCE OF BUTLER WITH HIS SISTER MAY. Ed. D[aniel] F. Howard. Berkeley and Los Angeles: University of California Press, 1962.

THE FAMILY LETTERS OF BUTLER, 1841-86. Ed. Arnold Silver. Stanford, Calif.: Stanford University Press, 1962.

LETTERS BETWEEN BUTLER AND MISS E.M.A. SAVAGE. Eds. G[eoffrey] Keynes and B. Hill. London: Cape, 1935.

Samuel Butler

THE SHREWSBURY EDITION OF THE WORKS. Eds. H[enry] F. Jones and A.T. Bartholomew. 20 vols. London: Cape, 1923-26.

> Volumes 10 and 11 contain THE LIFE AND LETTERS OF DR. SAMUEL BUTLER.

BIOGRAPHIES

Furbank, P.N. SAMUEL BUTLER. Cambridge: At the University Press, 1948.

> Begins by attacking the negative portrait of Butler that Muggeridge presented, below. Furbank proceeds to analyze the writings on evolution and Butler's relationship with Eliza Savage and his family.

Henderson, Philip. SAMUEL BUTLER: THE INCARNATE BACHELOR. New York: Barnes and Noble, 1953.

> Generally considered the best biography. Henderson notes that his short study is written because of his "delight in the personality of Butler."

Jones, Henry F. SAMUEL BUTLER: A MEMOIR. 2 vols. London: Macmillan, 1920.

> The most detailed biography, but makes no use of the family correspondence. Also includes a nine-page bibliography.

Muggeridge, Malcolm. THE EARNEST ATHEIST: A STUDY OF BUTLER. London: Eyre and Spottiswoode, 1936.

> A controversial study that severely criticizes Butler and his writings. See Furbank, above.

CRITICAL STUDIES

Angelo, Giovanni. "A Note on Samuel Butler in Sicily." EM, 22 (1971), 263-67.

Bekker, Willem G. AN HISTORICAL AND CRITICAL REVIEW OF SAMUEL BUTLER'S LITERARY WORKS. Rotterdam: Gedrukt, 1925; rpt. New York: Russell and Russell, 1964.

> A survey of Butler's works with chapters devoted to EREWHON, FAIR HAVEN, and THE WAY OF ALL FLESH. Bekker says Butler's work shows him to be "an optimist" who "opposed the deadening atmosphere emanating from the materialistic consequences of Darwinian theories."

Bisanz, Adam. "Samuel Butler: A Literary Venture Into Atheism and Beyond." OL, 29 (1974), 316-37.

 Examines the major works in an attempt "to view Butler's religious peregrinations from orthodox theism to atheism and ultimately toward a transcendental vision of polytheism."

_____. "Samuel Butler's 'College of Unreason.'" OL, 28 (1973), 1-22.

 Examines the two chapters on the Erewhonian system of education as "a masterpiece of satire."

Bissell, Claude T. "A Study of THE WAY OF ALL FLESH." NINETEENTH-CENTURY STUDIES. Eds. Herbert Davis; William C. DeVane; and R.C. Bald. Ithaca, N.Y.: Cornell University Press, 1940.

 Bissell writes it is a mistake to read THE WAY OF ALL FLESH as "a masterpiece of long drawn-out matricide and parricide." Instead, the novel presents "the conception of personality, the theory of the unconscious, and the biological approach to the problems of human conduct."

Canby, Henry S. "The Satiric Rage of Butler." In his DEFINITIONS. New York: Harcourt, Brace, 1922.

 Compares the two Erewhons and concludes that, according to Butler, political authority exploits the weaknesses of the masses for its own advantage.

Cannon, Gilbert. SAMUEL BUTLER: A CRITICAL STUDY. London: Martin Secker, 1915.

 Includes chapters on Butler as a satirist, Darwin and Butler, and the major writings: EREWHON, THE FAIR HAVEN, and THE WAY OF ALL FLESH.

Carey, Glenn O. "Samuel Butler's Theory of Evolution: A Summary." ELT, 7 (1964), 230-33.

 Analyzes LIFE AND HABIT, which "was humorously received by professional biologists and thought of as a vulgar joke."

Cockshut, A.O.J. "Samuel Butler: The Search for Paradox." In his THE UNBELIEVERS: ENGLISH AGNOSTIC THOUGHT, 1840-1890. New York: New York University Press, 1966.

 Discusses Butler as a "born protester" who "directed his blows with roughly equal force at Christianity, at agnostic morality, and at the new god of science."

Cole, George D.H. SAMUEL BUTLER. Denver, Colo.: Swallow, 1948.

A brief survey of Butler's work that claims "Butler's outlook was limited. Acute critic as he was of many Victorian values, he was very much a Victorian himself." Appendixes include a bibliography and a biographical sketch.

Copland, R.A. "Bulter's Metaphorical Man." AUMLA, 42 (1974), 163-74.

Examines Butler's "special type of metaphor," and anthropomorphism that is the "source of much of Butler's wit, especially of his paradoxes, and the basis of his most original theories."

Daniels, R. Balfour. "The Conscience of Samuel Butler (1835-1902)." FORUM, 4 (1964), 4-7.

──────. "God and Samuel Butler (1835-1902)." 1967 PROCEEDINGS OF THE CONFERENCE OF COLLEGE TEACHERS OF ENGLISH OF TEXAS. Lubbock: Texas Technical College Press, 1967.

──────. "The Wit and Humor of Samuel Butler." NDQ, 33 (1965), 44-49.

A slight examination of some humorous characters in Butler's works, including THE FAIR HAVEN and EREWHON.

DeLaura, David J. "Echoes of Butler, Browning, Conrad, and Pater in the Poetry of T.S. Eliot." ELN, 3 (1966), 211-21.

DeLaura finds echoes of EREWHON in "The Hollow Men" and the opening lines of "Burnt Norton."

Dollerup, Cay. "Man, He Said, Was a Machinate Mammal." N&Q, 18 (1971), 101.

Dupee, F.W. "Butler's Way." NYRB, 24 August 1967, pp. 28-31.

Dyson, A.E. THE CRAZY FABRIC: ESSAYS IN IRONY. New York: St. Martin's, 1965.

Dyson discusses Butler, Peacock, Thackeray, and Wilde.

Greenacre, Phyllis. THE QUEST FOR THE FATHER: A STUDY OF THE DARWIN-BUTLER CONTROVERSY. New York: International Universities Press, 1963.

"An examination of the vicissitudes and struggles of the oedipal relationship in these two creative individuals."

Greene, David. "The Strangest Work of Classical Scholarship: Samuel Butler and THE AUTHORESS OF THE ODYSSEY." MIDWAY, 8 (1967), 69-79.

Harling, Bruce S. "Samuel Butler." TLS, 16 June 1972, p. 689.

Holt, Lee Elbert. SAMUEL BUTLER. New York: Twayne, 1964.

>Holt bases his speculations about Butler's originality upon a reading of Freud and Jung; but he stresses the "pragmatic ambiguity" in Butler's works.

Joad, C.E.M. SAMUEL BUTLER. London: Parson's 1924.

>Includes a biographical note and chapters on "Butler's Influence on Modern Thought" and "Butler's Practical Philosophy."

Jones, Joseph. THE CRADLE OF EREWHON: SAMUEL BUTLER IN NEW ZEALAND. Austin: University of Texas Press, 1959.

>Discusses the milieu that influenced the creation of EREWHON, that "curious blending of candor and enigma, sense and perversity." Five appendixes examine the documentary notes on the text.

Kenner, Hugh. "Homer's Sticks and Stones." JJQ, 6 (1969), 285-89.

>Discusses Butler's version of Homer as an influence on Joyce's ULYSSES and concludes that "had it not obtruded that unacceptable female Homer, Butler's book might have been taken rather seriously."

Knoepflmacher, Ulrich C. "Ishmael or Anti-Hero? The Division of Self in THE WAY OF ALL FLESH." ELT, 4 (1961), 28-35.

>An analysis of the various narrative viewpoints from which the story is told.

Lange, Petronella J. de. BUTLER: CRITIC AND PHILOSOPHER. Zutphen, Netherlands: Thieme, 1925; rpt. New York: Haskell House, 1966.

>Includes chapters on "Butler's Satirical Works," "Butler's Criticism of Philosophical Thought," and "Butler's Development as an Evolutionist." Concludes that "Butler's philosophy in connection with his personality will probably remain his chief value as a writer."

LeMire, E[ugene] D. "Irony in Erewhon." HAB, 16 (1965), 27-36.

>Contrasts EREWHON and GULLIVER'S TRAVELS as ironic visions, "intellectually circular and morally ambiguous."

McNeisch, James. "The Man Who Wanted to Be Loved." NEW ZEALAND LISTENER, 67 (1971), 8-9.

Murry, John Middleton. ASPECTS OF LITERATURE. London: Collins, 1920.

>Contains a chapter on Butler.

Samuel Butler

Nickerson, Charles C. "Samuel Butler's Copying Process." VPN, 12 (1961), 26.

O'Connor, William Van. "Samuel Butler and Bloomsbury." FROM JANE AUSTEN TO CONRAD. Eds. Robert C. Rathburn and Martin Steinmann. Minneapolis: University of Minnesota Press, 1958.

>Explores Butler's influence on Virginia and Leonard Woolf, Lytton Strachey, John Maynard Keynes, and E.M. Forster.

Pritchett, Victor S. "A Victorian Son." In his THE LIVING NOVEL. New York: Reynal, 1946.

>Discusses THE WAY OF ALL FLESH as "one of the time-bombs of literature waiting to blow up the Victorian family and with it the whole great pillared and balustraded edifice of the Victorian novel."

Sharma, Govind Narain. "Samuel Butler and Edmund Burke: A Comparative Study in British Conservatism." DR, 53 (1973), 5-29.

>Sharma discusses Butler's conservative philosophical outlook and his "mental make-up," as well as his moral and intellectual outlook in relation to that of the age.

Shoenberg, Robert E. "The Literal-Mindedness of Samuel Butler." SEL, 4 (1964), 601-16.

>Discusses Butler's unimaginative tendencies, which caused him to confuse life and art and thereby weakened "his powers as a literary critic and artist." Butler is also criticized for revealing "naive notions that a work of imaginative literature contains a literal account of ideas."

Stillman, Clara G. BUTLER: A MID-VICTORIAN MODERN. New York: Viking, 1932.

>The major work on Butler's thought. Butler was "primarily a philosopher, and it is from the biological foundation that we must ascend to the wide reaches of his philosophic outlook." Also sees THE WAY OF ALL FLESH as the forerunner of modern psychoanalytic fiction.

Toynbee, Philip. "A Satirist in a World Beyond Satire." LISTENER, 47 (1952), 1038-42.

>Toynbee emphasizes Butler's attacks upon Christianity.

Wilding, M. "Samuel Butler at Barbourne." N&Q, 8 (1966), 15-19.

Wiley, Paul L. "Butler: The Counterplay of Recollection." TKR, 1 (1970), 141-53.

>Discusses the "double perspective" in THE WAY OF ALL FLESH and states that "Butler's originality lies in his grasp of two interdependent narrative rhythms, in which one kind of memory complements, and to some degree generates, a second."

Willey, Basil. DARWIN AND BUTLER: TWO VERSIONS OF EVOLUTION. New York: Harcourt, Brace; London: Chatto and Windus, 1960.

>This valuable study devotes two chapters to Butler: "Samuel Butler and Darwin" and "Butler and Religion." According to Willey, "Butler wanted Religion, but not the Creed; and he wanted Evolution, but not Darwin."

BIBLIOGRAPHIES

Gerber, H.E. "Bibliography [of Butler]." EFT, 1 (1957), 17-18.

Gerber, H.E., and Philip Armato. "Samuel Butler." ELT, 10 (1967), 211-12.

>An annotated bibliography that attempts to supplement the Harkness bibliography, below.

Harkness, Stanley B. THE CAREER OF SAMUEL BUTLER, 1835-1903; A BIBLIOGRAPHY. New York: Macmillan, 1955.

>The standard bibliography of Butler's works.

Hoppé, A.J. A BIBLIOGRAPHY OF THE WRITINGS OF BUTLER AND OF WRITINGS ABOUT HIM. London: Bookman's Journal, 1925.

>Also includes some letters between Butler and Rev. F.G. Fleay.

THOMAS CARLYLE (1795-1881)

PRINCIPAL PROSE WORKS

SARTOR RESARTUS; THE LIFE AND OPINIONS OF HERR TEUFELSDRÖCKH, 1836.

THE FRENCH REVOLUTION. A HISTORY. 3 vols. 1837.

LECTURES ON THE HISTORY OF LITERATURE, 1838.

CRITICAL AND MISCELLANEOUS ESSAYS. 4 vols. 1838.

CHARTISM, 1840.

ON HEROES, HERO-WORSHIP, AND THE HEROIC IN HISTORY, 1841.

PAST AND PRESENT, 1843.

LATTER-DAY PAMPHLETS, 1850.

LIFE OF JOHN STERLING, 1851.

THE HISTORY OF FRIEDRICH II OF PRUSSIA, CALLED FREDERICK THE GREAT. 6 vols. 1858-65.

REMINISCENCES. Ed. John A. Froude. 2 vols. 1881.

COLLECTED WORKS

A CARLYLE READER: SELECTIONS FROM THE WRITINGS OF THOMAS CARLYLE. Ed. G[eorge] B. Tennyson. New York: Modern Library, 1969.

Thomas Carlyle

SELECTED WORKS, REMINISCENCES, AND LETTERS BY THOMAS CARLYLE. Ed. Julian Symons. Cambridge, Mass.: Harvard University Press, 1955.

SELECTIONS. Ed. Arthur M.D. Hughes. Oxford: Clarendon Press, 1957.

This selection of Carlyle's writings also includes a selection of "Appreciations" by his contemporaries.

THOMAS CARLYLE: SELECTED WRITINGS. Ed. Alan Shelston. Harmondsworth, Engl.: Penguin, 1971.

TWO NOTE-BOOKS OF THOMAS CARLYLE, FROM 23 MARCH 1822 TO 16 MAY 1832. Mamaroneck, N.Y.: Appel, 1972.

Illustrated; contains materials not available in Traill, below.

THE WORKS OF THOMAS CARLYLE. Ed. H[enry] D. Traill. 30 vols. Boston: Scribner's, 1896-1901.

There is no definitive scholarly edition of Carlyle's work, but Traill's is considered the standard edition.

LETTERS

Cate, George A. "The Correspondence of Thomas Carlyle and John Ruskin." Ph.D. dissertation, Duke University, 1974. DAI, 28, 4120A.

THE COLLECTED LETTERS OF THOMAS AND JANE WELSH CARLYLE. Ed. Charles R. Sanders. Projected 40 vols. Durham, N.C.: Duke University Press, 1971-- .

This will be the definitive edition of Carlyle's letters--over 9,500 by him and 3,000 by his wife. Nearly half have never been published before. Four volumes have appeared as of 1976: volume 1: 1812-21; volume 2: 1822-23; volume 3: 1824-25; volume 4: 1826-28. See Hilles, p. 96, and Sanders, p. 103.

THE CORRESPONDENCE BETWEEN GOETHE AND CARLYLE. Ed. C.E. Norton. London: Macmillan, 1887.

THE CORRESPONDENCE OF EMERSON AND CARLYLE. Ed. Joseph [H.] Slater. New York: Columbia University Press, 1964.

Faulkner, Peter. "Carlyle's Letters to Charles Redwood." YES, 2 (1972), 139-80.

LETTERS, 1826-1836. Ed. C.E. Norton. 2 vols. New York: Macmillan, 1888.

Thomas Carlyle

LETTERS OF CARLYLE TO JOHN STUART MILL, JOHN STERLING, AND ROBERT BROWNING. Ed. Alexander Carlyle. London: Unwin, 1923.

THE LETTERS OF THOMAS CARLYLE TO HIS BROTHER ALEXANDER, WITH RELATED FAMILY LETTERS. Ed. Edwin W. Marrs. Cambridge, Mass.: Harvard University Press, 1969.

THE LOVE LETTERS OF THOMAS CARLYLE AND JANE WELSH. Ed. Alexander Carlyle. 2 vols. London: Lane, 1909.

NEW LETTERS OF THOMAS CARLYLE. Ed. Alexander Carlyle. London: Lane, 1904.

Shipley, John B. "A New Carlyle Letter." ES, 49 (1968), 441-44.

Tarr, Rodger [L.]. "Thomas Carlyle and Henry McCormac: Letters on the Condition of Ireland in 1848." SSL, 5 (1968), 253-56.

BIOGRAPHIES

Collis, John. THE CARLYLES: A BIOGRAPHY OF THOMAS AND JANE CARLYLE. London: Sidgwick and Jackson, 1973.

>A composite biography that is intended as "a truly succinct, yet comprehensive, account of their joint upbringing, courtship, and subsequent life together."

Froude, James A. THOMAS CARLYLE: A HISTORY OF HIS LIFE IN LONDON, 1834-1881. 2 vols. London: Longmans, Green, 1884.

>Froude's four volumes remain the standard biography despite the aura of controversy that has surrounded his work.

_____. THOMAS CARLYLE: A HISTORY OF THE FIRST FORTY YEARS OF HIS LIFE, 1795-1835. 2 vols. London: Longmans, Green, 1882.

Neff, Emery E. CARLYLE. New York: Columbia University Press, 1924.

>Generally considered the best single-volume treatment of Carlyle's life. Neff concludes that Carlyle is the "best representative" of Victorian thought and feeling, as well as the chief influence on the next generation.

Symons, Julian. THOMAS CARLYLE: THE LIFE AND IDEAS OF A PROPHET. London: Gollancz, 1952.

>Charts the general psychological influences that shaped Carlyle and

explores "the effects of his various frustrations on his attitude toward life, politics, and other human beings."

Wilson, David Alec. CARLYLE'S LIFE. 6 vols. New York: Dutton, 1923-34.

Wilson deliberately attempted to correct what he saw as erroneous pronouncements on Carlyle's character.

CRITICAL STUDIES

Alexander, Edward. "Thomas Carlyle and D.H. Lawrence: A Parallel." UTQ, 37 (1968), 248-67.

The parallel is that both writers experienced frustrations as artists seeking to transform society.

August, Eugene R., ed. THOMAS CARLYLE: THE NIGGER QUESTION; JOHN STUART MILL: THE NEGRO QUESTION. New York: Appleton-Century-Crofts, 1971.

August condemns Carlyle's opinions on the subject.

Baumgarten, Murray. "Carlyle and 'Spiritual Optics.'" VS, 11 (1968), 503-22.

Discusses J.A. Froude's analysis of Carlyle's religious beliefs as presented in Carlyle's unfinished essay "Spiritual Optics," in which we find "a writer seeking the tone and voice through which he can communicate his perceptions."

Bentley, Eric. A CENTURY OF HERO-WORSHIP. New York: Lippincott, 1944.

Stresses the philosophical similarities between Carlyle and Nietzsche.

Berger, Harold L. "Emerson and Carlyle--Stylists at Odds." ESQ, 33 (1963), 87-90.

Examines the differences in prose techniques.

――――. "Emerson and Carlyle: The Dissenting Believers." ESQ, 35 (1965), 61-65.

Emphasizes the spiritual similarities between the two.

Brookes, Gerry H. THE RHETORICAL FORM OF CARLYLE'S SARTOR RESARTUS. Berkeley and Los Angeles: University of California Press, 1972.

Attempts to discover how SARTOR RESARTUS' "fictions, its arrangement, its ideas fit together in relation to the effect the whole is intended to have and to understand what that effect is." Concludes that SARTOR RESARTUS is not a novel, but a persuasive essay.

Bufano, Randolph J. "Emerson's Apprenticeship to Carlyle, 1827-1848." ATQ, 13 (1972), 17-25.

Notes that Carlyle and Emerson "never really 'corresponded,' they merely exchanged monologues. In the most intense stage of their friendship they played roles, Emerson of apprentice, Carlyle of master."

Burwick, Frederick L. "Stylistic Continuity and Change in the Prose of Thomas Carlyle." STATISTICS AND STYLE. Eds. Lubomir Dolezel and Richard W. Bailey. New York: American Elsevier, 1969.

A highly technical exploration of the LIFE OF SCHILLER (1821), SARTOR RESARTUS, and EARLY KINGS OF NORWAY (1875), among others. Burwick claims that Carlyle's rhetoric became increasingly imaginative as he grew older.

Calder, Grace. THE WRITING OF PAST AND PRESENT. New Haven, Conn.: Yale University Press, 1949.

Calder analyzes the evolution of the work by comparing the manuscript at the British Museum and the page proofs at Yale.

Cameron, Kenneth W., ed. "Carlyle Evaluated and Criticized." ATQ, 5 (1970), 70-71.

Reprints an 1850 review of LATTER-DAY PAMPHLETS to examine Carlyle's American reputation.

Campbell, Ian. "Carlyle and the Negro Question Again." CRITICISM, 13 (1971), 279-90.

Campbell reviews Carlyle's opinions on slavery and race and claims to have found a "particular" source for his unpopular views: "On the West Indies Question," published in 1829-30 in the DUMPHRIES AND GALLOWAY COURIER.

_____. "Carlyle, Cromwell, and Kimbolton." BIBLIOTHECK, 3 (1970), 246-52.

_____. "Carlyle, Pictet, and Jeffrey Again." BIBLIOTHECK, 7 (1974), 1-15.

Analyzes Carlyle's early review of Pictet's "Theory of Gravitation" as an influence on Carlyle's later work. See Maxwell Goldberg, below.

_____. "Carlyle's Borrowings from the Theological Faculty of Edinburgh University." BIBLIOTHECK, 2 (1969), 165-68.

    Discusses Carlyle's early readings.

_____. "Edward Irving, Carlyle, and the Stage." SSL, 8 (1971), 166-73.

_____. THOMAS CARLYLE. London: Hamilton, 1974.

    Relies on the letters to discuss Carlyle's life and writings. After tracing his intellectual development, the study concludes with "Carlyle: A Portrait," which lists four major concerns: "religion, action, order, and the hero."

Castan, C. "Clough's 'Epi-Strauss-ium' and Carlyle." VP, 4 (1966), 54-56.

    Asserts that Clough's poem on Strauss used a central image from PAST AND PRESENT.

Christensen, Allan. "A Dickensian Hero Retailored: The Carlylean Apprenticeship of Martin Chuzzlewit." SNNTS, 3 (1971), 18-25.

Clubbe, John. "John Carlyle in Germany and the Genesis of SARTOR RESARTUS." ROMANTIC AND VICTORIAN: STUDIES IN MEMORY OF WILLIAM H. MARSHALL. Eds. W. Paul Elledge and Richard L. Hoffman. Rutherford, N.J.: Fairleigh Dickinson University Press, 1971.

    "Carlyle's image of Germany sharpened by [his brother's] letters and conversation, he was now well able to present a compelling picture of German life."

Confer, David. SAINT-SIMONIANISM IN THE RADICALISM OF THOMAS CARLYLE. Austin, Tex.: Van Boeckmann-Jones, 1931.

    Confer sees PAST AND PRESENT as the culmination of Carlyle's Saint-Simonianism.

Coulling, Sidney M.B. "Carlyle and Swift." SEL, 10 (1970), 741-58.

    Coulling's thesis is that Carlyle was too distrustful of satire to be Swift's disciple.

Crossman, R.H.S. "Carlyle and Froude." NST, 67 (1964), 81-82.

Daiches, David. CARLYLE AND THE VICTORIAN DILEMMA. Edinburgh: Carlyle Society, 1963.

    Analyzes Carlyle's attitudes toward nineteenth-century social and political realities: "One cannot help feeling that the increasing inadequacy of his remedies, like the growing stridency of his voice and repetitiveness of his arguments, is related in some way to the logical inadequacy of his positive creed."

Deen, Leonard W. "Irrational Form in SARTOR RESARTUS." TSLL, 5 (1963), 438-51.

Deen claims that the "disorder" of the work is due to Carlyle's "extraordinary ambitious intentions"--"to lay bare the social, political, moral, and religious problems and failures of the early nineteenth century."

DeLaura, David J. "Arnold and Carlyle." PMLA, 79 (1964), 104-29.

An important article that traces Carlyle's influence on Arnold and, more importantly, Arnold's "persistent ambivalence" toward Carlyle as a precursor. See Wilkinson, below.

———. "Ishmael as Prophet: HEROES AND HERO-WORSHIP and the Self-Expressive Basis of Carlyle's Art." TSLL, 11 (1969), 705-32.

DeLaura claims that the unity of HEROES lies in the "deeply personal character" of Carlyle's efforts to define the social role of the prophet, while the "ultimate hero" of the work is Carlyle himself.

Deneau, Daniel P. "Relationship of Style and Device in SARTOR RESARTUS." VN, 17 (1960), 17-20.

Claims that SARTOR RESARTUS is "a work of imaginative literature" and that "we must look closely at the elaborate device which Carlyle employed; we must examine, in addition, how effectively Carlyle was able to manipulate his style according to the demands imposed by the device"--the character of Teufelsdröckh.

Dibble, J.A. "Carlyle's British Reader and the Structure of SARTOR RESARTUS." TSLL, 16 (1974), 293-304.

Traces Carlyle's depiction of the British reader throughout every chapter of SARTOR RESARTUS and asserts that the reader "is as much a part of the fictive world as is Teufelsdröckh."

Dilthey, Wilhelm. "SARTOR RESARTUS: Philosophical Conflict, Positive and Negative Eras, and Personal Resolution." ClioW, 1 (1972), 40-60.

Dunn, Richard J. "Dickens, Carlyle, and the HARD TIMES Dedication." DSN, 2 (1971), 90-92.

———. "'Inverse Sublimity': Carlyle's Theory of Humour." UTQ, 40 (1970), 41-57.

"It was finally the incompatibility between his theory of humour and his views of the hero and the hero's function which made it impossible for him to sustain the kind of humour he described in his early critical essays." See Sutton, below.

Dunn, Waldo H. "Carlyle and the Eternal Verities." In his LECTURES ON THREE EMINENT VICTORIANS. Claremont, Calif.: Scripps College Papers, 1932.

    Dunn concludes that Carlyle's great virtue was supplying "moral energy."

———. FROUDE AND CARLYLE: A STUDY OF THE FROUDE-CARLYLE CONTROVERSY. London: Longmans, Green, 1930; rpt. New York: Kennikat Press, 1969.

    An attempt to vindicate Froude's biography of Carlyle.

Ebel, Henry. "The Primaeval Fountain of Human Nature: Mill, Carlyle, and the French Revolution." VN, 30 (1966), 13-18.

    Discusses the French Revolution as "the intellectual pivot" of Carlyle's career, the source of his "psychology of the Unconscious," by which he attempted "to comprehend the irrational and violent potentialities of the individual."

Ferguson, William. CARLYLE AS HISTORIAN. Edinburgh: Carlyle Society, 1966.

    "How did history appear to Carlyle, and through what processes did he arrive at his views?" Ferguson lists Hume, Robertson, Scott, and Schiller as influences.

Gascoyne, David. THOMAS CARLYLE. London: Longmans, Green, 1952; rpt. 1963.

    A short introduction to Carlyle that praises him: "more than a great Victorian writer, he is one of our great national prophets."

Gilbert, Elliot L. "A Wondrous Contiguity: Anachronism in Carlyle's Prophecy and Art." PMLA, 87 (1972), 432-42.

    Claims that Carlyle cannot be charged with "anachronism" because "in his writing he rejects the frame of reference out of which such attacks come; rejects, that is, the view that history consists of a series of events linked by a superficial causality."

Gohdes, Clarence. "The Correspondence of Emerson and Carlyle." SOR, 2 (1966), 471-75.

    Discusses the Slater edition, above, of correspondence between the two writers and disagrees with Slater's judgment that the letters form "a single work of art."

Goldberg, Maxwell H. "Carlyle, Pictet, and Jeffrey." MLQ, 7 (1946), 291-96.

An account of Carlyle's first acquaintance with the EDINBURGH REVIEW and Carlyle's opinion of Francis Jeffrey as editor. See Campbell, above.

Goldberg, Michael. CARLYLE AND DICKENS. Athens: University of Georgia Press, 1972.

Emphasizes the literary interaction and includes chapters on their contrasting styles and use of the grotesque.

Goodheart, Eugene. THE CULT OF THE EGO IN MODERN LITERATURE. Chicago: University of Chicago Press, 1968.

Includes an essay on "Goethe, Carlyle and THE SORROWS OF WERTHER," in which Carlyle is depicted as "antiromantic" and "antilibertarian."

Grierson, Herbert J. "Thomas Carlyle." PBA, 26 (1940), 301-25.

Grierson discusses Carlyle as a kind of Old Testament prophet.

Harrold, Charles F. CARLYLE AND GERMAN THOUGHT, 1819-1834. New Haven, Conn.: Yale University Press, 1934.

The definitive study of this topic. Harrold reviews other opinions and examines Carlyle's method in THE FRENCH REVOLUTION and the influence of Kant, Goethe, Schiller, and Novalis upon it. See Smeed, below.

──────. "Carlyle's General Method in THE FRENCH REVOLUTION." PMLA, 43 (1928), 1150-69.

Discusses Carlyle's use of "dull or hopelessly biased accounts" to "winnow that thing which he revered with his whole soul, the significant human fact." Concludes that Carlyle was not "a scientific historian" but an "artist."

Hilles, Frederick W. "Tom Carlyle and his Mocking Bonny Jane." YR, 60 (1971), 569-76.

Reviews the four volumes of the Duke-Edinburgh collection of the Carlyle letters, above.

Hopwood, Alison. "Carlyle and Conrad: PAST AND PRESENT and THE HEART

OF DARKNESS." RES, 23 (1972), 162-72.

 See parallels between the two works as evidence that Conrad echoed Carlyle, although in greatly altered form.

Hutton, Richard H. CRITICISM ON CONTEMPORARY THOUGHT AND THINKERS. 2 vols. London: Macmillan, 1894; rpt. Westmead, Australia: Gregg Publishers, 1969.

 Volume 1 contains "Carlyle's Faith," "Thomas Carlyle," and "Carlyle's Reminiscences."

Ikeler, A. Abbott. PURITAN TEMPER AND THE TRANSCENDENTAL FAITH: CARLYLE'S LITERARY VISION. Columbus: Ohio State University Press, 1972.

 Traces the ambiguities inherent in Carlyle's transcendental Puritan vision as revealed in his attitude toward literature. Ikeler discusses the major prose, Carlyle's religious development, and the sources of his thought.

Jones, Iva G. "Trollope, Carlyle, and Mill on the Negro: An Episode in the History of Ideas." JNH, 52 (1967), 185-99.

Jones, Joseph. "Carlyle, Whitman, and the Democratic Dilemma." ESA, 3 (1960), 179-97.

 Jones discusses Whitman's agreements and disagreements with Carlyle's "Shooting Niagara."

Kegel, Charles H. "Carlyle and Ruskin: An Influential Friendship." BYUS, 5 (1964), 219-29.

 Kegel studies details of the personal relationship.

Kenney, Blair G. "Carlyle and BLEAK HOUSE." DICKENSIAN, 66 (1970), 36-41.

 A study of Carlyle's influence on Dickens.

Kusch, Robert W. "Carlyle and the Milieu of 'Spontaneous Combustion.'" NM, 70 (1969), 339-44.

 Deals with Carlyle's use of metaphor in THE FRENCH REVOLUTION.

_____. "The Eighteenth Century as 'Decaying Organism' in Carlyle's THE FRENCH REVOLUTION." ANGLIA, 89 (1971), 456-70.

 Asserts that Carlyle "sees in metaphor a primary way of knowing and uses language for evocation as well as description." In his use of the phrase "decaying organism," metaphor and theme generate a "vitality which is his artistry at its best."

Thomas Carlyle

---------. "Pattern and Paradox in HEROES AND HERO-WORSHIP." SSL, 6 (1969), 146-55.

    Kusch criticizes the lack of aesthetic coherence in HEROES.

La Valley, Albert J. CARLYLE AND THE IDEA OF THE MODERN: STUDIES IN CARLYLE'S PROPHETIC LITERATURE AND ITS RELATION TO BLAKE, NIETZSCHE, MARX, AND OTHERS. New Haven, Conn.: Yale University Press, 1968.

    Discusses the "dominant modern pattern" in SARTOR, PAST AND PRESENT, and THE FRENCH REVOLUTION. La Valley sees Carlyle less as a philosopher than as a "prophetic prophet, the seer who is himself a quester into self and society."

Lea, Frank A. CARLYLE: PROPHET OF TODAY. London: Routledge and Kegan Paul, 1943.

    This psychological study claims that Carlyle's writings are intrinsically religious.

Lehman, B.H. CARLYLE'S THEORY OF THE HERO. Durham, N.C.: Duke University Press, 1928.

    Lehman emphasizes Carlyle's antidemocratic ideas.

Leicester, H.M. "The Dialectic of Romantic Historiography: Prospect and Retrospect in THE FRENCH REVOLUTION." VS, 15 (1971), 1-17.

    Leicester claims that Carlyle's work embodies "the tensions of historical dialectic."

Levine, George L. "The Use and Abuse of Carlylese." In his THE ART OF VICTORIAN PROSE. New York: Oxford University Press, 1968.

    Levine observes that, although Carlyle was committed to writing about practical problems, his readers have ignored those problems and attended only to his style, that is, considered him only as a poet.

Lindberg, John. "The Artistic Unity of SARTOR RESARTUS." VN, 17 (1960), 20-23.

---------. "The Decadence of Style: Symbolic Structure in Carlyle's Later Prose." SSL, 1 (1964), 183-95.

    Divides Carlyle's career into three phases, the last one characterized by a "style separated from reality and more dogmatically symbolic."

Mackerness, E.D. "The Voice of Prophecy: Carlyle and Ruskin." FROM DICKENS TO HARDY. Ed. Boris Ford. Harmondsworth, Engl.: Penguin, 1958.

>Contrasts the two writers and concludes that Carlyle's work "must be seen more narrowly within the framework of the period he belongs to."

McMaster, Rowland D. "Criticism of Civilization in the Structure of SARTOR RESARTUS." UTQ, 37 (1968), 268-80.

>Sees SARTOR RESARTUS as somewhat unified, for its various parts force the reader to view Teufelsdröckh and his era from different perspectives: "the apparently confused structure and chaotic jumble of ideas are a true symbolic reflection of the world."

Malin, James C. "Carlyle's Philosophy of Clothes and Swedenborg's." SS, 33 (1961), 155-68.

>Details the many striking similarities between the two writers and notes that their use of the Philosophy of Clothes "is a literary and philosophical coincidence of the first order of magnitude."

Marrs, Edwin W. "Dating the Writing of PAST AND PRESENT." N&Q, 14 (1967), 370-71.

>Marrs argues that the book was begun in November, 1842 and completed in March, 1843.

Martin, Peter. "Carlyle and Mill: The 'Anti-Self-Consciousness' Theory." THOTH, 6 (1965), 20-34.

>Martin discusses the two men as complements and opposites.

Mendel, Sydney. "Carlyle: Notes Towards a Revaluation." ESA, 10 (1967), 11-21.

>Attempts to compare Carlyle with Sartre.

Metzger, Lore. "SARTOR RESARTUS: A Victorian FAUST." CL, 13 (1961), 316-31.

>Metzger claims that FAUST stood at the "fixed center of the spiral of Carlyle's philosophy."

Mill, Anna J. CARLYLE AND MILL: TWO SCOTTISH UNIVERSITY RECTORS. Edinburgh: Carlyle Society, 1965.

>A short comparative study of their educational theories.

Mitford, Nancy. "Tom and Fritz: Carlyle and Frederick the Great." HT, 18 (1968), 3-13.

    Discusses the "oddity" of Carlyle's style.

Moore, Carlisle. "SARTOR RESARTUS and the Problems of Carlyle's Conversion." PMLA, 70 (1955), 662-81.

    Moore argues that it actually took Carlyle more than ten years to move from the "Everlasting No" to the "Everlasting Yea," although this progression is condensed in SARTOR.

──────. "Thomas Carlyle and Fiction, 1822-1834." NINETEENTH-CENTURY STUDIES. Eds. Herbert Davis, William C. DeVane, and R.C. Bald. Ithaca, N.Y.: Cornell University Press, 1940.

    Explores Carlyle's three attempts to write fiction, which "throw light on Carlyle's development as an artist and help to explain his transferred allegiance from fiction to fact, and from the novel to history."

Morgan, Peter F. "Carlyle and Macaulay as Critics of Literature and Life in the EDINBURGH REVIEW." SGG, 12 (1970), 131-44.

    Discusses Carlyle's views on literature as reflected in the seven articles he published in the EDINBURGH REVIEW, 1827-32.

Neff, Emery E. CARLYLE AND MILL: AN INTRODUCTION TO VICTORIAN THOUGHT. 2nd rev. ed. New York: Octagon, 1964.

    The definitive study of this topic, in which Neff contrasts the two writers as representatives of the Victorian period and analyzes their opposing temperaments as keys to understanding the political, economic, religious, and literary background of the period.

Obertello, Alfredo. CARLYLE'S CRITICAL THEORIES: THEIR ORIGIN AND PRACTICE. Genoa, Italy: Lupa Library Publications, 1948.

    Discusses the foreign sources of Carlyle's literary criticism, as well as analyzes his "Conception of the Poet" and "Theory of Literature." Contains two appendixes that discuss Carlyle's literary relationship to Germany and his attitude toward his English contemporaries.

Oddie, William. DICKENS AND CARLYLE: THE QUESTION OF INFLUENCE. London: Centenary Press, 1972.

    Explores Carlyle's influence on Dickens and concludes that "Carlyle offered an imprecise but consistent structure of ideas and opinions that happened to overlap with many of Dickens' disparate and disorganized feelings."

Pankhurst, Richard K.P. THE SAINT-SIMONIANS: MILL AND CARLYLE. London: Sidgwick and Jackson, 1957.

>Details the history of the Saint-Simonians in England, with emphasis on Mill and Carlyle as supporters who "wrote in glowing terms" about the movement.

Reed, Walter L. "The Pattern of Conversion in SARTOR RESARTUS." ELH, 38 (1971), 411-31.

>SARTOR presents a romantic rather than a Christian conversion.

Roberts, Mark. "Carlyle and the Rhetoric of Unreason." EIC, 18 (1968), 397-419.

>Discusses Carlyle's distinctive rhetorical devices in relation to substantive meaning in the works.

Roe, Frederick William. SOCIAL PHILOSOPHY OF CARLYLE AND RUSKIN. New York: Harcourt, Brace, 1921.

>Roe stresses their similarities.

_____. THOMAS CARLYLE AS A CRITIC OF LITERATURE. New York: Columbia University Press, 1910.

>Discusses Carlyle's relation to romantic and German literature and to the English essay tradition.

Roellinger, Francis X. "The Early Development of Carlyle's Style." PMLA, 72 (1957), 936-51.

>Uses early letters to show that Carlyle's early style was typical of his period, "a mildly Johnsonian mode," which changed only much later in his career. See Ryan, below.

Rogers, William Hudson. "A Study in Contrasts: Carlyle and Macaulay as Book Reviewers." FSUS, 5 (1952), 1-10.

>Carlyle "was the prosaic moralist, the enemy of conventionality, the crusader against materialism and hypocrisy--the greatest of all his reviews was that of Lockhart's LIFE OF BURNS."

Rosenberg, Philip. THE SEVENTH HERO: THOMAS CARLYLE AND THE THEORY OF RADICAL ACTIVISM. Cambridge, Mass.: Harvard University Press, 1974.

>Rosenberg argues that, between ages thirty-three and forty-eight, Carlyle was a radical and that his works were a development of his activism.

Thomas Carlyle

Ross, Donald. "Composition as a Stylistic Feature." STYLE, 4 (1971), 1-10.

> Ross discusses key words and methods of linking paragraphs in Carlyle, Emerson, and Thoreau.

Rutherford, Andrew. "Carlyle and Kipling." KJ, 158 (1966), 10-19; 159 (1966), 11-19; and 160 (1967), 11-16.

Ryan, Alvan S. "The Attitude Toward the Reader in Carlyle's SARTOR RESARTUS." VN, 23 (1963), 15-16.

> Discusses the editorial voice in an attempt to correct Roellinger's study, above.

――――. "Carlyle, Jeffrey, and the 'Helotage' Chapter of SARTOR RESARTUS." VN, 27 (1965), 30-32.

Sanders, Charles R. "The Byron Closed in SARTOR RESARTUS." SIR, 3 (1964), 108-20.

> Points out what Carlyle and Byron had in common, asserting that "Carlyle read and criticized Byron as a contemporary and, in many respects, as one Romantic speaking of a fellow Romantic."

――――. "Carlyle and Tennyson." PMLA, 76 (1961), 82-97.

> Examines the personal relationship as revealed through several letters. Also discusses Carlyle's estimate of Tennyson's poetry and the religious differences between the two.

――――. "Carlyle as Editor and Critic of Literary Letters." EUQ, 20 (1964), 108-20.

> Discusses Carlyle's editing of Oliver Cromwell's and John Sterling's letters, but focuses on Carlyle's attempt to edit his wife's letters after her death in 1866.

――――. "Carlyle, Poetry and the Music of Humanity." WHR, 16 (1962), 53-66.

> Discusses Carlyle's antipathy to poetry.

――――. "The Carlyles and Thackeray." NINETEENTH-CENTURY LITERARY PERSPECTIVES. Eds. Clyde de L. Ryals et al. Durham, N.C.: Duke University Press, 1974.

> "Despite important differences and philosophies of life, however, Carlyle and Thackeray found much to admire in one another and a considerable amount of common ground to stand on."

_____. "Editing the Carlyle Letters: Problems and Opportunities." EDITING NINETEENTH-CENTURY TEXTS. Ed. John M. Robson. Toronto: University of Toronto Press, 1967.

_____. "The Victorian Rembrandt: Carlyle's Portraits of His Contemporaries." BJRL, 39 (1967), 521-57.

> Sanders argues that Carlyle's portraits are keys to an understanding of his larger value system.

Seigel, Jules Paul, ed. THOMAS CARLYLE: THE CRITICAL HERITAGE. New York: Barnes and Noble, 1971.

> A useful collection of critical essays written about Carlyle by several of his contemporaries.

Sharrock, Roger. "Carlyle and the Sense of History." E&S, 19 (1966), 74-91.

> Discusses Carlyle's polemical style as well as his deterministic sense of history as reflected in THE FRENCH REVOLUTION.

Shine, Hill. CARLYLE AND THE SAINT-SIMONIANS: THE CONCEPT OF HISTORICAL PERIODICITY. Baltimore: Johns Hopkins University Press, 1941.

> Shine argues that Carlyle's exposure to Saint-Simonianism in 1830-31 influenced both SARTOR RESARTUS and PAST AND PRESENT.

_____. CARLYLE'S EARLY READINGS TO 1834. Lexington: University of Kentucky Press, 1953.

> Shine lists every work and author that Carlyle is known to have read before he moved to London.

_____. "Carlyle's Early Writing and Herder's IDEEN: The Concept of History." In his BOOKER MEMORIAL STUDIES. Chapel Hill: University of North Carolina Press, 1950.

> Shine examines Herder's influence on Carlyle's historiography. See Wellek, below.

_____. CARLYLE'S FUSION OF POETRY, HISTORY, AND RELIGION BY 1834. Chapel Hill: University of North Carolina Press, 1937.

> Shine traces the way Carlyle refined and assimilated his ideas until they gave way to Calvinism in his later years.

Sigman, Joseph. "'Diabolico-angelical Indifference': The Imagery of Polarity in SARTOR RESARTUS." SORA, 5 (1972), 207-24.

Thomas Carlyle

Smeed, J.W. GERMAN INFLUENCE ON THOMAS CARLYLE. Edinburgh: Carlyle Society, 1964.

    A valuable study on this topic. See Harrold, above.

Smith, Sheila M. "Blue Books and Victorian Novelists." RES, 21 (1970), 23-40.

    Smith argues that Carlyle inspired other writers to use official governmental statistics in their work.

Straka, Gerald M. "The Spirit of Carlyle in the Old South." HISTORIAN, 20 (1957), 39-57.

    Straka concentrates on the Southern response to Carlyle's writings on the "nigger question" in the 1850s.

Sutton, Max K. "'Inverse Sublimity' in Victorian Humor." VS, 10 (1966), 177-92.

    Attempts to recover the "elusive meaning" of Carlyle's term, for it "not only illuminates stylistic features that are common to Dickens's humor and his own, it also suggests the relationship between their fancifully distorted pictures of reality and the serious imaginative visions of the Romantic poets." See Richard Dunn, above.

Swanson, Donald R. "Carlyle on the English Romantic Poets." LHR, 11 (1969), 25-32.

    Swanson claims that "in spite of his final evaluation of them, the influence of the Romantic poets on Carlyle was far greater than he could ever consciously acknowledge."

_____. "Ruskin and His 'Master.'" VN, 31 (1967), 56-59.

    Swanson argues that Carlyle was Ruskin's "Master."

Tarr, Rodger [L.]. "Thomas Carlyle's Growing Radicalism: The Social Context of THE FRENCH REVOLUTION." COSTERUS, 1 (1974), 113-26.

    Examines THE FRENCH REVOLUTION for its "self-avowed didacticism."

Tarr, Rodger [L.], and Ian Campbell. "Carlyle's Early Study of German, 1819-1821." IQ, 34 (1971), 19-27.

    Explores the reasons behind Carlyle's early study of German, for it marks "the most crucial phase in the development of his philosophical and moral character." Begins by asserting that the basic obstacle to the acceptance of Carlyle to the modern mind is his conviction "that man has forgotten God."

Thomas Carlyle

Tennyson, G[eorge] B. SARTOR CALLED RESARTUS: THE GENESIS, STRUCTURE, AND STYLE OF THOMAS CARLYLE'S FIRST MAJOR WORK. Princeton, N.J.: Princeton University Press, 1965.

    A valuable study that traces Carlyle's "Apprenticeship, 1819-1827" and the influence of "Germany, 1824-1832." Sees SARTOR RESARTUS as unified through its use of imagery, themes, fragments, and allusions. Also contains a chronology of works written by Carlyle during 1814-33.

Thurman, William R. "Carlyle, Browning, and Ruskin on One Purpose of Art." SAB, 37 (1972), 52-57.

    "For Carlyle, as for Ruskin, the worth which we place upon the skill and product of the artist only reveals the shallowness and short-sightedness of man, who, dressed in a little brief authority values his own finite accomplishments above those of Divine creation."

Trowbridge, Ronald L. "Carlyle's 'Illudo Chartis' as a Prophetic Exercise in the Manner of Swift and Sterne." SSL, 6 (1968), 115-22.

    Discusses specific parallels and echoes of Swift and Sterne in Carlyle's works.

_____. "Thomas Carlyle's Masks of Humor." MIA, 3 (1970), 57-66.

    Discusses Carlyle as a humorist.

Turner, Frank M[iller]. "Victorian Scientific Naturalism and Thomas Carlyle." VS, 18 (1975), 325-43.

    Argues that Carlyle's relationship to science and rationalism is considerably more ambiguous than is generally recognized.

Vance, William S. CARLYLE AND THE AMERICAN TRANSCENDENTALISTS. Chicago: University of Chicago Press, 1944.

    Carlyle's relationship with Emerson is treated extensively.

Wellek, René. "Thomas Carlyle." In his A HISTORY OF MODERN CRITICISM, 1750-1950. Vol. 3. New Haven, Conn.: Yale University Press, 1965.

    "Strictly from the point of view of literary criticism, one must deplore that Carlyle chose the path of virtue: the shift to biography, didacticism, moralism, and the criterion of 'sincerity' have not advanced the cause of criticism."

_____. "Thomas Carlyle and the Philosophy of History." PQ, 23 (1944), 55-76.

Thomas Carlyle

Wellek challenges the views of Shine, above, and Young, below, on the nature of Carlyle's philosophy of history.

West, Paul. "Carlyle's Bravura Prophetics." COSTERUS, 5 (1972), 153-95.

"Carlyle, if he is anything, is a temperament exactly reproduced in his prose, and his opinions often seem the perfect extensions of his prose style. If there is sound and fury in his prose, then what is signified often seems to come second."

Wilkinson, D.R.M. "Carlyle, Arnold, and Literary Justice." PMLA, 86 (1971), 225-35.

This article is a response to DeLaura's unflattering portrait of Arnold, above.

Wilson, John R. "'Signs of the Times' and 'The Present Age': Essays of Crisis." WHR, 26 (1972), 369-74.

Discusses the similarities between Carlyle and Kierkegaard.

Witte, William. "Carlyle as a Critic of German Literature." In his SCHILLER AND BURNS AND OTHER ESSAYS. Oxford: Blackwell, 1959.

Witte discussed Carlyle's relation to German romanticism and emphasizes his more critical posture toward the first generation rather than the second generation of German writers.

Young, Louise. THOMAS CARLYLE AND THE ART OF HISTORY. Philadelphia: University of Pennsylvania Press, 1939.

An important study of Carlyle as an historian. Young's thesis is that Carlyle "perpetuated the tradition of literary history" of the eighteenth century, but revitalized the tradition by introducing romantic and German influences. See Wellek, above.

BIBLIOGRAPHIES

Buckley, Jerome. "Thomas Carlyle." In his VICTORIAN POETS AND PROSE WRITERS. Goldentree Bibliographies. New York: Appleton-Century-Crofts, 1966.

A selective listing suitable for introductory work.

Dyer, Isaac W. A BIBLIOGRAPHY OF THOMAS CARLYLE'S WRITINGS. Portland, Maine: Southworth Press, 1928; rpt. New York: Franklin, 1968.

The standard and most useful bibliography.

Moore, Carlisle. "Thomas Carlyle." THE ENGLISH ROMANTIC POETS AND

ESSAYISTS. Eds. C[arolyn] W. Houtchens and L[awrence] H. Houtchens. Rev. ed. New York: MLA, 1966.

In this valuable bibliographical essay, Moore discusses Carlyle as a transitional figure since some of his best work was done before 1832.

Tarr, Rodger L. CHECK-LIST OF TWENTIETH-CENTURY ENGLISH LANGUAGE ARTICLES ON THOMAS CARLYLE, 1900-1965. Columbia: University of South Carolina Press, 1972.

A valuable listing of secondary sources.

Tennyson, George B. "Thomas Carlyle." VICTORIAN PROSE: A GUIDE TO RESEARCH. Ed. David J. DeLaura. New York: MLA, 1973.

The most thorough and useful bibliographical essay on Carlyle.

WILLIAM COBBETT (1763-1835)

PRINCIPAL PROSE WORKS

THE LIFE AND ADVENTURES OF PETER PORCUPINE, 1796.

PORCUPINE'S GAZETTE, 1797-1800.

THE PORCUPINE, 1800-24.

COBBETT'S WEEKLY POLITICAL REGISTER, 1802-35.

A YEAR'S RESIDENCE IN THE UNITED STATES OF AMERICA, 1818-19.

A GRAMMAR OF THE ENGLISH LANGUAGE, 1818.

COBBETT'S SERMONS, 1822.

COBBETT'S POOR MAN'S FRIEND; OR, USEFUL INFORMATION FOR THE WORKING CLASSES, 1827.

HISTORY OF THE REGENCY AND REIGN OF KING GEORGE THE FOURTH. 2 vols. 1830.

RURAL RIDES IN THE COUNTIES OF SURREY, KENT, SUSSEX, . . . WITH ECONOMICAL AND POLITICAL OBSERVATIONS, 1830.

COBBETT'S TWO-PENNY TRASH. 2 vols. 1831-32.

COLLECTED WORKS

THE AUTOBIOGRAPHY OF WILLIAM COBBETT: THE PROGRESS OF A

PLOUGH-BOY TO A SEAT IN PARLIAMENT. Ed. William Reitzel. London: Faber and Faber, 1933; rev. ed. 1947.

> Reitzel compiled this "autobiography" from portions of A YEAR'S RESIDENCE, RURAL RIDES, LIFE AND ADVENTURES OF PETER PORCUPINE, and ADVICE TO YOUNG MEN.

PORCUPINE'S WORKS. 12 vols. London: Cobbett and Morgan, 1801.

THE WORKS OF PETER PORCUPINE. 2 vols. Philadelphia: Cobbett, 1795.

LETTERS

Also see Benjamin's biography, LIFE AND LETTERS, below.

Duff, Gerald A. "An Unpublished William Cobbett Letter." ELN, 4 (1966), 110-12.

LETTERS FROM WILLIAM COBBETT TO EDWARD THORNTON, 1797-1800. Ed. G[eorge] D.H. Cole. London: Oxford University Press, 1937.

LETTERS OF WILLIAM COBBETT. Ed. Gerald [A.] Duff. Salzburg: University of Salzburg Press, 1974.

> Contains a chronology of Cobbett's life and the letters written during 1800-1835.

Osborne, John W. "A Newly Acquired William Cobbett Letter." JRUL, 33 (1969), 28-30.

BIOGRAPHIES

Benjamin, Lewis S. [Lewis Melville]. THE LIFE AND LETTERS OF WILLIAM COBBETT. 2 vols. London: Lane, 1913.

> Relies heavily on Cobbett's letters, to which four chapters are devoted. Presents Cobbett as a radical champion of the poor and oppressed.

Bowen, Marjorie. PETER PORCUPINE: A STUDY OF WILLIAM COBBETT. London: Longmans, Green, 1936.

> An idealized portrait in which Cobbett is described as "the epitome and sublimation" of the English peasant, possessed of "noble simplicity and direct contact with the earth."

William Cobbett

Briggs, Asa. WILLIAM COBBETT. London: Oxford University Press, 1967.

>Presents Cobbett as "the great radical leader" during a turbulent transitional period.

Carlyle, E.I. COBBETT: A STUDY OF HIS LIFE AS SHOWN IN HIS WRITINGS. London: Constable, 1904.

>Dismisses Cobbett's social and political writings, but praises his

Chesterton, Gilbert K. WILLIAM COBBETT. London: Hodder and Stoughton, 1925.

>Chesterton presents Cobbett as a "self-made man" and an "amateur historian" who was concerned with "liberty, England, the family, and the honour of the yeoman."

Cole, G[eorge] D.H. THE LIFE OF WILLIAM COBBETT. London: Wilkinson, 1924.

>Generally considered the definitive biography of Cobbett, who is presented as a radical and leader of the working class. Also includes a chapter by F.E. Green on RURAL RIDES that presents a nostalgic view of rustic life.

Pemberton, William Baring. WILLIAM COBBETT. Harmondsworth, Engl.: Penguin, 1949.

>Rejects Cole's portrait, above, and presents Cobbett as a traditional, reactionary embodiment of "the serenity of a solid rural economy."

Sambrook, J. WILLIAM COBBETT. London: Routledge and Kegan Paul, 1973.

>Details the historical and intellectual background of Cobbett's era. Claims that the "myth" of Merry England, a "unifying image of the land and its workers," profoundly affected Cobbett and his writings.

Smith, Edward. WILLIAM COBBETT: A BIOGRAPHY. 2 vols. London: Low, Marston, Searle, and Rivington, 1878.

>An early biography that focuses on Cobbett as "the barometer of popular opinion, more or less, for thirty years."

CRITICAL STUDIES

Ausubel, Herman. "William Cobbett and Malthusianism." JHI, 13 (1952), 250-56.

Discusses Cobbett's play SURPLUS POPULATION (1831) as his severest denunciation of "the institutions, practices, and doctrines of Malthus." See Kegel, below.

Birrell, T.A. "THE POLITICAL REGISTER: Cobbett and English Literature." ES, 45 (1964), 213-19.

"Cobbett's great achievement is a political journalist," while "his chief affiliation is to the great political satirical tradition of the eighteenth century."

Duff, Gerald [A.]. "Scenic Description in William Cobbett's Rural Rides." MCNR, 18 (1967), 45-59.

_____. WILLIAM COBBETT AND THE POLITICS OF EARTH. Salzburg: University of Salzburg Press, 1972.

Discusses Cobbett's views on education, religion, history, and landscapes in relation to his age. One chapter examines Cobbett's prose style and suggests reasons why it reached such a wide audience.

_____. "William Cobbett and the Prose of Revelation." TSLL, 11 (1970), 1349-65.

Discusses Cobbett's style as a reflection of his desire to present faithful descriptions with an air of assurance.

Gaines, Pierce U. "William Cobbett's Account Book." PAAS, 78 (1968), 299-312.

Hultin, Neil C. "Inchiquin and Cobbett: American Letters and British Politics." N&Q, 19 (1972), 91-93.

Jensen, Jay. "William Cobbett: John Bull as Journalist." EUQ, 21 (1965), 173-82.

Presents a biographical sketch and concludes that "whatever his shortcomings as a thinker and as a social critic, his genius for expressing in concrete terms the interests and sentiments of the working classes made him the most popular and influential English journalist of his time."

Jones, Stanley. "Hazlitt, Cobbett, and the EDINBURGH REVIEW." NEO, 53 (1969), 69-76.

Discusses Hazlitt's attacks on Cobbett and Cobbett's supposed defense in 1807. Concludes that this incident "illustrates Hazlitt's imperfect knowledge of Cobbett's relations with the EDINBURGH REVIEW."

William Cobbett

Kegel, Charles H. "William Cobbett and Malthusianism." JHI, 19 (1958), 348-62.

> Reviews Cobbett's changing attitudes toward Malthus and concludes that Cobbett thought "man was not a mere animal, and he raised his voice against those who would treat man as such. Also, he saw in Malthusianism a rationalization for the injustices of the contemporary social patterns." See Ausubel, above.

Martin, E.W. "Cobbett and the Making of Modern England." HT, 10 (1960), 44-50.

Osborne, John W. WILLIAM COBBETT: HIS THOUGHT AND HIS TIMES. New Brunswick, N.J.: Rutgers University Press, 1966.

> This important study analyzes Cobbett's ideas and claims that he is radical only in techniques, not in objectives. States Cobbett was actually a "utopian reactionary" who looked back on an invented and romantic past.

―――. "William Cobbett's GRAMMAR and Its Purchasers." JRUL, 30 (1966), 8-11.

Palmer, Chris. "Facts are Facts: Cobbett's RURAL RIDES." CR, 15 (1972), 105-12.

Potter, J. "William Cobbett in North America." BAASB, 2 (1961), 4-28.

Thompson, Edward P. THE MAKING OF THE ENGLISH WORKING CLASS. New York: Pantheon Books, 1963; rpt. New York: Gollancz, 1966.

> This work explores the emergence of popular culture as seen through Cobbett's eyes.

Uttrachi, Patricia. "COBBETT'S TWO-PENNY TRASH." JRUL, 34 (1971), 53-62.

Weiner, M.J. "The Changing Image of William Cobbett." JBS, 13 (1974), 135-54.

> Surveys previous studies of Cobbett to analyze the shifts in his reputation. Concludes that "the history of Cobbett's changing reputation has come full circle: from posthumous dismissal to rehabilitation to a renewed note of dismissal." His reputation has always been, however, "a touchstone of fundamental social attitudes."

BIBLIOGRAPHIES

Gaines, Pierce [U.]. WILLIAM COBBETT AND THE UNITED STATES, 1792-1835: A BIBLIOGRAPHY WITH NOTES AND EXTRACTS. Worcester, Mass.: American Antiquarian Society, 1971.

Muirhead, Arnold M. AN INTRODUCTION TO A BIBLIOGRAPHY OF COBBETT. London: Library 4th Series, 1939.

Pearl, M.L. COBBETT: A BIBLIOGRAPHICAL ACCOUNT OF HIS LIFE AND TIMES. Oxford: Clarendon Press, 1953.

SAMUEL TAYLOR COLERIDGE (1772-1834)

PRINCIPAL PROSE WORKS

THE WATCHMAN, 1796.

THE FRIEND, 1809-10.

THE STATESMAN'S MANUAL, 1816.

BIOGRAPHIA LITERARIA, OR BIOGRAPHICAL SKETCHES OF MY LITERARY LIFE AND OPINIONS. 2 vols. 1817.

ON THE PROMETHEUS OF AESCHYLUS, 1825.

ON THE CONSTITUTION OF THE CHURCH AND STATE, 1830.

SPECIMENS OF THE TABLE-TALK OF THE LATE SAMUEL TAYLOR COLERIDGE. Ed. H.N. Coleridge. 2 vols. 1835.

THE LITERARY REMAINS OF SAMUEL TAYLOR COLERIDGE. Ed. H.N. Coleridge. 4 vols. 1836-39.

CONFESSIONS OF AN INQUIRING SPIRIT. Ed. H.N. Coleridge. 1840.

NOTES AND LECTURES UPON SHAKESPEARE AND SOME OF THE OLD POETS AND DRAMATISTS. Ed. Mrs. H.N. Coleridge. 2 vols. 1849.

COLLECTED WORKS

THE COLLECTED WORKS OF SAMUEL TAYLOR COLERIDGE. Eds. Kathleen

Coburn et al. Projected 24 volumes. Princeton, N.J.: Bollingen Foundation, 1969-- .

These volumes comprise the first comprehensive attempt to collect Coleridge's work and will constitute the standard edition. Six volumes have appeared so far: volume 1: LECTURES 1795: ON POLITICS AND RELIGION, eds. Lewis Patton and Peter Mann, 1971; volume 2: THE WATCHMAN, ed. Lewis Patton, 1970; volume 3: ESSAYS ON HIS TIMES, ed. David V. Erdman, 1974; volume 4: THE FRIEND, ed. Barbara Rooke, 2 vols., 1969; volume 6: LAY SERMONS, ed. R.J. White, 1972; volume 10: ON THE CONSTITUTION AND STATE, ed. John Colmer, 1975.

THE NOTEBOOKS OF SAMUEL TAYLOR COLERIDGE. Ed. Kathleen Coburn. Projected 5 volumes. New York: Bollingen Foundation, 1957-- .

Two volumes have appeared so far: volume 1 covers 1794-1804; volume 2 covers 1804-08. Both are annotated and contain a chronological table. For commentary, see Coburn under "Critical Studies," below.

LETTERS

THE COLLECTED LETTERS OF COLERIDGE. Ed. Earl L. Griggs. 6 vols. Oxford: Clarendon Press, 1956-71.

The definitive collection.

BIOGRAPHIES

Bate, Walter J. COLERIDGE. New York: Macmillan, 1968.

The best biography. Bate discusses the multifaceted nature of Coleridge's career, but stresses his "ideal of unity" as expressed in all his writings.

Chambers, Edmund K. SAMUEL TAYLOR COLERIDGE. Oxford: Clarendon Press, 1938.

Chambers presents an unsympathetic portrait of Coleridge.

Charpentier, John. COLERIDGE, THE SUBLIME SOMNAMBULIST. New York: Dodd, Mead, 1929.

Concentrates on Coleridge's later years and his philosophical criticism.

Elwin, Malcolm. THE FIRST ROMANTICS. New York: Russell and Russell, 1948.

Samuel Taylor Coleridge

>Studies Coleridge's personal relationships with Wordsworth and Southey up to 1802.

Fausset, Hugh I'Anson. SAMUEL TAYLOR COLERIDGE. London: Cape, 1926.

>A psychological interpretation that claims Coleridge was unable to cope with reality.

Hanson, Lawrence. THE LIFE OF SAMUEL TAYLOR COLERIDGE: THE EARLY YEARS. New York: Oxford University Press, 1938.

>Discusses the early relationship between Wordsworth and Coleridge and their views on the French Revolution.

House, Humphry. COLERIDGE. Philadelphia: Dufor, 1965.

>After proclaiming the "limitations of the historical approach" to Coleridge's life, House proceeds to examine Coleridge's "Mind and Personality," his "Creation, Emotion, and Will." Also includes a section on "Examples from the Notebooks." Concludes that "nobody can possibly pretend the formal published prose is not very uneven."

Margoliouth, H.M. WORDSWORTH AND COLERIDGE, 1795-1834. New York: Oxford University Press, 1953.

>A narrative of the famous friendship which concludes that "Coleridge and Wordsworth had in the end failed one another."

Potter, Stephen. COLERIDGE AND S.T.C. London: Cape, 1935.

>Potter presents a dichotomy between two Coleridges--the poet and the theologian.

CRITICAL STUDIES

Abrams, Meyer H. "Coleridge's 'A Light in Sound': Science, Metascience, and Poetic Imagination." PAPS, 116 (1972), 458-76.

Adams, Maurianne S. "Coleridge and the Victorians: Studies in the Interpretation of Poetry, Scripture, and Myth." Ph.D. dissertation, Indiana University, 1968. DAI, 28, 3662A.

Adams, Maurianne S., and Richard Haven. "Coleridge in Victorian Journalism." VPN, 2 (1968), 20-22.

>A report of work in progress on a "definitive" annotated and indexed bibliography of material on Coleridge (1794-1969). See "Bibliography," below.

Alkon, Paul K. "Critical and Logical Concepts of Method from Addison to Coleridge." ECS, 5 (1971), 97-121.

Alley, Alvin D. "Coleridge and Existentialism." SHR, 2 (1968), 451-61.

> Coleridge's "description of the Secondary Imagination is correspondent with the existential belief that life for man involves his total identity both as a part of the world and as an individual turned away from the world."

Appleyard, J.A. COLERIDGE'S PHILOSOPHY OF LITERATURE. Cambridge, Mass.: Harvard University Press, 1965.

> An important study that presents a chronological account of Coleridge's philosophical development, picturing Coleridge as "a Democrat and Physico-Theologian" influenced by Associationism, Transcendentalism, and Enthusiasm.

_____. "Structuring Coleridge's Ideas." MLQ, 32 (1971), 206-13.

> Reviews the studies by Haven, Barth, and McFarland, below, as evidence of "the present state of Coleridge investigations."

Badawi, Muhammed M. COLERIDGE: CRITIC OF SHAKESPEARE. New York: Cambridge University Press, 1973.

> "Attempts to understand the critical methods and assumptions in Coleridge's writings on Shakespeare, and secondly to define the nature of his contribution to the criticism of Shakespeare in England."

Baker, James V. THE SACRED RIVER: COLERIDGE'S THEORY OF IMAGINATION. Baton Rouge: Louisiana State University Press, 1957.

> Treats Coleridge's view of the opposition of "organism and machine." Asserts that Coleridge's philosophical views, critical theories, and metaphysics are unified and coherent.

Ball, Patricia M. "The Waking Dream: Coleridge and the Drama." THE MORALITY OF ART: ESSAYS PRESENTED TO G. WILSON KNIGHT BY HIS COLLEAGUES AND FRIENDS. Ed. D.W. Jefferson. London: Routledge and Kegan Paul, 1969.

> Discusses "Coleridge's investigations into the strange, associated regions of theatrical and dream experience" as they influenced his research into the workings of the mind.

Barfield, Owen. WHAT COLERIDGE THOUGHT. Middleton, Conn.: Wesleyan University Press, 1971.

Barfield discusses the "organic" development of Coleridge's thought on imagination, reason, science, God, and "Man in History and Society."

Barth, J. Robert. COLERIDGE AND CHRISTIAN DOCTRINE. Cambridge, Mass.: Harvard University Press, 1969.

>Barth deals with Coleridge's "profoundly modern" views on faith, scripture, God, and the church.

_____. "Symbol as Sacrament in Coleridge's Thought." SIR, 11 (1972), 320-31.

>In Coleridge's later thought, 1815-34, "symbol seems so often to be present. Whether he is talking of idea, of method, of faith, or of poetry, even when he does not use the word symbol, the concept always seems to be there."

Beer, J[ohn] B. COLERIDGE AND VISIONARY. London: Chatto and Windus, 1959.

>Attempts "to explore some of the field where poet and thinker meet, and thus to throw light on both the intellectual organization of the poetry and the imaginative qualities implicit in the philosophy."

_____, ed. COLERIDGE'S VARIETY: BICENTENARY STUDIES. London: Macmillan, 1974.

>A valuable collection of essays, including "Coleridge as Revealed in His Letters" by E.L. Griggs, "Coleridge and the Romantic Vision of the World" by Meyer H. Abrams, "Coleridge's Anxiety" by Thomas McFarland, and "Coleridge and Kant" by D.M. MacKinnon.

Blunden, Edmund, and Edward H. Griggs, eds. COLERIDGE: STUDIES BY SEVERAL HANDS. London: Constable, 1934.

>Contains several chapters from Hartley Coleridge's projected life of Coleridge, as well as Muirhead's essay, "Coleridge: Metaphysician or Mystic?"

Bostetter, Edward E. "Coleridge's Manuscript Essay 'On the Passions.'" JHI, 31 (1970), 99-108.

>Discusses 'On the Passions' as "one of the most daring of Coleridge's scientific speculations which throws considerable light on the psychological problems that plagued him and kept him from the completion of his OPUS MAXIMUM."

Boulger, James. COLERIDGE AS A RELIGIOUS THINKER. New Haven, Conn.: Yale University Press, 1961.

    Boulger argues that Coleridge tried to maintain a balance between intellect, will, and emotion in his religious thinking.

Brett, Raymond L., ed. SAMUEL TAYLOR COLERIDGE. London: Bell, 1971.

    A useful collection of essays, including "On Reading Coleridge" by George Whalley, "Coleridge and Religion" by Basil Willey, "Coleridge and Politics" by John Colmer, "Coleridge and Philosophy" by Dorothy Emmet, and two essays on "Coleridge and Criticism" by J.A. Appleyard and Richard H. Fogle.

Brinkley, R. Florence. COLERIDGE ON THE SEVENTEENTH CENTURY. Durham, N.C.: Duke University Press, 1955.

    Brinkley's thesis is that Coleridge's philosophical position was that of the seventeenth-century Cambridge Platonists.

Byatt, A.S. WORDSWORTH AND COLERIDGE IN THEIR TIME. London: Nelson, 1970.

    A heavily illustrated study that traces "the pattern of the relationship" and emphasizes the writers' social, political, and literary views.

Calleo, David P. COLERIDGE AND THE IDEA OF THE MODERN STATE. New Haven, Conn.: Yale University Press, 1966.

    Presents Coleridge as "a modern political theorist whose ideas remain potent." Concentrates on the political writings after 1815 in which Coleridge attempted "to spell out the nature of the good society" that would reconcile "traditional humanism and constitutionalism with the conditions of his time."

Christensen, Merton A. "Udolpho, Horrid Mysteries, and Coleridge's Machinery of the Imagination." WC, 2 (1971), 153-59.

    Coleridge was preeminent among the romantics in "his use of the Gothic in terms of the Imagination."

Coburn, Kathleen, ed. COLERIDGE: A COLLECTION OF CRITICAL ESSAYS. Englewood Cliffs, N.J.: Prentice-Hall, 1967.

    This collection of essays includes "Coleridge as Critic" by Herbert Read, "Coleridge's Historical Thought" by Robert O. Preyer, and "Coleridge on the Growth of the Mind" by Dorothy M. Emmet.

_____. "Coleridge and Restraint." UTQ, 38 (1969), 233-47.

Proposes to view Coleridge's "life-long sensitivity to restraint of diverse kinds; his passionate resistance to it and his consciousness of his own failure to resist at times." This dilemma "motivates much of his writings, often providing what is most prophetic in his thinking."

──────. "Editing the Coleridge Notebooks." EDITING TEXTS OF THE ROMANTIC PERIOD. Ed. John D. Baird. Toronto: Hakkert, 1972.

See THE COLLECTED WORKS, pp. 114-15.

──────. THE SELF-CONSCIOUS IMAGINATION: A STUDY OF THE COLERIDGE NOTEBOOKS IN CELEBRATION OF THE BI-CENTENARY OF HIS BIRTH. London: Oxford University Press, 1974.

Discusses "Coleridge's thoughts and feelings and insights as he confided them to his notebooks" and emphasizes Coleridge's education and spiritual outlook.

Colmer, John. COLERIDGE: CRITIC OF SOCIETY. Oxford: Clarendon Press, 1959.

Presents a "straightforward account of each of the political works, the circumstances of its publication, and a discussion of the social and political criticism contained therein."

──────. "Coleridge and the Life of Hope." SIR, 11 (1972), 332-41.

Analyzes Coleridge's religious writings to conclude that Coleridge's ideas about the importance of hope owed more to his own sufferings and patient self-analysis than to any other source."

Cooke, M.G. "Quisque Sui Faber: Coleridge in the BIOGRAPHIA LITERARIA." PQ, 50 (1971) 208-29.

Cooke claims that BIOGRAPHIA LITERARIA is a "brilliantly, intricately improvised autobiography."

DeLaura, David J. "Coleridge, Hamlet, and Arnold's 'Empedocles.'" PLL, 8 (1972), 17-25.

"Coleridge's portrait of Hamlet seems in a special way to have provided essential elements for the elaborate self-analysis indulged in by Arnold's brooding Empedocles."

DiPasquale, P. "Coleridge's Framework of Objectivity and Eliot's Objective Correlative." JAAC, 26 (1968), 489-500.

Discusses the "'organicism' of Coleridge's theory, with a complete diagram of the creative process as he envisions it," and compares this theory to Eliot's theory.

Samuel Taylor Coleridge

Doughty, Oswald. "Coleridge as Statesman." EM, 20 (1969), 241-55.

Erdman, David V. "Coleridge as Editorial Writer." POWER AND CONSCIOUSNESS. Eds. Conor Cruise O'Brien and William Vanech. London: University of London Press, 1969.

Fletcher, Angus. "'Positive Negation': Threshold, Sequence, and Personification in Coleridge." NEW PERSPECTIVES ON COLERIDGE AND WORDSWORTH. Ed. Geoffrey H. Hartman. New York: Columbia University Press, 1972.

> Discusses myth and metaphor in Coleridge's writing, stating that the romantic fascination with temples and labyrinths "gains its power from the hybrid nature of classical and Christian mythography."

Foakes, Reginald A. COLERIDGE ON SHAKESPEARE: THE TEXT OF THE LECTURES OF 1811-1812. Charlottesville: University Press of Virginia, 1971.

> The introduction discusses Collier's character and his motive for distorting Coleridge's lectures. Foakes also represents Collier's text with annotations.

──────. "The Text of Coleridge's 1811-1812 Shakespeare Lectures." SHS, 23 (1970), 101-11.

> Examines John P. Collier's edition of Coleridge's SEVEN LECTURES ON SHAKESPEARE AND MILTON (1856) and concludes that the preface, notes, and text are filled with inaccuracies and should be "treated with some caution."

Fogle, Richard H. "Hawthorne and Coleridge on Credibility." CRITICISM, 13 (1971), 234-41.

> Fogle argues that the BIOGRAPHIA had a pervasive influence on Hawthorne's theory of the imagination.

──────. THE IDEA OF COLERIDGE'S CRITICISM. Berkeley and Los Angeles: University of California Press, 1962.

> Fogle rejects Wellek's position, below, that Coleridge was substantially influenced by the German romantics.

Freedman, Ralph. "Eyesight and Vision: Forms of the Imagination in Coleridge and Novalis." THE RARER ACTION: ESSAYS IN HONOR OF FRANCIS FERGUSSON. Eds. Alan Cheuse and Richard Koffler. New Brunswick, N.J.: Rutgers University Press, 1970.

Frothingham, Richard. "The Unitarianism of Samuel Taylor Coleridge." Ph.D. dissertation, Columbia University, 1967. DAI, 27, 4250A.

Samuel Taylor Coleridge

Fruman, Norman. COLERIDGE: THE DAMAGED ARCHANGEL. New York: Braziller, 1971.

> A controversial work that discusses what are viewed as borrowings, lies, red herrings, exaggerated claims, and contradictions in Coleridge's prose.

Garrett, Clarke. "Coleridge's Utopia Revisited." SCUL, 55 (1972), 121-37.

> Discusses Coleridge's involvement in the pantisocratic scheme as a way of analyzing his educational, religious, and sexual attitudes.

Geckle, George. "Coleridge on MEASURE FOR MEASURE." SQ, 18 (1967), 71-73.

> Discusses Coleridge's distaste for the play because "it exasperated his sense of justice and common decency."

Gilpin, George H. "Coleridge: The Pleasure of Truth." SCB, 30 (1970), 191-94.

> Defines Coleridge's use of the word "pleasure" in chapter 14 of BIOGRAPHIA LITERARIA: "the word links metaphysics and psychology."

──────. "Coleridge and the Spiral of Poetic Thought." SEL, 12 (1972), 639-52.

> "Coleridge's epistemology inevitably shapes his artistic expression--his ideal aesthetic structure should be spiraling or serpentine--Coleridge conceives of the structure as a symbol of the creative mind."

Grant, Allen. A PREFACE TO COLERIDGE. New York: Scribner's, 1973.

> A valuable survey of Coleridge's work with chapters on "Coleridge's Bristol Circle," which discuss the political background of the period. Also includes "Coleridge as Romantic Critic," which explores the relation of Coleridge to Wordsworth and Kant.

Hall, Roland. "Words from Coleridge's BIOGRAPHIA LITERARIA." N&Q, 17 (1970), 171-74.

Harris, John. "Coleridge's Readings in Medicine." WC, 3 (1972), 85-95.

> Discusses Coleridge's extensive medical readings and examines his extensive marginalia and notebook jottings on psychosomatics.

Harris, Wendell [V.]. "The Shape of Coleridge's 'Public' System." MP, 68 (1970), 46-61.

> Insists that "at some point we must make a distinction and raise

a question about the use of all Coleridge's writings not published by himself."

Hassler, Donald M. "Coleridge, Darwin, and the Dome." SERIF, 4 (1967), 28-31.

Traces Coleridge's attitudes toward Erasmus Darwin's works and their impact on Coleridge's conception of nature, the sublime, and "pleasure domes."

Haven, Richard. "Coleridge, Hartley, and the Mystics." JHI, 20 (1959), 477-94.

Claims that Coleridge was forced to rationalize his spiritual experiences and insights to have them accepted by his society.

_____. "Coleridge on Milton: A Last Lecture." WC, 3 (1972), 21-24.

Reprints an account of Coleridge's lecture on Milton, which was found in THE RIFLEMAN (1812) and written by an anonymous witness.

_____. PATTERNS OF CONSCIOUSNESS: AN ESSAY ON COLERIDGE. Amherst: University of Massachusetts Press, 1969.

Psychology outweighs philosophy in this interpretation of Coleridge's thought. See McFarland, below.

Hayden, John O. "Coleridge, the Reviewers, and Wordsworth." SP, 68 (1971), 105-19.

Hayden observes that both Coleridge and the reviewers who criticized him shared the same Aristotelian and humanist critical standards.

Hayden, John O., ed. ROMANTIC BARDS AND BRITISH REVIEWERS: A SELECTED EDITION OF THE CONTEMPORARY REVIEWS OF THE WORKS OF WORDSWORTH, COLERIDGE, BYRON, KEATS, AND SHELLEY. London: Routledge and Kegan Paul, 1971.

Reprints the reviews of CHRISTABEL, THE FRIEND, and BIOGRAPHIA LITERARIA.

Hayter, Althea. OPIUM AND THE ROMANTIC IMAGINATION. Berkeley and Los Angeles: University of California Press; London: Faber and Faber, 1968.

Includes a discussion of Coleridge's addiction and its influence on his work.

_____. A VOYAGE IN VAIN: COLERIDGE'S JOURNEY TO MALTA IN

Samuel Taylor Coleridge

1804. London: Faber and Faber, 1973.

> A day-by-day account of Coleridge's journey, which stresses the trip as crucial to his psychological development. Concludes that during the trip Coleridge lost hope and realized "he would never be the man he aspired to be."

Heath, William. WORDSWORTH AND COLERIDGE: A STUDY OF THEIR LITERARY RELATIONS IN 1801-1802. Oxford: Clarendon Press, 1970.

> Heath studies the interrelations among Dorothy and William Wordsworth, the Hutchinson sisters, and the Coleridges from November 1801 through October 1802. Emphasizes their mutual concern for "the relation between the self and the circumambient universe" and their "sense of haunting destinies and enabling freedoms."

Holland, Norman. "The 'Willing Suspension of Disbelief' Revisited." CR, 11 (1967), 1-23.

> Claims that Coleridge's phrase "merely describes the phenomenon without explaining it." To do so, Holland utilizes Freudian theories.

Hough, Graham. "Coleridge and the Victorians." THE ENGLISH MIND. Ed. H[ugh] S. Davies. Cambridge: At the University Press, 1964.

> Hough surveys Coleridge's influence on Thomas Arnold, Newman, Disraeli, and Matthew Arnold.

Houston, Robert. "Coleridge's Psychometaphysics." THOTH, 9 (1968), 14-24.

> Discusses the relation of Coleridge's organic theory to his criticism and concludes that "a critic's job is first to ascertain ends, and from those to deduce rules."

Hume, Robert D. "Coleridge's Retention of Primary Imagination." N&Q, 16 (1969), 55-56.

_____. "Kant and Coleridge on Imagination." JAAC, 28 (1970), 485-96.

> Redefines the "context in which Coleridge's ideas should be viewed"--that is, from the field of faculty psychology. Proceeds to "draw a sharp distinction between Coleridge as theoretician and Coleridge as practical critic."

Hunt, Bishop C., Jr. "Coleridge and the Endeavor of Philosophy." PMLA, 91 (1976), 829-39.

> Discusses the "conversion" Coleridge made in later life to the "Platonic idealism" which provided him with "emotional as well as intellectual satisfaction."

Samuel Taylor Coleridge

Hutchings, Patrick. "Imagination: 'As the Sun Paints in the Camera Obscura.'" JAAC, 29 (1970), 63-76.

    Hutchings discusses the distinctions made in the BIOGRAPHIA between Milton and Wordsworth.

Jackson, James R. de J., ed. COLERIDGE: THE CRITICAL HERITAGE. New York: Barnes and Noble, 1970.

    Includes many contemporary reviews of Coleridge's works, including the first notices of THE FALL OF ROBESPIERRE and POETICAL WORKS. No newspaper reviews are included.

_____. "Free Will in Coleridge's Shakespeare." UTQ, 38 (1968), 34-50.

    Takes three points in Coleridge's Shakespeare criticism and argues that "each of them can be explained in terms of a pattern in Coleridge's thought of which we were already aware but which has seemed hitherto to have little or nothing to do with his views on literature."

_____. METHOD AND IMAGINATION IN COLERIDGE'S CRITICISM. Cambridge, Mass.: Harvard University Press, 1969.

    Discusses Coleridge's "Principles in Literary Ciriticism" and his "Method of Poetry"--both in theory and in practice. Concluding chapter treats Coleridge's transition from criticism to theology.

James, David G. THE ROMANTIC COMEDY. London: Oxford University Press, 1948.

    Coleridge combines romanticism and Christianity, and anticipates Newman.

Josephs, Lois. "Shakespeare and Coleridgean Synthesis: Cleopatra, Leontes, and Falstaff." SQ, 18 (1967), 17-21.

    Discusses Coleridge's Shakespeare criticism and notes that "in his analysis of the Shakespearean character, Coleridge most sharply draws his metaphysics--his attempt to synthesize what seems to be contraries--into practical critical focus."

Kauvar, Gerald B. "Coleridge, Hawkesworth, and the Willing Suspension of Disbelief." PLL, 5 (1969), 91-94.

    A discussion of Coleridge's critical terminology.

Kelly, Michael. "Coleridge and Dream Phenomenology." MSE, 1 (1967), 1-7.

    Analyzes Coleridge's discussion of dreams in relation to "existing

Samuel Taylor Coleridge

systems of psychology and epistemology" and concludes that "what Coleridge knew of dreams convinced him that the associationist psychology was inadequate as an explanation for all of the events of dreams."

Kennedy, Wilma L. THE ENGLISH HERITAGE OF COLERIDGE OF BRISTOL, 1798: THE BASIS IN EIGHTEENTH-CENTURY ENGLISH THOUGHT FOR HIS DISTINCTION BETWEEN IMAGINATION AND FANCY. Hamden, Conn.: Archon Books, 1969.

Kennedy argues that the roots of Coleridge's distinction are in Berkeley and Reynolds.

Keppel-Jones, David. "Coleridge's Scheme of Reason." LITERARY MONOGRAPHS. Vol. 1. Eds. Eric Rothstein and Thomas Dunseath. Madison: University of Wisconsin Press, 1967.

Knoepflmacher, U[lrich] C. "A Nineteenth-Century Touchstone: Chapter XV of BIOGRAPHIA LITERARIA." NINETEENTH-CENTURY LITERARY PERSPECTIVES. Eds. Clyde de L. Ryals et al. Durham, N.C.: Duke University Press, 1974.

"The chapter must be read as a deliberate preparation for those later sections of the book in which Coleridge more openly catalogues Wordsworth's strengths and weaknesses."

Kohli, Devindra. "Coleridge, Hazlitt, and Keats's Negative Capability." LC, 8 (1967), 21-26.

States that chapter 15 of BIOGRAPHIA LITERARIA is the source of the distinction between Shakespeare and Milton as "literary types."

Land, Stephen. "Coleridge, Freud, and the Tribe of Asra." L&P, 22 (1972), 49-50.

Discusses a possible source for Coleridge's anagrammatic name for Sara Hutchinson.

Lawrence, Berta. COLERIDGE AND WORDSWORTH IN SOMERSET. New York: Barnes and Noble, 1970.

Focuses on Coleridge, Tom Poole, and John Chester.

Lowes, John. THE ROAD TO XANADU: A STUDY IN THE WAYS OF THE IMAGINATION. 2nd ed. New York: Knopf, 1959.

A classic study of Coleridge's transformations of his sources which asserts that Coleridge's distinction between imagination and fancy is of little use in understanding his work. See Powell, below.

McDowell, Frederick P., ed. THE POET AS CRITIC. Evanston, Ill.: Northwestern University Press, 1967.

This collection of critical essays includes "Coleridge: The Method and the Poetry" by Elizabeth Sewell, who discusses Coleridge's development of critical method, in which "the self is raised to an allegorical or mythical power."

McFarland, Thomas. COLERIDGE AND THE PANTHEIST TRADITION. Oxford: Clarendon Press, 1969.

Claims that Coleridge's greatness does not lie in his poetry but in his prose criticism, which is "remarkably unified and cohesive." Discusses Coleridge's relation to Plato, Plotinus, Boehme, Kant, Descartes, Spinoza, Leibniz, and Swedenborg.

_____. "Coleridge and Wordsworth." YR, 60 (1970), 439-48.

Reviews books on Coleridge by Haven, above, and Sultana, below, and describes the state of Coleridge studies as "an eruption."

_____. "The Origin and Significance of Coleridge's Theory of Secondary Imagination." NEW PERSPECTIVES ON COLERIDGE AND WORDSWORTH. Ed. Geoffrey Hartman. New York: Columbia University Press, 1972.

Discusses Coleridge's threefold distinction in the BIOGRAPHIA LITERARIA, and asks, "where does the Secondary Imagination originate and in what context should we consider it?"

_____. "The Symbiosis of Coleridge and Wordsworth." SIR, 11 (1972), 263-303.

Describes the Wordsworth-Coleridge relationship: "Nothing less than a symbiosis, a development of attitude so diagonal and intertwined that in some instances not even the participants themselves could discern their respective contributions."

McKenzie, Gordon. ORGANIC UNITY IN COLERIDGE. Berkeley: University of California Press, 1939.

Contains chapters on Coleridge's theory of poetry and his dramatic criticism, stressing the organic nature of Coleridge's critical method.

Martin, Richard T. "Coleridge's Use of 'Sermoni Propriora.'" WC, 3 (1972), 71-75.

Analyzes Coleridge's use of attaching mottoes or prefaces to his works as "the tendency so often expressed in BIOGRAPHIA LITERARIA to garner support from the authority of a critical tradition."

Samuel Taylor Coleridge

Mehrotra, R.R. "Coleridge's Hobby-Horse: Psychology." IJES, 12 (1971), 22-32.

> "Coleridge becomes the first psychologist in criticism; indeed, the first literary critic, to make use of the very word 'psychology' in his criticism of literature. He presented for the first time a systematic and correct treatment of the 'subconscious' long before Freud."

Mill, John Stuart. MILL ON BENTHAM AND COLERIDGE. Ed. F[rank] R. Leavis. London: Chatto and Windus, 1950.

> Leavis contends that Mill's essays on both writers are "key documents" to any understanding of the opposing currents of thought in the nineteenth century.

Milne, Fred. "Pantisocracy: A Reflection of Coleridge's Opium Use?" ELN, 9 (1972), 177-82.

> Uses the poem "Pantisocracy" (1974) to substantiate the view that Coleridge's opium addiction had occurred at this early date.

Muirhead, John H. COLERIDGE AS PHILOSOPHER. New York: Macmillan, 1930.

> Presents a survey of the whole of Coleridge's thought and concludes that Coleridge was the "Father of modern psychology."

Munro, Hector. "Coleridge and Shelley." KSMB, 21 (1970), 35-38.

> Discusses Shelley's portrait of Coleridge in his parody of Wordsworth's "Peter Bell."

Orsini, G.N.G. COLERIDGE AND GERMAN IDEALISM: A STUDY IN THE HISTORY OF PHILOSOPHY. Carbondale: Southern Illinois University Press, 1969.

> Reexamines the question of Coleridge's relation to Kant, Fichte, and Schelling and asserts that "Coleridge is primarily a poet and a great poet. But he wrote splendid prose."

_____. "Coleridge and Schlegel Reconsidered." CL, 16 (1964), 97-118.

> Coleridge's greatness as a critic lies in his introduction into English literature of Kant's theory of teleological organism and Schelling's theory of organic philosophy. See Stempel, below.

_____. "Coleridge's Manuscript Treatise on Logic." The DISCIPLINES OF CRITICISM: ESSAYS IN LITERARY THEORY, INTERPRETATION AND HISTORY. Eds. Peter Demetz, Thomas Greene, and Lowry Nelson. New Haven, Conn.: Yale University Press, 1968.

Owen, Huw Parry. "The Theology of Coleridge." CRQ, 4 (1962), 59-67.

> Discusses Coleridge's prose style in his later theological writings, mainly AIDS TO REFLECTION and ESSAY IN FAITH. Compares Coleridge to St. Augustine and asserts that Coleridge "came to have a horror of pantheism."

Park, Roy. "Coleridge: Philosopher and Theologian as Literary Critic." UTQ, 38 (1968), 17-33.

> Asserts Coleridge demanded that "poetic symbols be directly related to his own conception of a Christian God."

———. "Coleridge and Kant: Poetic Imagination and Practical Reason." BJA, 8 (1968), 335-46.

> "The crucial distinction for Coleridge between Aristotle and Kant, on the one hand, and Plato and the Platonists, on the other, arose out of their respective attitudes to the ideas of pure speculative reason."

———. "Coleridge's Two Voices as Critic of Wordsworth." ELH, 36 (1969), 361-81.

> "In Coleridge's critical theory, the poetic imagination performs a function analogous in a general way to the function performed by practical reason in the ethical theory of Kant."

Parker, Reeve. COLERIDGE'S MEDITATIVE ART. Ithaca, N.Y.: Cornell University Press, 1975.

> A discussion of Coleridge's "intellectual and emotional activity" as it shaped his poetry and prose. The BIOGRAPHIA LITERARIA is discussed, as well as the early prose.

Parrish, Stephen M. "The Wordsworth-Coleridge Controversy." PMLA, 73 (1958), 367-74.

> What appeared on the surface to be a dispute over "diction" was actually a "disagreement about dramatic method."

Paul-Emile, Barbara T. "Coleridge as Abolitionist." ARIEL, 5 (1974), 59-75.

> Distinguishes three periods in Coleridge's thought on the slavery issue: youthful abolitionist phase, paternalistic concern for "civilizing" Africans, and conservative shock at partial emancipation.

Powell, Grosvenor. "Coleridge's 'Imagination' and the Infinite Regress of Consciousness." ELH, 39 (1972), 266-78.

> Disagrees with Lowes's claim, above, that Coleridge's distinction

between fancy and imagination is of little use. Instead, asserts that Coleridge's distinction is crucial because "it is an evaluative one" which has meaning within his metaphysical system.

Pradhan, S.V. "Coleridge's 'Philocrisy' and His Theory of Fancy and Secondary Imagination." SIR, 13 (1974), 235-54.

Insists that readers of Coleridge must integrate the aesthetic and philosophical aspects of his thought because "there is a demonstrable connexion between his theory of fancy and the secondary imagination and his 'philocrisy.'"

Prickett, Stephen. ROMANTICISM AND RELIGION: THE TRADITION OF COLERIDGE AND WORDSWORTH IN THE VICTORIAN CHURCH. Cambridge: At the University Press, 1976.

Includes two chapters on Coleridge: "The 'Living Educts[sic] of the Imagination': Coleridge on Religious Language" and "'A Liberty of Speculation which no Christian can Tolerate'--the later Coleridge."

Rahme, Mary. "Coleridge's Concept of Symbolism." SEL, 9 (1969), 619-32.

Asserts that Coleridge "was primarily concerned with the relationship of the symbol to 'reality.'" He thought of art as imitation of the creative process; "artistic symbols imitate neither subjective nature nor subjective feelings."

Rauber, D.F. "The Fragment as Romantic Form." MLQ, 30 (1969), 212-21.

The fragment "can be viewed as that form which more completely than any other embodies romantic ideals and aims. The intent of this paper is to lay some foundations for a theoretical treatment of this elusive form."

Read, Herbert [Sir]. COLERIDGE AS CRITIC. New York: Haskell House, 1964.

Originally delivered as a lecture in 1948, this essay claims that "we need not take too seriously those who try to dissociate the poet and the philosopher."

Reardon, Bernard M. [G.]. FROM COLERIDGE TO GORE. London: Longmans, 1971.

A survey of the religious thought of England that uses Coleridge's AIDS TO REFLECTION as its frame of reference.

Reid, S.W. "The Composition and Revision of Coleridge's Essay on Aeschylus' PROMETHEUS." SB, 24 (1971), 176-83.

Reid demonstrates that the 1821 version of the essay for Hartley Coleridge was revised by Coleridge.

Richards, I.A. COLERIDGE AND IMAGINATION. Bloomington: Indiana University Press, 1960.

    Richards states that he is writing as "a materialist trying to interpret the utterances of an extreme idealist."

Robinson, Charles E. "The Shelley Circle and Coleridge's THE FRIEND." ELN, 8 (1971), 269-74.

    Emphasizes Shelley's indebtedness to Coleridge by identifying the source for Shelley's phrase as Coleridge's THE FRIEND, 1809.

Sanders, Charles R. "'The Ancient Mariner' and Coleridge's Theory of Poetic Art." ROMANTIC AND VICTORIAN: STUDIES IN MEMORY OF WILLIAM H. MARSHALL. Eds. W. Paul Elledge and Richard L. Hoffman. Rutherford, N.J.: Fairleigh Dickinson University Press, 1971.

_____. COLERIDGE AND THE BROAD CHURCH MOVEMENT. Durham, N.C.: Duke University Press, 1942.

    A reinterpretation of Coleridge's philosophical and religious opinions that stresses the overlooked strains of humanitarianism and liberalism in his outlook. Also discusses Carlyle, F.D. Maurice, and Thomas Arnold.

Sanderson, David R. "Coleridge's Political 'Sermons': Discursive Language and the Voice of God." MP, 70 (1973), 319-30.

    Discusses LAY SERMONS to claim that "Coleridge grew continually more frustrated, finally turning away from an emphasis on his own discursive language and toward a greater dependence on the language of Scripture."

Schulz, Max F. "COMFORTS AND CONSOLATIONS: An Unwritten Work by Coleridge." CORANTO, 4 (1968), 3-11.

_____. "The New Coleridge." MP, 69 (1971), 142-51.

    Reviews four major studies of Coleridge published in 1969 and concludes that they all present Coleridge as a prose writer whose views, although not always "properly organized," had within themselves the principles of organization.

_____. "THE SOOTHER OF ABSENCE: An Unwritten Work by Coleridge." SORA, 2 (1967), 289-97.

Sewell, Elizabeth. "Bacon, Vico, Coleridge, and Poetic Method." GIAMBATTISTA VICO: AN INTERNATIONAL SYMPOSIUM. Eds. Giorgio Tagliacozzo and Hayden White. Baltimore: Johns Hopkins University Press, 1969.

Sewell stresses the similarities among the three writers.

⸺. "Coleridge on Revolution." SIR, 11 (1972), 342-59.

Explores "Coleridge's ambivalence in regard to revolution, his declared abhorrence of it accompanied by a life-long preoccupation with the idea and by numerous comments in which he seems to sympathize and even to identify himself with revolution."

Shaffer, Elinor. "Coleridge's Revolution in the Standard of Taste." JAAC, 28 (1969), 213-21.

Contrasts Coleridge's treatment of the sublime to Kant's and Schelling's and concludes that "the sublime can be said to have reached its apotheosis in Coleridge's theory."

⸺. "Coleridge's Theory of Aesthetic Interest." JAAC, 27 (1969), 399-408.

Disagrees with Wellek's opinion of Coleridge, below, and asserts that "Coleridge has succeeded in fusing into a unity precisely these 'irreconcilables'; Kant's theory of 'disinterest' as the essential mark of aesthetic appreciation, and the extreme sensationalist theory of Burke."

⸺. "Iago's Malignity Motivated: Coleridge's Unpublished 'Opus Magnus.'" SQ, 19 (1968), 195-203.

Uses Coleridge's NOTEBOOK comments on Iago to discuss his "most mature thought about the problems of evil and the maintenance of the self" and "the heart of the romantic conception of tragedy."

⸺. "Metaphysics of Culture: Kant and Coleridge's AIDS TO REFLECTION." JHI, 31 (1970), 199-218.

Asserts that "Coleridge's development of the 'aid to reflection' is a major contribution to the idealist effort to found and justify a mode of thought that will be aesthetic and moral without sacrificing rationality. It displays, moreover, the metaphysical roots of the idea of 'culture' that dominated religious humanism in the Victorian period."

⸺. "The 'Postulates in Philosophy' in the BIOGRAPHIA LITERARIA." CLS, 7 (1970), 297-313.

Discusses Coleridge's alterations of Schelling's theory: "Coleridge's cautious handling of the postulate governs his position on the nature of intuition, the validity of dialectic, the means of gaining access to the unconscious, and the relation of rational to aesthetic and moral thought."

Sinclair, Nora Rea. "Coleridge and Education." QQ, 74 (1967), 413-26.

Discusses Coleridge's educational theory: "most of his prose suggests improvements that, if implemented, bring about improvements in many aspects of modern life."

Snyder, Alice D. COLERIDGE ON LOGIC AND LEARNING. New Haven, Conn.: Yale University Press, 1920.

An important work that discusses Coleridge's views on these subjects in a number of his unpublished manuscripts.

Stempel, Daniel. "Coleridge and Organic Form: The English Tradition." SIR, 6 (1967), 89-97.

Disagrees with Orsini's argument, above, that Coleridge received his notion of organicism from Kant and Schelling; instead, concludes that he learned it from his opposite, "the despised Hume."

_____. "Revelation on Mount Snowdon: Wordsworth, Coleridge, and the Fichtean Imagination." JAAC, 29 (1971), 371-84.

Stempel claims that it was Fichte, not Schelling, to whom Coleridge was indebted for his aesthetic theories. Wordsworth, in turn, learned of Fichte's model of the mind from Coleridge.

Stephens, Fran. "The Coleridge Collection: A Sample." LCUT, 1 (1970), 32-38.

Describes the Coleridge family papers acquired by the University of Texas in 1964.

Sultana, Donald. SAMUEL TAYLOR COLERIDGE IN MALTA AND ITALY. New York: Barnes and Noble, 1969.

Concentrates on the political situation in the Mediterranean at the time of Coleridge's service there. See McFarland, above.

Szenczi, Nicholas J. "Reality and the English Romantics." HLQ, 31 (1968), 179-98.

A valuable discussion of the theory of the romantics' works as "intense and passionate responses to the stirring events of a revolutionary age. . . . The romantic theory of the imagination received in England its fullest elaboration at the hands of Coleridge."

Samuel Taylor Coleridge

Teich, Nathaniel. "Coleridge's BIOGRAPHIA LITERARIA and the Contemporary Controversy about Style." WC, 3 (1972), 61-70.

> Uses the BIOGRAPHIA LITERARIA to "provide necessary historical dimensions to the critical disputes involving the Lake Poets. As a result, the BIOGRAPHIA can be reaffirmed not only as the preeminent critical product of its time, but also as the influential source of theories of reconciliation and unity in twentieth-century criticism."

Tillotson, Geoffrey. "Ars Celare Artem?" STYLE, 1 (1967), 65-68.

> Discusses Coleridge's critical opinion of Southey's prose, which he praised for its "conversational" tone.

Todd, Ruthven. "Coleridge and Paracelsus, Honeydew and LSD." LONDON MAGAZINE, 6 (1967), 52-62.

Walsh, William. COLERIDGE: THE WORKS AND THE RELEVANCE. New York: Barnes and Noble, 1967.

> Discovers a genuine modernity in Coleridge as reflected in his educational theory.

Watson, George. "Wordsworth and Coleridge." In his THE LITERARY CRITICS. New York: Barnes and Noble, 1962.

> "For Coleridge, ultimately, only a theory of poetic creation matters: he analyzes, not so much poems as they exist, but the creative act that makes them what they are."

Watters, Reginald. COLERIDGE. London: Evans, 1971.

> Part of the "Literature in Perspective" series, which sets Coleridge's literary work against the background of his time. Includes a chapter on "The Poet as Critic," but treatment of the Notebooks, prose, and philosophical lectures is brief.

Weather, Winston. THE ARCHETYPE AND THE PSYCHE: ESSAYS IN WORLD LITERATURE. Tulsa, Okla.: University of Tulsa, 1968.

> A collection of essays that includes "Coleridge and the Epic Experience."

Webb, Timothy. "Coleridge and Shelley's 'Alastor': A Reply." RES, 18 (1967), 402-11.

> Disagrees with the theory advanced by Joseph Raben in "Coleridge as the Prototype of the Poet in Shelley's 'Alastor,'" (RES, 17 [1966], 278-92), and claims that "Coleridge had little or nothing to do with the conception of 'Alastor.'"

Wellek, René. "Coleridge." In his HISTORY OF MODERN CRITICISM. Vol. 2. New Haven, Conn.: Yale University Press, 1965.

"Coleridge as an aesthetician is fragmentary and derivative with wide gaps between his theory and practice." See Fogle, above.

_____. IMMANUEL KANT IN ENGLAND. Princeton, N.J.: Princeton University Press, 1931.

An important work that criticizes Coleridge's indebtedness to Kant: his adaptations are "heterogeneous, incoherent and even contradictory so that the study of Coleridge's philosophy is ultimately futile." See Shaffer, above.

Werkmeister, Lucyle. "Coleridge and Godwin in the Communication of Truth." MP, 55 (1958), 170-77.

Asserts that "Godwin's influence, even if it manifested itself only as a stimulus to Coleridge's own thinking, was more abiding than has heretofore been supposed."

Whalley, George. "Coleridge and the Royal Society of Literature." EDH, 35 (1969), 147-51.

Discusses Coleridge's membership in the Society and the only paper he delivered there, "On Prometheus."

_____. "Coleridge and Vico." VICO: AN INTERNATIONAL SYMPOSIUM. Eds. G. Tagliacozzo and H. White. Baltimore: Johns Hopkins University Press, 1969.

Discusses Coleridge's admiration of Vico; Coleridge, however, never completed any of his projected major works on Vico.

_____. "Coleridge Marginalia Lost." BC, 17 (1968), 428-42.

A list of 142 unlocated books containing manuscript notes by Coleridge; of these, sixty-eight are starred as never having been transcribed.

_____. "Coleridge Unlabyrinthed." UTQ, 32 (1963), 325-45.

Traces Coleridge's reputation, which Whalley believes began to revive with Lowes's study, above, and is being established with the editing of the COLLECTED WORKS, above.

_____. "The Harvest on the Ground: Coleridge's Marginalia." UTQ, 38 (1969), 248-76.

Discusses the significant annotations Coleridge made in his almost 400 books, now housed in the British Museum and Victoria College Library, Toronto.

Samuel Taylor Coleridge

―――. "On Editing Coleridge's Marginalia." EDITING TEXTS OF THE ROMANTIC PERIOD. Ed. John D. Baird. Toronto: Hakkert, 1972.

―――. "The Publication of Coleridge's PROMETHEUS Essay." N&Q, 16 (1969), 52-55.

―――. "Recent Wordsworth and Coleridge Studies." QQ, 76 (1969), 118-30.

> A review article that discusses two works published on Coleridge in 1967 and concludes there has been "an unhappy critical tendency to see them either as identical or strongly contrasted figures."

Wheeler, Charles B. "The People Versus Art: Coleridge's Testimony Reexamined." SAQ, 67 (1968), 40-52.

> Discusses some of the limitations of Coleridge's phrase, "Willing suspension of disbelief."

Whitehill, Joseph. "Samuel Taylor Coleridge: Prisoner and Prophet of System." AS, 37 (1968), 145-58.

> Uses the BIOGRAPHIA LITERARIA, chapter 17, to analyze Coleridge's communication theory in relation to modern linguistic theory: "Coleridge was one of the theory's ancestors."

Willey, Basil. SAMUEL TAYLOR COLERIDGE. Princeton, N.J.: Princeton University Press, 1957; rpt. New York: Norton, 1972.

> Willey states that his book attempts to outline "Coleridge's intellectual and spiritual biography."

Willson, Robert. "Landmarks of Criticism: Coleridge 'On Shakespeare as a Poet.'" SNL, 17 (1967), 58.

Wilson, Douglas B. "Two Modes of Apprehending Nature: A Gloss on the Coleridgean Symbol." PMLA, 87 (1972), 42-52.

> Asserts that "Coleridge's governing literary principles, the very assumptions behind his literary judgments, stem from his idea of the symbol."

Wojcik, Manfred. "Coleridge: Symbol, Organic Unity, and Modern Aesthetic Subjectivism." ZAA, 18 (1970), 355-90.

―――. "Coleridge: Symbolization, Expression, and Artistic Creativity." ZAA, 19 (1971), 117-54.

———. "Coleridge and the Problem of Transcendentalism." ZAA, 18 (1970), 30-58.

"Coleridge's aesthetic thought cannot simply be subsumed under the heading of transcendentalism. It must even be considered as directly opposed to a Platonizing conception of art."

———. "The Mimetic Orientation of Coleridge's Aesthetic Thought." ZAA, 17 (1969), 344-91.

Discusses how and why the mimetic basis of Coleridge's aesthetic has been interpreted to justify the prevalent formalism of modern criticism.

Zall, Paul M. "Coleridge and SONNETS FROM VARIOUS AUTHORS." CLJ, 2 (1967), 49-67.

———. "Sam Spitfire; or, Coleridge in THE SATIRIST." BNYPL, 71 (1967), 239-44.

BIBLIOGRAPHIES

Also see Adams and Haven, p. 116, and Whalley, p. 135, under "Critical Studies," above.

Brinkley, R. Florence. "Notes on Coleridge." HLQ, 8 (1945), 312-20.

Discusses the extensive Coleridge collection in the Huntington Library in San Marino, California, which is "approximately as rich as the British Museum." See Zall, below.

Crawford, Walter B., and Edward S. Lauterbach. "Coleridge in Narrative and Drama . . . Part I." WC, 3 (1972), 117-22.

A bibliography in process on various pieces of imaginative literature that utilize Coleridge as a figure in the work.

———. "Recent Coleridge Scholarship: A Survey." WC, 3 (1972), 186-92.

Hall, Thomas. "A Checklist of Coleridge Criticism." BB, 25 (1968), 124-31, 152-55, 172, 175-82.

Haney, John Louis. A BIBLIOGRAPHY OF SAMUEL TAYLOR COLERIDGE. Philadelphia: Private circulation, 1903.

Haven, Richard; Josephine Haven; and Maurianne [S.] Adams. SAMUEL TAYLOR COLERIDGE: AN ANNOTATED BIBLIOGRAPHY OF CRITICISM AND SCHOLARSHIP. Projected 2 vols. Boston: Hall, 1976-- .

The first volume includes over 1,907 bibliographical items covering 1793-1899. The second volume, when it appears, will bring the criticism up to 1969.

Kennedy, Virginia W., and Mary N. Barton. SAMUEL TAYLOR COLERIDGE: A SELECTED BIBLIOGRAPHY. Baltimore: Pratt, 1935; rpt. New York: Kraus Reprint, 1969.

Useful critical bibliography on secondary studies.

Wellek, René. "Coleridge's Philosophy and Criticism." THE ENGLISH RO-MANTIC POETS AND ESSAYISTS: A REVIEW OF RESEARCH. Ed. Frank Jordan, Jr. 3rd ed. New York: MLA, 1972.

A valuable bibliographical essay which discusses critical studies published through 1970.

Wise, Thomas J. A BIBLIOGRAPHY OF THE WRITINGS IN PROSE AND VERSE OF SAMUEL TAYLOR COLERIDGE. London: Bibliographical Society, 1913.

The basic formal bibliography.

Zall, P[aul] M. "Coleridge in the Huntington Library (1794-1834)." WC, 2 (1971), 1-16.

A checklist of holdings meant to supplement R.F. Brinkley's checklist, above.

THOMAS DE QUINCEY (1785-1859)

PRINCIPAL PROSE WORKS

CONFESSIONS OF AN ENGLISH OPIUM EATER, 1822.

KLOSTERHEIM, OR THE MASQUE, 1832.

THE LOGIC OF POLITICAL ECONOMY, 1844.

SELECTIONS GRAVE AND GAY, FROM WRITINGS, PUBLISHED AND UNPUBLISHED, OF THOMAS DE QUINCEY. Revised and arranged by himself. 14 vols. 1853-60.

COLLECTED WORKS

THE COLLECTED WRITINGS OF THOMAS DE QUINCEY. Ed. David Masson. 14 vols. Edinburgh: Black, 1889-90.

> The standard edition, with critical annotations, index, and notes. Volume 14 contains a bibliography.

DE QUINCEY MEMORIALS. BEING LETTERS AND OTHER RECORDS HERE FIRST PUBLISHED. Ed. A.H. Japp. 2 vols. 1891.

DE QUINCEY'S LITERARY CRITICISM. Ed. Helen Darbishire. London: Frowde, 1909.

> This collection has an interesting introduction, which presents De Quincey as a romantic critic, a mystic, and a lover of symbolism.

A DIARY OF THOMAS DE QUINCEY FOR 1803. Ed. H[orace] A. Eaton. London: Douglas, 1927.

Thomas De Quincey

NEW ESSAYS BY DE QUINCEY: HIS CONTRIBUTIONS TO THE EDINBURGH SATURDAY POST, AND THE EDINBURGH EVENING POST, 1827-28. Ed. Stuart M. Tave. Princeton, N.J.: Princeton University Press, 1966.

>Includes thirty-nine new additions to the De Quincey canon.

POSTHUMOUS WORKS OF DE QUINCEY. Ed. A.H. Japp. 2 vols. London: Heinemann, 1891-93.

SELECTED ESSAYS ON RHETORIC BY THOMAS DE QUINCEY. Ed. Frederick L. Burwick. Carbondale: Southern Illinois University Press, 1968.

THOMAS DE QUINCEY'S WRITINGS. Ed. J.T. Field. 23 vols. Boston: Ticknor, 1851-59.

THE WORKS OF THOMAS DE QUINCEY. 12 vols. 3rd ed. Boston: Houghton, 1877.

>Known as the "American Edition."

LETTERS

DE QUINCEY AT WORK: AS SEEN IN 130 NEW AND NEWLY EDITED LETTERS. Ed. W.H. Bonner. Buffalo: Airport Publishers, 1936.

Eaton, H[orace] A. "The Letters of De Quincey to Wordsworth, 1803-1807." ELH, 3 (1936), 15-30.

Moore, E.H. "Some Unpublished Letters of Thomas De Quincey." RES, 9 (1933), 176-85.

>Prints and discusses letters relating to De Quincey's financial straits.

BIOGRAPHIES

Eaton, Horace A. THOMAS DE QUINCEY: A BIOGRAPHY. Oxford: Clarendon Press, 1936.

>A very sound work, nearly exhaustive as a source of De Quincey information.

Elwin, Malcolm. DE QUINCEY. London: Duckworth, 1935; rpt. New York: Kennikat Press, 1972.

>Elwin depicts De Quincey as a "dual personality" who succeeded

because he developed both his intellectual and imaginative faculties.

Hogg, James, ed. DE QUINCEY AND HIS FRIENDS: PERSONAL RECOLLECTIONS, SOUVENIRS AND ANECDOTES. London: Low, Marston, 1895.

> Hogg's edition contains several biographical essays written by De Quincey's contemporaries.

Metcalf, John. DE QUINCEY: A PORTRAIT. Cambridge, Mass.: Harvard University Press, 1940.

> Presents a sympathetic portrait of De Quincey.

Sackville-West, Edward. A FLAME IN SUNLIGHT. London: Bodley Head, 1936.

> Published in America as THOMAS DE QUINCEY: HIS LIFE AND WORK, this interpretive biography emphasizes the importance of opium in De Quincey's life.

CRITICAL STUDIES

Bilsland, John W. "De Quincey on Poetic Genius." DR, 48 (1968), 200-214.

> Examines De Quincey's critical gifts for "close analysis and discrimination" as they apply to his attempts to define the nature of the poet. Concludes that De Quincey's distinctions among poets tend to separate them into "classical" or "romantic" groups.

Burwick, Frederick [L.]. "The Dream-Visions of Jean Paul and Thomas De Quincey." CL, 20 (1968), 1-26.

> Clarifies De Quincey's indebtedness to Richter by demonstrating that Jean-Paul provided De Quincey with definitions for a number of literary concepts which recur in his essays.

Byrns, Richard H. "De Quincey's Revisions in the 'Dream-Fugue.'" PMLA, 77 (1962), 97-101.

> Byrns claims that De Quincey's revisions "intensify the emotional quality" and increase the flowing movment of the prose.

Chilcott, Tim. "De Quincey and THE LONDON MAGAZINE." CLB, 1 (1973), 9-19.

> Focuses on the CONFESSIONS OF AN ENGLISH OPIUM EATER as "the centre of De Quincey's association with the LONDON." Also examines and reprints De Quincey's essay "On the LONDON

MAGAZINE"--a significant analysis of "the general influence of periodical literature in Regency England."

Davies, H[ugh] S. THOMAS DE QUINCEY. London: Longmans, Green, 1964.

Considers De Quincey's life in relation to his writings. Assesses the literary criticism and concludes with a discussion of CONFESSIONS OF AN ENGLISH OPIUM EATER.

DeLuca, Vincent A. "Satanic Fall and Hebraic Exodus: An Interpretation of De Quincey's 'Revolt of the Tartars.'" SIR, 8 (1969), 95-108.

Illustrates De Quincey's "considerable equivocation in attitude toward rebellious forces." By examining "The Revolt of the Tartars," DeLuca observes that De Quincey treats rebellious assertion as a "necessary step of liberation from constriction" and as a form of "self-destruction."

——. "'The Type of a Mighty Mind': Mutual Influence in Wordsworth and De Quincey." TSLL, 13 (1971), 239-47.

Suggests that De Quincey's CONFESSIONS OF AN ENGLISH OPIUM EATER influenced Wordsworth's revisions of the Snowdon passage in THE PRELUDE: "this is a characteristically Romantic instance of literary reciprocity."

Durham, Weldon B. "The Elements of Thomas De Quincey's Rhetoric." SM, 37 (1970), 240-48.

Examines De Quincey's rhetoric by analyzing his essay on that topic. Concludes that "De Quincey's treatment of the teleology of rhetoric may be summarized . . . in terms of the four Aristotelian causes."

Fowler, J.H. DE QUINCEY AS LITERARY CRITIC. London: English Association, 1922.

Claims that De Quincey's distinction between "literature of knowledge" and "literature of power" is false.

Goldman, Albert. THE MIND AND THE MINT: SOURCES FOR THE WRITINGS OF DE QUINCEY. Carbondale: Southern Illinois University Press, 1965.

Asserts that De Quincey saw himself as "the bold and original thinker posing traditional problems in a new light and offering novel and paradoxical solutions." Attempts to reform present notions of De Quincey by showing that his scholarly and intellectual works "are almost all derived from printed sources," and that the study of De Quincey's writings in relation to their sources tends "to enhance his literary reputation" by providing evidence of his imaginative capacities.

Grant, Douglas. "Thomas De Quincey." SOME BRITISH ROMANTICS: A COLLECTION OF ESSAYS. Eds. James V. Logan et al. Columbus: Ohio State University Press, 1966.

> Examines De Quincey's relationship with Coleridge and its influence on CONFESSIONS OF AN ENGLISH OPIUM EATER. Concludes by noting that "the principal weakness of De Quincey's miscellaneous essays lies in his constitutional disability to set a straight course and come deliberately to a point."

Haltresht, Michael. "The Meaning of De Quincey's 'Dream-Fugue on . . . Sudden Death.'" L&P, 26 (1976), 31-36.

> Analyzes De Quincey's essay as "a paradigm for human helplessness and sense of betrayal in the face of any form of suffering and disaster."

Hayter, Althea. OPIUM AND THE ROMANTIC IMAGINATION. Berkeley and Los Angeles: University of California Press; London: Faber and Faber, 1968.

> Contains a section on De Quincey.

Herbert, C. "De Quincey and Dickens." VS, 17 (1974), 247-63.

> Contends that the opening paragraph of EDWIN DROOD is modelled on De Quincey's style and that "Dickens' literary connection with De Quincey extends throughout Dickens' career. The themes of memory, loss, and guilt link De Quincey and Dickens."

Hopkins, Robert. "De Quincey on War and the Pastoral Design of THE ENGLISH MAIL-COACH." SIR, 6 (1967), 129-51.

> Contends that THE ENGLISH MAIL-COACH is not a "loose strung-together series of purple passages," but rather a "coherent, imaginative prose work" by a "conservative first-generation Romantic trying to sum up the profound significance of the Napoleonic Wars for himself and for the Victorian era."

Jack, Ian. "De Quincey Revises His CONFESSIONS." PMLA, 72 (1957), 122-46.

> Examines the original version of CONFESSIONS with reference to the revised edition that De Quincey prepared for SELECTIONS GRAVE AND GAY. Contends that a comparison of the two forms of the CONFESSIONS "throws a great deal of light on De Quincey's development."

Jordan, John E. DE QUINCEY AND WORDSWORTH: A BIOGRAPHY OF A

Thomas De Quincey

RELATIONSHIP. Berkeley and Los Angeles: University of California Press, 1962.

    Jordan discusses the relationship between the two writers, emphasizing De Quincey's early attitude was of a worshipping acolyte who later became disillusioned.

──────. "De Quincey on Wordsworth's Theory of Diction." PMLA, 68 (1953), 764-78.

    Clarifies De Quincey's stand on poetic diction by comparing it with the beliefs of Wordsworth and Coleridge.

──────. "De Quincey's Dramaturgic Criticism." ELH, 18 (1951), 32-49.

    Jordan compares De Quincey's "theatrical" view of Shakespeare to his contemporaries' views.

──────. THOMAS DE QUINCEY, LITERARY CRITIC. Berkeley and Los Angeles: University of California Press, 1952.

    Jordan discusses De Quincey as a practicing critic.

Kobayashi, Shozo. RHYTHM IN THE PROSE OF THOMAS DE QUINCEY. Tokyo: Dainippon, 1956.

Lyon, Judson. THOMAS DE QUINCEY. New York: Twayne, 1969.

    Proposes to "reconsider De Quincey in the light of the principal results of recent critical evaluation . . . and to present him, in a balanced account and estimate, as he appears today."

Murray, James G. "Mill on De Quincey: ESPRIT CRITIQUE Revoked." VN, 37 (1970), 7-12.

    Mill's review of De Quincey's LOGIC (1842) reveals "the new Mill" who has "changed his views on debate, logic, error, and truth."

Patterson, Charles I. "De Quincey's Conception of the Novel." PMLA, 70 (1955), 375-89.

    Patterson discusses De Quincey's attitude toward the Gothic novel.

Proctor, Sigmund. THOMAS DE QUINCEY'S THEORY OF LITERATURE. Ann Arbor: University of Michigan Press, 1943.

    Discusses De Quincey's philosophical knowledge. Also contains an appendix by C.D. Thorpe on De Quincey's efforts to spread German philosophical thought in England.

Salt, H.S. DE QUINCEY. London: Bell, 1904.

> Salt's discussion centers on De Quincey as "one of the great mystics of literature."

Stapleton, Laurence. "The Virtù of De Quincey." In his THE ELECTED CIRCLE: STUDIES IN THE ART OF PROSE. Princeton, N.J.: Princeton University Press, 1973.

> Examines De Quincey's criticism and concludes that in his best prose "he is able simultaneously to narrate, to interpret, and to intensify."

Warren, Leland E. "A Sudden Vision of Life: De Quincey's THE ENGLISH MAIL-COACH." STUDIES IN THE HUMANITIES. Ed. William F. Grayburn. Indiana: Indiana University of Pennsylvania Press, 1971.

Watson, George. "Lamb, Hazlitt, De Quincey." In his THE LITERARY CRITICS. New York: Barnes and Noble, 1962.

> "There is an underlying austerity in De Quincey's criticism, a faculty for reasoning at length, and a conscientious determination to get the right answers."

Wellek, René. "De Quincey's Status in the History of Ideas." PQ, 23 (1944), 248-72.

> Wellek claims De Quincey had little originality as a thinker.

———. "Thomas De Quincey." In his HISTORY OF MODERN CRITICISM, 1750-1950. Vol. 3. New Haven, Conn.: Yale University Press, 1965.

> Contends that "in literary theory, De Quincey belongs not to the Coleridgean and German dialectical symbolism but to the empirical psychological tradition of the British and to the emotionalist trend."

Wells, John E. "Wordsworth and De Quincey in Westmoreland Politics, 1818." PMLA, 55 (1940), 1080-1128.

> Wells discusses De Quincey's early Tory thinking, which led to his editorship of the WESTMORELAND GAZETTE.

Woolf, Virginia. THE COMMON READER. 2nd series. London: Hogarth Press, 1935.

> Woolf claims that De Quincey's autobiographical writings are anticipations of modern literary expressions of psychological theories and insights.

Wright, Brooks. "The Cave of Trophonius: Myth and Reality in De Quincey." NCF, 8 (1954), 290-99.

> Wright's thesis is that De Quincey used myths to express symbolically his own internal state of mind and his personal relationships.

BIBLIOGRAPHIES

Green, John A. THOMAS DE QUINCEY: A BIBLIOGRAPHY. Manchester, Engl.: Moss Library, 1908.

> Green lists periodical publications and describes the various editions of De Quincey's work. He also lists critical studies published before 1908.

Jordan, John E. "Thomas De Quincey." THE ENGLISH ROMANTIC POETS AND ESSAYISTS. Eds. C[arolyn] W. Houtchens and L[awrence] H. Houtchens. Rev. ed. New York: MLA, 1966.

> A thorough and valuable bibliographical essay which discusses critical studies published by 1965.

WILLIAM GODWIN (1756-1836)

PRINCIPAL PROSE WORKS

ITALIAN LETTERS: OR THE HISTORY OF THE COUNT DE ST. JULIAN, 1783.

AN ENQUIRY CONCERNING THE PRINCIPLES OF POLITICAL JUSTICE, AND ITS INFLUENCE ON GENERAL VIRTUE AND HAPPINESS. 2 vols. 1793.

THINGS AS THEY ARE: OR THE ADVENTURES OF CALEB WILLIAMS. 3 vols. 1794.

THE ENQUIRER: REFLECTIONS ON EDUCATION, MANNERS, AND LITERATURE, 1797.

ST. LEON: A TALE OF THE SIXTEENTH CENTURY. 4 vols. 1799.

FLEETWOOD: OR THE NEW MAN OF FEELING. 3 vols. 1805.

MANDEVILLE: A TALE OF THE SEVENTEENTH CENTURY IN ENGLAND. 3 vols. 1817.

OF POPULATION: AN ANSWER TO MR. MALTHUS'S ESSAY, 1820.

HISTORY OF THE COMMONWEALTH OF ENGLAND FROM ITS COMMENCEMENT TO THE RESTORATION OF CHARLES THE SECOND. 4 vols. 1824-28.

COLLECTED WORKS

WILLIAM GODWIN'S UNCOLLECTED WRITINGS (1785-1822): ARTICLES IN PERIODICALS AND SIX PAMPHLETS, ONE WITH COLERIDGE'S MARGINALIA. Eds. Jack W. Marken and Burton R. Pollin. Gainesville, Fla.: Scholar's Facsimiles & Reprints, 1968.

William Godwin

LETTERS

Also see Cameron under "Critical Studies," below.

GODWIN AND MARY: LETTERS OF WILLIAM GODWIN AND MARY WOLLSTONECRAFT. Ed. Ralph [M.] Wardle. Lawrence: University of Kansas Press, 1966.

BIOGRAPHIES

Brown, Ford K. THE LIFE OF WILLIAM GODWIN. London: Dent, 1926.

> Brown surveys Godwin's life and works, including POLITICAL JUSTICE and CALEB WILLIAMS. Includes a discussion of the political pamphlets and a bibliography of Godwin's writings.

Paul, Charles K. WILLIAM GODWIN. 2 vols. London: King & Co., 1876.

> This early biography relies heavily on Godwin's letters. Volume 1 covers 1756-1800, volume 2 1801-36.

Woodcock, George. WILLIAM GODWIN: A BIOGRAPHICAL STUDY. London: Porcupine Press, 1946.

> Stresses Godwin's relevance as a political theorist to later generations: "His teachings apply not merely to social institutions of his own day, but to society in general, and most of POLITICAL JUSTICE can be read with as much profit today as in the eighteenth century."

CRITICAL STUDIES

Albrecht, William P. "Godwin and Malthus." PMLA, 70 (1955), 552-55.

> Defends Godwin's OF POPULATION against Hazlitt's charge that it was plagiarized from Malthus.

Allentuck, Marcia. "An Unpublished Account of Encounters with William Godwin in 1804." KSJ, 20 (1971), 19-21.

> Discusses Joseph Carrington Cabell's firsthand account of his meeting with Godwin in 1804.

Brailsford, Henry N. SHELLEY, GODWIN AND THEIR CIRCLE. London: Oxford University Press, 1951.

> Includes a general chapter on "The French Revolution in England,"

as well as chapters on "Godwin and the Revolution," "POLITICAL JUSTICE," "Godwin and the Reaction," and "Godwin and Shelley."

Brinton, Crane. POLITICAL IDEAS OF THE ENGLISH ROMANTICS. London: Milford, 1926.

> Discusses the importance of Godwin's political writings.

Cameron, Kenneth [H.], and Donald W. Reiman, eds. SHELLEY AND HIS CIRCLE, 1773-1822. Cambridge, Mass.: Harvard University Press, 1961-- .

> Volume 1 contains a large collection of Godwin letters, as well as a biographical sketch and a testimonial written by a contemporary. Also see indexes in volumes 4 and 6 for other Godwin references.

Cobban, Alfred. EDMUND BURKE AND THE REVOLT AGAINST THE EIGHTEENTH CENTURY. London: Allen and Unwin, 1929.

> Cobban emphasizes Godwin's importance to early nineteenth-century attitudes.

Colmer, John. "Godwin's MANDEVILLE and Peacock's NIGHTMARE ABBEY." RES, 21 (1970), 331-36.

> Colmer believes that NIGHTMARE ABBEY parodies Godwin's work.

Crutwell, Patrick. "On CALEB WILLIAMS." HR, 11 (1958), 87-95.

> CALEB WILLIAMS "shows a Godwin for whom the romantic poets could easily feel a kinship, who shared with them the tastes of nightmare, for abnormal psychology, for the thriller and mystery, and for the persecuted rejects of society."

Deen, Floyd. "The Genesis of Martin Faber in CALEB WILLIAMS." MLN, 59 (1944), 315-17.

> MARTIN FABER by William Simms (1833) "grew out of the work of Godwin." Proceeds to detail some striking similarities.

Driver, Cecil H. "William Godwin." THE SOCIAL AND POLITICAL IDEAS OF THE REVOLUTIONARY AGE. Ed. Fossey J.C. Hearnshaw. London: Harrap, 1931.

> Says POLITICAL JUSTICE belongs to the tradition of empirical philosophy, and Godwin is a disciple of Locke and Hartley. See Priestley, below.

Dumas, Donald G. "Things as They Were: The Original Ending of CALEB WILLIAMS." SEL, 6 (1966), 575-97.

William Godwin

Discusses the conclusion in the light of what is perceived of as a "split" between Godwin the philosopher and Godwin the novelist. See McCracken, below.

Evans, Frank B. "Shelley, Godwin, Hume, and the Doctrine of Necessity." SP, 37 (1940), 632-40.

Claims that Shelley's concept of "Necessity" derives not from Godwin, but from Hume's ENQUIRY.

Fleisher, David. WILLIAM GODWIN: A STUDY IN LIBERALISM. New York: Kelley, 1951.

Generally considered the best study of Godwin's themes and intellectual concerns as expressed in POLITICAL JUSTICE. Fleisher praises Godwin's notion of human and social perfectability, but concludes that "a fatal flaw lies at the heart of Godwin's system--and exaggerated notion of the power of reason over human conduct."

Furbank, P.N. "Godwin's Novels." EIC, 3 (1955), 214-18.

Claims that "the novels are not reflections of the political writings; they are the complement of them, and in some ways a counterblast to them."

Grob, Alan. "Wordsworth and Godwin: A Reassessment." SIR, 6 (1967), 98-119.

Discusses the writers' personal and intellectual relationship and asserts that Godwin was never a strong influence on Wordsworth's major work.

Grylls, Rosalie. WILLIAM GODWIN AND HIS WORLD. London: Odhams, 1953.

A study of Godwin in relation to his age, with chapters on "The English Jacobins at Home and in France" and "Charles Lamb and His Circle."

Lund, Mary G. "Mary Shelley's Father." DISCOURSE, 22 (1969), 130-35.

Reviews the study of Godwin by the Smiths, below, but emphasizes Godwin's relationship with his daughter, Mary Shelley.

McCelvey, G. GODWIN'S NOVELS: THEME AND CRAFT. Durham, N.C.: Duke University Press, 1964.

McCelvey observes that Godwin's novels are in the eighteenth-century confessional tradition.

McCracken, David. "Godwin's CALEB WILLIAMS: A Fictional Rebuttal of Burke." SBHT, 11 (1969-70), 1442-52.

> McCracken claims that Godwin's novel should be read in light of the political tensions of the 1790s.

_____. "Godwin's Literary Theory: The Alliance Between Fiction and Political Philosophy." PQ, 49 (1970), 113-33.

> Disagrees with the views of Dumas, above, and claims that Godwin was "at least aware of the possible antagonism between philosophy and fiction, and that he clearly saw intellectual links between the two as he practiced them."

_____. "Godwin's Reading in Burke." ELN, 7 (1970), 264-70.

> Contends that "Godwin's reading in Burke, in fact, had an important and direct effect not only on POLITICAL JUSTICE but also on CALEB WILLIAMS."

Marken, Jack [W.]. "The Canon and Chronology of William Godwin's Early Works." MLN, 69 (1954), 176-80.

> Gives the complete list of Godwin's early works, exclusive of his writings for such periodicals as the ENGLISH REVIEW, the NEW ANNUAL REGISTER, and the POLITICAL HERALD AND REVIEW.

Monro, David H. GODWIN'S MORAL PHILOSOPHY. London: Cumberlege, 1953.

> Examines Godwin as a "moralist" and outlines his theory of ethics, the relation between reason and feeling in ethics, his views on the influence of society on our behavior, and his debt to Montesquieu.

Murry, John Middleton. "William Godwin: The Protestant Dream." In his HEAVEN AND EARTH. London: Cape, 1938. Rpt. as "William Godwin: The Independent's Dream," in his HEROES OF THOUGHT (New York: Messner, 1938).

> Analyzes Godwin's independence; he was "perhaps as near as a modern mind can get to what a seventeenth-century Independent [Cromwell] imagined."

Pollin, Burton R. EDUCATION AND ENLIGHTENMENT IN THE WORKS OF WILLIAM GODWIN. New York: Las Americas Publishing Co., 1962.

> A study of Godwin's works, concentrating on the role of the educated elite in the enlightenment of society.

_____. "Godwin's Account of Shelley's Return in September, 1814: A Letter to John Taylor." KSMB, 21 (1970), 21-31.

>Reprints Godwin's letter to John Taylor, which gives Godwin's version of the "tangled relationship" among the Taylor-Godwin-Shelley households. Also traces the financial relations between Taylor and Godwin.

_____. "Godwin's MANDEVILLE in Poems of Shelley." KSMB, 19 (1968), 33-40.

>Describes Shelley's enthusiastic review of Godwin's novel (1817), and claims that the characters in MANDEVILLE influenced both "Ozymandias" and "Love's Philosophy."

Preu, James. THE DEAN AND THE ANARCHIST. Tallahassee: Florida State University Press, 1959.

>A comparative study of Swift and Godwin.

_____. "Swift's Influence on Godwin." JHI, 15 (1954), 371-83.

>Claims that Godwin "drew much of his inspiration from the fourth book of GULLIVER'S TRAVELS."

Priestley, F.E.L. "Platonism in William Godwin's POLITICAL JUSTICE." MLQ, 4 (1943), 63-69.

>Disagreed with Driver's view, above, and instead places Godwin "with the Platonic rationalists rather than with the empiricists, with Cudworth and Clarke rather than with Hobbes and Helvetius."

Rodway, A.E. GODWIN AND THE AGE OF TRANSITION. London: Harrap, 1952.

>A discussion of Godwin's life and works with emphasis on his literary influence in the period.

Rosen, Frederick. "Godwin and Holcroft." ELN, 5 (1968), 183-86.

>Discussed the literary friendship during 1788-1805. It ended when Godwin depicted a son's suicide in FLEETWOOD and Holcroft felt that Godwin had based the incident on an event which actually occurred in Holcroft's family.

_____. "The Principle of Population as Political Theory: Godwin's OF POPULATION and the Malthusian Controversy." JHI, 31 (1970), 33-48.

>Examines the reception of Godwin's OF POPULATION and compares it to Malthus' theories.

Sherburn, George. "Godwin's Later Novels." SIR, 1 (1962), 65-82.

>Examines five of Godwin's later novels for their thematic contempt "for law and control." Concludes that "the core of interest in Godwin's study of minds lies in his obsession with guilt arising from misanthropy and from criminal violation of conscience."

Smith, Elton E., and Esther G. Smith. WILLIAM GODWIN. New York: Twayne, 1966.

>Discusses all of Godwin's works, with a chapter devoted to POLITICAL JUSTICE. Stresses Godwin "as the heir of Locke's epistemology, radical Protestantism, Roman republicanism, Rousseau's naturalism, and the political theories of Helvetius and d'Holbach." See Lund, above.

Werkmeister, Lucyle. "Coleridge and Godwin on the Communication of Truth." MP, 55 (1958), 170-77.

>Explores Godwin's influence on Coleridge, which "was still in evidence as late as 1809."

BIBLIOGRAPHIES

Cordasco, Francesco. WILLIAM GODWIN: A HANDLIST OF CRITICAL NOTICES AND STUDIES. Brooklyn, N.Y.: Long Island University Press, 1950.

Pollin, Burton R. "Bibliography--Studies of Godwin." In his EDUCATION AND ENLIGHTENMENT IN THE WORKS OF WILLIAM GODWIN. New York: Las Americas Publishing Co., 1962.

>Lists Godwin's works for adults and children, as well as critical studies of his works.

─────. GODWIN CRITICISM: A SYNOPTIC BIBLIOGRAPHY. Toronto: University of Toronto Press, 1967.

>The definitive bibliography of Godwin's works. Also contains a listing of critical studies published before 1967.

WILLIAM HAZLITT (1778-1830)

PRINCIPAL PROSE WORKS

THE ROUND TABLE: A COLLECTION OF ESSAYS ON LITERATURE, MEN AND MANNERS. With Leigh Hunt. 2 vols. 1817.

CHARACTERS OF SHAKESPEAR'S PLAYS, 1817.

A VIEW OF THE ENGLISH STAGE; OR, A SERIES OF DRAMATIC CRITICISMS, 1818.

LECTURES ON THE ENGLISH POETS, 1818.

LECTURES ON THE ENGLISH COMIC WRITERS, 1819.

POLITICAL ESSAYS, WITH SKETCHES OF PUBLIC CHARACTERS, 1819.

LECTURES CHIEFLY ON THE DRAMATIC LITERATURE OF THE AGE OF ELIZABETH, 1820.

TABLE TALK; OR, ORIGINAL ESSAYS. 2 vols. 1821-22.

LIBER AMORIS; OR, THE NEW PYGMALION, 1823.

THE SPIRIT OF THE AGE: OR CONTEMPORARY PORTRAITS, 1825.

THE PLAIN SPEAKER: OPINIONS ON BOOKS, MEN, AND THINGS. 2 vols. 1826.

THE LIFE OF NAPOLEON BUONAPARTE. 4 vols. 1828-30.

William Hazlitt

LITERARY REMAINS OF THE LATE WILLIAM HAZLITT. With a notice of his life, by his son. 2 vols. 1836.

SKETCHES AND ESSAYS. Now first collected by his son. 1839.

COLLECTED WORKS

THE BEST OF HAZLITT. Ed. P.P. Howe. London: Methuen, 1923.

THE COLLECTED WORKS OF WILLIAM HAZLITT. Eds. A[lfred] R. Waller and A. Glover. 13 vols. London: Dent, 1902-06.

THE COMPLETE WORKS OF WILLIAM HAZLITT. Ed. P.P. Howe. 21 vols. London: Dent, 1930-34.
> The standard, definitive edition of the works.

SELECTED ESSAYS OF HAZLITT. Ed. John R. Nabholtz. New York: Appleton, 1970.

SELECTED WRITINGS OF HAZLITT. Ed. Ronald Blythe. Baltimore: Penguin, 1970.

LETTERS

LAMB AND HAZLITT: FURTHER LETTERS AND RECORDS. Ed. W.C. Hazlitt. New York: Dodd, 1899; rpt. New York: AMS, 1973.
> This volume was edited by Hazlitt's grandson, who was concerned with presenting his grandfather in a favorable light.

MEMOIRS OF HAZLITT, WITH PORTIONS OF HIS CORRESPONDENCE. Ed. W.C. Hazlitt. 2 vols. London: Bentley, 1867.
> There is no complete edition of Hazlitt's letters, although one is currently being prepared by Herschel M. Sikes.

BIOGRAPHIES

Baker, Herschal. WILLIAM HAZLITT. Cambridge, Mass.: Harvard University Press, 1962.
> The definitive biography.

Howe, P.P. THE LIFE OF WILLIAM HAZLITT. London: Hamilton, 1922; rev. ed. 1947.

Howe attempts to correct the portrait of Hazlitt created by his grandson. See W.C. Hazlitt, above.

Maclean, Catherine M. BORN UNDER SATURN. New York: Macmillan, 1944.

Emphasizes Hazlitt's Nonconformist religious background and his political beliefs, calling his life a "struggle in the service of Liberty."

Wardle, Ralph M. HAZLITT. Lincoln: University of Nebraska Press, 1971.

Since Baker's study, above, stresses the development of Hazlitt's thought in relation to his time, Wardle's study attempts to supplement Howe's biography, above.

CRITICAL STUDIES

Albrecht, William P. HAZLITT AND THE CREATIVE IMAGINATION. Lawrence: University of Kansas Press, 1965.

Albrecht says Hazlitt's concept of the imagination is the key to his writings.

_____. "Hazlitt, Keats, and the Sublime Pleasures of Tragedy." THE NINETEENTH-CENTURY WRITER AND HIS AUDIENCE: SELECTED PROBLEMS IN THEORY, FORM, AND CONTENT. Eds. Harold Orel and George J. Worth. Lawrence: University of Kansas Press, 1969.

Discusses Hazlitt's definition of "imagination," "tragedy," and the "sublime," and concludes that, for Hazlitt, tragedy "provided unity, coalesced sublime masses of ideas, and brought all the faculties into play in a self-identifying knowledge of evil."

_____. "Hazlitt on Wordsworth; or, The Poetry of Paradox." SIX STUDIES IN NINETEENTH-CENTURY ENGLISH LITERATURE AND THOUGHT. Eds. Harold Orel and George J. Worth. Lawrence: University of Kansas Press, 1962.

"Although always a great defender of the French Revolution, humanity, and nature, especially as the gauge of art, Hazlitt put the poetry of paradox at the bottom of a scale of excellence."

_____. "Hazlitt's Preference for Tragedy." PMLA, 71 (1956), 1042-51.

Discusses Hazlitt's preference for tragedy by analyzing "his theory of imagination as it affects his definition and evaluation of both tragedy and comedy." Sylvan Barnet responds to this article (PMLA, 73 [1958], 443-45) by stating that Hazlitt preferred tragedy because of a "recurring sadistic strain" in his personality.

Albrecht, William P., and James D. O'Hara. "More on Hazlitt and the Functions of the Imagination (An Exchange)." PMLA, 83 (1968), 151-54.

>Albrecht disagrees with O'Hara's disparagement of the role of "sympathy" in Hazlitt's criticism, stating that sympathy is the "integration of thought, feeling, and directed toward a kind of selfless self-realization." Albrecht contends that "Hazlitt sees this sympathy as the greatest possibility for man."

Bullitt, John M. "Hazlitt and the Romantic Conception of the Imagination." PQ, 24 (1945), 343-61.

>Discusses Hazlitt's concept of the imagination as "both instinctive and immediate" and concludes that Hazlitt's "confidence in the reality of what is immediately influenced" had a profound influence on Keats.

Carver, P.L. "Hazlitt's Contributions to the EDINBURGH REVIEW." RES, 4 (1928), 385-93.

>Identifies six articles contributed by Hazlitt to the EDINBURGH REVIEW and not previously identified by Waller and Glover's bibliography in their edition of the COLLECTED WORKS (see "Collected Works," above).

Cecil, David. "Hazlitt's Occasional Essays." In his THE FINE ART OF READING. Indianapolis: Bobbs-Merrill, 1957.

>Discusses Hazlitt's life as reflected in his prose: "he takes every opportunity to air his idiosyncrasies and prejudices and preferences. Yet when we try to analyze this personality, we find ourselves baffled."

Chandler, Zilpha E. AN ANALYSIS AND SYNOPSIS OF THE STYLISTIC TECHNIQUE OF ADDISON, JOHNSON, HAZLITT, AND PATER. 2 vols. Iowa City: University of Iowa Humanistic Studies, 1928.

>An early attempt to use quantitative methods to study prose style. Includes statistics on derivations of words and distribution of phrases. Concludes that Hazlitt's style is "more expressive than Johnson's."

Coburn, Kathleen. "Hazlitt on the Disinterested Imagination." SOME BRITISH ROMANTICS. Eds. James Logan et al. Columbus: Ohio State University Press, 1966.

>Hazlitt as the argumentative social critic has been overshadowed by "the ardent play-goer, the reviewer, the journalist, the tabletalker, the familiar essayist." Coburn focuses on Hazlitt's biography of Napoleon and his ON THE PRINCIPLES OF HUMAN ACTION to examine the sources of his work.

William Hazlitt

DeLaura, David J. "Arnold and Hazlitt." ELN, 9 (1972), 277-83.

    Explores Hazlitt's influence on Arnold.

Dobrée, Bonamy. MILTON TO OUIDA. London: Cass, 1970.

    Includes an essay on Hazlitt.

―――. "William Hazlitt, 1778-1830." REL, 2 (1961), 30-37.

    Reviews Hazlitt's writings and concludes that he is less a critic than an essayist: "certainly as an essayist he is invigorating to read, if only for the vitality of the language which so well expresses the virility of his being."

Friedman, Martin B. "Hazlitt, Jerrold, and Home: LIBER AMORIS Twenty Years After." RES, 22 (1971), 455-62.

    Friedman argues that Jerrold's story, "The Metaphysician and the Maid," is a satire of Hazlitt's LIBER AMORIS.

Garrod, H.W. "The Place of Hazlitt in English Criticism." In his THE PROFESSION OF POETRY AND OTHER LECTURES. Oxford: Oxford University Press, 1929.

    Garrod predicts that Hazlitt's SPIRIT OF THE AGE will one day be considered the greatest work of English criticism.

Griggs, Earl L. "Hazlitt's Estrangement from Coleridge and Wordsworth." MLN, 48 (1933), 173-76.

    Discusses the unfavorable CHRISTABEL review that Coleridge attributed to Hazlitt, although it was in fact the work of Jeffrey.

Hayden, John O. "Hazlitt Reviews Hazlitt?" MLR, 44 (1969), 20-26.

    Hayden argues that Hazlitt reviewed his own and Hunt's publications for the EDINBURGH MAGAZINE in November 1817.

Houck, James A. "Hazlitt on the Obligations of the Critic." WC, 4 (1974), 250-58.

    Hazlitt "views the true critic as one in a long line of preservers or guardians: it is the duty of each critic to preserve for his time the reputations of the geniuses of the past."

Jones, Stanley. "Dating Hazlitt's 'Essay on Taste.'" EA, 22 (1969), 68-71.

―――. "Hazlitt, Cobbett, and the EDINBURGH REVIEW." NEO, 53 (1969), 69-76.

Discusses Hazlitt's portrait of Cobbett (1821) as a revelation of Hazlitt's "imperfect knowledge of Cobbett's relations with the EDINBURGH REVIEW."

_____. "Hazlitt's Journal of 1823: Some Notes and Emendations." LIBRARY, 26 (1971), 325-36.

Klingopulos, G.D. "Hazlitt as Critic." EIC, 4 (1956), 386-403.

Concludes that Hazlitt reveals "not fanaticism or misanthropy but responsible intelligence, and so represents an important link in the contininuities of English life."

Law, Marie H. THE ENGLISH FAMILIAR ESSAY IN THE EARLY NINETEENTH CENTURY. Philadelphia: University of Pennsylvania Press, 1934.

Contains a discussion of Hazlitt's essays.

McAleer, John J. "William Hazlitt--Shakespeare's 'Advocate and Herald.'" SHN, 22 (1972), 4.

Margolis, John D. "Keats's 'Men of Genius' and 'Men of Power.'" TSLL, 40 (1970), 1333-47.

Margolis discusses Keats's attitudes toward Haydon, Wordsworth, and Hazlitt.

Mills, Howard. PEACOCK: HIS CIRCLE AND HIS AGE. London: Cambridge University Press, 1969.

Discusses Hazlitt in relation to Peacock.

Milner, Perry L. "William Hazlitt on the Genius of Shakespeare." SOQ, 5 (1966), 64-71.

Discusses Hazlitt's "distrust of abstractions, confidence in concrete nature, and his sympathetic and emotional immediacy" as reflected in his views of Shakespeare.

Noxon, James. "Hazlitt as Moral Philosopher." ETHICS, 73 (1963), 279-83.

Explores Hazlitt's rejection of the epistemological, psychological, and moral elements of the "modern philosophy."

O'Hara, James D. "Hazlitt and Romantic Criticism of the Fine Arts." JAAC, 27 (1968), 73-85.

Claims that Hazlitt broke with neoclassic terminology and thus prepared the way for new views of art: "Hazlitt made out of the vague and inconsistent aesthetic attitudes of his time a useful aesthetic approach."

William Hazlitt

———. "Hazlitt and the Functions of the Imagination." PMLA, 81 (1966), 552-62.

> States that it is not sufficient to recognize sympathy in Hazlitt's theory of the imagination. Instead, O'Hara "investigates the major supplements in Hazlitt's criticism--associational aesthetics and the formative imagination." See Albrecht, above.

Park, Roy. "Hazlitt and Bentham." JHI, 30 (1969), 369-84.

> Explores the differences between Hazlitt's and Bentham's concept of utilitarianism.

———. HAZLITT AND THE SPIRIT OF THE AGE: ABSTRACTION AND CRITICAL THEORY. Oxford: Clarendon Press, 1971.

> Park presents a thorough analysis of Hazlitt's attitude about the dangers of abstraction. According to Park, Hazlitt anticipates Mill and Arnold.

———. "The Painter as Critic: Hazlitt's Theory of Abstraction." PMLA, 85 (1970), 1072-81.

> Discusses Hazlitt as "primarily a painter and philosopher." Until 1814 he invested his efforts in developing "a highly individual and revolutionary theory of abstraction that was to become the basis of his response both to life and to art."

Patterson, Charles I. "Hazlitt as a Critic of Prose Fiction." PMLA, 68 (1953), 1001-16.

> Patterson discusses Hazlitt's opinions of James Fenimore Cooper, Fielding, Sterne, and Smollett.

Priestley, John B. WILLIAM HAZLITT. London: Longmans, Green, 1960.

> A short introduction to Hazlitt's work that discusses him as an essayist rather than a critic: "His main subject was not other men's work but himself. He preferred above anything else to tell us what Hazlitt thought and felt about everything."

Sallé, J.C. "Hazlitt the Associationist." RES, 15 (1964), 38-51.

> Sallé emphasizes Hazlitt's connection with eighteenth-century associationalism.

———. "Identifications of Three Allusions in Hazlitt's Essays." N&Q, 19 (1972), 99-100.

Schneider, Elizabeth W. THE AESTHETICS OF HAZLITT. Philadelphia: University of Pennsylvania Press, 1933; rpt. New York: Octagon, 1952.

> Contains a chapter on Hazlitt's philosophy as it relates to his attitudes on literature. Schneider emphasizes that Hazlitt believed "truth is not one but many."

Stapleton, Laurence. "William Hazlitt: The Essayist and the Moods of the Mind." In his THE ELECTED CIRCLE: STUDIES IN THE ART OF PROSE. Princeton, N.J.: Princeton University Press, 1973.

> "Hazlitt speaks in his own person. He comes straight forward and utters an incisive sentence reflecting a personal conviction."

Story, Patrick L. "Byron's Death and Hazlitt's SPIRIT OF THE AGE." ELN, 7 (1969), 42-46.

> Discusses Hazlitt's unfavorable portrait of Byron in SPIRIT OF THE AGE and the "coda" he attached after Byron's death.

_____. "A Contemporary Continuation of Hazlitt's SPIRIT OF THE AGE." WC, 1 (1970), 59-65.

> Discusses the attempt by Sir William Allan (1782-1850) to begin "a fragmentary continuation of Hazlitt's text in the manner of a collected biography."

Stouck, David. "The Modernity of Hazlitt's Familiar Essays." HAB, 21 (1970), 10-14.

> Compares Hazlitt's "On Going a Journey" to Wordsworth's "Tintern Abbey" to illustrate "the frustrations of social life and the quest for self-renewal in a pastoral setting."

Thorpe, Clarence D. "Keats and Hazlitt." PMLA, 62 (1947), 487-502.

> States that Keats's early admiration for many contemporary writers cooled, but Hazlitt was "among those he first admired, and was virtually the sole exception to a modified estimate."

Wardle, Ralph [M.]. "Hazlitt on 'The Beggar's Opera.'" SAQ, 70 (1971), 256-64.

> Discusses Hazlitt's review as a revelation of Hazlitt's own principles; "his insistence on the moral purpose of literature, the remedial nature of comedy, his independence, and his naive perversity."

Watson, George. "Lamb, Hazlitt, De Quincey." In his THE LITERARY CRITICS. New York: Barnes and Noble, 1964.

> "Hazlitt's language has at times a certain splendour, but a splendour flyblown and empty of significance, like a schoolboy in a

hurry with his homework anxious to impress a master with a taste for rhetoric."

Wellek, René. "William Hazlitt." In his A HISTORY OF MODERN CRITICISM, 1750-1950. Vol. 2. New Haven, Conn.: Yale University Press, 1965.

    Wellek's essay places Hazlitt in the earlier literary tradition.

Wilcox, Stewart. HAZLITT IN THE WORKSHOP. Baltimore: Johns Hopkins University Press, 1943.

    Wilcox reprints Hazlitt's manuscript of "The Fight" and discusses his method of revision.

Wright, William C. "Hazlitt, Ruskin, and Nineteenth-Century Art Criticism." JAAC, 32 (1974), 509-23.

    Explores "the relationship of Hazlitt's views of the fine arts to those held by Ruskin early in his career."

Zeitlin, Jacob. HAZLITT ON ENGLISH LITERATURE. New York: Oxford University Press, 1913.

    Zeitlin discusses Hazlitt as a literary critic by analyzing his style and his influence on others.

BIBLIOGRAPHIES

Houghton, Walter E., et al., eds. THE WELLESLEY INDEX TO VICTORIAN PERIODICALS. Projected 4 volumes. Toronto: University of Toronto Press, 1966-- .

    See volume 1, p. 934 for a listing of Hazlitt's contributions to various periodicals.

Ireland, Alexander. A LIST OF THE WRITINGS OF WILLIAM HAZLITT AND LEIGH HUNT. London: Smith, 1868; rpt. New York: Franklin, 1970.

Keynes, Geoffrey. BIBLIOGRAPHY OF HAZLITT. London: Nonesuch Press, 1931.

    The standard descriptive bibliography of Hazlitt's works.

Schneider, Elizabeth W. "William Hazlitt." THE ENGLISH ROMANTIC POETS AND ESSAYISTS: A REVIEW OF RESEARCH AND CRITICISM. Eds. C[arolyn] W. Houtchens and L[awrence] H. Houtchens. Rev. ed. New York: MLA, 1966.

    A valuable bibliographical essay that discusses critical studies published through 1965.

LEIGH HUNT (1784-1859)

PRINCIPAL PROSE WORKS

CRITICAL ESSAYS ON THE PERFORMERS OF THE LONDON THEATRES, 1807.

THE ROUND TABLE: A COLLECTION OF ESSAYS ON LITERATURE, MEN AND MANNERS. With William Hazlitt. 2 vols. 1817.

LORD BYRON AND SOME OF HIS CONTEMPORARIES; WITH RECOLLECTIONS OF THE AUTHOR'S LIFE, AND OF HIS VISIT TO ITALY. 2 vols. 1828.

IMAGINATION AND FANCY; WITH AN ESSAY IN ANSWER TO THE QUESTION WHAT IS POETRY?, 1844.

MEN, WOMEN AND BOOKS; A SELECTION OF SKETCHES, ESSAYS, AND CRITICAL MEMOIRS. 2 vols. 1847.

THE AUTOBIOGRAPHY OF LEIGH HUNT; WITH REMINISCENCES OF FRIENDS AND CONTEMPORARIES. 3 vols. 1850.

TABLE TALK: TO WHICH ARE ADDED IMAGINARY CONVERSATIONS OF POPE AND SWIFT, 1851.

THE RELIGION OF THE HEART: A MANUAL OF FAITH AND DUTY, 1853.

COLLECTED WORKS

THE AUTOBIOGRAPHY OF LEIGH HUNT. Ed. J.E. Morpurgo. London: Cresset Press, 1949.

>   The scholarly edition of this work. In his introduction Morpurgo discusses Hunt as a journalist.

LEIGH HUNT'S DRAMATIC CRITICISM, 1808-1831. Eds. C[arolyn] W. Houtchens and L[awrence] H. Houtchens. New York: Columbia University Press, 1962.

>An annotated edition that collects Hunt's reviews from the EXAMINER and the TATLER.

LEIGH HUNT'S LITERARY CRITICISM. Eds. C[arolyn] W. Houtchens and L[awrence] H. Houtchens. New York: Columbia University Press, 1956.

>Also includes an essay by C.D. Thorpe, "Hunt as Man of Letters."

LEIGH HUNT'S POLITICAL AND OCCASIONAL ESSAYS. Eds. C[arolyn] W. Houtchens and L[awrence] H. Houtchens. New York: Columbia University Press, 1962.

>This edition collects Hunt's articles from the EXAMINER. Also includes an essay by Carl Woodring, "Hunt as Political Essayist."

LEIGH HUNT'S PREFACES, MAINLY TO HIS PERIODICALS. Ed. R.B. Johnson. Chicago: Hill, 1927.

>Johnson's introduction discusses Hunt's status as a journalist.

LETTERS

Barnes, Warner. "Leigh Hunt's Letters in the Luther Brewer Collection: Plans for a New Edition." BI, 3 (1965), 10-14.

THE CORRESPONDENCE OF LEIGH HUNT. Ed. Thornton Hunt. 2 vols. London: Smith Elder, 1862.

>Compiled by his son, this collection does not include hundreds of letters that could have presented an unfavorable picture of Hunt. See Tatchall under "Critical Studies," below.

Sanders, Charles R. "The Correspondence and Friendship of Carlyle and Hunt: The Early Years." BJRL, 45 (1963), 439-85; BJRL, 46 (1963), 179-216.

BIOGRAPHIES

Blunden, Edmund. LEIGH HUNT: A BIOGRAPHY. London: Cobden-Sanderson, 1930; rpt. Hamden, Conn.: Archon Books, 1970.

>Published in America as LEIGH HUNT AND HIS CIRCLE, Blunden's biography is generally considered the best and only complete biography in English.

CRITICAL STUDIES

Blunden, Edmund. LEIGH HUNT'S EXAMINER EXAMINED. London: Cobden-Sanderson, 1928; rpt. Hamden, Conn.: Archon Books, 1967.

    Discusses the EXAMINER as a "journal of progress and vision." He analyzes the contents year-by-year, 1808-25. The second section of the book contains selections written by Leigh, Robert Hunt, and Charles Lamb.

Brack, O.M. "Lord Byron, Leigh Hunt, and THE LIBERAL: Some New Evidence." BI, 4 (1966), 36-38.

    Reprints an unpublished letter by Byron (1822) which characterizes Hunt as "a bore and a proser."

Cheney, David. "Leigh Hunt's Efforts to Encourage an Appreciation of Classical Music." KSJ, 17 (1968), 89-96.

    Discusses Hunt's "efforts to encourage the appreciation of classical music, both in the musical evening at Novello's and in the manuscript MUSICAL EVENINGS, as largely failures."

――――. "Leigh Hunt's 'Evening the First' of MUSICAL EVENINGS." KSMB, 18 (1967), 39-42.

    Presents new evidence to argue that "Evening the First" may have been completed.

David, James Atterbury. "Leigh Hunt and John Forster." RES, 19 (1968), 25-40.

    David discusses Forster's association with Hunt as both business manager and literary adviser.

Duff, Gerald. "Leigh Hunt's Criticism of the Novel." CLAJ, 13 (1969), 109-18.

    Focuses on "why Hunt wrote proportionately so little about a genre which he admittedly admired and enjoyed." Also explores "what characterized the novel for him and what critical criteria did he apply in a discussion of it."

Fenner, Theodore. LEIGH HUNT AND OPERA CRITICISM, 1808-1821. Lawrence: University of Kansas Press, 1972.

    Discusses early influences on Hunt's musical development, evaluates the extent of his talents, and estimates the importance of music in his social relationships. Concludes that Hunt was "profoundly aware of the relationship between music, politics, and society."

_____. "The Making of an Opera Critic: Leigh Hunt." MQ, 55 (1969), 439-63.

    Discusses Hunt's musical reviews published in the EXAMINER and concludes that "his prose is nowhere more vivid and energetic than in his reviews of operas."

Fielding, K.J. "Leigh Hunt and Skimpole: Another Remonstrance." DICKENSIAN, 64 (1968), 5-9.

    Fielding discusses Dickens' satire of Hunt as Harold Skimpole in BLEAK HOUSE.

Fisher, Walter. "Hunt as Friend and Critic of Keats: 1816-59." LHR, 1 (1962), 27-42.

    "Traces the relationship from Hunt's point of view" and concludes that "Hunt's affection for Keats never wavered from their meeting in 1816 until Hunt's death in 1859."

Fleece, Jeffrey. "Hunt's Shakespearian Criticism." In his ESSAYS IN HONOR OF WALTER C. CURRY. Nashville, Tenn.: Vanderbilt University Press, 1955.

    A useful analysis of Hunt's theatrical reviews.

Fogle, Stephen F. "Leigh Hunt and the End of Romantic Criticism." SOME BRITISH ROMANTICS. Eds. James V. Logan et al. Columbus: Ohio State University Press, 1966.

    Analyzes IMAGINATION AND FANCY (1844) as the conclusion of romantic criticism: "a summing-up and explanation, a charting of ground already won, rather than an attempt to explore the future."

_____. "Leigh Hunt, Thomas Powell, and the FLORENTINE TALES." KSJ, 14 (1965), 78-87.

    Fogle claims that internal evidence points to Hunt as author of the TALES.

Gates, Payson G. "Hunt's Review of Shelley's Posthumous Poems." PBSA, 42 (1948), 1-40.

    Reprints and discusses the text of Hunt's unpublished review.

Green, David B. "The Publication of Hunt's IMAGINATION AND FANCY." SB, 12 (1959), 227-30.

    Contradicts an early account of the circumstances of the publication by citing a heretofore unpublished letter from Hunt.

Kendall, Kenneth E. LEIGH HUNT'S REFLECTOR. New York: Humanities Press, 1971.

>   Examines "the nature of the period, 1810-1812," and Hunt's and Lamb's involvement with the journal. A final chapter discusses the REFLECTOR's historical and literary significance.

Landré, Louis. "Hunt: A Few Remarks About the Man." KSMB, 10 (1959), 1-6.

>   Written by the prominent French biographer of Hunt, this essay evaluates Hunt's strengths and weaknesses.

──────. "Hunt: His Contribution to English Romanticism." KSJ, 8 (1959), 133-44.

>   Concludes that Hunt was not "a mere follower" among the great romantics. He was influential through his criticism, poetry, essays, and "idealistic temperament."

Law, Marie H. THE ENGLISH FAMILIAR ESSAY IN THE EARLY NINETEENTH CENTURY. Philadelphia: University of Pennsylvania Press, 1934.

>   Law emphasizes Hunt's later work.

Leary, Lewis. "Leigh Hunt in Philadelphia." ROMANTIC AND VICTORIAN: STUDIES IN MEMORY OF WILLIAM H. MARSHALL. Eds. W. Paul Elledge and Richard L. Hoffman. Rutherford, N.J.: Fairleigh Dickinson University Press, 1971.

>   Discusses Hunt's attitudes toward the American piracies of his works.

Levy, Robert H. "On the Pleasures of Forensic Rhetoric: Brougham and Gibbs in REX versus JOHN AND LEIGH HUNT." RMS, 15 (1971), 85-102.

>   Discusses the rhetoric used during the Hunts' trial.

McCartney, Hunter. "English Writer Leigh Hunt: Victim of Journalistic McCarthyism." JQ, 50 (1973), 92-96.

>   Makes comparisons between Hunt's trial for libel and the McCarthy era in the 1950s.

Marshall, William. BYRON, SHELLEY, HUNT, AND THE LIBERAL. Philadelphia: University of Pennsylvania Press, 1960.

>   A valuable discussion of this literary partnership.

Mills, Howard. PEACOCK: HIS CIRCLE AND HIS AGE. London: Cambridge University Press, 1969.

Mills contrasts Peacock with several other literary contemporaries, among them Hunt.

Misenheimer, James B. "Leigh Hunt: A 'Great Introducer' in English Romanticism." YES, 1 (1971), 135-40.

Concludes that Hunt "was hardly a mere spectator when the literature of England was taking a new course; he himself was helping to shape that course."

Moore, Doris L. "Byron, Hunt and the Shelleys: New Light on Certain Old Scandals." KSMB, 10 (1959), 20-29.

Discusses Hunt's bitter attack on Byron, which was an attempt to increase Shelley's reputation at the expense of Byron's.

Nowell-Smith, Simon. "Leigh Hunt as Bellman." TLS, 2 April 1970, p. 367.

Also see TLS, 2 April 1970, p. 430.

Pickering, Leslie P. LORD BYRON, LEIGH HUNT, AND THE LIBERAL. New York: Haskell, 1966.

Another discussion of this shortlived journalistic venture.

Roberts, Michael. "Hunt's Place in the Reform Movement, 1808-1810." RES, 11 (1935), 58-65.

Discusses Hunt's editorship of the EXAMINER and his involvement in the political disputes between Tories and Whigs: "the brilliant humanity of Hunt is united to a political judgment."

Saunders, Beatrice. PORTRAITS OF GENIUS. London: Murray, 1959.

Includes an essay on Hunt.

Severn, Derek. "Leigh Hunt versus the Tories and the Prince Regent." CORNHILL, 1066 (1970-71), 288-312.

Gives a detailed account of the muckraking done by the EXAMINER in 1808-12.

Stout, George D. "Leigh Hunt on Wordsworth and Coleridge." KSJ, 6 (1957), 59-73.

"The graph of Hunt's reactions to Coleridge runs an almost exactly contrary course to that of his reactions to Wordsworth." In Hunt's opinion, Coleridge rose to preeminance and remained there, while Wordsworth rose and then declined.

Leigh Hunt

_____. "Leigh Hunt's Shakespeare: A 'Romantic' Concept." In his STUDIES IN MEMORY OF FRANK M. WEBSTER. St. Louis, Mo.: Washington University Press, 1951.

> Stout explains that the type and arrangement of ideas that we think are characteristically "Romantic" are prevalent in Hunt's writings on Shakespeare.

_____. THE POLITICAL HISTORY OF HUNT'S EXAMINER." St. Louis, Mo.: Washington University Press, 1949.

> Discusses the EXAMINER as "the most influential Radical journal" and examines "the political side of the journal under Hunt's editorship."

Tatchall, Molly. "Thornton Hunt." KSMB, 20 (1969), 13-20.

> A discussion of Hunt's son, editor of his correspondence.

Watson, Melvin R. "The SPECTATOR Tradition and the Development of the Familiar Essay." ELH, 13 (1946), 189-215.

> Includes a discussion of Hunt as editor of the EXAMINER and the REFLECTOR. Concludes that Hunt "remained loyal to Addison and Steele throughout his life."

Welch, Jack. "The Leigh Hunt-William Moxon Dispute of 1836." WVUPP, 18 (1971), 30-41.

> Reprints a series of letters between Hunt and Moxon, his solicitor, in which Hunt "was literally forced to bargain for his own freedom" because of overdue debts.

Wellek, René. "Leigh Hunt." In his A HISTORY OF MODERN CRITICISM, 1750-1950. Vol. 2. New Haven, Conn.: Yale University Press, 1965.

> "Hunt has historical importance as a propagandist of imaginative 'pure' poetry, as a mediator of older Italian literature, as an early champion of Keats and Shelley. But he lacks theoretical power, as his loose derivative theory of the imagination shows."

BIBLIOGRAPHIES

Brewer, Luther A. MY LEIGH HUNT LIBRARY: THE FIRST EDITIONS. Cedar Rapids, Iowa: Private circulation, 1932.

> Includes detailed discussions of Hunt's first editions.

Houtchens, C[arolyn] W., and L[awrence] H. Houtchens. "Leigh Hunt." In their THE ENGLISH ROMANTIC POETS AND ESSAYISTS. Rev. ed. New York: MLA, 1966.

A valuable bibliographical essay which discusses critical studies published before 1965.

Ireland, Alexander. A LIST OF THE WRITINGS OF WILLIAM HAZLITT AND LEIGH HUNT. London: Smith, 1868; rpt. New York: Franklin, 1970.

Besides providing a bibliography, this work also contains a section entitled "Opinions of Leigh Hunt's Character, Genius, and Writing," written by his contemporaries.

Mitchell, Alexander. "A Bibliography of the Writings of Leigh Hunt." In his BIBLIOGRAPHIES OF MODERN AUTHORS. 3rd series. London: Bookman's Journal, 1931.

CHARLES LAMB (1775-1834)

PRINCIPAL PROSE WORKS

ELIA: ESSAYS WHICH HAVE APPEARED UNDER THAT SIGNATURE IN THE LONDON MAGAZINE, 1823.

THE LAST ESSAYS OF ELIA: BEING A SEQUEL TO ESSAYS PUBLISHED UNDER THAT NAME, 1833.

RECOLLECTIONS OF CHRIST'S HOSPITAL, 1835.

ELIANA: BEING THE HITHERTO UNCOLLECTED WRITINGS. Ed. J.E. Babson, 1864.

COLLECTED WORKS

LAMB: PROSE AND POETRY. Ed. G.S. Gordon. Oxford: Clarendon Press, 1921.

LAMB'S CRITICISM: A SELECTION. Ed. E.M.W. Tillyard. Cambridge: At the University Press, 1923.

THE WORKS IN PROSE AND VERSE OF CHARLES AND MARY LAMB. Ed. T. Hutchinson. 2 vols. Oxford: Clarendon Press, 1908.

THE WORKS OF CHARLES AND MARY LAMB. Ed. E[dward] V. Lucas. 7 vols. London: Methuen, 1903-05.
    The standard edition. Volumes 6 and 7 contain the letters.

THE WORKS OF CHARLES LAMB. Ed. William McDonald. 12 vols. London: Dent, 1903-04.

LETTERS

Barnett, George L. "Corrections in the Text of Lamb's Letters." HLQ, 18 (1955), 147-58.

>Barnett attempts to make all the most important corrections to Lucas' edition of LETTERS, below.

_____. "A Critical Analysis of the Lucas Edition of Lamb's Letters." MLQ, 9 (1948), 303-14.

>The article criticizes the Lucas text: "it cannot be the final text for scholars who demand accuracy in every detail."

Green, David B. "Three New Letters of Charles Lamb." HLQ, 27 (1963), 83-86.

>Discusses Lamb's correspondence with Basil Montagu.

THE LETTERS OF CHARLES AND MARY ANN LAMB. Ed. Edwin W. Marrs, Jr. Projected 6 vols. Ithaca, N.Y.: Cornell University Press, 1975-- .

>The latest collection of letters, which will supersede the earlier editions when the projected six volumes (two have been published so far) are complete. There will be 1,150 letters in all. The 70-page introduction in volume 1 is particularly valuable for its discussion of the publishing history of Lamb's letters.

THE LETTERS OF CHARLES LAMB. Ed. Guy Pocock. 2 vols. New York: Dutton, 1946.

>Pocock's collection is a revision of Lucas' edition, below, and contains additional letters.

THE LETTERS OF CHARLES LAMB, TO WHICH ARE ADDED THOSE OF HIS SISTER, MARY LAMB. Ed. E[dward] V. Lucas. 3 vols. New Haven, Conn.: Yale University Press, 1935.

>Generally considered the standard edition, although it does have errors. See Barnett and other commentators in this section.

Schneider, Duane [B.]. "The Lucas Edition of Lamb's Letters: Corrections and Notes." N&Q 21 (1974), 171-74.

>Corrects Lucas' edition of the LETTERS, above, by examining those in the British Museum and the Bodleian Library.

BIOGRAPHIES

Blunden, Edmund. CHARLES LAMB. London: Longmans, Green, 1954; rev. ed. 1964.

A brief biographical sketch and estimate of the works. Discusses
Lamb's varied talents, early influences, and the prose: "elaborate
in design where the theme suggests a specially imaginative movement."

⎯⎯⎯⎯⎯. CHARLES LAMB AND HIS CONTEMPORARIES. Cambridge: At the University Press, 1933.

Includes chapters on Lamb's childhood, his relationship with his
sister, his ELIA essays, and his literary reputation in his own age.

Blunden, Edward, ed. CHARLES LAMB: HIS LIFE RECORDED BY HIS CONTEMPORARIES. London: Hogarth Press, 1934.

Blunden has compiled impressions of Lamb under such headings as
"Elia and His Admirers." "The Superannuated Man," and "Prose
Elegies."

Howe, Will. CHARLES LAMB AND HIS FRIENDS. Indianapolis: Bobbs-Merrill, 1964.

Howe emphasizes Lamb's traits of character as well as his personal
relationships.

Jerrold, Walter. CHARLES LAMB. London: Bell, 1905.

A useful introduction to Lamb's life.

Lucas, Edward V. THE LIFE OF LAMB. 2 vols. London: Methuen, 1905.

Still considered the standard biography, although it is at present
out of print.

CRITICAL STUDIES

Ades, J.I. "Charles Lamb: Romantic Criticism and the Aesthetics of Sympathy." DELTA EPSILON SIGMA BULLETIN, 6 (1961), 106-14.

Contends that the lack of scholarly attention to Lamb's criticism
is caused by its "appreciativeness, personal response, and brevity,"
all of which make Lamb an "amateur critic."

⎯⎯⎯⎯⎯. "Charles Lamb, Shakespeare, and Early Nineteenth-Century Theatre." PMLA, 85 (1970), 514-26.

Argues for the seriousness of Lamb's Shakespearean criticism which,
like Coleridge's, shared the "standard Romantic opposition to the
neo-classic critical view as to the importance of the unities."

Charles Lamb

Bald, R.C. "Lamb and the Elizabethans." STUDIES IN HONOR OF A.H.R. FAIRCHILD. Ed. Charles Prouty. Columbia: University of Missouri Press, 1946.

>Bald emphasizes Lamb's shortcomings as a critic.

Barnet, Sylvan. "Charles Lamb and the Tragic Malvolio." PQ, 33 (1954), 178-88.

>Examines Lamb's estimate of Robert Bensley as Malvolio because "an understanding of Lamb's theory of acting is inextricably related to his theory of the nature of drama."

_____. "Lamb's Contributions to the Theory of Dramatic Illusion." PMLA, 69 (1954) 1150-59.

>Maintains that Lamb's comments on dramatic illusion, although brief and often contradictory, are "subtle, incisive, and worthy of attention."

Barnett, George L. CHARLES LAMB: THE EVOLUTION OF ELIA. Bloomington: Indiana University Press, 1964.

>Explores "the development of Lamb's career as a writer and of his essays in particular" by focusing on the "factors in his early life which informed and directed the literary talents of the subsequent Elia." Also asks, "was Lamb aware of what his predecessors in the essay had done and of his position in the tradition?"

_____. "The Pronunciation of Elia." SIR, 5 (1965), 51-55.

>Concludes that "Lamb himself pronounced the name with the short e, not with the a accented as Lucas transcribed it."

Brier, Peter. "Dramatic Characterization in the Essays of Charles Lamb." CORANTO, 8 (1973), 3-24: 9 (1973), 17-31.

>This two-part article discusses Lamb's use of character: "If his characterization of others is 'dramatic,' Lamb's own persona, Elia, is no exception. Elia, more successfully than any of the other characters in the essays, embodies the 'antithetical manner' --the ability to alternate freely between feeling and wit, compassion and detachment."

Conarroe, Joel O. "Melville's BARTLEBY and Charles Lamb." SSF, 5 (1968), 113-18.

>Asserts that "both in tone and in structure BARTLEBY is patterned on the familiar essay as written by Lamb."

Davies, Hugh S. "Charles Lamb and the Romantic Style." CLB, 5 (1974), 153-57.

> Analyzes Lamb's prose style and concludes that it is characterized by "moods of reverie, of memory" and "so far as its intonations and main structure go, it is based solidly on the English of his own day."

Fukuda, Tsutomu. A STUDY OF LAMB'S ESSAYS OF ELIA. Tokyo: Hokuseido, 1964.

> The first part presents an analysis of Lamb's prose style.

Haven, Richard. "The Romantic Art of Lamb." BLH, 30 (1963), 137-46.

> Haven discusses "Old China" and "The Old Benchers" as examples of romantic sensibility.

Henderson, Arnold. "Some Constants of Charles Lamb's Criticism." SIR, 7 (1968), 104-16.

> Attempts to "extract some constants from the mass of Lamb's critical fragments and suggest where Lamb is at one with his friends [particularly Coleridge]." Also "places Lamb's essays on drama in the context of his principles and methods."

Houghton, Walter E. "Lamb's Criticism of Restoration Comedy." ELH, 10 (1943), 61-72.

> Houghton argues that Lamb's critical pronouncements on this comedy are not as eccentric as they are usually thought to be.

Iseman, Joseph S. A PERFECT SYMPATHY: CHARLES LAMB AND SIR THOMAS BROWNE. Cambridge, Mass.: Harvard University Press, 1937.

Jessup, Bertram. "The Mind of Elia." JHI, 15 (1954), 246-59.

> Points out the similarities between Lamb and his creation, Elia, and concludes that Elia is "a person--which is generally recognized; and he has a mind, acute, consistent, and remarkably whole."

Johnson, Edith. LAMB ALWAYS ELIA. London: Methuen, 1935.

> Johnson disagrees with Morley's view of Lamb, below. She claims that Lamb's evolution as an essayist was a regular, understandable process.

Johnson, Robert V. "Aesthetic Traits in Charles Lamb." SOR, 3 (1968), 151-58.

> Johnson discusses Pater's essay on Lamb (in APPRECIATIONS) as

reflecting "a genuine affinity between Lamb and Victorian aestheticism."

Kelly, Michael. "Claggart's 'Equivocal Words' and Lamb's 'Popular Fallacies.'" SSF, 9 (1972), 183-86.

Concludes that Melville's phrase in BILLY BUDD was taken from Lamb's essay (1833) and is a "means of exploring the ambiguities of appearances."

Law, Marie H. THE ENGLISH FAMILIAR ESSAY IN THE EARLY NINETEENTH CENTURY. Philadelphia: University of Pennsylvania Press, 1934.

Law emphasizes the relation between Lamb's letters and his essays.

Lieb, Michael. "The Aesthetics of Nostalgia: The Three Worlds of Lamb's 'Dream Children.'" XUS, 7 (1968), 17-26.

Analyzes the essay's tone, which is "made complex and highly ironic by the dramatic revelation of three worlds that interact and contrast with each other as the essay develops."

Morley, F.V. LAMB BEFORE ELIA. London: Cape, 1932.

Morley draws a distinction between Lamb before and after he wrote the ELIA ESSAYS. He also emphasizes the escapism in Lamb's works. Also see Johnson, Edith, above.

Mulcahy, David J. "Charles Lamb: The Antithetical Manner and the Two Planes." SEL, 3 (1963), 517-42.

Characterizes the "antithetical manner" as Lamb's method of character-sketching, as well as his approach to art and life in general: "thesis and antithesis, each presenting the reader with 'no full front,' but at most 'a feature or sideface' of Truth."

Murti, K.V.S. "Charles Lamb's 'Dream-Children': A Syntactic Approach to Sublimation." RRL, 15 (1970), 31-36.

Studies the essay sentence-by-sentence for length, variety, parentheses, and subject-verb sequence in order to "project a scientific explanation."

Nabholtz, John R. "Drama and Rhetoric in Lamb's Essays of the Imagination." SEL, 12 (1972), 683-703.

Nethery, Wallace. CHARLES LAMB IN AMERICA TO 1848. Worcester, Mass.: A.J. St. Onge, 1963.

_____. ELIANA AMERICANA: CHARLES LAMB IN THE UNITED STATES, 1849-1866. Los Angeles: Plantin Press, 1971.

>Both of Nethery's books discuss Lamb's reputation and reception in America.

Orage, A.R. "The Danger of the Whimsical." SELECTED ESSAYS AND CRITICAL WRITINGS. Eds. [Sir] Herbert Read and Denis Saurat. London: Nott, 1935.

>A critique of Lamb's essays.

Pater, Walter. "Charles Lamb." In his APPRECIATIONS. London: Macmillan, 1889.

>Generally considered one of the most important essays on Lamb. Pater praises him for his ability to see life as an organic whole.

Patterson, Charles I. "Lamb's Insight Into the Nature of the Novel." PMLA, 67 (1952), 375-82.

>Concludes that Lamb read deeply in the eighteenth-century novelists, Fielding, Smollet, Defoe, and Goldsmith: "He exhibited the same genial attitude toward books as toward people; he never expected too much of either, and was therefore seldom disappointed."

Randel, Fred V. "Eating and Drinking in Lamb's ELIA ESSAYS." ELH, 37 (1970), 57-76.

>Concludes that Lamb's memories of his mother surface in his utilization of eating and drinking imagery.

_____. THE WORLD OF ELIA. Port Washington, N.Y.: Kennikat Press, 1975.

>Relies on Lamb's letters and uses modern critical techniques to discuss Lamb's psychological characteristics, his oral cravings, and his humor.

Reed, Mark. "Blake, Wordsworth, Lamb, Etc.: Further Information from Henry Crabb Robinson." BN, 3 (1970), 76-84.

>Discusses Lamb's characterization of Blake as a "mad Wordsworth."

Reiman, Donald H. "Thematic Unity in Lamb's Familiar Essays." JEGP, 64 (1965), 470-78.

>Analyzes three essays in order "to show that Lamb strove for artistic excellence and, because his judgment was equal to his genius, he succeeded in molding disparate and apparently trivial subjects and ideas into artistic unities of thematic significance."

Schwartz, Lewis M. "A New Review of Coleridge's CHRISTABEL." SIR, 9 (1970), 114-24.

> Schwartz attempts to identify Lamb as the reviewer in THE TIMES, 20 May 1816, and in the COURIER, 4 June 1816.

Scoggins, James. "Images of Eden in the ESSAYS OF ELIA." JEGP, 71 (1972), 198-210.

> Asserts that the "one root theme" in the essays is that of "modern Adam living in a time of great crisis, uncertain of his beliefs and values, and blessed and cursed by the same new freedom."

Tillotson, Geoffrey. "The Historical Importance of Certain ESSAYS OF ELIA." SOME BRITISH ROMANTICS. Eds. James V. Logan et al. Columbus: Ohio State University Press, 1966.

> Discusses Lamb's essays as "irremovable masterpieces in their own right," for they "represent life as it is."

Watson, George. "Lamb, Hazlitt, De Quincey." In his THE LITERARY CRITICS. New York: Barnes and Noble, 1964.

> Considers Lamb as "a sound Johnsonian critic, partly romanticized by his reverence for Coleridge."

Watson, Melvin R. "The SPECTATOR Tradition and the Development of the Familiar Essay." ELH, 13 (1946), 189-215.

> Discusses Lamb's contributions to the REFLECTOR as "Lamb at his best--chatty, vivid, intimate. The early essays have many virtues, but they are most important for showing Lamb as an artist in transition."

Webb, Alice. "Charles Lamb's Use of the Character." SOQ, 1 (1963), 273-84.

> Focuses on the characters in Lamb's familiar essays and concludes that character writing as a literary movement should be extended through Lamb.

Whalley, George. "Coleridge's Debt to Lamb." E&S, 11 (1958), 68-85.

> Whalley claims that Coleridge reached his peak as a poet after a year of correspondence with Lamb.

Willey, Basil. "Charles Lamb and Coleridge." CLB, 1 (1973), 1-9.

> Outlines the relationship between the two writers by emphasizing their personal interchanges and mutual influence.

BIBLIOGRAPHIES

Barnett, George L., and Stuart M. Tave. "Charles Lamb." THE ENGLISH ROMANTIC POETS AND ESSAYISTS. Eds. C[arolyn] W. Houtchens and L[awrence] H. Houtchens. Rev. ed. New York: MLA, 1966.

> A valuable bibliographical essay that discusses critical studies published before 1965.

Braendel, Doris. "The Lamb Collection at the Rosenbach Foundation." WC, 2 (1970), 80-91.

Brier, Peter. "Charles Lamb in the Huntington Library (1796-1833)." WC, 3 (1972), 123-46.

> A checklist.

Thomson, Joseph C. A BIBLIOGRAPHY OF THE WRITINGS OF CHARLES AND MARY LAMB. Hull: Tutin, 1908.

> A fully annotated bibliography that discusses all the Lambs's writings.

WALTER SAVAGE LANDOR (1775-1864)

PRINCIPAL PROSE WORKS

IMAGINARY CONVERSATIONS OF LITERARY MEN AND STATESMEN. 3 vols. 1824-28. 2nd series. 2 vols. 1829.

THE LETTERS OF A CONSERVATIVE: IN WHICH ARE SHOWN THE ONLY MEANS OF SAVING WHAT IS LEFT OF THE ENGLISH CHURCH, 1836.

THE HELLENICS OF WALTER SAVAGE LANDOR, 1847.

IMAGINARY CONVERSATIONS OF GREEKS AND ROMANS, 1853.

THE LAST FRUIT OFF AN OLD TREE, 1853.

COLLECTED WORKS

THE COMPLETE WORKS OF WALTER SAVAGE LANDOR: PROSE. Ed. T.E[arle] Welby. 12 vols. London: Chapman and Hall, 1927-31.

>   The only complete edition of the prose; it has been criticized, however, for its lack of index and annotations.

THE WORKS AND LIFE OF LANDOR. Ed. John Forster. 8 vols. London: Chapman and Hall, 1876.

>   Volume 1 contains the LIFE.

LETTERS

THE LETTERS OF WALTER SAVAGE LANDOR PRIVATE AND PUBLIC. Ed. S.

Wheeler. London: Duckworth, 1899.

    Also contains Landor's EXAMINER articles.

Mariani, John F. "The Letters of Walter Savage Landor to Marguerite Countess of Blessington." Ph.D. dissertation, Columbia University, 1974. DAI, 34, 3414A.

Rouff, A. LaVonne. "Landor's Letters to His Family: 1802-1825." BJRL, 52 (1971), 465-500.

    Rouff discusses and reprints sixteen new letters.

_____. "Landor's Letters to the Reverend William Brick: Landor's Latin Poetry." BJRL, 51 (1968), 200-261.

Super, Robert H. "Landor's Letters to Wordsworth and Coleridge." MP, 55 (1957), 73-83.

    Analyzes Landor's attitude toward Wordsworth by discussing the letters between the two: "the influence of the correspondence upon Landor was greater than upon Wordsworth; the latter's admiration for Landor's English poetry unquestionably was responsible for Landor's return to that form of writing."

BIOGRAPHIES

Colvin, Sidney. LANDOR. London: Harper, 1881.

    Although written almost a century ago, this study is still considered a valuable critical biography.

Elwin, Malcolm. SAVAGE LANDOR. New York: Macmillan, 1941.

    Elwin revised this biography of Landor and republished it as LANDOR: A REPLEVIN (London: MacDonald, 1958). Elwin declares that his biography challenges Super's, below, which he charges with "misrepresentation." Also see Leavis under "Critical Studies," below.

Evans, Edward W. LANDOR: A BIOGRAPHY. New York: Putnam's, 1892; rpt. Port Washington, N.Y.: Kennikat Press, 1970.

    An early study on "Landor as a Man of Letters," with chapters on the poetry and prose. Concludes with negative pronouncements on Landor's "scientific, philosophical, and religious conceptions, his criticism and politics."

Forster, John. LANDOR: A BIOGRAPHY. 2 vols. London: Boston, Fields,

Osgood, 1869; rpt. St. Clair Shores, Mich.: Scholarly Press, 1969.

> Forster was Landor's executor and friend. This work also contains many of Landor's letters to his family and to Southey.

Super, Robert H. WALTER SAVAGE LANDOR: A BIOGRAPHY. New York: New York University Press, 1954.

> The definitive biography. See Elwin, above.

Van Thal, Herbert, ed. LANDOR: A BIOGRAPHICAL ANTHOLOGY. London: Allen and Unwin, 1973.

> Gives "an outline of Landor's life and works," including a bibliography of his works. Also contains an informative introduction by Elwin.

CRITICAL STUDIES

Becker, George J. "Landor's Political Purpose." SP, 35 (1938), 446-55.

> Becker claims that the crucial concern in all of Landor's works is politics.

Chambers, Edmund K. "Some Notes on Landor." RES, 20 (1944), 145-54.

> Chambers discusses Landor's youth in Wales and western England.

Dilworth, Ernest. WALTER SAVAGE LANDOR. New York: Twayne, 1971.

> Surveys Landor's works, including two chapters on his prose. The final chapter, "Style and Substance," concludes that "there is an inner rightness as if the ear were an instant judge, though the outlying form may lack proportion." Includes an annotated bibliography.

Elkin, Felice. LANDOR'S STUDIES OF ITALIAN LIFE AND LITERATURE. Philadelphia: University of Pennsylvania Press, 1934.

> Focuses on estimating "the importance of Italy in Landor's development and achievement." Also "compares his contribution to our knowledge of Italy with that of other English men of letters."

Gossman, Anne. "Landor and the 'Higher Fountains.'" CJ, 50 (1955), 303-07.

> A valuable study of Landor's HELLENICS--his epigrams on love, fame, and death.

Hamilton, G. Rostrevor. WALTER SAVAGE LANDOR. London: Longmans, Green, 1960.

A brief introduction to Landor's life and works, including an assessment of his prose: "whether as critic or essayist, Landor devoted meticulous attention to detail, the shape and sound of a sentence or a line."

Henderson, W.B.D. SWINBURNE AND LANDOR. London: Macmillan, 1918.

Discusses Landor's great influence on Swinburne.

Leavis, Frank R. "Landor and the Seasoned Epicure." SCRUTINY, 11 (1942), 148-50.

In this review of Elwin's biography, above, Leavis states, "it seems worse than pointless to keep up the pretense that Landor is, or should be, [a] current classic."

Mercier, Vivian. "The Future of Landor Criticism." SOME BRITISH ROMANTICS. Eds. James V. Logan et al. Columbus: Ohio State University Press, 1966.

Discusses Landor's neglect by the critics and suggests "a number of critical approaches that may still prove fruitful."

Perrine, Laurence. "Landor and Immortality." VP, 2 (1964), 50-57.

Discusses Landor's understanding of the soul's immortality.

Prasher, A. LaVonne. "The Censorship of Landor's IMAGINARY CONVERSATIONS." BJRL, 49 (1967), 427-63.

Recounts, by narration and letters, the attempts made by Landor's publisher to prune pages from his IMAGINARY CONVERSATIONS.

Proudfit, Charles L. "Landor's Hobbyhorse: A Study in Romantic Orthography." SIR, 7 (1968), 207-17.

Discusses the eccentricities of Landor's spelling.

Robinson, David M. "Landor's Knowledge of the Classics." CJ, 51 (1955), 25-26.

Discusses Landor's critical understanding of Sappho, Aeschylus, and Pindar.

Rouff, A. LaVonne. "The Publication of Landor's IMAGINARY CONVERSATIONS: 1825-38." JEGP, 72 (1973), 32-47.

Discusses and reprints several letters between Landor and the publishers of IMAGINARY CONVERSATIONS.

———. "Walter Savage Landor's Criticism of Horace: The Odes and Epodes." ARION, 9 (1970), 189-204.

>Discusses Landor's ambivalent response to Horace and concludes that Landor "never believed that Horace was equal to his beloved Catullus."

Selincourt, Ernest de. "Landor's Prose." In his WORDSWORTHIAN AND OTHER STUDIES. Oxford: Clarendon Press, 1947.

>A valuable discussion of IMAGINARY CONVERSATIONS.

Super, Robert H. "A Grain of Truth about Wordsworth and Browning, Landor and Swinburne." MLN, 67 (1952), 419-21.

>Discusses Gosse's portrait of the meeting between Landor and Swinburne, contained in Gosse's 1925 biography of Swinburne.

———. "Landor and the 'Satanic School.'" SP, 42 (1945), 793-810.

>"Landor, guided largely by the reports of his friends, plunged into the fray, only to find himself uncomfortably on the wrong side for his temperament and sympathies."

Williams, Stanley [T.]. "Landor and His Contemporaries." In his STUDIES IN VICTORIAN LITERATURE. New York: Dutton, 1923.

>Williams claims that it was Landor's uncompromising ideals that were most influential in his own time.

———. "Landor as a Critic of Literature." PMLA, 38 (1923), 906-28.

>After analyzing IMAGINARY CONVERSATIONS, Williams concludes that Landor was a critic with "no method or body of criteria."

BIBLIOGRAPHIES

Proudfit, Charles [L.]. "More Unrecorded Periodical Contributions of Walter Savage Landor." N&Q, 18 (1971), 90-91.

>Proudfit identifies fourteen letters and articles Landor published in newspapers in 1848-56.

Super, Robert H. THE PUBLICATION OF LANDOR'S WORKS. London: Bibliographical Society, 1954.

>Intended as a supplement to the Wise and Wheeler bibliography, below.

———. "Walter Savage Landor." THE ENGLISH POETS AND ESSAYISTS. Eds. C[arolyn] W. Houtchens and L[awrence] H. Houtchens. Rev. ed. New York: MLA, 1966.

    A valuable bibliographical essay that discusses critical studies published before 1965.

Wise, Thomas J. A LANDOR LIBRARY. London: Private circulation, 1928.

Wise, Thomas J., and Stephen Wheeler. A BIBLIOGRAPHY OF THE WRITINGS IN PROSE AND VERSE OF WALTER SAVAGE LANDOR. London: Blades, East, & Blades, 1919; rpt. Folkestone, Engl.: Dawson's, 1971.

    Lists Landor's works with full descriptions. A valuable resource.
    Also see Super, above.

JOHN STUART MILL (1806-73)

PRINCIPAL PROSE WORKS

A SYSTEM OF LOGIC, RATIOCINATIVE AND INDUCTIVE, 1843.

PRINCIPLES OF POLITICAL ECONOMY. 2 vols. 1848.

THOUGHTS ON PARLIAMENTARY REFORM, 1859.

ON LIBERTY, 1859.

CONSIDERATIONS ON REPRESENTATIVE GOVERNMENT, 1861.

UTILITARIANISM, 1863.

EXAMINATION OF SIR WILLIAM HAMILTON'S PHILOSOPHY, 1865.

AUGUSTE COMTE AND POSITIVISM, 1865.

ON THE SUBJECTION OF WOMEN, 1869.

AUTOBIOGRAPHY, 1873.

THREE ESSAYS ON RELIGION, 1874.

COLLECTED WORKS

THE COLLECTED WORKS OF JOHN STUART MILL. Eds. F.E.L. Priestley, J[ohn] M. Robson et al. Projected 25 vols. Toronto: University of Toronto Press, 1963-- .

   The standard edition. Of 25 volumes, 11 have appeared so far:

THE EARLIER LETTERS, 2 vols., 1963; PRINCIPLES OF POLITICAL ECONOMY, 2 vols., 1965; ESSAYS ON ECONOMICS AND SOCIETY, 2 vols., 1967; ESSAYS ON ETHICS, RELIGION, AND SOCIETY, 1969; LATER LETTERS, 4 vols., 1972. The edition should be completed by 1980. See Robson under "Critical Studies," below.

THE ESSENTIAL WORKS OF JOHN STUART MILL. Ed. Max Lerner. New York: Bantam, 1961.

JOHN STUART MILL: LITERARY ESSAYS. Ed. Edward Alexander. Indianapolis: Bobbs-Merrill, 1967.

JOHN STUART MILL AND HARRIET TAYLOR MILL: ESSAYS ON SEX EQUALITY. Ed. Alice S. Rossi. Chicago: University of Chicago Press, 1970.

> Rossi's collection includes sections by Mill and his wife on marriage and divorce, as well as Harriet Taylor's essay, "The Enfranchisement of Women."

THE LITERARY CRITICISM OF JOHN STUART MILL. Ed. F.P. Sharpless. New York: Humanities Press; The Hague: Mouton, 1967.

MILL'S ESSAYS ON LITERATURE AND SOCIETY. Ed. Jerome Schneewind. New York: Collier, 1965.

SELECTED WRITINGS OF JOHN STUART MILL. Ed. Maurice Cowling. New York: New American Library, 1968.

LETTERS

THE EARLIER LETTERS OF JOHN STUART MILL. Eds. Frederick A. von Hayek and Francis [E.] Mineka. 2 vols. Toronto: University of Toronto Press, 1963.

> These two volumes are numbered 12 and 13 in the COLLECTED WORKS, above.

THE LATER LETTERS OF JOHN STUART MILL. Eds. Francis [E.] Mineka and Dwight N. Lindley. 4 vols. Toronto: University of Toronto Press, 1972.

> These four volumes are numbered 14-17 in the COLLECTED WORKS, above.

BIOGRAPHIES

Borchard, Ruth. JOHN STUART MILL, THE MAN. London: Watts, 1957.

> Borchard's biography supplements Packe's, below.

John Stuart Mill

Cranston, Maurice. JOHN STUART MILL. London: Longmans, Green, 1958.

    A useful introduction to Mill's life and works.

Hayek, Frederick A. von, ed. JOHN STUART MILL AND HARRIET TAYLOR: THEIR FRIENDSHIP AND SUBSEQUENT MARRIAGE. London: Routledge and Kegan Paul, 1951.

    This work has been very important in the debate over Mill's relationship with his wife. See Pappe, p. 198.

Packe, Michael St. J. THE LIFE OF JOHN STUART MILL. New York: Macmillan, 1954.

    The standard biography. Packe stresses Mill's dependence on his wife's guidance. Also see Borchard, above, and Pappe, p. 198.

CRITICAL STUDIES

Albee, Ernest. A HISTORY OF ENGLISH UTILITARIANISM. London: Allen and Unwin, 1901; rpt. New York: Macmillan, 1957.

    Albee devotes three chapters to the importance of Mill.

Alexander, Edward. "Disinterested Virtue: Dickens and Mill in Agreement." DICKENSIAN, 65 (1969), 163-70.

    The anti-utilitarian views of Dickens and the utilitarian philosophy of Mill have a common ground in their respective critiques of Bentham.

_____. "John Stuart Mill on Dogmaticism, 'Liberticide,' and Revolution." VN, 37 (1970), 12-18.

    Defends Mill as true to his ideals. According to Alexander, Mill fought the partisans of dogmatism in religion and politics even when sympathetic to their principles.

_____. MATTHEW ARNOLD AND JOHN STUART MILL. New York: Columbia University Press; London: Routledge and Kegan Paul, 1965.

    The definitive study of their relationship and their reciprocal influence.

_____. "Mill's Marginal Notes on Carlyle's 'Hudson's Statue.'" ELN, 7 (1969), 120-23.

    Alexander discusses Mill's irritation with Carlyle's essay.

_____. "Mill's Theory of Culture: The Wedding of Literature and Democracy." UTQ, 35 (1965), 75-88.

> Article attempts to relate Mill's literary attitudes to his views on other subjects.

Annan, Noel. "John Stuart Mill." THE ENGLISH MIND. Ed. H[ugh] S. Davies. Cambridge: At the University Press, 1964.

> "Mill adorns a famous tradition of thought and he cannot be seen in perspective until we stop regarding him as the man who tried and failed to spiritualize utilitarianism."

Anschutz, Richard. THE PHILOSOPHY OF JOHN STUART MILL. Oxford: Clarendon Press, 1953.

> Discerns "two strains in Mill. The sensitive temperament and the systematic scientist." Includes chapters on Mill's theories of syllogism, induction, mathematics, and democracy.

August, Eugene R. "Mill as Sage: The Essay on Bentham." PMLA, 89 (1974), 142-53.

> "Mill employed many of the techniques of the literary artist" in order to capture Bentham's importance to his age.

_____. "Mill's AUTOBIOGRAPHY as Philosophic COMMEDIA." VP, 11 (1973), 143-62.

> Defends Mill against charges of literary indistinction. The essay on Bentham employs metaphor, imagery, and effective allusions.

Axelrod, Rise B. "Argument and Strategy in Mill's THE SUBJECTION OF WOMEN." VN, 46 (1974), 10-14.

> "Mill's approach to the woman question, as well as his solutions, are indicative of his characteristic attitude of mind. THE SUBJECTION is not a freak of circumstances but a logical development of Mill's lifelong thought."

Backes, James G. "J.S. Mill and His Preposterous Notion." WS, 34 (1970), 90-99.

> The "preposterous notion" was female suffrage, presented to the House of Commons in 1867. Examines the speech within the context of Mill's training and career as an orator.

Baker, William J. "Gradgrindery and the Education of J.S. Mill." WHR, 24 (1970), 49-56.

> Baker's thesis is that Mill's education was in several ways the op-

posite of Gradgrind's system as interpreted in Dickens' HARD TIMES.

Billings, John R. "J.S. Mill's Quantity-Quality Distinction." MNL, 7 (1971), 6-16.

"I do not wish to argue that Mill's distinction is tenable, but that it may not be dismissed in the summary manner in which philosophers have dismissed it." See Graff, below.

Britton, Karl. JOHN STUART MILL. Baltimore: Penguin, 1953.

Britton concentrates on Mill's philosophy.

_____. "Perpetuating a Mistake about Mill's THREE ESSAYS ON RELIGION." MNL, 5 (1970), 6-7.

Claims that Mill's ESSAYS were written in 1850-58 and that, in them, Mill discusses "the bearing of Darwin's doctrine on the marks of design in nature."

Brown, Donald G. "Mill on Liberty and Morality." PHR, 81 (1972), 133-58.

Explores the roots of these two concepts in Mill and finds that they cannot coexist without tension.

Buchdahl, Gerd. "Inductivist versus Deductivist Approaches in the Philosophy of Science as Illustrated by Some Controversies between Whewell and Mill." MONIST, 55 (1971), 343-67.

Contrasts Mill and Whewell's theories of "formulation, explication, probation, consolidation, and validation of hypotheses."

Cockshut, A.O.J. "J.S. Mill: The Half-Circle." In his THE UNBELIEVERS: ENGLISH AGNOSTIC THOUGHT, 1840-1890. New York: New York University Press, 1966.

"Mill presents us with a perfect mirror-image of the more usual kind of Victorian doubt, where nostalgia is felt for the religious comforts of childhood."

Cooney, Seamus. "'The Heart of That Mystery': A Note on J.S. Mill's Theory of Poetry." VN, 21 (1962), 20-23.

Cooney argues that Mill's interest in poetry declined as he grew older.

_____. "Mill, Poets, and Other Men." VN, 17 (1960), 23-25.

"Mill distinguishes between the poet by nature and the poet by culture. The distinction functions less as a means of discriminating meaningfully among poets than as a means of discriminating among men."

Cowling, Maurice. MILL AND LIBERALISM. Cambridge: At the University Press, 1963.

>   Presents Mill as a "moral totalitarian" whose "liberalism was a dogmatic, religious one and whose emphasis was on social cohesion and moral consensus." Includes chapters on "Liberalism and the Religion of Humanity" and "ON LIBERTY." Also see Rees, below.

Day, John P. "On Liberty and the Real Will." PHILOSOPHY, 45 (1970), 177-92.

>   Sees affinities in Mill with Rousseau's and Hegel's notion of a Real (or General) Will and explores its relation to Mill's concept of liberty and freedom.

Donagan, Alan. "Victorian Philosophical Prose: J.S. Mill and F.H. Bradley." THE ART OF VICTORIAN PROSE. Eds. George L. Levine and William A. Madden. New York: Oxford University Press, 1968.

>   Donagan discusses the evolution of prose style from Berkeley to Bradley and places Mill in the polemical tradition as opposed to the classical style of Bradley.

Dyke, C. "Collective Decision-Making in Rousseau, Kant, Hegel, and Mill." ETHICS, 80 (1969), 21-37.

>   Contrasts the four philosophers' ideas with that of the modern welfare state and, through them, explores the metaphysical assumptions underlying the liberal political heritage.

Ebel, Henry. "'The Primaeval Fountain of Human Nature': Mill, Carlyle, and the French Revolution." VN, 30 (1966), 13-18.

>   "Mill, then, is a study in conflict. And nowhere do we see a more sustained refraction of this inner clash [between rationalism and romanticism] than in his successive dealings with the French Revolution."

Ellery, John. JOHN STUART MILL. New York: Twayne, 1964.

>   A general discussion of Mill that also contains a section on his speeches.

Feltes, Norman N. "'Bentham' and 'Coleridge': Mill's 'Completing Counterparts.'" MNL, 2 (1967), 2-7.

Discusses Mill's essays on the two as representative of the age's counterbalancing viewpoints.

Foulk, Gary J. "Kendall's Criticisms of J.S. Mill." PERSON, 51 (1970), 314-23.

Examines Kendall's article, "The 'Open Society' and Its Fallacies" (see Radcliffe's collection, below), and charges that the author misrepresents many of Mill's ideas and intentions in his case against the philosopher's liberalism.

Friedman, Richard B. "A New Exploration of Mill's Essay 'On Liberty.'" PS, 14 (1966), 281-304.

Friedman defends what some critics have seen as Mill's ambiguity in his famous essay.

Graff, J.A. "Mill's Quantity-Quality Distinction: A Defence." MNL, 7 (1972), 14-18.

Examines charges that Mill's arguments for qualities of pleasure are meaningless and outlines how Mill's position can be defended. See Billings, above.

Grube, John. "ON LIBERTY as a Work of Art." MNL, 5 (1969), 2-6.

"Mill's essay is a celebrated defence of liberty, but it is also a very great work of art. As one begins to respond to the essay in this way, it becomes the 'objective correlative' to his AUTOBIOGRAPHY."

Hainds, John R. "J.S. Mill and the Saint-Simonians." JHI, 7 (1946), 103-12.

A reply to Hill Shine's article on the same subject, below. Hainds argues that Mill was interested only in tolerance, not in advancing the views of Saint-Simonians.

――――. "J.S. Mill's EXAMINER Articles on Art." JHI, 11 (1950), 215-34.

Relies on the several unsigned notices and reviews, heretofore unknown, that elaborate Mill's interest in music, the theater, and poetry, and presents a comprehensive view of his theoretical and critical opinions.

Hall, Roland. "Further Addenda to the Diction of Mill." N&Q, 17 (1970), 10-11.

――――. "Still More Addenda to the Diction of Mill." N&Q, 17 (1970), 368-69.

Hamburger, Joseph. INTELLECTUALS IN POLITICS: JOHN STUART MILL AND THE PHILOSOPHIC RADICALS. New Haven, Conn.: Yale University Press, 1965.

    Claims that the Philosophic Radicals "tried to be both philosophers and politicians" and in exploring this theme stresses their "doctrinarism, which is examined both from their point of view and its relation to the broad spectrum of political opinion." Includes chapters on "Mill as Philosophical Radical" and "Mill--Last Spokesman for Philosophical Radicalism."

Harris, Wendell V. "The Warp of Mill's 'Fabric' of Thought." VN, 37 (1970), 1-7.

    Traces a shifting pattern in Mill's intellectual life, but believes that "the basic Benthamite principles and methods of thought were never discarded."

Hayek, Frederick A. von. "John Stuart Mill at the Age of Twenty-Five." In Mill's THE SPIRIT OF THE AGE. Ed. von Hayek. Chicago: University of Chicago Press, 1942.

    In this introductory essay, Hayek sketches Mill's education.

Heertje, Arnold, and Evert Schoorl. "Jean-Baptiste Say and the Education of J.S. Mill." MNL, 8 (1972), 10-15.

    Reprints letters between Mill and Say and concludes that they reveal Say was influential "in the development of Mill's economic thinking."

Himmelfarb, Gertrude. ON LIBERTY AND LIBERALISM: THE CASE OF JOHN STUART MILL. New York: Knopf, 1974.

    Examines the conflict between Mill, author of ON LIBERTY, and the "other" Mill, the bulk of whose work, it is argued here, represents a "quite different mode of liberal thought." This "other" Mill "belongs to the older liberal tradition of Montesquieu, Burke, and Tocqueville."

Hollis, Martin. "J.S. Mill's Political Philosophy of Mind." PHILOSOPHY, 47 (1972), 334-47.

    Believes that the collapse of Mill's liberalism, through the tension between liberty and freedom in his philosophy, can be avoided, but only by rejecting key theses in his logic.

Holthoon, F.L. von. THE ROAD TO UTOPIA: A STUDY OF JOHN STUART MILL'S SOCIAL THOUGHT. Assen, Netherlands: Royal Van Gorcum, 1971.

    Focuses on Mill's "endeavours at synthesis"--"how he thought out a modus operandi for reconciling conflicting ideas." Concludes that in Mill's thought "realism and far-reaching idealism went hand in hand."

Hughes, William H. "More on Mill's Socialism." MNL, 7 (1972), 9-13.

"Mill's own utilitarian criteria would have forced him to give up his attachment to the system of private property had he become aware of the way the system has developed in the one hundred years since his death."

Jackson, Reginald. AN EXAMINATION OF THE DEDUCTIVE LOGIC OF J.S. MILL. London: Oxford University Press, 1941.

Discusses SYSTEM OF LOGIC and Mill's writings on Hamilton for their epistemological, syllogistic, and verbal aspects.

Kendall, Willmoore, and George W. Carey. "The 'Roster Device': J.S. Mill and Contemporary Elitism." WPQ, 21 (1968), 20-39.

Finds an elitist perspective in modern liberalism to be partially rooted in Mill's tendency to convert political issues into moral ones, these to be resolved only by the intellectually expert.

Kubitz, Oskar. THE DEVELOPMENT OF J.S. MILL'S SYSTEM OF LOGIC. Urbana: University of Illinois Press, 1932.

Kubitz attempts to analyze Mill's evolution as a logician in 1825-43.

Lang, Berel, and Gary Stahl. "Mill's 'Howlers' and the Logic of Naturalism." PPR, 29 (1969), 562-74.

Surveys some of the traditional attacks against Mill and finds all of them based on misreadings and misinterpretations.

Levi, Albert W. "The Idea of Socrates: The Philosophic Hero in the Nineteenth Century." JHI, 17 (1956), 89-108.

Examines Mill's use of Socrates in ON LIBERTY to symbolize both the authentic voice of science and the martyrdom of civil liberties.

_____. A STUDY IN THE SOCIAL PHILOSOPHY OF JOHN STUART MILL. Chicago: University of Chicago Press, 1940.

A discussion of "the problem of a planned society as historically localized in the social philosophy of John Stuart Mill."

_____. "The Writing of Mill's AUTOBIOGRAPHY." ETHICS, 61 (1951), 284-96.

"Although the AUTOBIOGRAPHY is neither religious, sentimental, nor pathetic, it is by no means, I think, the purely intellectual exercise for which it is often mistaken."

Lewisohn, David H. "J.S. Mill's 'Logic of the Moral Sciences.'" MNL, 7 (1971), 18-19.

A thesis abstract in which Lewisohn examines "Mill's aims in writing LOGIC" and the "relation between Mill's work on the methods of social science and earlier Utilitarian social thought."

―――. "Mill and Comte on the Methods of Social Science." JHI, 33 (1972), 315-24.

Lewisohn claims that Comte's influence on Mill has been overemphasized.

Lichtman, R. "Surface and Substance of Mill's Defense of Freedom." SOCIAL RESEARCH, 30 (1963), 469-95.

Considers ON LIBERTY and asserts that "at the most vital points in the argument the actual structure of Mill's position is quite different from his stated position, and paradoxically, it is the unannounced defense of freedom that is the real source of Mill's strength."

Lindley, Dwight N. "J.S. Mill: The Second Greatest Influence." VN, 11 (1957), 25-26.

Discusses Mill's association with the Saint-Simonians.

McCallum, Robert B. "The Individual in the Mass: Mill on Liberty and the Franchise." 1859: ENTERING AN AGE OF CRISIS. Eds. Philip Appleman et al. Bloomington: Indiana University Press, 1959.

"Wonderful as was his work as a political thinker, the evils which Mill feared have been averted not by the use of his prescribed safeguards but by forces in human nature which he was by temperament and education little fitted to understand."

McCloskey, H.J. JOHN STUART MILL: A CRITICAL STUDY. London: Macmillan, 1971.

This work is intended for students. It devotes chapters to each of the major areas of Mill's philosophical thought: logic, metaphysics, ethical and political theory, and the philosophy of religion.

Man, K.S. "The Imaginative Dimension in the Writings of John Stuart Mill." MNL, 6 (1970), 21-23.

"The AUTOBIOGRAPHY, the "Bentham" and "Coleridge" essays,

and the essays on poetry project their author's private feelings and desires by their structure and by such stylistic elements as tone, metaphor, and imagery."

Mandelbaum, Maurice. "On Interpreting Mill's 'Utilitarianism.'" JHP, 6 (1968), 35-46.

> Tries to improve on "fragmentary criticism" of Mill's treatise by examining some of the neglected but important ideas of the work in a hostile manner.

Martin, Rex. "A Defense of Mill's Qualitative Hedonism." PHILOSOPHY, 47 (1972), 140-51.

> Examines Mill's famous distinction between "higher" and "lower" pleasures and believes that, despite numerous philosophers' criticism of the distinction, it is logically and empirically sound.

Matthews, Charles. "Argument through Metaphor in J.S. Mill's ON LIBERTY." L&S, 4 (1971), 221-28.

> Believes that Mill's famous treatise is a "masterpiece of rhetoric" and concentrates on the author's use of figurative language and the "almost allegorical drama" which is played out by the metaphors to illustrate his point.

Mazlish, Bruce. JAMES AND J.S. MILL: FATHER AND SON IN THE NINETEENTH CENTURY. New York: Basic Books, 1975.

> Claims his study is a "psychohistory": "Taken together, the relations of the two make up one of the great father and son stories of the nineteenth century." And, "as key figures in the political and intellectual changes of their time, both father and son became prototypic protagonists in what Freud was later to call the Oedipal conflict."

Megill, A.D. "J.S. Mill's Religion of Humanity and the Second Justification for the Writing of ON LIBERTY." JP, 34 (1972), 612-32.

> Shows the persistence of Mill's adherence to a religion of humanity, but shows that he was not unaware of dangers in it.

Mill, Anna J. CARLYLE AND MILL: TWO SCOTTISH UNIVERSITY RECTORS. Edinburgh: Carlyle Society, 1965.

> A short comparative study of their educational theories.

─────. "J.S. Mill and the Picturesque." VS, 14 (1970), 151-63.

> Contends that Mill was a devoted student of the picturesque and

that this interest in natural beauties is evident in his walking-tour journals.

———. "Some Notes on Mill's Early Friendship with Henry Cole." MNL, 4 (1969), 2-8.

> Relies on Cole's own journal entries to describe a relationship that is not mentioned in Mill's AUTOBIOGRAPHY.

Mineka, Francis E. "The AUTOBIOGRAPHY and the Lady." UTQ, 32 (1963), 301-06.

> Discusses Mrs. Mill's influence on Mill's thought and work.

———. "J.S. Mill and Neo-Malthusianism, 1873." MNL, 8 (1972), 3-10.

> Considers the significance of Mill's distribution of birth-control literature in the early 1830s.

Miyoshi, Masao. "Mill and 'Pauline': The Myth and Some Facts." VS, 11 (1965), 154-63.

> Discusses Mill's influence on Browning's theory of poetry. Also see Peterson, below.

Mueller, Iris W. JOHN STUART MILL AND FRENCH THOUGHT. Urbana: University of Illinois Press, 1956.

> Mill's study of French political movements and French thought had most to do with determining the nature of his final attitude toward liberty." See Pappe, below.

Murray, James G. "Mill on De Quincey: ESPRIT CRITIQUE Revoked." VN, 37 (1970), 7-12.

> Sees Mill's benevolent treatment of De Quincey as a focal point of his changed ideas and hence as a key to the thought of the "new Mill."

Myers, C.J. "The Moral Economist." DR, 49 (1969), 110-15.

> A review article of Robson's study, below, which presents Mill as "primarily a moralist who subordinates all practice to his ethical philosophy."

Nagel, Ernest. "The Enforcement of Morals." HUMANIST, 28 (1968), 20-27.

> "Mill made individual freedom an absolute good to which he formally subordinated all other objectives--though his actual evaluations of social practices and his recommendations of changes in them are not always consonant with his formal principles."

John Stuart Mill

Neff, Emery E. CARLYLE AND MILL: AN INTRODUCTION TO VICTORIAN THOUGHT. 2nd rev. ed. New York: Octagon, 1964.

> The major study on this subject, in which Neff contrasts the two writers as representative men of the Victorian period.

Pankhurst, Richard K.P. THE SAINT-SIMONIANS: MILL AND CARLYLE. London: Sidgwick and Jackson, 1957.

> A general history of Saint-Simonianism in England, including sections on Mill and Carlyle as avid supporters of the movement.

Pappe, H.O. J.S. MILL AND THE HARRIET TAYLOR MYTH. Melbourne: Melbourne University Press, 1960.

> Disagrees with statements in the biographies by von Hayek and Packe, p. 188, and claims that Mrs. Mill did not exercise a crucial influence on Mill.

──────. "Mill and Tocqueville." JHI, 25 (1964), 217-34.

> Assesses evidence used by Mueller, above, to determine the extent of Mill's debt to the French political writer.

Peterson, William S., and Fred L. Standley. "The J.S. Mill Marginalia in Browning's 'Pauline': A History and Transcription." PBSA, 66 (1972), 135-70.

> Reprints the edited text and describes how the marginalia "provides an illuminating glimpse of a crucial moment in their respective careers." Also see Miyoshi, above.

Radcliffe, Peter, ed. LIMITS OF LIBERTY: STUDIES OF MILL'S ON LIBERTY. Belmont, Calif.: Wadsworth, 1966.

> Includes a number of essays: "The Value of Freedom: Mill's Liberty" by Albert Levi, "Paternalism and the Enforcement of Morality" by H.L.A. Hart, "A Re-Reading of Mill on Liberty" by J.C. Rees, and "The 'Open Society' and Its Fallacies" by Willmoore Kendall (see Foulk, above).

Randall, John H. "J.S. Mill and the Working-out of Empiricism." JHI, 26 (1965), 59-88.

> Believes that SYSTEM OF LOGIC is a "masterpiece of confusion, contradiction, inconsistency."

Rees, John C. MILL AND HIS EARLY CRITICS. Leicester, Engl.: University College Press, 1956.

> "Mill's essay was more critically received in the journals of the time than we usually tend to allow."

———. "A Re-Reading of Mill on Liberty." PS, 8 (1960), 113-29.

Rees claims that the major dichotomy in ON LIBERTY is between public and private interests.

———. "Was Mill for Liberty?" PS, 14 (1966), 72-77.

A critique of Cowling's criticisms of Mill, above.

Remnant, Peter. "The Relevance of Mill." QQ, 77 (1970), 513-29.

Asks "to what extent is Mill's principle of individual liberty applicable in today's society?"

Robbins, Larry M. "Mill and MIDDLEMARCH: The Progress of Public Opinion." VN, 31 (1967), 37-39.

Robbins emphasizes the similarities between Mill's and Eliot's ethical principles.

Robson, John M. "Harriet Taylor and J.S. Mill: Artist and Scientist." QQ, 73 (1966), 167-86.

Believes that Harriet Taylor was an inspirational force on Mill, but deflates larger claims that she was a true "coauthor" of ON LIBERTY and the AUTOBIOGRAPHY.

———. THE IMPROVEMENT OF MANKIND: THE SOCIAL AND POLITICAL THOUGHT OF J.S. MILL. Toronto: University of Toronto Press, 1968.

A valuable study in which Robson discusses Mill's relation to Comte, Carlyle, the Saint-Simonians, Coleridge, and Tocqueville. Emphasizes the "central importance of the utilitarian ethic, as Mill defined it, to his theoretical and practical work." See Myers, above.

———. "'Joint Authorship' Again: The Evidence in the Third Edition of Mill's 'Logic.'" MNL, 6 (1971), 15-20.

"While it is virtually clear that Harriet Taylor had no part in the original composition of the LOGIC, we may infer that they together went through both the LOGIC and the PRINCIPLES in 1851 and 1852."

———. "J.S. Mill and J. Bentham, with Some Observations on James Mill." ESSAYS IN ENGLISH LITERATURE FROM THE RENAISSANCE TO THE VICTORIAN AGE. Eds. Millar MacLure and F.W. Watt. Toronto: University of Toronto Press, 1964.

Discusses J.S. Mill's "ambiguous" attitude toward Bentham, which was caused by Bentham's association with Mill's father, James: "All of Mill's comments on Bentham should be read with this sensitivity in mind."

_____. "Mill and Matthew Arnold: Liberty and Culture." HAB, 12 (1961), 20-32.

Emphasizes the apparent conflict between the social and political views in ON LIBERTY and CULTURE AND ANARCHY.

_____. "Mill's AUTOBIOGRAPHY: The Public and the Private Voice." CCC, 16 (1965), 97-101.

Relies on evidence of chronology in the construction of the AUTOBIOGRAPHY, as the narration progresses, to account for the transition from private experience to public exhortation.

_____. "Principles and Methods in the Collected Edition of John Stuart Mill." In his EDITING NINETEENTH-CENTURY TEXTS. Toronto: University of Toronto Press, 1967.

Rockmore, Tom. "The Moral Philosophy of J.S. Mill Revisited." PERSON, 55 (1974), 380-87.

Seriously challenges the well-known claim that Mill was a "rule utilitarian."

Rossi, Alice S. "Sentiment and Intellect: The Story of J.S. Mill and Harriet Taylor Mill." MIDWAY, 10 (1970), 29-51.

"It is not only Mill's own development, but the history of his relationship with Harriet Taylor that must be examined if we are to understand why Mill wrote a book on women and why the book has such remarkable survival power and impact."

Ryan, Alan. JOHN STUART MILL. New York: Pantheon, 1970.

The "aim of this book is to present Mill as the author of a philosophical system, 'inductivism.'" Includes chapters on "Induction and Its Canons," "Mathematics as an Inductive Science," and "Toward Rationality in Ethics."

Sanderson, David R. "Metaphor and Method in Mill's ON LIBERTY." VN, 34 (1968), 22-25.

"I should like to demonstrate how one feature of Mill's prose style--the absence of metaphor--is consistent with, and in fact depends upon, his mode of thinking--the incisive method of analysis."

Scanlon, James P. "Mill and the Definition of Freedom." ETHICS, 68 (1958), 194-206.

Examines 'On Social Freedom' as "a curious document that sheds light on an important element in Mill's thought"--the place of the emotions.

Schneewind, Jerome, ed. MILL: A COLLECTION OF CRITICAL ESSAYS. New York: Doubleday, 1968.

A valuable collection of essays. Among others, it contains Burns' "Mill and Democracy, 1829-61," and Halliday's very useful "Some Recent Interpretations of Mill."

Schwartz, Pedro. THE NEW POLITICAL ECONOMY OF J.S. MILL. London: Weidenfeld and Nicolson, 1968.

"Mill's thought on policy is the key to understanding his work as an economist. Mill sought to transform the political economy of his masters from what he thought was a narrow sense into an instrument for social progress."

Sharpless, Francis P. "William Johnson Fox and Mill's Essay on Poetry." VN, 27 (1965), 18-21.

Examines the letters exchanged between Mill and Fox, a Unitarian minister and supporter of liberal causes. He suggests that Fox influenced Mill's aesthetic viewpoints.

_____, ed. THE LITERARY CRITICISM OF JOHN STUART MILL. New York: Humanities Press; The Hague: Mouton, 1967.

This study is the first on this topic and emphasizes Bentham's influence.

Shine, Hill. "J.S. Mill and an Open Letter to the Saint-Simonian Society in 1832." JHI, 6 (1945), 102-08.

Shine emphasizes Mill's belief in Saint-Simonianism as a useful force for reform. See Hainds, above.

Steele, E.D. "J.S. Mill and the Irish Question: Reform and the Integrity of the Empire, 1865-1870." HIJ, 13 (1970), 419-50.

Steele's thesis is that Mill was less radical on the Irish situation than is generally thought.

_____. "J.S. Mill and the Irish Question: The Principles of Political Economy, 1848-1865." HIJ, 13 (1970), 216-36.

Examines Mill's ENGLAND AND IRELAND and concludes that "Mill was less libertarian but less radical than is often supposed because he very largely shared the complacency of his contemporaries, was a patriot and even an 'imperialist.'"

John Stuart Mill

Stephen, Leslie. THE ENGLISH UTILITARIANS. 3 vols. London: Duckworth, 1900; rpt. New York: Smith, 1950.

> Volume 3 is devoted to Mill's life and to his political, economic, and philosophical ideas.

Stillinger, Jack. "The Text of J.S. Mill's AUTOBIOGRAPHY." BJRL, 43 (1960), 220-42.

> A discussion of the text used by Stillinger in his edition of Mill's AUTOBIOGRAPHY AND OTHER WRITINGS (Boston: Houghton Mifflin, 1969).

Stocker, Michael. "Mill on Desire and Desirability." JHP, 7 (1969), 199-201.

> Defends Mill's "famous controversial proof of utilitarianism in the third paragraph of chapter four of UTILITARIANISM" by stating that it should be read in the context of his other works. Also see Wertz and West, below.

Tatalovich, Anne. "J.S. Mill, THE SUBJECTION OF WOMEN: An Analysis." SOQ, 12 (1973), 87-105.

> Sketches the main lines of Mill's argument, his opinions on the female role in politics, and Mill's attempts to implement his support of suffrage.

Ten, C.L. "Mill and Liberty." JHI, 30 (1969), 47-68.

> Ten concludes that to view Mill as anything other than a great liberal would be to make a serious error in historical judgment.

_____. "Mill's Stable Society." MNL, 7 (1971), 2-6.

> Discusses Book 6 of SYSTEM OF LOGIC as a list of three requirements for a stable society: a disciplining educational system, a sense of loyalty to something, and a feeling of common interest among citizens.

Thomas, William E. "J.S. Mill and the Uses of Autobiography." HISTORY, 56 (1971), 341-59.

> Thomas' thesis is that Mill altered and subordinated his early activities to his later goals in the AUTOBIOGRAPHY.

Viner, Jacob. "Bentham and J.S. Mill: The Utilitarian Background." In his THE LONG VIEW AND THE SHORT: STUDIES IN ECONOMIC THEORY AND POLICY. Glencoe, Ill.: Free Press, 1958.

> A valuable discussion of Mill's thinking on economics in relation to Bentham's philosophical and political beliefs.

Watson, D.R. "Clemenceau and Mill." MNL, 6 (1970), 13-19.

> Believes that Clemenceau's liberalism was greatly influenced by Mill and traces affinities between them.

Wellek, René. "John Stuart Mill." In his A HISTORY OF MODERN CRITICISM, 1750-1950. Vol. 3. New Haven, Conn.: Yale University Press, 1965.

> Discusses Mill's writings on literature, particularly "What is Poetry?"--"Mill's single important contribution to a theory of poetry."

Welty, Gordon A. "Mill's Principle of Government as a Basis of Democracy." MONIST, 55 (1971), 51-60.

> ON LIBERTY is examined for "its individualist thesis, its simplicity, and its widespread recognition." These virtues account for its "recurrence in contemporary ethical theory."

Wertz, S.K. "Composition and Mill's Utilitarian Principle." PERSON, 52 (1971), 417-31.

> Gives critical attention to the controversial section in chapter 4 of UTILITARIANISM wherein Mill extends the individual theory of good to the general happiness of the whole. At stake are several principles of logic. Also see Stocker, above, and West, below.

West, Henry R. "Reconstructing Mill's 'Proof' of the Principle of Utility." MIND, 81 (1972), 256-57.

> "Mill's primary argument in Chapter IV of UTILITARIANISM is to establish individualistic hedonism as the ultimate principle of human valuation on the basis of an analysis of the psychology of desiring a thing for its own sake."

Woods, Thomas. POETRY AND PHILOSOPHY: A STUDY IN THE THOUGHT OF J.S. MILL. London: Hutchinson, 1961.

> Woods utilizes Mill as a "test case" to "define the influence that poets and their poetry have on philosophers and their philosophy." Includes chapters on "Mill and Benthamism" and "Mill, Wordsworth, and Poetry."

BIBLIOGRAPHIES

Hascall, Dudley, and J[ohn] M. Robson. "A Bibliography of Writings on Mill." MNL, 5 (1970), 8-11.

MacMinn, Ney, J[ohn] R. Hainds, and James McCrimmon. THE BIBLIOGRAPHY OF THE PUBLISHED WRITINGS OF J.S. MILL. Evanston, Ill.: Northwestern

University Press, 1945; rpt. Lincoln: University of Nebraska Library, 1970.

>The standard bibliography, based on the careful list Mill compiled of all his publications.

Robson, John M. "John Stuart Mill." VICTORIAN PROSE: A GUIDE TO RESEARCH. Ed. David J. DeLaura. New York: MLA, 1973.

>A valuable bibliographical essay that discusses critical studies published before 1972.

_____. "A Note on Mill Bibliography." UTQ, 34 (1964), 93-97.

>This listing supplements the MacMinn bibliography, above.

WILLIAM MORRIS (1834-96)

PRINCIPAL PROSE WORKS

THE DECORATIVE ARTS, THEIR RELATION TO MODERN LIFE AND PROGRESS, 1878.

HOPES AND FEARS FOR ART: FIVE LECTURES, 1882.

THE TABLES TURNED, OR NUPKINS AWAKENED: A SOCIALIST INTERLUDE, 1887.

SIGNS OF CHANGE: SEVEN LECTURES, 1888.

A DREAM OF JOHN BALL AND A KING'S LESSON, 1888.

NEWS FROM NOWHERE, OR AN EPOCH OF REST, 1891.

GOTHIC ARCHITECTURE, 1893.

THE WELL AT THE WORLD'S END, 1896.

COLLECTED WORKS

THE COLLECTED WORKS OF WILLIAM MORRIS. Ed. May Morris. 24 vols. London: Blackwell, 1936; rpt. New York: Russell and Russell, 1966.
>   The standard edition.

MORRIS: ARTIST, WRITER, SOCIALIST. Ed. May Morris. 2 vols. London: Blackwell, 1936; rpt. New York: Russell and Russell, 1966.
>   These two volumes are supplements to the COLLECTED WORKS.

William Morris

ON ART AND SOCIALISM. Ed. Holbrook Jackson. London: Lehmann, 1947.

This collection contains a selection of Morris' lectures.

THE POLITICAL WRITINGS OF WILLIAM MORRIS. Ed. A.L. Morton. Berlin: Seven Seas, 1973.

SELECTIONS FROM THE PROSE WORKS OF WILLIAM MORRIS. Ed. A.H.R. Ball. Cambridge: At the University Press, 1931.

THE UNPUBLISHED LECTURES OF WILLIAM MORRIS. Ed. Eugene [D.] LeMire. Detroit: Wayne State University Press, 1969.

This collection of ten lectures also contains a schedule of Morris' public lectures.

WILLIAM MORRIS: STORIES IN PROSE, STORIES IN VERSE, SHORTER POEMS, LECTURES, AND ESSAYS. Ed. G[eorge] D.H. Cole. London: Nonesuch Press, 1934.

Generally considered the best single-volume collection of Morris' writings. Cole's introduction is particularly valuable.

LETTERS

Also see Arnot's biography, below.

THE LETTERS OF MORRIS TO HIS FAMILY AND FRIENDS. Ed. Philip Henderson. London: Longmans, Green, 1950.

This collection, although it contains over 400 letters, is not a complete edition. That is being prepared by Norman Kelvin for Stanford University Press.

THE UNPUBLISHED LETTERS OF MORRIS. Ed. R.P. Arnot. London: Trinity Trust, 1951.

BIOGRAPHIES

Arnot, R[obert] Page. MORRIS: THE MAN AND THE MYTH. New York: Monthly Review Press, 1964.

Arnot presents Morris as "belonging to the revolutionary working class of Great Britain." Also contains forty-six letters written by Morris to the Socialist League.

Bloomfield, Paul. THE LIFE AND WORK OF MORRIS. London: Barker, 1934.

Celebrates Morris as a "poet-moralist who wanted to establish his flower-garden, his Paradise, on earth, and to throw it open to all men."

Cary, Elizabeth L. MORRIS: POET, CRAFTSMAN, SOCIALIST. New York: Putnam's, 1902.

Relies heavily on Mackail's version of Morris' life, below, but includes chapters on "Public Life and Socialism," "Literature of the Socialist Period," and "Later Writings."

Grennan, Margaret. MORRIS: MEDIEVALIST AND REVOLUTIONARY. New York: King's Crown Press, 1945.

Claims that Morris "used the medieval more consistently than any other writer." Includes chapters on A DREAM OF JOHN BALL and "Prose Romances."

Henderson, Philip. WILLIAM MORRIS: HIS LIFE, WORK, AND FRIENDS. New York: McGraw-Hill, 1967.

Henderson's focus is Morris as an artist, a designer of the civilized life based on equality and personal creativity. See Johnson, p. 211.

Jackson, Holbrook. WILLIAM MORRIS: CRAFTSMAN, SOCIALIST. London: Cape, 1908; rev. ed. 1926.

Includes chapters on "Morris's Idea of Handicraft," "The Kelmscott Press," and "Man of Letters" which concludes that "with Morris literature was if not entirely, at least in the nature of a by-product."

Mackail, John W. THE LIFE OF WILLIAM MORRIS. 2 vols. London: Longmans, Green, 1899; rpt. New York: Blom, 1968.

Mackail's is the official standard biography.

Macleod, Robert D. MORRIS WITHOUT MACKAIL. Glasgow: Holmes, 1954.

A collection of biographical observations about Morris that present him differently than does the "official" portrait in Mackail, above.

_____. WILLIAM MORRIS AS SEEN BY HIS CONTEMPORARIES. London: Holmes, 1957.

"Our aim has been merely to endeavour to find the real Morris by going beyond Mackail by presenting the views and opinions of other writers and artists, who, unlike Mackail, were not writing to commission but merely reminiscing on Morris as they themselves found him."

Thompson, Edward P. MORRIS: ROMANTIC TO REVOLUTIONARY. London: Lawrence & Wishart, 1955.

>Generally considered the most useful recent biography, definitive in its interpretation of Morris' politics. See Johnson, p. 211.

CRITICAL STUDIES

ADDRESSES COMMEMORATING THE ONE-HUNDREDTH ANNIVERSARY OF THE BIRTH OF WILLIAM MORRIS. New Haven, Conn.: Overbrook Press, 1934.

>This collection includes, among others, "Morris as a Poet" by C.B. Tinker and "The Ordeal of William Morris" by C. Rollins.

Antippas, Andy. "William Morris and 'The Murder of Art.'" TSE, 16 (1968), 49-62.

>Discusses Morris' views on the industrial revolution's effect on art; "all the arts had become debased, affected, imitative, narrow."

Arnot, Robert Page. BERNARD SHAW AND WILLIAM MORRIS. London: Morris Society, 1957.

>Discusses the influence "Morris's personality and outlook on art and life, especially his social outlook," had on Shaw's socialist theory.

Broers, B.C. "William Morris." In his MYSTICISM IN THE NEO-ROMANTICS. Amsterdam: Paris Publishers, 1923.

>Also includes chapters on Rossetti and Swinburne.

Castle, Barbara. "The Vision Splendid." NST, 82 (1971), 450-51.

>Discusses Morris' prose romance, "The Water of the Wondrous Isles."

Cole, George D.H. WILLIAM MORRIS AS A SOCIALIST. London: Morris Society, 1960.

>Complains that Morris' utopias are unreal and that Morris writes "like a child who is remaking the world."

Collins, John. "Harry Buxton Forman and William Morris: A Preliminary Enquiry." BC, 21 (1972), 503-23.

Dunlap, Joseph. THE BOOK THAT NEVER WAS: THE ARGUMENT, HOW MORRIS AND BURNE-JONES ATTEMPTED TO MAKE OF 'THE EARTHLY

PARADISE' A BIG BOOK WITH 'LOTS OF STORIES AND PICTURES': HOW THEY FAILED IN THIS ENDEAVOUR: AND HOW THEIR DREAM, THOUGH IT EVADED THEM, HAS YET OUTLIVED THEM. New York: Oriole, 1971.

    The title sums up this history of the work.

Evans, B. Ifor. "William Morris, His Influence and Reputation." COR, 145 (1934), 315-23.

    Reviews Morris' writings and concludes that "it becomes apparent that he is closely related to our own age."

Faulkner, Peter. "Senghor and Morris: Socialists." JWMS, 11 (1971), 2-7.

    Contrasts Morris with Leopold Senghor: "Both men seek to complete an economic analysis with a moral critique, and in so doing they make use of an ethical vocabulary scorned by exponents of scientific socialism."

_____. "William Morris and the Two Cultures." JWMS, 6 (1966), 9-12.

    Discusses the split between humanists and scientists as expounded by C.P. Snow and F.R. Leavis: "Morris is important at this point because he asked the most incisive question about his society--how far does it promote the happiness of all its members?"

_____. "William Morris and Yeats." JWMS, 3 (1963), 19-23.

    "In both writers there is the late-Romantic tendency to the picturesque rather than the dramatic, the dreamy rather than the intense."

_____, ed. MORRIS: THE CRITICAL HERITAGE. London: Routledge and Kegan Paul, 1973.

    A collection of essays written about Morris by his contemporaries and arranged under the major writings.

Ford, George H. KEATS AND THE VICTORIANS. New Haven, Conn.: Yale University Press, 1944.

    Includes a chapter on Morris' interest in Keats.

Glasier, Bruce. WILLIAM MORRIS AND THE EARLY DAYS OF THE SOCIALIST MOVEMENT. London: Longmans, Green, 1921.

    Glasier discusses Morris as a social agitator and political propagandist.

Goode, John. "Gissing, Morris, and English Socialism." VS, 12 (1968), 201-26.

Compares NEWS FROM NOWHERE with Gissing's THE NETHER WORLD to explore "the relation of the novel to historical accuracy."

_____. "William Morris and the Dream of Revolution." LITERATURE AND POLITICS IN THE NINETEENTH CENTURY. Ed. John Lucas. New York: Barnes and Noble, 1971.

Analyzes A DREAM OF JOHN BALL as "a formal response to the realities of Morris's own situation," that is, "a revolutionary literature which dramatized the tensions of the revolutionary mind."

Gordon, Jan B. "William Morris' Destiny of Art." JAAC, 27 (1968), 271-79.

"Morris was forced to confuse a sociology of the arts with a theory of aesthetics. Such a confusion takes on a unique tone when aesthetic facts must be harmonized with a mythology of aesthetic development."

Gordon, Walter R. "Pre-Raphaelitism and the OXFORD AND CAMBRIDGE MAGAZINE." JRUL, 29 (1966), 42-51.

Discusses Morris' leadership of the periodical, "a workshop for the early efforts of Morris which gave him an opportunity to form the ideas, values, and attitudes which were to determine the course of his mature life."

Harris, S. Dale. "Evaluating William Morris." QNL, 33 (1967), 3-10.

Morris is difficult to evaluate because of "the sheer multifariousness of his gifts and the energy with which he expressed them."

Henderson, Philip. WILLIAM MORRIS. London: Longmans, Green, 1952; rev. ed. 1963.

A short introduction to Morris' life and works. Concludes that NEWS FROM NOWHERE "appears now like Morris's masterpiece, for into it he put not only his social philosophy and hopes for the future, but also his love of the earth."

Hoare, Dorothy. THE WORKS OF MORRIS AND YEATS IN RELATION TO EARLY SAGA LITERATURE. Cambridge: At the University Press, 1937.

Compares the writers and concludes that they both "escaped from life to the sagas" and then "from the actuality which the sagas reveal to the dreaming and stilled refuge, with all harshness eliminated, which they made of them."

Hollow, John W. "William Morris and the Judgment of God." PMLA, 86 (1971), 446-51.

"Morris was careless of metaphysics and religion because he thought men should not concern themselves about God."

Hulse, James W. REVOLUTIONISTS IN LONDON: A STUDY OF FIVE UNORTHODOX SOCIALISTS. New York: Oxford University Press, 1970.

Discusses Morris as "The Pilgrim of Hope," in which Morris' socialism is described as "catholic, borrowed from the Middle Ages and from Russian nihilism, as well as from Mill and from Marx."

Irvine, A.L. "Morris at Oxford and Dublin." JWMS, 8 (1968), 3-5.

Relates a contemporary version of speeches Morris made at political meetings in 1884 and 1886.

Johnson, Fridolf. "William Morris." AMERICAN ARTIST, 32 (1968), 43-49.

Reviews the biographies by Thompson and Henderson, above, and emphasizes Morris' artistic innovations.

Jordan, R. Furneaux. THE MEDIEVAL VISION OF WILLIAM MORRIS. London: Morris Society, 1960.

"Morris's socialism can only begin to be understood as part of his medieval vision, as seen against a wholly medieval world of guilds, free cities, masonry and the subsistence economy of those centuries."

Kocmanova, Jesse. "The Aesthetic Opinions of William Morris." CLS, 4 (1967), 409-24.

Analyzes Morris' "social conception of art" and concludes that "the intimate union of matter and form can be found in his life-long search for poetic and prose expression, governed not by the desire to produce 'literature,' but by the endeavour to find the perfect medium for expressing a particular meaning."

_____. "The Living Language of William Morris." BSE, 9 (1970), 17-34.

Morris' prose is "romantic" in that it utilizes "syntactical and metaphoric devices designed to excite an affective response." Further, the prose is "based on the living speech which Morris used in his daily life and in this sense it is related to the main tradition of English prose."

_____. "Two Uses of the Dream Form as a Means of Confronting the Present with the National Past." BSE, 2 (1960), 113-48.

Contrasts A DREAM OF JOHN BALL with Svatopluk Cech's saga

(1888): "Both describe in the form of a dream a situation which is historically impossible, with the object of offering a contrast to the world of today which the author wishes to criticize."

Lewis, Clive S. "William Morris." In his REHABILITATIONS AND OTHER ESSAYS. London: Oxford, 1939.

Lewis discusses Morris' poetry and art.

Lindsay, Jack. WILLIAM MORRIS, WRITER. London: William Morris Society, 1961.

Lindsay claims that instead of the craftsman or socialist, it was the poet in Morris who provided "the continuity and the dynamic force in all aspects of his development."

Litzenberg, Karl. "The Social Philosophy of Morris and the Doom of the Gods." ESSAYS AND STUDIES IN ENGLISH AND COMPARATIVE LITERATURE OF THE UNIVERSITY OF MICHIGAN, 10 (1933), 183-203.

———. "William Morris and the Literary Tradition." MICHIGAN ALUMNUS, 53 (1946), 48-55.

"Examines the origins of what is frequently called the socialism or communism of Morris to show that it has more to do with art and literature than with life and society."

McAlindon, T. "The Idea of Byzantium in William Morris and W.B. Yeats." MP, 64 (1967), 307-19.

McAlindon argues that Morris viewed Byzantium as an ideally unified culture, "a constant preoccupation" in his pamphlets and essays.

Mackail, John W. WILLIAM MORRIS AND HIS CIRCLE. Oxford: Clarendon Press, 1907.

Emphasizes Rossetti's influence and the Oxford days.

Maurer, Oscar. "William Morris and GESTA ROMANORUM." STUDIES IN LANGUAGE, LITERATURE AND CULTURE OF THE MIDDLE AGES AND LATER. Ed. E.B. Atwood and A.A. Hill. Austin: University of Texas Press, 1969.

Mauer discusses how Morris transformed three medieval tales to create his own vision of kingship in "The Earthly Paradise."

———. "William Morris and the Poetry of Escape." NINETEENTH-CENTURY STUDIES. Eds. H. Davis; William C. DeVane; and R.C. Bald. Ithaca, N.Y.: Cornell University Press, 1940.

Asserts that Morris "found in socialism the only valid means for healing the dangerous breach between escapist art on the one hand and Philistinism on the other. It was this dilemma that convinced him of the necessity for social reform."

Mumford, Lewis. "A Universal Man." NYRB, 23 May 1968, pp. 8-15.

Munby, Lionel. "William Morris's Romances and the Society of the Future." ZAA, 10 (1962), 56-70.

> Concludes that Morris' prose in the later Romances is appropriate to his vision of social utopias.

Murry, John Middleton. "William Morris: The Church Re-edified." In his HEROES OF THOUGHT. New York: Messner, 1938.

> Discusses Morris' educational, political and religious beliefs, concluding that "Morris was pure-bred Victorian bourgeois, and he escaped the new insidious bourgeois culture."

Short, Clarice. "William Morris and Keats." PMLA, 59 (1944), 513-23.

> Short discusses Morris' reliance on Keatsian imagery.

Smith, Jack. "William Morris and His Theory of Art: Its Bases and Its Meaning." SOQ, 7 (1968), 59-71.

> Discusses the influences that shaped Morris' theory of art--Oxford, Ruskin, the Pre-Raphaelite Brotherhood--and concludes that "the dignity of labor and the unity of art and craftsmanship were the very core of his theory."

Sparing, Henry H. THE KELMSCOTT PRESS AND WILLIAM MORRIS, MASTER CRAFTSMAN. London: Macmillan, 1924.

> Written by Morris' son-in-law, this work treats Morris as a printer and publisher; the emphasis is on the book as an art form.

Stevenson, Lionel. THE PRE-RAPHAELITE POETS. Chapel Hill: University of North Carolina Press, 1972.

> Includes a section on Morris.

Swannell, J.N. WILLIAM MORRIS AND OLD NORSE LITERATURE. London: William Morris Society, 1961.

> Concludes that Old Norse literature was "Morris's greatest single inspiration; the source of his finest verse and his most characteristic prose . . . after his discovery of this most vital and human of great literatures there was no danger of his withdrawal forever into a nebulous world of dreams."

Talbot, Norman C. "THE GIRL'S JOURNEY AND THE LAD'S QUEST: A Study in the Romances of William Morris." AUSTRALASIAN UNIVERSITIES LANGUAGE AND LITERATURE ASSOCIATION. Ed. A.P. Treweek. Sydney: AULLA, 1970.

──────. "Women and Goddesses in the Romances of William Morris." SORA, 3 (1969), 339-57.

> Distinguishes between women as "archetypes" and "emanations"-- "one of the devices by which Morris develops an image of a complex anima with double functions."

Thompson, Paul R. THE WORK OF WILLIAM MORRIS. New York: Viking, 1967.

> Includes a brief introduction to Morris' life and works that "takes into account all of the important research" and "reconsiders the relation of Morris as an artist to the Victorian period."

Tillotson, Geoffrey. "Morris and Machines" and "William Morris, Word Spinner." In his ESSAYS IN CRITICISM AND RESEARCH. Cambridge: At the University Press, 1942.

> The "Word Spinner" article discusses Morris' conception of poetry and its audience: "Morris refused to realize that poetry in the nineteenth century was a sophisticated pleasure experienced in solitude through the eye." The "Morris and Machines" article analyzes Morris' attitude toward machines: "they brought misery and boredom into workshops."

Tompkins, J.M.S. "The Work of William Morris: A Cord of Triple Strand." DR, 50 (1970), 97-111.

> Tompkins discusses the "interwoven" nature of Morris' art, writing, and politics.

Wahl, John R. NO IDLE SINGER. Cape Town: Balkema, 1964.

> Analyzes the sources "on which Morris drew in writing THE LOVERS OF GUDRUN and SIGURD THE VOLSUNG."

Wall, Bernard. "William Morris and Karl Marx." DUR, 202 (1938), 39-47.

> An important article that outlines the differences between Morris' socialism and Marx's theory.

Welby, T. Earle. THE VICTORIAN ROMANTICS: THE EARLY WORK OF ROSSETTI, MORRIS, BURNE-JONES, SOLOMON, AND THEIR ASSOCIATES. London: Howe, 1929.

Considers Morris' effects on the others in his circle, especially Swinburne. Generally an appreciative rather than a critical study.

BIBLIOGRAPHIES

Ehrsam, Theodore G., and Robert H. Deily. "William Morris." In their BIBLIOGRAPHIES OF TWELVE VICTORIAN AUTHORS. New York: Wilson, 1936; rpt. New York: Octagon, 1968.

Forman, H. Buxton. BOOKS OF WILLIAM MORRIS. London: Hallings, 1897.

Gives considerable information about the publishing details of Morris' writings.

Fredeman, William E. "William Morris." In his PRE-RAPHAELITISM: A BIBLIOCRITICAL STUDY. Cambridge, Mass.: Harvard University Press, 1965.

A selective bibliographical essay which supplements the others done by Fredeman.

──────. "William Morris." VICTORIAN POETS. Ed. F[rederic] E. Faverty. Rev. ed. Cambridge, Mass.: Harvard University Press, 1965.

A valuable bibliographical essay which discusses critical studies published through the early 1960s.

──────. "William Morris and His Circle: Selective Bibliography of Publications, 1960-62; 1963-65." JWMS, 1-2 (1964-66).

Jones, Howard M[umford]. "The Pre-Raphaelites." VICTORIAN POETS. Ed. F[rederic] E. Faverty. Cambridge, Mass.: Harvard University Press, 1965.

Jones's bibliographical essay discusses critical studies published in 1936-56.

Scott, Temple. A BIBLIOGRAPHY OF THE WORKS OF MORRIS. London: Bell, 1897.

Scott attempts to list all of Morris' writings, including his periodical pieces. There is also a useful list of very early critical studies.

Vaughan, C.E. "Bibliography of the Works of William Morris." In his BIBLIOGRAPHIES OF SWINBURNE, MORRIS, ROSSETTI. Oxford: Hart, 1914.

LESLIE STEPHEN (1832-1904)

PRINCIPAL PROSE WORKS

ESSAYS ON FREE THINKING AND PLAIN SPEAKING, 1873.

HOURS IN A LIBRARY, Series 1-3. 1874-79.

HISTORY OF ENGLISH THOUGHT IN THE EIGHTEENTH CENTURY, 2 vols. 1876.

SAMUEL JOHNSON, 1878.

ALEXANDER POPE, 1880.

SCIENCE OF ETHICS, 1882.

SWIFT, 1882.

DICTIONARY OF NATIONAL BIOGRAPHY. Ed. Leslie Stephen, 1882-91.

WHAT IS MATERIALISM? A DISCOURSE, 1886.

AN AGNOSTIC'S APOLOGY, AND OTHER ESSAYS, 1893.

SOCIAL RIGHTS AND DUTIES. 2 vols. 1896.

STUDIES OF A BIOGRAPHER. 4 vols. 1898-1902.

THE ENGLISH UTILITARIANS. 3 vols. 1900.

GEORGE ELIOT, 1902.

ROBERT LOUIS STEVENSON, 1903.

ENGLISH LITERATURE AND SOCIETY IN THE EIGHTEENTH CENTURY, 1904.

COLLECTED WORKS

COLLECTED ESSAYS, LITERARY AND CRITICAL. Introductions by James Bryce and Herbert [W.] Paul. 10 vols. New York: Putnam's, 1907.

> There is no complete edition of all of Stephen's writings, but COLLECTED ESSAYS contains HOURS IN A LIBRARY, STUDIES OF A BIOGRAPHER, SCIENCE OF ETHICS, ESSAYS ON FREE THINKING AND PLAIN SPEAKING, and ENGLISH LITERATURE AND SOCIETY IN THE EIGHTEENTH CENTURY.

MEN, BOOKS, AND MOUNTAINS. Ed. Samson O.[A.] Ullman. Minneapolis: University of Minnesota Press, 1956.

> This collection includes several short essays by Stephen, including "The Study of English Literature," "The Essayists," and "Thoughts on Criticism by a Critic." Ullman contends that, except for Matthew Arnold, "no other Victorian produced so large a body of distinguished criticism."

LETTERS AND BIOGRAPHIES

Maitland, Frederic W. THE LIFE AND LETTERS OF LESLIE STEPHEN. London: Duckworth, 1906; rpt. Detroit: Gale, 1968.

> This is the definitive biography and contains the only substantial number of Stephen's letters in print.

CRITICAL STUDIES

Annan, Noel. "The Intellectual Aristocracy." STUDIES IN SOCIAL HISTORY: A TRIBUTE TO G.M. TREVELYAN. Ed. J[ohn] H. Plumb. London: Longmans, Green, 1955.

> Annan places the Stephen family in the intellectual milieu of their day.

──────. LESLIE STEPHEN: HIS THOUGHT AND CHARACTER IN RELATION TO HIS TIMES. Cambridge, Mass.: Harvard University Press, 1951.

> An important study of Stephen's life and personality. Annan criti-

cizes Stephen's literary criticism for its overt morality, but claims that Stephen was "Arnold's disciple" who "did for English fiction what Arnold has tried to do for poetry." See Sheen, below.

Bell, Quentin. "The Mausoleum Book." RES, 6 (1965), 9-18.

Bell describes the "letter" Stephen composed for his children after his second wife died.

Bicknell, John W. "Leslie Stephen's ENGLISH THOUGHT IN THE EIGHTEENTH CENTURY: A Tract for the Times." VS, 5 (1962), 103-20.

Explains the "gap between Stephen's theory and his practice as an historian" by examining ENGLISH THOUGHT as "a notable document in the history of Victorian rationalism, a manifestation of a search for a usable past."

Burrell, Sidney A. "Sir Leslie Stephen." SOME MODERN HISTORIANS OF BRITAIN. Ed. Herman Ausubel. New York: Dryden Press, 1951.

Burrell treats Stephen as an intellectual historian.

Grosskurth, Phyllis. LESLIE STEPHEN. London: Longmans, Green, 1968.

A useful general introduction to Stephen's life and works.

Himmelfarb, Gertrude. "Mr. Stephen and Mr. Ramsay: The Victorian as Intellectual." PARTISAN R, 19 (1952), 664-79.

Himmelfarb uses Virginia Woolf's portrait of her father in TO THE LIGHTHOUSE to compare Stephen's public and private images.

Leavis, Queenie D. "Leslie Stephen: Cambridge Critic." SCRUTINY, 7 (1939) 404-15.

Leavis praises Stephen's literary criticism and claims that he was the founder of the Cambridge tradition in literary criticism.

Maurer, Oscar. "Leslie Stephen and the CORNHILL MAGAZINE, 1871-1882." SE, 32 (1953), 67-95.

Maurer discusses Stephen's editorship and the magazine's eventual financial collapse.

Sanders, Charles. "Stephen, Coleridge, and Two Coleridgeans." PMLA, 55 (1940), 795-801.

Sanders discusses Stephen's attitude toward F.D. Maurice and Coleridge.

Sheen, Edwin. "Stephen and Modern Criticism." CLAJ, 2 (1958), 1-14.

    Sheen defends Stephen against Annan's criticism, above. He relies on essays Stephen wrote for the SATURDAY REVIEW.

Ullman, Samson O.[A.]. "The Philistine Pose: A Study in the Literary Criticism of Leslie Stephen." Ph.D. dissertation, Harvard University, 1954. DAI, 21, 261.

    Claims that Stephen's pose as a philistine allowed him to undermine the position of contemporaries taking extreme sides on literary and social issues.

Vogeler, Martha S. "Leslie Stephen's DRYASDUST." VPN, 14 (1972), 23-26.

    Reprints an article by Stephen in which he discusses organizing and cataloging the "vast masses" of periodical literature of his time.

Wellek, René. "Leslie Stephen." In his A HISTORY OF MODERN CRITICISM, 1750-1950. Vol. 4. New Haven, Conn.: Yale University Press, 1965.

    Wellek criticizes Stephen's literary criticism for its severe morality and scientism.

_____. "Stephen's Stature as a Literary Critic." VN, 11 (1957), 19-22.

    Severely criticizes Stephen's aesthetic theories: "Stephen simply distrusts art . . . apart from morality and truth Stephen has no standards or theory for literature." Concludes that Stephen has "great historical merits, but we must admit the grave limitations of sensibility."

Wilson, John D. LESLIE STEPHEN AND MATTHEW ARNOLD AS CRITICS OF WORDSWORTH. Cambridge: At the University Press, 1939; rpt. New York: Haskell House, 1972.

    Presents "a discussion of the different views of Wordsworth's poetry held by Stephen and Arnold," differences caused by their religious views.

Woolf, Virginia. THE CAPTAIN'S DEATH BED AND OTHER ESSAYS. New York: Harcourt, 1950.

    Includes an essay assessing her father.

Zink, David D. LESLIE STEPHEN. New York: Twayne, 1972.

    A helpful, basic introduction to Stephen's life and works.

Leslie Stephen

BIBLIOGRAPHIES

Bicknell, John W. "The Unbelievers: Leslie Stephen." VICTORIAN PROSE: A GUIDE TO RESEARCH. Ed. David J. DeLaura. New York: MLA, 1973.

The most valuable bibliographical essay on Stephen scholarship.

MEN, BOOKS, AND MOUNTAINS. Ed. Samson O.[A.] Ullman. Minneapolis: University of Minnesota Press, 1956.

Ullman's edition of Stephen essays contains the most thorough bibliography of Stephen's publications, including his periodical writings.

ROBERT LOUIS STEVENSON (1850-94)

PRINCIPAL PROSE WORKS

AN INLAND VOYAGE, 1878.

TRAVELS WITH A DONKEY, 1879.

VIRGINIBUS PUERISQUE, 1881.

NEW ARABIAN NIGHTS. 2 vols. 1882.

FAMILIAR STUDIES OF MEN AND BOOKS, 1882.

TREASURE ISLAND, 1883.

THE SILVERADO SQUATTERS, 1883.

THE STRANGE CASE OF DR. JEKYLL AND MR. HYDE, 1886.

KIDNAPPED, 1886.

MEMORIES AND PORTRAITS, 1887.

THE MASTER OF BALLANTRAE, 1889.

ACROSS THE PLAINS, WITH OTHER MEMORIES AND ESSAYS, 1892.

COLLECTED WORKS

RLS: FROM SCOTLAND TO SILVERADO. Ed. James Hart. Cambridge, Mass.: Harvard University Press, 1966.

Robert Louis Stevenson

This collection contains all of Stevenson's writings about his California journey, 1879-80.

THE WORKS OF ROBERT LOUIS STEVENSON. Ed. Sidney Colvin. 24 vols. New York: Scribner's, 1905-39.

THE WORKS OF ROBERT LOUIS STEVENSON. South Seas Edition. 32 vols. New York: Scribner's, 1925.

Since this is the last of the large collected works, it contains the most letters.

THE WORKS OF ROBERT LOUIS STEVENSON. Tusitala Edition. 35 vols. London: Heinemann, 1923-24.

THE WORKS OF ROBERT LOUIS STEVENSON. Vailima Edition. 26 vols. New York: Scribner's, 1921-23; rpt. New York: AMS Press, 1971.

This collection includes introductory material by Stevenson, his wife, and her son.

LETTERS

Booth, Bradford A. "The Vailima Letters of Stevenson." HLB, 15 (1967), 117-28.

This article discusses the editorial deletions made by Colvin, below. Booth died before he could re-edit Stevenson's letters.

THE LETTERS OF STEVENSON TO HIS FAMILY AND FRIENDS, SELECTED. Ed. Sidney Colvin. 2 vols. London: Methuen, 1899; rpt. new ed. 4 vols. New York: Scribner's, 1911.

Colvin made many editorial omissions in this collection of letters.

RLS: STEVENSON'S LETTERS TO CHARLES BAXTER. Eds. DeLancey Ferguson and Marshall Waingrow. Port Washington, N.Y.: Kennikat Press, 1956.

Contains some 250 letters with annotations.

Smith, Janet A., ed. HENRY JAMES AND ROBERT LOUIS STEVENSON: A RECORD OF FRIENDSHIP AND CRITICISM. London: Hart-Davis, 1948.

A valuable collection of letters and the critical reactions of both authors to one another.

VAILIMA LETTERS; BEING CORRESPONDENCE ADDRESSED BY STEVENSON

TO SIDNEY COLVIN, NOVEMBER 1890-OCTOBER 1894. Ed. Sidney Colvin. London: Methuen, 1895.

>Colvin bowdlerized Stevenson's letters to present him as an idealized figure.

BIOGRAPHIES

Aldington, Richard. PORTRAIT OF A REBEL: THE LIFE AND WORKS OF ROBERT LOUIS STEVENSON. London: Evans, 1957.

>Emphasizes Stevenson's religious upbringing and concludes that, as a writer, "the work of art and the potboiler were always contending."

Balfour, Graham. THE LIFE OF ROBERT LOUIS STEVENSON. 2 vols. London: Methuen, 1901.

>The basic source for most biographical information. Generally considered the official biography, although it presents an idealized Stevenson.

Caldwell, Elsie. LAST WITNESS FOR ROBERT LOUIS STEVENSON. Norman: University of Oklahoma Press, 1960.

>An account of Stevenson's last years in the Pacific. Includes a chapter on THE MASTER OF BALLANTRAE.

Chesterton, Gilbert K. ROBERT LOUIS STEVENSON. New York: Sheed and Ward, 1928; rpt. 1955.

>One of the best studies of Stevenson, claiming that he was "a Christian theologian without knowing it." Stevenson's fault as a stylist was that "he simplified so much that he lost some of the complexity of real life."

Colvin, Sidney, et al., eds. STEVENSON: HIS WORK AND PERSONALITY. London: Hodder and Stoughton, 1924.

>A collection of reminiscences by Stevenson's contemporaries.

Cooper, Lettice. ROBERT LOUIS STEVENSON. Denver: Swallow, 1948.

>A brief biography with chapters on the major writings.

Daiches, David. ROBERT LOUIS STEVENSON AND HIS WORLD. London: Thames & Hudson, 1973.

>Contains over a hundred illustrations and a chronology of Stevenson's life. Concludes that the Stevenson legend remains because

"it embodies something central both in modern literature and modern personality--a sense of endurance."

Dark, Sidney. ROBERT LOUIS STEVENSON. New York: Hodder and Stoughton, 1931.

>Another glowing portrait of Stevenson and the "irresistable charm of his personality."

Ellison, Joseph. TUSITALA OF THE SOUTH SEAS. New York: Hastings House, 1953.

>A study of Stevenson's last years in Samoa. Although Stevenson was "a man with his full complement of human frailties, he nevertheless shines forth again, a radiant, gallant, magnetic personality."

Furnas, J.C. VOYAGE TO WINDWARD: THE LIFE OF ROBERT LOUIS STEVENSON. New York: Sloane, 1951.

>Furnas is generally considered the best of Stevenson's biographers. This work contains a useful 20-page bibliography of publications about Stevenson, published during 1885-1950.

Hellman, George. THE TRUE STEVENSON: A STUDY IN CLARIFICATION. Boston: Little, Brown, 1925.

>Includes chapters on "The Sex Question" and "The Henley Mystery," concluding that Stevenson was promiscuous and "an egoist."

Hennessy, James P. ROBERT LOUIS STEVENSON. New York: Simon and Schuster, 1975.

>Intended for the general reader. Presents Stevenson as a "major Romantic" whose charm lies in his "disarming candour."

Hinkley, Laura. THE STEVENSONS: LOUIS AND FANNY. New York: Hastings House, 1950.

>Criticizes the legends about Stevenson's Edinburgh days and depicts Henley as a villain. Presents Stevenson as Fanny Stevenson wanted him to be remembered. See Daiches, pp. 225-26.

Nakajima, Atsushi. LIGHT, WIND, AND DREAMS: AN INTERPRETATION OF THE LIFE AND MIND OF STEVENSON. Trans. Akira Miwa. Tokyo: Hokuseido, 1962.

>The author attempts to write a diary-style account of Stevenson's own thoughts about his life.

Osbourne, Lloyd. AN INTIMATE PORTRAIT OF ROBERT LOUIS STEVENSON. New York: Scribner's, 1924.

>Written by Stevenson's stepson.

Rice, E.E. JOURNEY TO UPOLU: ROBERT LOUIS STEVENSON, VICTORIAN REBELS. New York: Dodd, 1974.

>Intended for the general reader and amply illustrated. Emphasizes Stevenson's "modern" concerns and attacks on Victorian conventions.

Smith, Janet [A.]. ROBERT LOUIS STEVENSON. London: Duckworth, 1937.

>A brief biography with sections on "The Popularity of JEKYLL AND HYDE" and "Fanny's Influence on Stevenson's Work."

Stephen, Leslie. "The Style and Genius of Stevenson." In his STUDIES OF A BIOGRAPHER. Vol. 4. New York: Putnam's, 1907.

Steuart, J.A. STEVENSON: MAN AND WRITER: A CRITICAL BIOGRAPHY. 2 vols. London: Low, Martin, 1924.

>A valuable study that exposes the myths surrounding Stevenson's life and accuses Stevenson of "egoism" in both his life and works.

Swinnerton, Frank Arthur. ROBERT LOUIS STEVENSON: A CRITICAL STUDY. London: Doran, 1915.

>The first attack on the Stevenson legend perpetuated by Balfour, above. Extremely critical of the LIFE and all of Stevenson's literary works.

CRITICAL STUDIES

Brown, George A. A BOOK OF R.L.S. London: Methuen, 1919.

>A useful compilation of a great deal of miscellaneous information about Stevenson.

Butts, Denis. ROBERT LOUIS STEVENSON. London: Sydney, Bodley Head, 1966.

>Includes a biographical sketch and chapters on TREASURE ISLAND and Stevenson's prose. Intended for the general reader.

Daiches, David. ROBERT LOUIS STEVENSON. Norfolk, Conn.: New Directions Books, 1947.

>A short, excellent introduction to Stevenson's work. Criticizes

Stevenson's essays as "a self-conscious form of literary apprenticeship, in which he was endeavouring to develop a style."

_____. "Which R.L.S.?" NCF, 6 (1952), 61-70.

Contrasts the view of Elwin, below, and Hinkley, p. 224, concludes that "it is a mistake to write biographies of Stevenson in too partisan a frame of mind (or as Elwin has done on the other side)."

Dalglish, Doris N. PRESBYTERIAN PIRATE: A PORTRAIT OF ROBERT LOUIS STEVENSON. London: Oxford University Press, 1937.

Contains chapters on Stevenson's poetry, fiction, artistic technique, and "Essays and Miscellaneous Prose." The latter concludes that "if the essays fail, it is rather because of a flatness which has robbed his seriousness of its wider lyricism and restricted its cadences to a too conversational level."

Egan, Joseph J. "From History to Myth: A Symbolic Reading of THE MASTER OF BALLANTRAE." SEL, 8 (1968), 699-710.

Analyzes the relationship between the brothers in the novel as "representatives of the opposing Jacobite and Whig forces in eighteenth-century Scotland."

_____. "MARKHEIM: A Drama of Moral Pyschology." NCF, 20 (1966), 377-84.

Stevenson's intention in MARKHEIM was "to present not a short story as such, but a moral fable in the form of an exploration of his main character's mind." The novel is thus "symbolic," in that "the setting of the story gradually becomes the central character's own mind."

_____. "The Relationship of Theme and Art in THE STRANGE CASE OF DR. JEKYLL AND MR. HYDE." ELT, 9 (1966), 28-32.

Discusses the "artistic design of the story" as presenting "the idea of the self-contradictory impulses and mingled strains for good and evil within the same man."

Eigner, Edwin. ROBERT LOUIS STEVENSON AND ROMANTIC TRADITION. Princeton, N.J.: Princeton University Press, 1967.

Compares Stevenson's fiction to the tradition of nineteenth-century prose romance: "Through the comparisons, I have attempted to define this tradition and at the same time to establish Stevenson's rightful place within it."

Elwin, Malcolm. OLD GODS FALLING. New York: Macmillan, 1939.

    Contains two chapters on Stevenson that conclude Stevenson was "defeated by convention."

_____. THE STRANGE CASE OF ROBERT LOUIS STEVENSON. London: MacDonald, 1950.

    Claims that Stevenson's fiction suffered under the censorship of the "prurient prudery of popular taste." Elwin attacks the legend created by Balfour, p. 223, and blames Stevenson's wife for her "restrictive influence" on his career. Also see Daiches, above.

Hannah, Barbara. STRIVING TOWARDS WHOLENESS. New York: Putnam's, 1971.

    Includes a chapter on Stevenson that analyzes JEKYLL AND HYDE from a Jungian viewpoint: "the conflict between the ego and the shadow is bound to end in a deadlock if the anima or animus is not discovered."

Kiely, Robert. STEVENSON AND THE FICTION OF ADVENTURE. Cambridge, Mass.: Harvard University Press, 1964.

    Uses Freudian themes to analyze Stevenson's adventure stories, which eventually became a "symbolic chart of the formidable risks in which life involves all men."

MacPherson, Harriet. ROBERT LOUIS STEVENSON: A STUDY IN FRENCH INFLUENCE. New York: Institute of French Studies, 1930.

    Claims that Stevenson's residence at Fontainebleau was a "formative" influence, as was his study of Montaigne, Flaubert, Balzac, and Dumas.

Miyoshi, Masao. "Dr. Jekyll and the Emergence of Mr. Hyde." CE, 27 (1966), 470-80.

    Disagrees with critics who have called JEKYLL AND HYDE merely "crude science fiction or cruder moral allegory." Contends that the novel does "yield insights into certain aspects of the late Victorian society that was its milieu."

Muirhead, J[ohn] H. "Stevenson's Philosophy of Life." In his PHILOSOPHY AND LIFE. London: Swan, Sonnenschein, 1902.

    Attempts "to do justice to Stevenson's moral ideas which are not only his stock-in-trade in his essays, but underlie even his lighter studies, while they are the soul and essence of his greatest."

Saposnik, Irving. ROBERT LOUIS STEVENSON. New York: Twayne, 1974.

Saposnik's general survey of Stevenson's life and works concludes that his essays are "elaborate and overly self-conscious."

Snyder, Alice D. "Paradox and Antithesis in Stevenson's Essays: A Structural Study." JEGP, 19 (1920), 540-59.

Claims that the structure of the essays "parallels so interestingly with the structure of the typical lyric" with its reliance on opposition, paradox, thesis, and antithesis.

Stern, Gladys B. ROBERT LOUIS STEVENSON. London: Longmans, Green, 1952.

A brief introduction to Stevenson's life and works, concluding that "for some perplexing reason, Stevenson is not always readable; he demands an effort."

Torossian, Aram. "Stevenson as a Literary Critic." UNIVERSITY OF CALIFORNIA CHRONICLE, 27 (1925), 43-60.

Discusses Stevenson in some detail as an "impressionistic critic" who had a "strong moral sense" and "an abiding faith in human nature, even in the most lowly."

BIBLIOGRAPHIES

Ehrsam, Theodore G., and Robert H. Deily. "Robert Louis Stevenson." In their BIBLIOGRAPHIES OF TWELVE VICTORIAN AUTHORS. New York: Wilson, 1936; rpt. New York: Octagon, 1968.

A useful bibliography that lists critical studies published before 1935.

McKay, George L. A STEVENSON LIBRARY: CATALOGUE OF A COLLECTION OF WRITINGS BY AND ABOUT ROBERT LOUIS STEVENSON FORMED BY EDWIN J. BEINECKE. 6 vols. New Haven, Conn.: Yale University Library, 1951-64.

A careful bibliographical catalog of the most extensive Stevenson collection. Like Wainwright, below, it supplements Prideaux.

Prideaux, W.F. A BIBLIOGRAPHY OF THE WORKS OF ROBERT LOUIS STEVENSON. London: Hollings, 1903; rpt. New York: Franklin, 1968.

Generally considered the standard bibliography of Stevenson's works. Includes all of his contributions to periodicals, as well as early secondary studies.

Slater, J[oseph] H. A BIBLIOGRAPHY OF ROBERT LOUIS STEVENSON. London: Bell, 1914.

Attempts to supplement Prideaux's bibliography, above.

Wainwright, Alexander. ROBERT LOUIS STEVENSON: A CATALOGUE OF THE GERTSLEY STEVENSON COLLECTION, THE STEVENSON SECTION OF THE PARRISH COLLECTION OF VICTORIAN NOVELISTS, AND ITEMS FROM OTHER COLLECTIONS OF THE PRINCETON UNIV. LIBRARY. Princeton, N.J.: Princeton University Press, 1971.

A valuable supplement to Stevenson bibliography.

AESTHETIC

WALTER HORATIO PATER (1839-94)

PRINCIPAL PROSE WORKS

STUDIES IN THE HISTORY OF THE RENAISSANCE, 1873.

MARIUS THE EPICUREAN: HIS SENSATIONS AND IDEAS. 2 vols. 1885.

IMAGINARY PORTRAITS, 1887.

APPRECIATIONS, WITH AN ESSAY ON STYLE, 1889.

PLATO AND PLATONISM: A SERIES OF LECTURES, 1893.

AN IMAGINARY PORTRAIT [THE CHILD IN THE HOUSE], 1894.

GREEK STUDIES. Ed. C.L. Shadwell. 1895.

COLLECTED WORKS

ESSAYS ON LITERATURE AND ART. Ed. Jennifer Uglow. London: Dent, 1973.
> Contains "Style," "Charles Lamb," and extracts from the major prose works.

SELECTED ESSAYS OF WALTER PATER. Ed. H.G. Rawlinson. London: Macmillan, 1927.

SELECTED PROSE OF WALTER PATER. Ed. D. Patmore. London: Falcon, 1949.

Walter Horatio Pater

SELECTED WORKS OF WALTER PATER. Ed. Richard Aldington. New York: Duell, Sloan, Pearce, 1948.

SELECTED WRITINGS OF WALTER PATER. Ed. Harold Bloom. New York: New American Library, 1974.

THE WORKS OF WALTER PATER. 10 vols. London: Macmillan, 1910; rpt. London: Blackwell, 1971.

> There is no complete edition of all of Pater's work. This is the only one that collects most of his writings.

LETTERS

THE LETTERS OF WALTER PATER. Ed. Lawrence Evans. New York: Oxford University Press, 1970.

> Containing over 300 letters, this is the first collection of Pater's letters.

BIOGRAPHIES

Benson, Arthur. WALTER PATER. London: Macmillan, 1906.

> Benson's is the official biography, since he worked with materials provided by Pater's sisters.

Wright, Thomas. THE LIFE OF WALTER PATER. 2 vols. New York: Putnam's, 1907.

> Wright's biography has been criticized for relying on suspect information and giving authority to mistaken statements about Pater's life.

CRITICAL STUDIES

Appleman, Philip. "Darwin, Pater, and a Crisis in Classicism, 1859." In his 1859: ENTERING A YEAR OF CRISIS. Bloomington: Indiana University Press, 1959.

> "I shall attempt to establish that Darwin's influence on Pater was more significant than is usually assumed; that this influence led Pater's literary criticism toward two antithetical positions, the impressionistic and the historical."

Bizot, Richard. "Pater in Transition." PQ, 52 (1972), 129-41.

> Examines PLATO AND PLATONISM as an example of the "continual rethinking and reshaping of his ideas."

———. "Pater's 'The Child in the House' in Perspective." PLL, 8 (1972), 79-95.

    The first of Pater's IMAGINARY PORTRAITS is "essential to an understanding of the man and his work," both for "formal" and autobiographical reasons.

Bloom, Harold. THE RINGERS IN THE TOWER: STUDIES IN ROMANTIC TRADITION. Chicago: University of Chicago Press, 1971.

    Includes a study of MARIUS THE EPICUREAN.

———. "Walter Pater: The Intoxication of Belatedness." YFS, 50 (1974), 163-89.

    "Pater's great achievement, in conjunction with Swinburne and the pre-Raphaelites, was to empty Ruskin's aestheticism of its moral basis, and so to purify a critical stance appropriate for the apprehension of Romantic art."

Boas, George. "The Mona Lisa in the History of Taste." JHI, 1 (1940), 207-24.

    Aligns Pater with Gautier in the belief that the Mona Lisa is "a symbol of metempsychosis."

Bowra, Maurice. "Walter Pater." SR, 57 (1949), 378-400.

    Bowra praises Pater's efforts to define the place of art in life and of the artist in society.

Buckley, Jerome. "Pater and the Suppressed 'Conclusion.'" MLN, 65 (1950), 249-51.

    Buckley discusses the differences between the first and second editions of the HISTORY OF THE RENAISSANCE.

Cecil, David. "Walter Pater." In his THE FINE ART OF READING. Indianapolis: Bobbs-Merrill, 1957.

    Pater "was that rare hybrid, the scholar-artist" who, "as no one else before or since, put into words the scholar's distinctive sense of the beautiful."

Chandler, Edmund. PATER ON STYLE. Copenhagen: Rosenkild and Baggar, 1958.

    Attempts to "show the manner and extent that Pater applied the principles of the essay on 'Style' when revising MARIUS."

Chandler, Zilpha E. AN ANALYSIS AND SYNOPSIS OF THE STYLISTIC TECHNIQUE OF ADDISON, JOHNSON, HAZLITT, AND PATER. 2 vols. Iowa City: University of Iowa Humanistic Studies, 1928.

> Focuses on Pater's diction, sentence structure, and rhetorical method and concludes that "his style is seldom clear and never, in any sense, forceful."

Child, Ruth C. THE AESTHETIC OF WALTER PATER. New York: Macmillan, 1940.

> Defends Pater's philosophy of art by claiming that Pater did place value on the moral qualities and function of art, and was not totally "impressionistic."

Court, Franklin E. "Change and Suffering in Pater's Fictional Heroes." MFS, 13 (1967-68), 443-53.

> Court examines the heroes in Pater's fiction and claims that each embodies "some form of revolt" and a "pattern of change and suffering."

———. "Pater and the Subject of Duality." ELT, 15 (1972), 21-35.

> Examines Pater's debt to his contemporaries as well as to the Renaissance humanists for his belief that "man is directed toward the 'Ideal' naturally because he has a natural affinity for it."

———. "Virtue Sought 'As a Hunter His Sustenance': Pater's 'Amoral Aesthetic.'" ELH, 40 (1974), 549-63.

> "Pater's interest in the concept of virtue underlies the fundamentally ethical nature of his too frequently misunderstood aesthetic vision."

Cox, Catherine. "Pater's 'Apollo in Picardy' and Mann's DEATH IN VENICE." ANGLIA, 86 (1968), 143-54.

> Enumerates the many similarities between the two works--plot, heroes, godlike youths, artistic creativity, and death. Concludes that both are "stories of the artist's destiny."

Crinkley, Richmond. WALTER PATER: HUMANIST. Lexington: University Press of Kentucky, 1970.

> Crinkley attempts to put Pater's major works into the context of his life, which he claims was a search for a multisided vision of culture.

DeLaura, David J. "Pater and Eliot: The Origin of the 'Objective Correlative.'" MLQ, 26 (1965), 426-31.

DeLaura believes that Pater was the source for Eliot's condemnation of impressionistic, romantic criticism.

——. "Pater and Newman: The Road to the Nineties." VS, 10 (1967), 39-69.

DeLaura explores the influence of Newman on Pater's later work, particularly the essay on "Style" (1885).

——. "ROMOLA and the Origin of the Paterian View of Life." NCF, 21 (1966), 225-33.

DeLaura claims that Pater liked ROMOLA best among all of Eliot's novels and that it influenced MARIUS. Also see Hill, below.

——. "The 'Wordsworth' of Arnold and Pater: 'The Supreme Artistic View of Life.'" SEL, 6 (1966), 651-67.

DeLaura analyzes the interaction between Pater's and Arnold's view of "humanism."

Downes, David A. THE TEMPER OF VICTORIAN BELIEF: STUDIES IN THE RELIGIOUS NOVELS OF PATER, KINGSLEY, AND NEWMAN. New York: Twayne, 1972.

Includes a discussion of MARIUS THE EPICUREAN.

——. VICTORIAN PORTRAITS: HOPKINS AND PATER. New York: Bookman, 1965.

Downes claims that the major link between the two writers is their spiritual vision.

Duffy, John J. "From Essay to Portrait: Walter Pater after THE RENAISSANCE." THOTH, 6 (1965), 3-15.

"The concern of this study is to direct attention to the fiction that Pater wrote during the twenty years after THE RENAISSANCE and thus suggest how these expressions of Pater's sensibility reveal a desire to go beyond his famous dicta from THE RENAISSANCE."

——. "Walter Pater's Prose Style: An Essay in Theory and Analysis." STYLE, 1 (1967), 45-63.

Asserts that Pater's prose style cannot be described simply as "musical." Instead it "demonstrates at least two different sets of characteristics--melodic and pictorial."

Eliot, T.S. "Arnold and Pater." In his SELECTED ESSAYS. New York: Harcourt, 1932; rpt. London: Faber and Faber, 1961.

> Claims that Pater's "art for art's sake" is a direct result of the influence of Arnold's concept of culture. Pater, however, was "primarily a moralist, he was incapable of seeing any work of art simply as it is."

Fletcher, Ian. WALTER PATER. Rev. ed. London: Longmans, Green, 1972.

> A valuable study that emphasizes the "idea of style" as "a mode of of perception" in Pater's work.

Fraser, George S. "Walter Pater: His Theory of Style, His Style in Practice, His Influence." THE ART OF VICTORIAN PROSE. Eds. George L. Levine and William A. Madden. New York: Oxford University Press, 1968.

> This article discusses Pater's essay on "Style" and its influence on Butler, Beerbohm, and Saintsbury.

Frazier, Sloane. "Two Pagan Studies: Pater's 'Denys L'Auxerrois' and 'Apollo in Picardy.'" FOLKLORE, 81 (1970), 280-85.

> "Pater triumphs here in making mythic heroes live again in the eternal recurrence of human history."

Goff, Penrith. "Hugo von Hofmannsthal and Walter Pater." CLS, 7 (1970), 1-11.

> "Hofmannsthal admired Pater as a great critic, experimented with Pater's critical method, but took exception to what he felt was too subjective a stance."

Gordon, Jan B. "THE IMAGINARY PORTRAITS: Pater's Aesthetic Pilgrimage." UR, 35 (1968), 29-39.

> Gordon states that the transformation of life into art "not only pervades the characters of the IMAGINARY PORTRAITS and the criticism, but also Pater himself."

_____. "Pater's Gioconda Smile: A Reading of 'Emerald Uthwart.'" SSF, 6 (1968), 136-43.

> Gordon makes comparisons between "Emerald Uthwart," MARIUS, and PLATO AND PLATONISM.

Gross, Beverly. "Walter Pater and the Aesthetic Fallacy." SAQ, 68 (1969), 220-30.

> Gross argues that "the same basic aesthetic commitment" will explain the contradictions in Pater's prose.

Harris, Wendell V. "Arnold, Pater, Wilde, and the Object as in Themselves

They See It." SEL, 11 (1971), 733-47.

> "The relativism of all perceptions and impressions stated in the Conclusion of THE RENAISSANCE implies the aesthetic doctrines developed in the Preface and the essay on 'Style.'"

Harrison, John S. "Pater, Heine, and the Old Gods of Greece." PMLA, 39 (1924), 655-86.

> An early in-depth study of the classical influences on Pater.

Heffernan, James A. "Centripetal Vision in Pater's MARIUS." VN, 35 (1969), 13-17.

> Heffernan claims that MARIUS can be interpreted as a personal defense of Pater's own vision, although it "ironically reveals the crucial weaknesses of the centripetal approach to all experience."

Hidden, Norman. "Walter Pater: Aesthetic Standards or Impressionism?" USE, 2 (1969), 13-18.

> Defends Pater by claiming that he was guided by objective critical standards.

──────. "Walter Pater: A Victorian View on Hedonism." USE, 1 (1968), 22-31.

> Hidden disagrees with critics who have charged Pater with hedonism.

Hill, Charles G. "Walter Pater and the Gide-DuBos Dialogue." RLC, 31 (1967), 367-84.

> Discusses Pater's influence on Gide and DuBos.

Hill, Donald L. "Pater's Debt to ROMOLA." NCF, 22 (1968), 361-77.

> Hill disagrees with DeLaura, above, and claims that Pater seems not to have been influenced by Eliot's novel.

Inman, Billie A. "Pater's Appeal to His Readers: A Study of Two of Pater's Prose Styles." TSLL, 14 (1972), 643-65.

> Contrasts the "Animula Vagula" chapter of MARIUS with the conclusion of THE RENAISSANCE in order to claim that "the stylistic differences can best be explained by differences in Pater's purpose in writing the two works. The former was written to persuade an unaesthetic reader, the latter was written as an apology."

Johnson, Robert V. "Pater and the Victorian Anti-Romantics." EIC, 4 (1954), 42-57.

"My aim is to indicate the conception of romanticism held by Victorian critics who were in conscious reaction against it and to indicate further how that conception is exemplified in the writings of Pater, particularly in his theory of literature."

_____. WALTER PATER: A STUDY OF HIS CRITICAL OUTLOOK AND ACHIEVEMENT. Melbourne: Melbourne University Press, 1961.

A useful introduction to Pater's essays.

Knoepflmacher, U[lrich] C. "Pater's Religion of Sanity: PLATO AND PLATONISM as a Document of Victorian Unbelief." VS, 6 (1962), 151-68.

"Forever dependent on the impressions of the individual, Pater's 'religion of sanity' is perhaps the least comprehensive, but also the most intimate of all the personal cults of Victorian unbelief."

Lyons, Richard S. "The 'Complex, Many-Sided' Unity of THE RENAISSANCE." SEL, 12 (1972), 765-81.

"The unifying concept of THE RENAISSANCE is Pater's idea of expression--the unique and untranslatable character of art that gives the critic his special function and art its privileged role in human life."

McKenzie, Gordon. THE LITERARY CHARACTER OF WALTER PATER. Berkeley and Los Angeles: University of California Press, 1967.

McKenzie discusses Pater's use of mythology and symbolism, and his philosophy, fiction, and criticism.

Mason, Mary G. "Wordsworth and Pater's First Imaginary Portrait." HLB, 19 (1971), 194-203.

Pater is a transitional figure because "he intensely admires Wordsworth's sense of the whole and absolutes, but he is not able to retain that certainty himself."

Millhauser, Milton. "Walter Pater and the Flux." JAAC, 11 (1953), 214-23.

Millhauser discusses Pater's continual consciousness of death, which Pater alleviated by a search for artistic harmony and ethical commitment.

Monsman, Gerald. "Pater, Hopkins, and Fichte's Ideal Student." SAQ, 70 (1971), 365-76.

Monsman discusses Pater's activities at Oxford during the 1860s.

_____. "Pater, Hopkins, and the Self." VN, 46 (1974), 1-5.

"The distinction between Pater and Hopkins is that whereas Hopkins' inscapes participate in the time-transcending and eternally complete nature of Christ, Pater's selves participate in a gradually self-realizing World-Spirit."

_____. "Pater's Aesthetic Hero." UTQ, 40 (1971), 136-51.

"To make one's life a work of art: it was Pater who first conceived that as an ideal, just as it was Pater, not Wilde, who first quoted Gautier and Dante on the visible world and the worship of beauty."

_____. PATER'S PORTRAITS: MYTHIC PATTERNS IN THE FICTION OF WALTER PATER. Baltimore: Johns Hopkins University Press, 1967.

Monsman holds that it was through "portraiture"--the fictional creation of his characters--that Pater expressed his views on the relation between life and art.

Monsman, Gerald, and Samuel Wright. "Walter Pater: Style and Text." SAQ, 71 (1972), 106-23.

Discusses the prose techniques Pater employed in THE RENAISSANCE.

Morse, Samuel. "Wallace Stevens, Bergson, Pater." ELH, 31 (1964), 1-34.

Analyzes Stevens' poetry for "echoes of the final paragraphs of THE RENAISSANCE."

Pierle, Robert C. "Walter Pater and Epicureanism." SOQ, 7 (1969), 131-40.

Describes "some of the major tenets of the Epicurean philosophy and analyzes whatever correspondence may be found to exist in the writings of Pater."

Read, Sir Herbert. "Walter Pater." In his THE TENTH MUSE. Freeport, N.Y.: Books for Libraries, 1957.

Praises Pater's "amazing modernity" and "enduring vitality," while in his best writings "one is aware that our language is, perhaps for the first time, being used in the full measure of its music and meaning."

Roellinger, Francis X. "Intimations of Winckelmann in Pater's DIAPHANEITE." ELN, 2 (1965), 277-82.

Shows that Pater borrowed from his own earlier writing to describe Winckelmann in this later essay.

Rosenblatt, Louise. "The Genius of Pater's MARIUS THE EPICUREAN." CL, 14 (1962), 242-60.

> Claims that Arnold and Renan were the primary sources for Pater's novel, which Rosenblatt considers "both a document in intellectual history and a work of art."

Schoen, Max. "Pater on the Place of Music Among the Arts." JAAC, 1 (1942), 12-23.

> Discusses Pater's aesthetic theory and claims that, according to his theory, "music necessarily becomes the measure of the arts."

Schuetz, Lawrence F. "Pater's MARIUS: The Temple of God and the Palace of Art." EFT, 15 (1972), 1-19.

> Schuetz contends that the myth of Cupid and Psyche underlies the novel.

―――. "The Suppressed 'Conclusion' to THE RENAISSANCE and Pater's Modern Image." ELT, 17 (1974), 251-58.

> "In spite of a recent renewal of critical interest in him, our perspective of Pater seems invariably colored by the yellow filter of Wilde and the excesses of the Nineties when he ought to be seen in the clear light of objective critical judgment."

Shmiefsky, Marvel. "A Study in Aesthetic Relativism: Pater's Poetics." VP, 6 (1968), 105-24.

> Shmiefsky's thesis is that Pater's "most characteristic stance emphasizes the aesthetic end of art. Moral principles he regards as derivative."

Shuter, William F. "History as Palingenesis in Pater and Hegel." PMLA, 86 (1971), 411-21.

> Shuter claims that the rebirth metaphors in Pater are proof of Hegel's influence on Pater's historicism.

Small, I.C. "Plato and Pater: Fin-de-siècle Aesthetics." BJA, 12 (1972), 369-83.

> Analyzes PLATO AND PLATONISM because "it provides both a focus for a whole tradition of Platonic criticism and a focus for many of the major concerns in Pater's work."

Stein, Richard L. "The Private Themes of Pater's RENAISSANCE." PSYCHOANALYSIS AND LITERARY PROCESS. Ed. Frederick C. Crews. Cambridge, Mass.: Harvard University Press, 1970.

Presents a Freudian reading of THE RENAISSANCE.

Sullivan, William H. "Four Early Studies from Pater's RENAISSANCE: The Aesthetics for a Humanist Myth." VN, 60 (1971), 1-7.

>Discusses "Poems by Morris," "Leonardo da Vinci," "Botticelli," and "Winckelmann."

Symons, Arthur. A STUDY OF WALTER PATER. London: Sawyer, 1932.

>An appreciative memoir: "Everything in Pater was in harmony, when you got used to its particular forms of expression."

Temple, Ruth Z. "The Ivory Tower as Lighthouse." EDWARDIANS AND LATE VICTORIANS. Ed. Richard Ellmann. New York: Columbia University Press, 1960.

>Analyzes Pater's aestheticism and concludes that Pater's method elevated "the critic to the status of creator."

Tillotson, Geoffrey. "Arnold and Pater: Critics Historical, Aesthetic, and Unlabelled." In his CRITICISM AND THE NINETEENTH CENTURY. London: Athlone Press, 1951.

>Describes Pater as "more a painter-like poet than a critic" who "extended the bounds of the aesthetic critic illegitimately."

──────. "Pater, Mr. Rose, and the 'Conclusion' of THE RENAISSANCE." In his CRITICISM AND THE NINETEENTH CENTURY. London: Athlone Press, 1951.

>Discusses William Hurrell Mallock's portrait of Pater as Mr. Rose in his novel THE NEW REPUBLIC. According to Tillotson, Mallock's Mr. Rose "pushed Pater's views a step further than Pater pushed them, bringing them to the test."

Ward, Anthony. WALTER PATER: THE IDEA IN NATURE. London: MacGibbon and Kee, 1966.

>Ward claims that Pater's conservatism, idealization of mother and child, and search for security are understood only in relation to what he saw as a breakdown of traditional values.

Wellek, René. "Walter Pater's Literary Theory and Criticism." In his A HISTORY OF MODERN CRITICISM, 1750-1950. Vol. 4. New Haven, Conn.: Yale University Press, 1965.

>Wellek concludes that "none of Pater's work has escaped the limitations of nineteenth-century aestheticism."

West, Alick. "Walter Pater and Oscar Wilde." In his THE MOUNTAIN IN THE SUNLIGHT. London: Lawrence & Wishart, 1958.

>A Marxist analysis of Pater's social criticism.

West, Paul. "A Narrowed Humanism: Pater and Malraux." DR, 37 (1957), 278-84.

>West claims that both writers attempted to worship an aesthetic ideal.

_____. "Pater and the Tribulations of Taste." UTQ, 27 (1958), 424-32.

>"It is my intention to affirm the desirability of revaluing as a whole the achievement of Pater. And this intention entails his being detached from a few catchwords and from all their pejorative implications."

_____. "Pater's Cordial Canon." ENGLISH, 14 (1963), 185-88.

>Pater's criticism "is a fragmentary and allusive philosophy" and "to attempt to relate his critical valuations to his beliefs is to lose in darkness any guidance that our taste has been offered."

Young, Helen H. THE WRITINGS OF WALTER PATER: A REFLECTION OF BRITISH PHILOSOPHICAL OPINION FROM 1860 TO 1890. Lancaster, Pa.: Lancaster Press, 1933; rpt. New York: Haskell House, 1965.

>A valuable study that places Pater's writings in the context of contemporary thought and analyzes the changes in the meaning of his central concepts.

BIBLIOGRAPHIES

Evans, Lawrence. "Walter Pater." VICTORIAN PROSE: A GUIDE TO RESEARCH. Ed. David J. DeLaura. New York: MLA, 1973.

>A valuable bibliographical essay that discusses critical studies published through 1972.

Stonehill, Charles A., and H. Winthrop. "Walter Pater." In their BIBLIOGRAPHIES OF MODERN AUTHORS. 2nd series. London: Castle, 1925.

Wright, Samuel. A BIBLIOGRAPHY OF THE WRITINGS OF WALTER H. PATER. New York: Garland, 1975.

>The first complete and definitive bibliography of all of Pater's writings. An important addition to the Pater canon.

JOHN RUSKIN (1819-1900)

PRINCIPAL PROSE WORKS

MODERN PAINTERS, 5 vols., 1843-60.

THE SEVEN LAMPS OF ARCHITECTURE, 1849.

THE STONES OF VENICE. 3 vols. 1851-53.

PRE-RAPHAELITISM, 1851.

GIOTTO AND HIS WORKS IN PADUA, 1854.

LECTURES ON ARCHITECTURE AND PAINTING, 1854.

THE POLITICAL ECONOMY OF ART, 1857.

UNTO THIS LAST. FOUR ESSAYS ON THE FIRST PRINCIPLES OF POLITICAL ECONOMY, 1862.

SESAME AND LILIES, 1865.

THE CROWN OF WILD OLIVE. THREE LECTURES ON WORK, TRAFFIC, AND WAR, 1866.

FORS CLAVIGERA. LETTERS TO THE WORKMEN AND LABOURERS OF GREAT BRITAIN. 8 vols. 1871-84.

MUNERA PULVERIS. SIX ESSAYS ON THE ELEMENTS OF POLITICAL ECONOMY, 1872.

PRAETERITA. OUTLINES OF SCENES AND THOUGHTS PERHAPS WORTHY OF MEMORY IN MY PAST LIFE. 3 vols. 1886-88.

COLLECTED WORKS

THE ART CRITICISM OF JOHN RUSKIN. Ed. Robert Herbert. New York: Anchor, 1964.

THE BRANTWOOD DIARY OF JOHN RUSKIN: TOGETHER WITH SELECTED RELATED LETTERS AND SKETCHES OF PERSONS MENTIONED. Ed. Helen Gill Viljoen. New Haven, Conn.: Yale University Press, 1971.

THE DIARIES OF JOHN RUSKIN, 1835-1889. Eds. Joan Evans and John H[oward] Whitehouse. 3 vols. London: Oxford University Press, 1955-59.

THE GENIUS OF JOHN RUSKIN: SELECTIONS FROM HIS WRITINGS. Ed. John D. Rosenberg. London: Allen and Unwin, 1963.

THE LAMP OF BEAUTY: WRITINGS ON ART BY JOHN RUSKIN. Ed. Joan Evans. New York: Doubleday, 1959.

THE LITERARY CRITICISM OF JOHN RUSKIN. Ed. Harold Bloom. New York: Anchor, 1965.

RUSKIN TODAY. Ed. [Sir] Kenneth [M.] Clark. London: Murray, 1964.

SELECTED WRITINGS OF JOHN RUSKIN. Ed. Peter Quennell. New York: Anchor, 1952.

THE WORKS OF JOHN RUSKIN. Eds. Sir Edward T. Cook and Alexander D.O. Wedderburn. 39 vols. London: Allen; New York: Longmans, Green, 1903-12.

> This is the standard, definitive collection of Ruskin's works. Volume 38 contains a valuable bibliography; also see Halliday under "Bibliographies," below.

LETTERS

DEAREST MAMA TALBOT: A SELECTION OF LETTERS BY JOHN RUSKIN TO MRS. FANNY TALBOT. Ed. Margaret Spence. London: Allen and Unwin, 1966.

DeLaura, David J. "Ruskin and the Brownings: Twenty-five Unpublished Letters." BJRL, 54 (1972), 314-56.

JOHN RUSKIN AND EFFIE GRAY: THE STORY OF JOHN RUSKIN, EFFIE

GRAY, AND JOHN EVERETT MILLAIS TOLD FOR THE FIRST TIME IN THEIR UNPUBLISHED LETTERS. Ed. Sir William J. James. New York: Scribner's, 1947.

THE LETTERS OF JOHN RUSKIN TO LORD AND LADY MOUNT-TEMPLE. Ed. John Lewis Bradley. Columbus: Ohio State University Press, 1964.

MILLAIS AND THE RUSKINS. Ed. Mary Lutyens. London: Murray, 1967.

A study of the relationship based on the correspondence.

THE RUSKIN FAMILY LETTERS: THE CORRESPONDENCE OF JOHN JAMES RUSKIN, HIS WIFE, AND THEIR SON, JOHN, 1801-1843. Ed. Van A. Burd. 2 vols. Ithaca, N.Y.: Cornell University Press, 1973.

RUSKIN IN ITALY: LETTERS TO HIS PARENTS, 1845. Ed. Harold I. Shapiro. Oxford: Clarendon Press, 1972.

RUSKIN'S LETTERS FROM VENICE, 1851-1852. Ed. John L[ewis] Bradley. New Haven, Conn.: Yale University Press, 1955.

Contains over 200 letters, many published here for the first time.

Spence, Margaret. "Ruskin's Correspondence with Miss Blanche Atkinson." BJRL, 42 (1959), 194-219.

SUBLIME AND INSTRUCTIVE: LETTERS FROM JOHN RUSKIN TO LOUISA, MARCHIONESS OF WATERFORD, ANNA BLUNDEN, AND ELLEN HEATON. Ed. Virginia Surtees. London: Joseph, 1972.

Ruskin's letters to female correspondents, 1853-75.

THE WINNINGTON LETTERS: JOHN RUSKIN'S CORRESPONDENCE WITH MARGARET ALEXIS BELL AND THE CHILDREN AT WINNINGTON HALL. Ed. Van A[kin] Burd. Cambridge, Mass.: Harvard University Press, 1969.

YOUNG MRS. RUSKIN IN VENICE: UNPUBLISHED LETTERS OF MRS. JOHN RUSKIN WRITTEN FROM VENICE BETWEEN 1849-1852. Ed. Mary Lutyens. New York: Vanguard, 1967.

BIOGRAPHIES

Bell, Quentin. JOHN RUSKIN. Edinburgh: Oliver & Boyd, 1963.

A general introduction to Ruskin's life.

Evans, John. JOHN RUSKIN. New York: Oxford, 1954.

Usually considered the best recent biography.

Leon, Derrick. RUSKIN: THE GREAT VICTORIAN. London: Routledge and Kegan Paul, 1949.

> Also contains several letters between Ruskin and Rose LaTouche.

Mather, Marshall. JOHN RUSKIN: HIS LIFE AND TEACHING. London: Warne, 1897; rpt. New York: Haskell House, 1972.

> A biography that stresses Ruskin's "teachings" on social science, education, art, and political economy.

Quennell, Peter. JOHN RUSKIN: THE PORTRAIT OF A PROPHET. New York: Viking, 1949.

> Quennell's thesis is that the frustrations of Ruskin's private life "finally brought an end to his career of public usefulness."

Rosenberg, John D. THE DARKENING GLASS: A PORTRAIT OF RUSKIN'S GENIUS. New York: Columbia University Press, 1961.

> Rosenberg's theme is "Ruskin's mind, its wayward genius, its sickness, its essential sanity. Because Ruskin was the most personal of writers, the book is also about his life, but only in so far as it shaped--or warped--what he wrote."

Viljoen, Helen G[ill]. RUSKIN'S SCOTTISH HERITAGE. Urbana: University of Illinois Press, 1956.

> Focuses on the formative influences in Ruskin's life by examining his parents' religious and social beliefs.

Wilenski, Reginald. JOHN RUSKIN: AN INTRODUCTION TO FURTHER STUDY OF HIS LIFE AND WORK. London: Faber and Faber, 1933.

> This important study pioneered modern Ruskin biography.

CRITICAL STUDIES

Alexander, Edward. "Art Amidst Revolution: Ruskin in 1848." VN, 40 (1970), 8-13.

> Alexander's thesis is that Ruskin valued art for its civilizing restraint on society.

———. "PRAETERITA: Ruskin's Remembrance of Things Past." JEGP, 73 (1974), 351-62.

> "Proust's discovery of the secret of his own quest for the past in Ruskin's PRAETERITA enabled him to see that the unity of such a work as PRAETERITA lies not in the logical ordering of episodes and ideas but in the recurrent use of certain motifs and images."

———. "Ruskin and Science." MLR, 64 (1969), 508-21.

> Alexander discusses Ruskin's fears about the encroaching powers of science.

Arvidson, K.O. "Ruskin's Aesthetic: An Approach to the English Elements in the Decadence." AUSTRALASIAN UNIVERSITIES LANGUAGE AND LITERATURE ASSOCIATION. Melbourne: AULLA, 1971.

Bradley, John Lewis. AN INTRODUCTION TO RUSKIN. Boston: Houghton Mifflin, 1971.

> Bradley's is a useful general work on Ruskin's life and works. Also contains an annotated bibliography.

Burd, Van Akin. "Background to the MODERN PAINTERS: The Tradition and the Turner Controversy." PMLA, 74 (1959), 254-67.

> "This paper will develop Ruskin's projection of the controversy over Turner's pictures, as he witnessed it after 1836, against the tradition of which it was a product."

———. "Ruskin, Rossetti, and William Bell Scott: A Second Arrangement." PQ, 48 (1969), 102-07.

> Discusses the photographs taken of Ruskin by F.J. Sharp in 1863.

———. "Ruskin's Defense of Turner: The Initiative Phase." PQ, 37 (1958), 465-83.

> Examines Ruskin's 1836 version of the defense of Turner for "its significance in the development of Ruskin's ideas."

———. "Ruskin's Quest for a Theory of Imagination." MLQ, 17 (1956), 60-72.

> Analyzes Ruskin's unpublished correspondence to his father during his 1845 Italian tour, to chart the growth in his ideas between the first and second volumes of MODERN PAINTERS.

Colburn, William E. "Ruskin and Browning: The Poet's Responsibility." SLI, 1 (1968), 37-46.

> Discusses the resemblance between Browning's poetry and THE STONES OF VENICE.

Curtin, Frank D. "Aesthetics in English Social Reform: Ruskin and His Followers." NINETEENTH-CENTURY STUDIES. Eds. Herbert Davis, William C. DeVane; and R.C. Bald. Ithaca, N.Y.: Cornell University Press, 1940.

> Asserts that "the attitudes and ideas of Ruskin, so often dismissed as sentimental and unpractical in his own time and after, were seminal in the social criticism of the late nineteenth century."

———. "Ruskin in French Criticism: A Possible Reappraisal." PMLA, 77 (1962), 102-08.

"A substantial and varied body of criticism in French concentrates on Ruskin--a dozen books and some thirty lesser studies; from the first, Ruskin's aesthetics and his art criticism were their especial concern."

Dearden, James S. "The Ruskin Circle in Italy in 1872." CONNOISSEUR, 179 (1972), 240-45.

Reviews Arthur Severn's account of Ruskin's trip to Italy with several friends.

Dellamora, Richard J. "The Revaluation of 'Christian' Art: Ruskin's Appreciation of Fra Angelico, 1845-1860." UTQ, 43 (1974), 143-50.

Analyzes "Ruskin's changing presentation to his readers of the art of Fra Angelico" in terms of "the dialectic of 'Christian' and 'Pagan' or classical art in Romantic and early Victorian aesthetics."

Dollarhide, Louis E. "The Paradox of Ruskin's Admiration of Renaissance English Writers." UMSE, 8 (1967), 7-12.

Concludes that Ruskin admired the Renaissance writers because of "their unbroken links with the spirit of the Middle Ages--a unified faith, a spiritual rest or repose, in which he perceives true beauty, and the penetrative, intuitive power called imagination."

Doughtery, Charles T. "Of Ruskin's Gardens." MYTH AND SYMBOL: CRITICAL APPROACHES AND APPLICATIONS. Eds. Northrop Frye et al. Lincoln: University of Nebraska Press, 1963.

Doughtery analyzes two of Ruskin's symbols, the garden and the idealized female.

Fain, John T. RUSKIN AND THE ECONOMISTS. Nashville, Tenn.: Vanderbilt, 1956.

Fain discusses Ruskin's attacks on orthodox economists by analyzing his distinctions between the medieval and the modern systems of exchange.

Feltes, Norman N. "The Quickset Hedge: Ruskin's Early Prose." VN, 34 (1968), 18-22.

Feltes applies the hedge metaphor to Ruskin's peculiar prose style.

Fishman, Solomon. THE INTERPRETATION OF ART: ESSAYS ON THE ART CRITICISM OF JOHN RUSKIN, WALTER PATER, CLIVE BELL, ROGER FRY,

AND HERBERT READ. Berkeley and Los Angeles: University of California Press, 1963.

Fleming, Gordon H. THAT NE'ER SHALL MEET AGAIN: ROSSETTI, MILLAIS, HUNT. London: Young, 1971.

> Fleming discusses the Ruskin marriage and the broken friendships among Rossetti, Millais, and Hunt.

Fontaney, Pierre. "Death and Champagnole: A Contribution to the Reading of THE SEVEN LAMPS OF ARCHITECTURE." UTQ, 43 (1974), 132-42.

> Asserts that Ruskin's "conception of beauty remains objective throughout and firmly grounded in the divine. What is pre-eminently perceptible, though, is the massive new emphasis on life and the human."

_____. "Ruskin and PARADISE REGAINED." VS, 12 (1969), 347-56.

> Fontaney attempts a Jungian analysis of the images in Ruskin's description of the Rhone.

Fulford, Roger. "Ruskin's Notes on Carlyle." TLS, 16 April, 1971, p. 453.

> Discusses Ruskin's unpublished marginalia on Carlyle. Also see letter from Martha S. Vogeler, TLS, 7 May 1971, p. 535.

Greenberg, Robert A. "Ruskin, Pugin, and the Contemporary Context of 'The Bishop Orders His Tomb.'" PMLA, 84 (1969), 1588-94.

> Stresses both Ruskin's and Browning's debt to Pugin's writings on the Renaissance. "Ruskin in retrospect found Browning's poem exemplary of his own position."

Harris, Wendell V. "The Gothic Structure of Ruskin's PRAISE OF THE GOTHIC." UTQ, 40 (1971), 109-18.

> Asserts that Maria Edgeworth's stories serve "as a paradigm for Ruskin's almost invariable approach to any problem, and many of the strengths and weaknesses of his work are precisely those of that method."

Hayman, John. "John Ruskin and the Art of System-Making." YES, 4 (1974), 197-202.

> Analyzes Ruskin's notion of "system-making" as a means of understanding "the underlying structure of Ruskin's rhetoric, Ruskin's habitual cast of mind, and the metaphysical basis of his thought."

Hiton, Timothy. THE PRE-RAPHAELITES. London: Thames, 1970.

John Ruskin

Surveys the aesthetics of the Pre-Raphaelites by discussing Ruskin's critical works on art.

Johnson, Wendell Stacy. "'The Bride of Literature': Ruskin, the Eastlakes, and Mid-Victorian Theories of Art." VN, 26 (1964), 23-28.

John discusses the nineteenth-century attacks on Ruskin's aesthetics.

Joseph, Robert J. "John Ruskin: Radical and Psychotic Genius." PR, 56 (1969), 425-41.

Joseph diagnoses Ruskin as a sadomasochist who spent his last years as a schizophrenic.

Jump, John D. "Ruskin's Reputation in the Eighteen-Fifties: The Evidence of the Three Principal Weeklies." PMLA, 63 (1948), 678-85.

Jump analyzes the reviews of Ruskin's works in the SPECTATOR, the SATURDAY REVIEW, and the ATHENAEUM.

Kitson, Michael. "Ruskin and English Taste." LISTENER, 87 (1972), 205-07.

Considers Ruskin as an art critic who "combined the primitive and the Christian with the artistic in his efforts to effect a Gothic revival."

Ladd, Henry. THE VICTORIAN MORALITY OF ART: AN ANALYSIS OF RUSKIN'S AESTHETICS. New York: Long & Smith, 1932.

Until Landow's study, below, Ladd's was generally considered the standard work on this topic.

Landow, George P. THE AESTHETIC AND CRITICAL THEORIES OF JOHN RUSKIN. Princeton, N.J.: Princeton University Press, 1971.

The definitive study of this subject. Supersedes Ladd's study, above.

──────. "J.D. Harding and John Ruskin on Nature's Infinite Variety." JAAC, 28 (1970), 369-80.

Landow believes that Ruskin was influenced by Harding's aesthetic theories.

──────. "Ruskin and Baudelaire on Art and Artist." UTQ, 37 (1968), 295-308.

Landow claims that both writers applied romantic literary principles to judgments on painting.

———. "Ruskin's Refutations of False Opinions Held Concerning Beauty." BJA, 8 (1968), 60-72.

Discusses Ruskin's attempts to link Beauty with the Divine.

———. "Ruskin's Revisions of the Third Edition of MODERN PAINTERS, Volume 1." VN, 33 (1968), 12-16.

Landow analyzes how Ruskin incorporated changes based on contemporary critiques of the second edition.

———. "Ruskin's Version of 'Ut Pictura Poesis.'" JAAC, 26 (1968), 521-28.

Examines the notion of ut pictura poesis and "the idea of art based on expression of emotion." Also "investigates the ways in which these views, in the form Ruskin encountered them, were occassionally in conflict."

Lucas, John. "Conservatism and Revolution in the 1880's." In his LITERATURE AND POLITICS IN THE NINETEENTH CENTURY. New York: Barnes and Noble, 1971.

Analyzes the Conservative reorganization in the first half of the 1880s and discusses Ruskin's FORS CLAVIGERA as emblematic of "the fear of social anarchy which lumped together names like anarchist, radical, democrat and socialist, as though they all meant the same thing."

Lutyens, Mary. "The Millais-LaTouche Correspondence." CORNHILL, 1051 (1967), 1-18.

Analyzes the relationship as it is reflected in the correspondence. See also Leon's biography, p. 248.

———. THE RUSKINS AND THE GRAYS. London: Murray, 1972.

A study of the relationship between Ruskin and his in-laws, the Grays.

Mackerness, E.D. "The Voice of Prophecy: Carlyle and Ruskin." FROM DICKENS TO HARDY. Ed. Boris Ford. Baltimore: Penguin, 1958.

"Ruskin's major writings retain that sense of immediacy and inner power that is shared by all durable literature."

McLean, Robert S. "Altruistic Ideals versus Leisure Class Values: An Irreconcilable Conflict in John Ruskin." JAAC, 31 (1973), 347-56.

McLean claims that Ruskin campaigned for the imperfect because he was "a victim of unconscious self-contradiction" and "unknowingly professed leisure class ideas under the guise of altruism."

Millett, Kate. "The Debate over Women: Ruskin versus Mill." SUFFER AND BE STILL: WOMEN IN THE VICTORIAN AGE. Ed. Martha Vicinus. Bloomington: Indiana University Press, 1972.

    Compares Ruskin's "Of Queen's Gardens" to Mill's SUBJECTION OF WOMEN to contrast their views on the nature, education, and domestic role of women. Also see Doughtery, above.

Morris, Bertram. "Ruskin on the Pathetic Fallacy, or on How a Moral Theory of Art May Fail." JAAC, 14 (1955), 248-66.

    "My purpose is to show what seems to be Ruskin's chief purport in explaining the nature of the pathetic fallacy, how the statement of the fallacy implicates a whole theory of the relationships of man and nature and art, and why this theory, together with the fallacies it recognizes, has relevance to our more contemporary outlook."

Pevsner, Sir Nickolaus. RUSKIN AND VIOLLET-LE-DUC: ENGLISHNESS AND FRENCHNESS IN THE APPRECIATION OF GOTHIC ARCHITECTURE. London: Thames, 1969.

Quennell, Peter. JOHN RUSKIN. London: Longmans, Green, 1956.

    A useful introduction to Ruskin's writings.

Roellinger, Francis X. "Ruskin on Education." JGE, 5 (1950), 38-47.

    Ruskin "thinks of education as related to everything else, as an inference from the nature of man, of religion, and of society."

Rosenberg, John D. "The Genius of John Ruskin." VN, 23 (1963), 4-6.

    An excerpt from Rosenberg's introduction to his edition of a Ruskin anthology. Concludes that when the caricature is replaced, Ruskin's "genius will be recognized for what it is--a unique fusion of the capacity to see with the amazed eyes of a child and to reason with a mind as swift and penetrating as any that England has produced."

_____. "The Geopoetry of John Ruskin." EA, 22 (1969), 42-48.

    "Ruskin is nowhere more archaic, more out of tune with his own and our time, than in his conviction that the earth is man's devinely appointed home."

_____. "Style and Sensibility in Ruskin's Prose." THE ART OF VICTORIAN PROSE. Eds. George L. Levine and William A. Madden. New York: Oxford University Press, 1968.

    Rosenberg concludes that Ruskin "has no single style, or, more

accurately, shed his style as he became himself, in another sense
his styles were as various as the subjects he wrote upon and the
audiences he addressed."

Ross, Malcolm Mackenzie. "Ruskin, Hooker, and 'The Christian Theoria.'"
ESSAYS IN ENGLISH LITERATURE FROM THE RENAISSANCE TO THE VICTO-
RIAN AGE. Eds. Millar MacLure and F.W. Watt. Toronto: University of
Toronto Press, 1964.

"Within a framework broadly Christian, Ruskin occupies a series
of positions incompatible with one another. It will therefore be
necessary to specify the perdurable 'quarter' of Ruskin's theory of
art, extricate it from entanglements and contradictions."

San Juan, Epifanio. "Ruskin and Exuberance: Control in Literature." OL,
23 (1968), 257-64.

Analyzes Ruskin's notion of the "pathetic fallacy" and concludes
that "Ruskin thus reconciles the traditional conflict between 'classical' and 'romantic' standards."

Shapiro, Harold I. "The Poetry of Architecture: Ruskin's Preparation for
MODERN PAINTERS." RMS, 15 (1971), 70-84.

Shapiro analyzes Ruskin's ideas about architecture, 1837-38.

Sherburne, James C. JOHN RUSKIN OR THE AMBIGUITIES OF ABUNDANCE.
Cambridge, Mass.: Harvard University Press, 1973.

An examination of Ruskin's economic and social theories as they
relate to his milieu.

Sonstroem, David. "John Ruskin and the Nature of Manliness." VN, 40
(1971), 14-17.

Sonstroem attempts a sexual interpretation of THE STONES OF
VENICE.

Stanonik, Janez. "Ruskin's Theory of Literature as Communication." AN, 3
(1970), 3-26.

"The purpose of the present study is to determine to what extent
was Ruskin aware of and interested in the problem of the communi-
cativeness of arts, especially of literature, and what he considered
to be the consequences of this problem both for the author and for
the reader."

Stein, Roger B. JOHN RUSKIN AND AESTHETIC THOUGHT IN AMERICA,
1840-1900. Cambridge, Mass.: Harvard University Press, 1967.

The standard work on this topic.

John Ruskin

Stevens, L. Robert. "John Ruskin, God, and the Happening." SAQ, 71 (1972), 149-54.

> Stevens claims that Ruskin's writings prepared the way for a new sociology of business.

Stroupe, John H. "Ruskin, Lawrence, and Gothic Naturalism." BSUF, 11 (1970), 3-9.

> Claims that Ruskin's "influence on Lawrence is more significant than has been acknowledged. Lawrence's use of mechanical industry depends on Ruskinesque language and terminology."

Sussman, Herbert [L.]. "Hunt, Ruskin, and 'The Scapegoat.'" VS, 12 (1968), 83-90.

> Sussman discusses Ruskin's defense of Hunt's symbolic painting.

Swanson, Donald R. "Ruskin and His 'Master.'" VN, 31 (1967), 56-59.

> Discusses Carlyle's important influence on Ruskin.

Townsend, Francis G. RUSKIN AND THE LANDSCAPE FEELING: A CRITICAL ANALYSIS OF HIS THOUGHT DURING THE CRUCIAL YEARS OF HIS LIFE, 1843-1860. Urbana: University of Illinois Press, 1951.

> Townsend analyzes MODERN PAINTERS as a record of Ruskin's personal psychology.

Unrau, John. "A Note on Ruskin's Reading of Pugin." ES, 48 (1967), 335-37.

> Unrau claims that Ruskin read far more of Pugin than he ever admitted.

_____. "Ruskin's Use of the Adjective 'Moral.'" ES, 52 (1971), 339-47.

> Unrau stresses that Ruskin's use of the word "moral" was highly variable.

Waller, John O. "Ruskin on Slavery: A Semantic Controversy." VN, 28 (1965), 13-16.

> Waller isolates at least seven meanings Ruskin had for the word "slavery."

Watson, Francis. "The Devil and Mr. Ruskin." ENCOUNTER, 38 (1972), 64-70.

> Discusses Ruskin's bouts with madness, which culminated in 1878 in his obsession that he was struggling with the Devil.

Wellek, René. "John Ruskin." In his A HISTORY OF MODERN CRITICISM, 1750-1950. Vol. 3. New Haven, Conn.: Yale University Press, 1965.

> "Ruskin's aesthetics apply to literature, for he always refused to draw a line between painter and poet." His aesthetic theory is "an impressive restatement of romantic organicism."

Wesling, Donald. "Ruskin and the Adequacy of Landscape." TSLL, 9 (1967), 253-72.

> "This essay focuses on Ruskin as a writer for whom the movement from aesthetic to social criticism did not involve a repudiation of earlier concerns and methods, but instead their extension and development into a fairly coherent ethical view of what made for breakdown, what for health, in Victorian society."

Whitehouse, J[ohn] Howard, ed. RUSKIN THE PROPHET AND OTHER CENTENARY STUDIES. London: Allen and Unwin, 1920; rpt. New York: Folcroft, 1973.

> A collection that contains "Ruskin" by John Masefield, "Ruskin and Plato" by Dean Inge, "Ruskin the Prophet" by C.F.G. Masterman, and "Ruskin as Political Economist" by J.A. Hobson.

Wright, William C. "Hazlitt, Ruskin, and Nineteenth-Century Art Criticism." JAAC, 32 (1974), 509-23.

> "The relationship of Hazlitt's views of the fine arts to those held by Ruskin early in his career is the specific concern of this study."

BIBLIOGRAPHIES

Also see volume 38 of Cook and Wedderburn's edition of WORKS, above.

Halladay, Jean. "Some Errors in the Bibliography of the Library Edition of John Ruskin's Works." PBSA, 62 (1968), 127-29.

> Halladay attempts to correct some errors in the Cook and Wedderburn edition of Ruskin's WORKS, above.

Townsend, Francis G. "John Ruskin." VICTORIAN PROSE: A GUIDE TO RESEARCH. Ed. David J. DeLaura. New York: MLA, 1973.

> A valuable bibliographical essay which discusses critical studies published before 1972.

Wise, Thomas J., and J.P. Smart. A COMPLETE BIBLIOGRAPHY OF THE WRITINGS IN PROSE AND VERSE OF JOHN RUSKIN. London: Clay, 1889-93; rpt. 2 vols. London: Dawson's, 1964.

HISTORICAL

JAMES ANTHONY FROUDE (1818-94)

PRINCIPAL PROSE WORKS

THE NEMESIS OF FAITH, 1849.

THE HISTORY OF ENGLAND FROM THE FALL OF WOLSEY TO THE DEATH OF ELIZABETH. 12 vols. 1856-70.

SHORT STUDIES ON GREAT SUBJECTS. 2 vols. 1867.

THE CAT'S PILGRIMAGE, 1870.

THE ENGLISH IN IRELAND IN THE EIGHTEENTH CENTURY. 3 vols. 1872-74.

BUNYAN, 1880.

THOMAS CARLYLE: A HISTORY OF THE FIRST FORTY YEARS OF HIS LIFE, 1795-1835. 2 vols. 1882.

LUTHER: A SHORT BIOGRAPHY, 1883.

HISTORICAL AND OTHER SKETCHES. Ed. D.H. Wheeler, 1883.

THOMAS CARLYLE: A HISTORY OF HIS LIFE IN LONDON, 1834-1881. 2 vols. 1884.

OCEANA: OR, ENGLAND AND HER COLONIES, 1886.

MY RELATIONS WITH CARLYLE, TOGETHER WITH A LETTER FROM THE LATE SIR JAMES STEPHEN, 1886.

James Anthony Froude

THE ENGLISH IN THE WEST INDIES: OR, THE BOW OF ULYSSES, 1888.

LORD BEACONSFIELD, 1890.

THE SPANISH STORY OF THE ARMADA AND OTHER ESSAYS, 1892.

LIFE AND LETTERS OF ERASMUS, 1893.

COLLECTED WORKS

J.A. FROUDE'S WORKS. London: New Universal Library, 1905.

SELECTED ESSAYS OF J.A. FROUDE. Ed. H.G. Rawlinson. London: Longmans, Green, 1900.
> Includes a short biography and critical notes.

LETTERS

Bennett, R.M., ed. "The Letters of J.A. Froude." JRUL, 25 (1961), 10-23; 26 (1962), 14-22.

O'Connor, Peter. "An Unpublished Letter from J.A. Froude to Ruskin." N&Q, 11 (1964), 233-35.

Viljoen, Helen Gill, ed. THE FROUDE-RUSKIN FRIENDSHIP AS REPRESENTED THROUGH LETTERS. New York: Pageant, 1967.

BIOGRAPHIES

Dunn, Waldo H. JAMES ANTHONY FROUDE, A BIOGRAPHY: 1818-1894. 2 vols. New York: Oxford University Press, 1961-63.
> The definitive biography based on material given to Dunn by Froude's daughter. The first volume details Froude's youth and life until age thirty-eight. The second volume centers on his career as historian and biographer.

Kelly, Marshall. J.A. FROUDE. London: Drane, 1907.

Paul, Herbert [W.]. THE LIFE OF J.A. FROUDE. New York: Scribner's, 1905.
> Paul discusses Froude as "the Man, the Historian, and the Biographer."

CRITICAL STUDIES

Angus-Butterworth, L.M. TEN MASTER HISTORIANS. Aberdeen, Scotland: University Press, 1961.

    Contains a study of Froude.

Badger, K. "The Ordeal of Froude, Protestant Historian." MLQ, 13 (1952), 41-55.

    Discusses the history of Froude's religious opinions.

Dunn, Waldo H. FROUDE AND CARLYLE: A STUDY OF THE FROUDE-CARLYLE CONTROVERSY. London: Longmans, Green, 1930; rpt. New York: Kennikat Press, 1969.

    Dunn attempts to defend Froude's biography of Carlyle.

McCraw, Harry W. "Two Novelists of Despair: James A. Froude and William Hale White." SOQ, 13 (1974), 21-51.

    Discusses THE NEMESIS OF FAITH as one of the "classic Victorian studies of unresolved doubt." Concludes that the novel is "a projection and catharsis of Froude's experience on the imaginative level."

Maurer, Oscar. "Froude and FRASER'S MAGAZINE, 1860-74." SE, 28 (1949), 213-43.

    Maurer discusses Froude's editorship of FRASER'S.

Reynolds, B. "J.A. Froude." SOME MODERN HISTORIANS OF BRITAIN. Ed. Herman Ausubel. New York: Dryden, 1951.

    Reynolds contrasts modern appraisals of Froude's work to those of his contemporaries.

Rollins, Hyder E. "Charles Eliot Norton and Froude." JEGP, 57 (1958), 651-64.

    Rollins discusses Norton's part in the Froude-Carlyle controversy and concludes that Norton was motivated by "emotion rather than reason."

Strachey, Lytton. "One of the Victorians." In his CHARACTERS AND COMMENTARIES. London: Chatto and Windus, 1936.

Wilson, David Alec. MR. FROUDE AND CARLYLE. London: Heinemann, 1898.

    One of the first attacks on Froude's biography of Carlyle.

THOMAS BABINGTON MACAULAY (1800-1859)

PRINCIPAL PROSE WORKS

CRITICAL AND HISTORICAL ESSAYS, CONTRIBUTED TO THE <u>EDINBURGH REVIEW</u>. 3 vols. 1843.

THE HISTORY OF ENGLAND FROM THE ACCESSION OF JAMES II. 5 vols. 1849-61.

THE MISCELLANEOUS WRITINGS OF LORD MACAULAY. Ed. T.F. Ellis. 2 vols. 1860.

BIOGRAPHIES BY LORD MACAULAY CONTRIBUTED TO THE <u>ENCYCLOPAEDIA BRITANNICA</u>: WITH EXTRACTS FROM HIS LETTERS AND SPEECHES, 1860.

THE INDIAN EDUCATION MINUTES OF LORD MACAULAY. Ed. H. Woodrow, 1862.

COLLECTED WORKS

MACAULAY: PROSE AND POETRY. Ed. G[eorge] M. Young. Cambridge, Mass.: Harvard University Press, 1952.

THE READER'S MACAULAY. Eds. Walter H. French and Gerald D. Sanders. New York: American Book, 1936.

    Also includes a short biography.

THOMAS B. MACAULAY: SELECTED WRITINGS. Eds. John Clive and Thomas Pinney. Chicago: University of Chicago Press, 1972.

    A valuable collection that contains some items not usually reprinted.

THE WORKS OF LORD MACAULAY. Ed. Thomas F. Henderson. 9 vols. London: New Universal Library, 1905-07.

> The only annotated edition.

THE WORKS OF LORD MACAULAY. Ed. Lady Trevelyan. 8 vols. London: Longmans, 1866; rpt. as the Albany Edition, 12 vols. London: Longmans, 1898.

> The standard edition of Macaulay's works.

LETTERS

See also Trevelyan's biography, p. 266.

Clark, Peter. "A Macaulay Letter." N&Q, 14 (1967), 369.

> An unpublished letter to Henry Hallam.

THE LETTERS OF T.B. MACAULAY. Ed. Thomas Pinney. Cambridge: At the University Press, 1974-- .

> The only collection of Macaulay's letters; publication is in progress. Volume 1 covers 1807-31; volume 2 covers 1831-33; volume 3 covers 1834-41; volume 4 covers 1841-48. The collection, when complete, will contain over 2,500 letters. Includes an introductory sketch of Macaulay and notes on his correspondents.

BIOGRAPHIES

Arnold, Frederick. THE PUBLIC LIFE OF LORD MACAULAY. London: Tinsley, 1862.

> Emphasizes Macaulay's political activities and reprints several of his speeches.

Beatty, Richard Croom. LORD MACAULAY: VICTORIAN LIBERAL. Norman: University of Oklahoma Press, 1938.

> Beatty defines Macaulay's liberalism as "an economy designed to minister to the materialistic ambitions of a single class."

Bryant, [Sir] Arthur. MACAULAY. London: Davies, 1932.

> A useful introduction.

St. Aubyn, Giles. MACAULAY. London: Falcon, 1952.

> A popularized account of Macaulay s life.

Trevelyan, George O. LIFE AND LETTERS OF LORD MACAULAY. 2 vols. New York: Harper's, 1876.

>The standard biography, generally considered to be a classic Victorian biography. Includes about 500 letters written by Macaulay.

CRITICAL STUDIES

Clark, Harry H. "The Vogue of Macaulay in America." TWA, 34 (1962), 237-92.

>Discusses responses to Macaulay's work by American critics.

Clive, John. MACAULAY: THE SHAPING OF THE HISTORIAN. New York: Knopf, 1973.

>Clive traces the "familial, intellectual, political, and personal" forces which transformed an awkward young man into a prominent historian.

_____. "Macaulay's Historical Imagination." REL, 1 (1960), 20-28.

>Clive defends Macaulay's prose style against Arnold's criticism. He also praises Macaulay's imaginative powers.

Cutts, Elmer. "The Background of Macaulay's MINUTE." AHR, 58 (1953), 824-53.

>Discusses the religious milieu that influenced Macaulay's attitudes toward Indian education.

Dahl, Curtis. "Macaulay, Henry Taylor, and Swinburne's Trilogy." PLL, 2 (1966), 166-69.

>Dahl claims that Macaulay's history was an influence upon Swinburne's Mary-Queen-of-Scots trilogy.

Das Gupta, R.K. "Macaulay's Writings on India." HISTORIANS OF INDIA, PAKISTAN AND CEYLON. Ed. Cyril Philips. London: Oxford University Press, 1961.

>Defends Macaulay's essays on India against charges that they express imperialism.

Davies, Godfrey. "The Treatment of Constitutional History in Macaulay's HISTORY OF ENGLAND." HLQ, 2 (1939), 179-204.

>An important essay which traces Macaulay's treatment of law from the early Stuarts.

De Beer, Esmond S. "Macaulay and Croker." RES, 10 (1959), 388-97.

    Discusses Macaulay's hatred for Croker, editor of Boswell.

Firth, Sir Charles. COMMENTARY ON MACAULAY'S HISTORY OF ENGLAND. London: Macmillan, 1938.

    A defense of Macaulay's historical writings, although there is a chapter on Macaulay's errors.

Fleishman, Avrom. THE HISTORICAL NOVEL. Baltimore: Johns Hopkins University Press, 1971.

    In this work, Fleishman compares Macaulay's HISTORY to Thackeray's HENRY ESMOND.

Fong, David. "Macaulay: The Essayist as Historian." DR, 51 (1971), 38-48.

    Fong contends that Macaulay's essays can be seen as a series leading to the HISTORY.

_____. "Macaulay and Johnson." UTQ, 40 (1970), 27-39.

    "Macaulay's 1831 review [of Croker's edition of Boswell's LIFE] shows only one side--an immature one at that--of his relationship to Johnson, and the purpose of this essay is to explore the others."

Fraser, George S. "Macaulay's Style as an Essayist." REL, 1 (1960), 9-19.

    Fraser claims that, among the styles of all the great Victorian essayists, Macaulay's was "the most striking and lastingly imitable."

Gay, Peter. STYLE IN HISTORY. New York: Basic Books, 1974.

    Gay discusses Macaulay as a historiographer and compares him to Gibbon and Burkhardt.

Geyl, Pieter. "Macaulay in His Essays." In his DEBATES WITH HISTORIANS. New York: Meridian, 1955.

    Geyl sees Macaulay as an eighteenth-century stylist, more concerned with reason than imagination.

Gooch, George P. "Some Great English Historians." COR, 190 (1956), 344-49.

    Gooch characterizes Macaulay as "the trumpeter of the radical Whigs" and the "first English writer to make history attractive to the multitude."

Thomas Babington Macaulay

Griffin, John R. THE INTELLECTUAL MILIEU OF LORD MACAULAY. Ottawa: University of Ottawa Press, 1966.

> Includes chapters on "Macaulay and the 'Edinburgh Review,'" "Macaulay and the Idea of History," and "Macaulay's Theory of Literature and Criticism." According to Griffin, "Macaulay was actually using a traditional theory of literature, common to the Scottish philologists and critics."

Hartley, Lodwick. "A Late Augustan Circus: Macaulay on Johnson, Boswell, and Walpole." SAQ, 67 (1968), 513-26.

> Hartley concludes that Macaulay's vehement attacks on Johnson and Boswell were mistaken and derivative.

Horn, Robert D. "Addison's 'Campaign' and Macaulay." PMLA, 63 (1948), 886-902.

> Accuses Macaulay of simply fusing two conflicting accounts of Marlborough's victory at Blenheim.

Knowles, D. David. LORD MACAULAY, 1800-1859. Cambridge: At the University Press, 1960.

> Praises Macaulay "as a master of historical and descriptive narrative" who "illuminates the men and the literature of the past not by analysis, but by the communication of his own intense appreciation."

Levine, George L. "Macaulay: Progress and Retreat." In his BOUNDARIES OF FICTION. Princeton, N.J.: Princeton University Press, 1968.

> Levine discusses Macaulay's HISTORY as a piece of romantic and escapist writing.

Madden, William A. "Macaulay's Style." THE ART OF VICTORIAN PROSE. Eds. George L. Levine and William A. Madden. New York: Oxford University Press, 1968.

> Madden believes that Macaulay adapted his basic prose style, not only to the needs of his Victorian audience, but to his urgent private needs as well.

Magoun, Francis P. "Lord Macaulay, a Singer of Tales." NM, 73 (1972), 686-89.

> Analyzes Macaulay's four "Lays of Ancient Rome" for their "frequent and consistent use of stock epithets paralleling Homer."

Millgate, Jane. "Father and Son: Macaulay's EDINBURGH Debt." RES, 21 (1970), 159-67.

Discusses Macaulay's first publication in the EDINBURGH REVIEW.

──────. "History and Politics: Macaulay and Ireland." UTQ, 42 (1973), 110-21.

Analyzes the construction of the twelfth chapter of Macaulay's HISTORY OF ENGLAND as "an opportunity for watching the historian put together different kinds of material to form an effective whole."

──────. MACAULAY. London: Routledge and Kegan Paul, 1973.

Millgate concentrates on specific texts to analyze Macaulay's focus on his audience and his narrative.

──────. "Macaulay at Work: An Example of His Use of Sources." TCBS, 5 (1970), 90-98.

Millgate analyzes Macaulay's sources to show how thoroughly he transformed them.

Milne, Alexander T. "The Victorian Historian." COLORADOQ, 15 (1967), 301-17.

Discusses Macaulay in comparison with lesser known historians of the era, including James A. Froude. Concludes that Macaulay's work "influenced all subsequent historical writing of any value."

Morgan, H.A. "Boswell and Macaulay." COR, 192 (1958), 27-29.

Explores Macaulay's criticisms of Boswell.

Morgan, Peter F. "Carlyle and Macaulay as Critics of Literature and Life in the 'Edinburgh Review.'" SGG, 12 (1970), 131-44.

In his thirty-six contributions to the periodical, Macaulay "appears to be essentially concerned less with writings than with authors, and perhaps less even with the events of history than with the characters of great men."

──────. "Macaulay on Periodical Style." VPN, 1 (1968), 26-27.

"Macaulay's goal of imbuing learning with vivacity for the sake of the general reader thus marked both his HISTORY and the essays. It was the laudable ideal of many of the periodical writers contemporary with him."

Munby, Alan N.L. "Germ of a History: Twenty-three Quarto Pages of a Macaulay Cambridge Prize Essay." TLS, 1 May 1969, pp. 468-69.

Reprints the 1822 essay for the first time.

Thomas Babington Macaulay

———. MACAULAY'S LIBRARY. Glasgow: Jackson, 1966.

Munby surveys the books that Macaulay owned for their marginalia. Concludes that "Macaulay annotated his books far less in the forties than in the thirties and that the best marginalia belong to the Indian period."

Otten, Terry. "Macaulay's Critical Theory of Imagination and Reason." JAAC, 28 (1969), 33-43.

"I propose to examine Macaulay's idea of poetry as he expressed it between 1824 and 1842: Macaulay's notion is that imaginative poetry tends to develop rapidly and early in a nation's culture and then to decline."

Pinney, Thomas. "Notes on Macaulay's Unacknowledged and Uncollected Writings." PBSA, 67 (1973), 17-31.

Lists and annotates Macaulay's contributions to periodicals, his miscellaneous articles, official and public papers, speeches, and "Doubtful Attributions."

Plumb, John H. "Thomas Babington Macaulay." UTQ, 26 (1956), 17-31.

"In spite of all the criticism which can be levelled against it, the HISTORY remains a great work of literature and scholarship. Macaulay was an intellectual giant and although he lacked the imagination, the poetry, the sense of tragedy which is present in the very greatest writers, these were almost all that he lacked."

Potter, George R. MACAULAY. London: Longmans, Green, 1959.

A brief general survey of Macaulay's life and works.

Rogers, William Hudson. "A Study in Contrasts: Carlyle and Macaulay as Book Reviewers." FSUS, 5 (1952), 1-10.

"Macaulay was preeminently the 'Edinburgh Reviewer' supreme. The Addison and Lord Clive papers are considered models of English prose. As examples of good writing, they have scarcely a peer."

Schuyler, Robert L. "Macaulay and his HISTORY--A Hundred Years After." PSQ, 63 (1948), 161-93.

Schuyler claims that Macaulay wrote his HISTORY with both "sales-consciousness and fame-consciousness."

Sirkin, Gerald, and Natalie R. Sirkin. "The Battle of Indian Education: Macaulay's Opening Salvo Newly Discovered." VS, 14 (1971), 407-28.

Discusses a newly-discovered letter by Macaulay to John Tytler that outlines Macaulay's position in the struggle between Anglicists and Orientalists over control of Indian educational policy.

Stokes, Eric. THE ENGLISH UTILITARIANS AND INDIA. Oxford: Clarendon Press, 1959.

Discusses Macaulay as a Whig and a Utilitarian.

Svaglic, Martin J. "Classical Rhetoric and Victorian Prose." THE ART OF VICTORIAN PROSE. Eds. George L. Levine and William A. Madden. New York: Oxford University Press, 1968.

Article concentrates on Macaulay's essay "Milton" as an example of Victorian rhetoric employing classical devices.

Thomson, Mark A. MACAULAY. London: Historical Society, 1959.

A survey of Macaulay as a historian: "there are errors of fact in the HISTORY, but relative to its size the amount of factual error is very small."

Trevelyan, George O. "Macaulay and the Sense of Optimism." IDEAS AND BELIEFS OF THE VICTORIANS. Ed. Harman Grisewood. London: Sylvan Press, 1959.

Claims that Macaulay and Carlyle were responsible for creating the Victorian interest in history.

Trevor-Roper, Hugh. "Macaulay." LISTENER, 74 (1965), 565-67.

Argues that Macaulay's uniqueness was due to his emphasis on the interaction between history and politics.

──────. THE ROMANTIC MOVEMENT AND THE STUDY OF HISTORY. London: Athlone Press, 1969.

Discusses Scott's influence on Macaulay.

Valenti, Jack. "Macaulay and His Critics." SR, 30 April 1966, pp. 22-23.

A defense of Macaulay's historical writings.

Weber, Ronald. "Singer and Seer: Macaulay on the Historian as Poet." PLL, 3 (1967), 210-19.

Weber claims that Macaulay saw the historian as a reconciler of reason and the imagination.

Wellek, René. "Thomas Babington Macaulay." In his A HISTORY OF MOD-

Thomas Babington Macaulay

ERN CRITICISM, 1750-1950. Vol. 3. New Haven, Conn.: Yale University Press, 1965.

> Macaulay is praised for "his knowledge and memory, the clarity of his prose, the expository skill, the vividness of the presentation. But his intolerance and cocksureness, his lack of analytical patience, and his contempt for theory point to the limitations of his mind."

Wood, Margaret. "Lord Macaulay, Parliamentary Speaker: His Leading Ideas." QJS, 44 (1958), 375-84.

> "Although oratory was probably not the sole cause of Macaulay's influence in politics, he probably owed his political advancement to the fact that he was an outstanding Parliamentary speaker."

Yoder, Edwin M. "Macaulay Revisited." SAQ, 63 (1964), 542-51.

> Criticizes Macaulay's "Victorian censoriousness." As a historian, Macaulay was "in thralldom to Victorian ethical structures" but did have a "knack for vivid portraiture."

BIBLIOGRAPHIES

Bufano, R[andolph] J. "Lord Macaulay's Critics, 1825-1970: An Annotated Bibliography Together with a Survey." Ph.D. dissertation, University of Pennsylvania, 1973. DAI, 34, 1895A.

Clive, John, and Thomas Pinney. "T.B. Macaulay." VICTORIAN PROSE: A GUIDE TO RESEARCH. Ed. David J. DeLaura. New York: MLA, 1973.

> The most valuable bibliographical essay on Macaulay's works and critical studies about him.

Cunningham, Donald H. "T.B. Macaulay: A Bibliography of Twentieth-Century Periodical Articles and Speeches." BB, 28 (1971), 19-21.

> This "161-item bibliography, limited to articles (other than book reviews) and speeches, indicates part of the interest of our century in Macaulay."

Houghton, Walter E., et al., eds. THE WELLESLEY INDEX TO VICTORIAN PERIODICALS. Projected 4 volumes. Toronto: University of Toronto Press, 1966-- .

> See volume 1, p. 988 for a listing of Macaulay's contributions to various periodicals.

JOURNALISTIC

FRANCIS JEFFREY (1773-1850)

PRINCIPAL PROSE WORKS

ESSAY ON BEAUTY, 1824.

CONTRIBUTIONS TO THE EDINBURGH REVIEW. 4 vols. 1844.

JONATHAN SWIFT, 1853.

SAMUEL RICHARDSON, 1853.

COLLECTED WORKS

JEFFREY'S LITERARY CRITICISM. Ed. D. Nichol Smith. Oxford: Clarendon, 1910.
> Also includes a bibliography listing Jeffrey's articles in the EDINBURGH REVIEW. Must be supplemented by the WELLESLEY INDEX, p. 278.

LETTERS

THE LETTERS OF JEFFREY TO UGO FOSCOLO. Ed. J. Purves. Edinburgh: Oliver & Boyd, 1934.

BIOGRAPHIES

Cockburn, Henry T. THE LIFE OF JEFFREY: WITH A SELECTION FROM HIS CORRESPONDENCE. 2 vols. Edinburgh: Black, 1852.
> The only full-length biography. Also contains a bibliography of Jeffrey's journalistic writings.

Francis Jeffrey

CRITICAL STUDIES

Bald, Robert C. "Francis Jeffrey as a Literary Critic." NC, 97 (1925), 201-05.

> Sees Jeffrey as "the mean, or midway post, in criticism." Yet his "essentially practical outlook" conflicts with the fact that he "clearly belongs to the Romantic movement."

Beatty, J.M. "Lord Jeffrey and Wordsworth." PMLA, 38 (1923), 221-35.

> Beatty praises Jeffrey's "classical ideal of decorum" and his "commonsense criticism" of Wordsworth.

Daniel, Robert. "Jeffrey and Wordsworth: The Shape of Persecution." SR, 50 (1942), 195-213.

> Discusses six reasons why Jeffrey "persecuted" Wordsworth: to increase the circulation of the "Edinburgh Review," animosity toward Wordsworth's "verboseness," the fact that "Jeffrey was carried away by his own style," and that Wordsworth was a means of indirectly attacking Southey, and finally, "Jeffrey wrote in haste and was opportunistic." Claims that Jeffrey's native common sense was at war with his sentimentality.

Gates, Lewis E. THREE STUDIES IN LITERATURE. New York: Macmillan, 1899.

> Includes a 60-page essay on Jeffrey that focuses on his reputation, his literary criticism, and his involvement with the EDINBURGH REVIEW. Concludes that "Jeffrey's dry intellectuality and his shallow associational psychology seemed unequal to the vital problems in art and in ethics that the new age was canvassing."

Greig, James A. FRANCIS JEFFREY OF THE EDINBURGH REVIEW. Edinburgh: Oliver & Boyd, 1948.

> Discusses Jeffrey's criticism of John Wilson, Leigh Hunt, Coleridge, and the literary activities of the era. Includes a chapter on "Fundamental Principles," which analyzes Jeffrey's ESSAY ON BEAUTY. See Wellek, below.

Guyer, Byron. "Jeffrey's ESSAY ON BEAUTY." HLQ, 13 (1949), 71-85.

> Contends that Jeffrey's ESSAY was "adaptation of Archibald Alison's essay on Taste, while Jeffrey's acceptance of Alison places him much nearer the center of romanticism than has been generally realized."

———. "The Philosphy of Jeffrey." MLQ, 11 (1950), 17-26.

"Jeffrey's romanticism is Scottish, having its roots in Hume, Gerard, Alison, and MacKenzie; nevertheless, his critical viewpoint is fundamentally similar to that of his own age."

Hatch, Ronald B. "'This Will Never Do.'" RES, 21 (1970), 56-62.

Hatch uses Jeffrey's four reviews of Crabbe to reveal the discrepancies between the texts in CONTRIBUTIONS TO THE EDINBURGH REVIEW and the original reviews. He concludes that the CONTRIBUTIONS is inaccurate.

Hughes, Merritt Y. "The Humanism of Jeffrey." MLR, 16 (1921), 243-51.

Discusses Jeffrey as "the Platonist of nineteenth-century criticism."

Morgan, Peter F. "Carlyle, Jeffrey, and the 'Edinburgh Review.'" NEO, 54 (1970), 297-310.

Examines "the relationship between Carlyle and Jeffrey, its chronological development, and its literary fruition in Carlyle's contributions to the EDINBURGH REVIEW."

――――. "Principles and Perspective in Jeffrey's Criticism." SSL, 4 (1967), 179-93.

"Jeffrey's principles concern language, feeling and society; and Wordsworth offends against them all. As a critic Jeffrey is a conservative intellectual, yet he shares in and leads the reaction against the neo-classical element of the eighteenth century."

――――. "Wordsworth and Jeffrey." HAB, 19 (1968) 17-28.

Discusses Jeffrey's criticism of Wordsworth's EXCURSION and claims that "Wordsworth's extreme poetic individualism eroded to a certain degree under the influence of pressures, some of which were given verbal expression in Jeffrey's criticism."

Noyes, Russell. WORDSWORTH AND JEFFREY IN CONTROVERSY. Bloomington: Indiana University Publications, 1941.

Noyes attempts to counter previous views that praised Jeffrey's conduct in the critical battle with Wordsworth, which he sees as "one of the most significant controversies in English literary history." See Wellek, below.

Owen, W.J.B. "Wordsworth and Jeffrey in Collaboration." RES, 15 (1964), 161-67.

Reviews the critical controversy, but concludes that the two writers were closer than is generally recognized; in fact, "each was curiously indebted to the other."

Peters, John U. "Jeffrey's Keats Criticism." SSL, 10 (1973), 175-85.

> Attempts to "clarify Jeffrey's methodology" as a critic of Keats: "Jeffrey's critical reception of Keats displays a bifurcation of method reflecting what Jeffrey calls 'two tastes.'"

Thomson, D. Cleghorn. "Francis Jeffrey: Charles Dickens's Friend and Critic." REL, 2 (1961), 52-54.

> Reprints some letters between the two and traces their personal friendship.

Wain, John, ed. CONTEMPORARY REVIEWS OF ROMANTIC POETRY. London: Harrap, 1953.

> Wain's collection reprints six of Jeffrey's essays on the romantics. In the introduction, Wain discusses the historical development of nineteenth-century literary criticism and discusses Jeffrey as a reforming Whig.

Wellek, René. A HISTORY OF MODERN CRITICISM, 1750-1950. Vol. 3. New Haven, Conn.: Yale University Press, 1965.

> Wellek adopts a middle position on Jeffrey's criticism, disagreeing with Greig, above, who praises Jeffrey's principles, and Noyes, above, who criticizes Jeffrey in favor of Wordsworth.

BIBLIOGRAPHIES

Also see Cockburn's biography, p. 275.

Dwyer, J. Thomas. "A Checklist of Primary Sources of the Bryon-Jeffrey Relationship." N&Q, 7 (1960), 256-59.

> Lists "primary sources for the Byron-Jeffrey relationship as a tool for additional research." The list includes references to letters and reviews which trace Jeffrey's attacks on Byron and Byron's replies.

Houghton, Walter E., et al., eds. THE WELLESLEY INDEX TO VICTORIAN PERIODICALS. Projected 4 volumes. Toronto: University of Toronto Press, 1966-- .

> Volume 1, of the two published at present, contains a complete listing of Jeffrey's contributions to the "Edinburgh Review."

SYDNEY SMITH (1771-1845)

PRINCIPAL PROSE WORKS

SIX SERMONS, 1800.

ELEMENTARY SKETCHES OF MORAL PHILOSOPHY, 1804.

SERMONS PREACHED AT ST. PAUL'S, 1846.

ESSAYS SOCIAL AND POLITICAL, 1802-1825, 1874.

ESSAYS, 1802-27. 2 vols. 1874-80.
   Reprinted from the EDINBURGH REVIEW.

COLLECTED WORKS

LETTERS ON THE SUBJECT OF THE CATHOLICS, TO MY BROTHER ABRAHAM, WHO LIVES IN THE COUNTRY. BY PETER PLYMLEY. 4 vols. London: Budd, 1807-08; rpt. as THE LETTERS OF PETER PLYMLEY, WITH OTHER SELECTED WRITINGS, SERMONS, AND SPEECHES. Ed. G.C. Heseltine. London: Dent, 1929.

   Smith used the pseudonym "Peter Plymley" in these letters to express his Whig position.

THE SELECTED WRITINGS OF SYDNEY SMITH. Ed. W.H. Auden. New York: Farrar, Straus, & Cudahy, 1956.

SELECTIONS FROM THE WRITINGS OF SYDNEY SMITH. 2 vols. London: Longmans, 1855.

Sydney Smith

THE WIT AND WISDOM OF SMITH; WITH A BIOGRAPHICAL MEMOIR AND NOTES. Ed. E.A. Duyckinck. New York: Longmans, 1858.

THE WORKS OF SYDNEY SMITH. 4 vols. London: Longmans, 1839-40.

THE WORKS OF SYDNEY SMITH. New York: Taylor, 1844.

LETTERS

Dilworth, Ernest. "The Letters of Sydney Smith." N&Q, 11 (1964), 419-21.
> Reprints eight letters, 1825-43, with annotations.

Heseltine, G.C. "Five Letters of Sydney Smith." LONDON MERCURY, 21 (1930), 512-17.

THE LETTERS OF SYDNEY SMITH. Ed. Nowell C. Smith. 2 vols. Oxford: Clarendon Press, 1953.

Schneider, Duane B. "Unpublished Letters of Sydney Smith." N&Q, 14 (1967), 307-08.

BIOGRAPHIES

Bell, Alan. SYDNEY SMITH, RECTOR OF FOSTON, 1806-29. York, Engl.: St. Anthony's Press, 1972.
> Emphasizes Smith's career as a country parson, but notes that "he developed over the years a characteristically witty and incisive style which gives many of his review-articles a permanent value as literature."

Bullett, Gerald. SYDNEY SMITH: A BIOGRAPHY AND A SELECTION. London: Joseph, 1951.
> Contains a good deal of hitherto unpublished material.

Burdett, Osbert. THE REVEREND SMITH. London: Chapman & Hall, 1934; rpt. 1951.
> Burdett emphasizes the development of Smith's philosophical system as found in his ELEMENTARY SKETCHES.

Holland, Lady Sara. A MEMOIR OF SYDNEY SMITH BY HIS DAUGHTER: WITH A SELECTION FROM HIS LETTERS. Ed. Mrs. Austin. London: Private circulation, 1855.

Holland's biography is generally considered the best as a portrait of Smith with his family and in society.

Pearson, Hesketh. THE SMITH OF SMITHS. New York: Hamish Hamilton, 1935.

A popular biography that concentrates on Smith's political and social activities.

Reid, Stuart J. A SKETCH OF THE LIFE AND TIMES OF SYDNEY SMITH. London: Sampson, Low, 1884.

An early collection of reminiscences by Smith's contemporaries.

Russell, George W.E. SYDNEY SMITH. London: Macmillan, 1905.

A useful source of information about Smith's life and works.

CRITICAL STUDIES

Auden, W.H. "Portrait of a Whig." EM, 3 (1952), 141-58.

Discusses Smith as a "polemical" writer and concludes that he was "a perfect expression of the Whig mentality."

Halpern, Sheldon. SYDNEY SMITH. New York: Twayne, 1966.

Halpern discusses Smith as an essayist on relevant topics--"Toleration, the relationship between church and state, the purposes of education, and the equality of justice." Also includes a useful annotated bibliography.

McLean, Robert S. "Tory Noodles in Sydney Smith and Charles Dickens: An Unnoticed Parallel." VN, 38 (1970), 24-25.

"There is a source in which 'noodle' is used in the context of anti-Tory satire that parallels that of Dickens [in BLEAK HOUSE] and to which the novelist may be indebted."

Murphy, James. "Some Plagiarisms of Sydney Smith." RES, 14 (1938), 199-205.

"To think of him as a confirmed plagiarist would be unjust, but his occasional borrowings are substantial."

Richardson, Joanna. "The Smith of Smiths." HT, 21 (1971), 433-39.

Reviews Smith's life, emphasizing his fight for the Catholic Emancipation Bill and his involvement with the EDINBURGH REVIEW.

Sparrow, John. INDEPENDENT ESSAYS. London: Faber, 1963.

> Includes an essay on the letters of Johnson and Smith.

_____. "Jane Austen and Smith." TLS, 2 July 1954, p. 429.

Sullivan, John P., ed. "Sydney Smith on Classics and Classicists." ARION, 4 (1965), 167-79.

> Reprints an essay by Smith that "represents the standpoint of the educational opposition to the classical establishment which prevailed in the English school system."

Williams, Stanley T. "The Literary Criticism of Sydney Smith." MLN, 38 (1923), 416-19.

> Williams concludes that Smith was of minor importance as a literary critic.

BIBLIOGRAPHIES

Halpern, Sheldon. "Sydney Smith in the EDINBURGH REVIEW: A New List." BNYPL, 66 (1962), 589-602.

Houghton, Walter E., et al., eds. THE WELLESLEY INDEX TO VICTORIAN PERIODICALS. Projected 4 volumes. Toronto: University of Toronto Press, 1966-- .

> Volume 1, of the two published at present, contains a complete listing of Smith's writings for the EDINBURGH REVIEW.

Schneider, Duane B. "Sydney Smith in America to 1900: Two Checklists." BNYPL, 70 (1966), 538-43.

> Lists American reprints of his works, 1809-93, and critical studies about him, 1844-1900.

JOHN WILSON ["CHRISTOPHER NORTH"] (1785-1854)

PRINCIPAL PROSE WORKS

THE RECREATIONS OF CHRISTOPHER NORTH. 3 vols. 1842.

THE NOCTES AMBROSIANAE OF BLACKWOOD'S. 4 vols. 1843.

SPECIMENS OF THE BRITISH CRITICS, 1846.

ESSAYS CRITICAL AND IMAGINATIVE. Ed. James Ferrier. 4 vols. 1856.

COLLECTED WORKS

THE WORKS OF PROFESSOR WILSON OF THE UNIVERSITY OF EDINBURGH. Ed. James Ferrier. 12 vols. Edinburgh: Blackwood, 1855-58.

BIOGRAPHIES

Gordon, Mary. CHRISTOPHER NORTH: A MEMOIR OF JOHN WILSON, COMPILED FROM FAMILY PAPERS AND OTHER SOURCES. 2 vols. Edinburgh: Edmonston & Douglas, 1862.
    Also lists Wilson's contributions to BLACKWOOD'S.

Swann, E. CHRISTOPHER NORTH. Edinburgh: Oliver & Boyd, 1934.
    A full-length biography that also includes a twenty-page bibliography and critical studies.

CRITICAL STUDIES

Gravely, William H. "Christopher North and the Genesis of 'The Raven.'" PMLA, 66 (1951), 149-61.

John Wilson

Explores Wilson's influence on Poe's conception of poetry.

Saintsbury, George. ESSAYS IN ENGLISH LITERATURE, 1780-1860. 3rd ed. London: Rivington, 1896.

Includes a study of Wilson.

_____. A HISTORY OF NINETEENTH-CENTURY LITERATURE, 1780-1895. New York and London: Macmillan, 1896.

Discusses "The Development of Periodicals" and includes comments on Cobbett, Jeffrey, Smith, and Wilson.

Strout, Alan L. "Christopher North on Tennyson." RES, 14 (1938), 428-39.

Strout discusses Wilson's criticisms of Tennyson and disagrees with the views of Lounsbury in THE LIFE AND TIMES OF TENNYSON.

_____. "Concerning the NOCTES AMBROSIANAE." MLN, 51 (1935), 493-504.

Discusses the evolution and development of the NOCTES during 1822-35.

_____. "John Wilson as a Shakespeare Critic: A Study of Shakespeare and the English Romantic Movement." SHJB, 72 (1936), 93-123.

Reprints several excerpts from Wilson's Shakespeare criticism and concludes that "though he is desultory, chaotic, contradictory, boisterous and emotional--he is always stimulating."

_____. "The NOCTES AMBROSIANAE and James Hogg." RES, 13 (1937), 46-63; 177-89.

This two-part article explores Wilson's attempts to make a real person fictitious, that is, to poetically transform James Hogg into the Ettrick Shepherd.

_____. "Purple Passages in the NOCTES AMBROSIANAE." ELH, 2 (1935), 327-31.

Discusses Wilson's "high spirits and Brobdingnagian humor" in the NOCTES.

_____. "A Study in Periodical Patchwork: Wilson's RECREATIONS OF CHRISTOPHER NORTH, 1842." MLR, 38 (1943), 88-105.

Discusses the RECREATIONS as "productions certainly of a deep feeling but by no means a deeply thinking mind." Strout proceeds to consider "the relation between the RECREATIONS and the original articles in BLACKWOOD'S and the RECREATION as literature."

_____. "Wilson, Champion of Wordsworth." MP, 31 (1934), 383-94.

Strout establishes the authorship of three letters in BLACKWOOD'S defending Wordsworth against Jeffrey's charges.

Wain, John, ed. CONTEMPORARY REVIEWS OF ROMANTIC POETRY. London: Harrap, 1953.

Wain reprints four of Wilson's critical essays on the romantics. In the introduction he discusses Wilson's writings as "realistic fantasy" with "a fantastic degree of mystification in order to shuffle off the responsibility for the virulent attacks" he made on poets.

BIBLIOGRAPHIES

Also see Swann, p. 283.

Houghton, Walter E., et al., eds. THE WELLESLEY INDEX TO VICTORIAN PERIODICALS. Projected 4 volumes. Toronto: University of Toronto Press, 1966-- .

Volume 1, of the two volumes published at present, contains a list of Wilson's contributions to BLACKWOOD'S.

RELIGIOUS

RICHARD HURRELL FROUDE (1803-36)

PRINCIPAL PROSE WORKS

TRACTS FOR THE TIMES, 1833-35 (Nos. 9, 59, 63, and, probably, part of 35 are by Froude).

FROUDE'S REMAINS: PART 1. Eds. J. Keble and J[ohn] H[enry] Newman. 2 vols. 1838.

FROUDE'S REMAINS: PART 2. Ed. J.B. Mozley. 2 vols. 1839.

CRITICAL STUDIES

Baker, William J. "Hurrell Froude and the Reformers." JEH, 21 (1970), 243-59.

> Baker claims that Froude was "a notorious critic of the English Reformation" and that his "perverse indictments and inadequate historical method" reduced polemical history "to the point of the ridiculous."

Brendan, Piers. HURRELL FROUDE AND THE OXFORD MOVEMENT. London: Elek, 1974.

> Brendan's study is the first full-length treatment of Froude's influence and ideas. Brendan sees Froude as representing the "heroic, chivalric, self-sacrificing aspect" of the Oxford Movement.

──────. "Newman, Keble, and Froude's REMAINS." EHR, 87 (1972), 697-716.

> Brendan thinks publication of the REMAINS pushed Oxford closer to a new Anglo-Catholic extremism.

Richard Hurrell Froude

Clegg, Herbert. "Froude's REMAINS." CQR, 167 (1966), 166-79.

> Analyzes Froude's influence on Newman and discusses the adverse reaction to the publication of Froude's REMAINS: "it made enemies for the Tractarians, their cause was not forwarded, and Newman again received unfavorable notice at national level."

Guiney, Louise I. HURRELL FROUDE: MEMORANDA AND COMMENTS. New York: Dutton, 1904.

> Guiney observes that her compilation of materials aims at being "not a disquisition, not even a biography, but simply a convenient rearrangement of obvious data for the study of a temperament." Also contains a collection of Froude's letters to Keble and Newman.

Harper, Gordon H. THE FROUDE FAMILY IN THE OXFORD MOVEMENT. Baltimore: Johns Hopkins University Press, 1933.

> Discusses Newman's relations with both Hurrell and William Froude.

MacKay, H.F.B. THE LIFE OF HURRELL FROUDE. London: Allan, 1932.

> A laudatory summary of Froude's life and religious writings.

O'Halloran, Bernard C. "Richard Hurrell Froude: His Influence on John Henry Newman and the Oxford Movement." Ph.D. dissertation, Columbia University, 1966. DAI, 26, 4636.

> Froude's friendship with Newman "accelerated the movement of Newman away from Evangelicalism toward a more dogmatic religion, gave Newman an appreciation of Catholic practices, and eventually undermined Newman's belief in the validity of his 'via media' theory."

JOHN KEBLE (1792-1866)

PRINCIPAL PROSE WORKS

THE CHRISTIAN YEAR. 15 vols. 1827-73.

NATIONAL APOSTASY CONSIDERED IN A SERMON, 1833.

TRACTS FOR THE TIMES, 1834-41. (Nos. 4, 13, 40, 52, 54, 57, 60, and 89 are by Keble.)

PRIMITIVE TRADITION RECOGNIZED IN HOLY SCRIPTURE: A SERMON, 1836.

THE CASE OF CATHOLIC SUBSCRIPTION TO THE XXXIX ARTICLES, 1841.

SERMONS, ACADEMICAL AND OCCASIONAL, 1847.

ON EUCHARISTICAL ADORATION, 1857.

SERMONS, OCCASIONAL AND PAROCHIAL, 1868.

VILLAGE SERMONS ON THE BAPTISMAL SERVICE. Ed. E.B. Pusey. 1869.

LETTERS OF SPIRITUAL COUNSEL AND GUIDANCE. Ed. R.F. Wilson. 1870.

SERMONS FOR THE CHRISTIAN YEAR. 11 vols. 1875-80.

OCCASIONAL PAPERS AND REVIEWS. Ed. E.B. Pusey. 1877.

BIOGRAPHIES

Battiscombe, Georgina. JOHN KEBLE: A STUDY IN LIMITATIONS. New York: Knopf, 1963.

The first modern biography; it praises Keble's "very understated, English type of holiness which went hand in hand with a humorous English oddity." Battiscombe also emphasizes Froude's relation to and influence on Keble.

Coleridge, John T. A MEMOIR OF THE REV. JOHN KEBLE. 2 vols. Oxford: Parker, 1868; rpt. Westmead, Australia: Gregg, 1969.

Early, enthusiastic appreciation for Keble. Also contains a valuable collection of Keble's correspondence.

Lock, Walter. JOHN KEBLE: A BIOGRAPHY. London: Methuen, 1893.

Appendix 2 contains a complete bibliography of Keble's published works.

Wood, Edward F.L. JOHN KEBLE. London: Mowbray, 1909.

Emphasizes Keble's work as "The Parish Priest." Concludes that if "the measure of a life's worth is taken by exclusive reference to its record of visible result, Keble's would be most inadequate . . . and yet the battles he waged have been in great part won."

CRITICAL STUDIES

Beek, Willem J. JOHN KEBLE'S LITERARY AND RELIGIOUS CONTRIBUTION TO THE OXFORD MOVEMENT. Nijmegen, Netherlands: Central Drukkerij, 1959.

Discusses Wordsworth's and Butler's influence on Keble's literary theories. Also contains a complete bibliography of Keble's works.

Chadwick, Owen. "The Limitations of Keble." THEOLOGY, 45 (1964), 46-52.

Concludes that "Keble was no theologian," but he managed to turn his "limitations" into advantages, which "helped him to frame high and poetic aspirations."

Fairchild, Hoxie N. "Catholic Christianity." In his RELIGIOUS TRENDS IN ENGLISH POETRY, 1830-80. Vol. 4. New York: Columbia University Press, 1957.

Discusses Keble in relation to Newman.

Ingram, Archibald Kenneth. JOHN KEBLE. London: Allan, 1933.

Includes chapters on "The Personality of Keble," "Poet and Pastor," and "The Message of Keble in Modern Times." Ingram praises

Keble's "sturdy aestheticism which mingled with his delicate artistic sensitiveness."

Prickett, Stephen. ROMANTICISM AND RELIGION: THE TRADITION OF COLERIDGE AND WORDSWORTH IN THE VICTORIAN CHURCH. Cambridge: At the University Press, 1976.

Includes an essay on "Keble's 'Two Worlds,'" which discusses Keble's "total union of thought and feeling." Analyzes Wordsworth's impact on Keble, in whose "hands Wordsworth's ideas undergo a strange sea-change."

JOHN HENRY NEWMAN (1801-90)

PRINCIPAL PROSE WORKS

TRACTS FOR THE TIMES. 6 vols. 1834-41.
    Newman wrote the following numbers: volume 1: 1, 2, 6, 7, 8, 10, 11, 19, 20, 21, 34, 38, 41, 45; volume 2: 47; volume 3: 71, 73, 75; volume 4: 79, 82; volume 5: 83, 85, 88; volume 6: 90.

PAROCHIAL SERMONS. 6 vols. 1834-42.

LECTURES ON JUSTIFICATION, 1838.

THE CHURCH OF THE FATHERS, 1839.

PLAIN SERMONS BY CONTRIBUTORS TO THE TRACTS FOR THE TIMES, vol. 5 by Newman (in PAROCHIAL AND PLAIN SERMONS, 1868).

SERMONS BEARING ON SUBJECTS OF THE DAY, 1843.

SERMONS, CHIEFLY ON THE THEORY OF RELIGIOUS BELIEF, 1843.

AN ESSAY ON THE DEVELOPMENT OF CHRISTIAN DOCTRINE, 1845.

LOSS AND GAIN, 1848.

LECTURES ON CERTAIN DIFFICULTIES FELT BY ANGLICANS IN SUBMITTING TO THE CATHOLIC CHURCH, 1850.

LECTURES ON THE PRESENT POSITION OF CATHOLICS IN ENGLAND, 1851.

DISCOURSES ON THE SCOPE AND NATURE OF UNIVERSITY EDUCATION, ADDRESSED TO THE CATHOLICS OF DUBLIN, 1852.

John Henry Newman

LECTURES AND ESSAYS ON UNIVERSITY SUBJECTS, 1859.

APOLOGIA PRO VITA SUA: BEING A REPLY TO A PAMPHLET [by Charles Kingsley] ENTITLED 'WHAT, THEN, DOES DR. NEWMAN MEAN?', 1864.

AN ESSAY IN AID OF A GRAMMER OF ASSENT, 1870.

ESSAYS, CRITICAL AND HISTORICAL. 2 vols. 1872.

HISTORICAL SKETCHES. 3 vols. 1872-73.

TRACTS, THEOLOGICAL AND ECCLESIASTICAL, 1874.

MEDITATIONS AND DEVOTIONS, 1893.

COLLECTED WORKS

AUTOBIOGRAPHICAL WRITINGS OF J.H. NEWMAN. Ed. Henry Tristam. London: Sheed and Ward, 1956.

CARDINAL NEWMAN'S BEST PLAIN SERMONS. Ed. Vincent F. Blehl. New York: Herder and Herder, 1965.

CARDINAL NEWMAN'S WORKS. 40 vols. London: Longmans, Green, 1874-1921.
> The only complete edition of Newman's works. The index was compiled by J. Rickaby.

THE ESSENTIAL NEWMAN. Ed. Vincent F. Blehl. New York: New American Library, 1963.

A NEWMAN COMPANION TO THE GOSPELS: SERMONS OF J.H. NEWMAN. Ed. Armel J. Coupet. London: Burns and Oates, 1966.

THE PHILOSOPHICAL NOTEBOOK OF J.H. NEWMAN. Vol. 1, GENERAL INTRODUCTION TO THE STUDY OF NEWMAN'S PHILOSOPHY. Ed. Edward J. Sillem. Louvain, Belgium: Neuwelaerts, 1969.

REALIZATIONS: NEWMAN'S SELECTION OF HIS PAROCHIAL AND PLAIN SERMONS. Ed. Vincent F. Blehl. London: Darton, Longman, Todd, 1964.

John Henry Newman

LETTERS

CARDINAL NEWMAN AND WILLIAM FROUDE, F.R.S., A CORRESPONDENCE. Ed. Gordon H. Harper. Baltimore: Johns Hopkins University Press, 1934.

> A collection of letters that covers 1838-79.

THE CORRESPONDENCE OF J.H. NEWMAN AND JOHN KEBLE AND OTHERS, 1839-45. London: Longmans, Green, 1917.

LETTERS AND CORRESPONDENCE OF J.H. NEWMAN DURING HIS LIFE IN THE ENGLISH CHURCH. Ed. Anne Mozley. 2 vols. London: Longmans, Green, 1898.

THE LETTERS AND DIARIES OF J.H. NEWMAN. Ed. Charles Stephen Dessain. 11 vols. London: Nelson, 1963-72.

> This is the definitive collection of Newman's correspondence and covers 1846-66.

THE LETTERS OF J.H. NEWMAN. Eds. Derek Stanford and Muriel Spark. London: Owen, 1957.

> Contains a brief biography and the letters from both the Anglican and Catholic periods.

NEWMAN FAMILY LETTERS. Ed. Dorothea Mozley. London: Society for Promoting Christian Knowledge (S.P.C.K.), 1962.

BIOGRAPHIES

Abbott, Edwin A. THE ANGLICAN CAREER OF CARDINAL NEWMAN. 2 vols. London: Macmillan, 1892.

> An early attempt to counter the effusive praise of Newman.

Barry, William. NEWMAN. New York: Scribner's, 1905.

> A short, useful introduction to Newman's life.

Bouyer, Louis. NEWMAN: HIS LIFE AND SPIRITUALITY. Trans. J.L. May. London: Burns and Oates, 1958.

> Father Bouyer's biography is a study of Newman's "inner life," emphasizing his conversion and his "introspectivism and sensitiveness."

Bremond, Henri. THE MYSTERY OF NEWMAN. Trans. H.C. Corrance. London: Williams and Norgate, 1907.

Attempts to present Newman's "inner life" because all of his work is said to be a revelation of his mind; discusses Newman's emotional, intellectual, and literary life.

Cross, Frank L. JOHN HENRY NEWMAN. London: Allan, 1933.

Emphasizes Newman's earlier Anglican career.

Dessain, Charles Stephen. JOHN HENRY NEWMAN. London: Nelson, 1966.

A biography that emphasizes Newman's "devotion to the cause of Revealed Religion."

Trevor, Meriol. NEWMAN: LIGHT IN WINTER. New York: Doubleday, 1963.

_____. NEWMAN: THE PILLAR OF THE CLOUD. New York: Doubleday, 1962.

Trevor's 2-volume biography is filled with minute detail and new material from the Birmingham Oratory. Her study is a valuable source of information, but has been criticized as being almost a hagiography.

Ward, Maisie. YOUNG MR. NEWMAN. London: Sheed and Ward, 1948.

A popular study of Newman's family life and career at Oxford through age forty-four.

Ward, Wilfrid. THE LIFE OF JOHN HENRY CARDINAL NEWMAN BASED ON HIS PRIVATE JOURNALS AND CORRESPONDENCE. 2 vols. London: Longmans, Green, 1927.

The standard biography, particularly valuable for Newman's Catholic period.

CRITICAL STUDIES

Altholz, Josef L[ewis]. THE LIBERAL CATHOLIC MOVEMENT IN ENGLAND: THE RAMBLER AND ITS CONTRIBUTORS, 1848-1864. London: Burns and Oates, 1962.

A study of the "Catholic Revival" in England, including chapters on "The 'Rambler,' the Bishops, and Newman, 1859" and "Father Newman Consults the Laity."

_____. "Newman and History." VS, 7 (1964), 285-94.

The "religious attitude, which is the basis of Newman's greatness, is also the measure of his limitations as an historian. In Newman, the historian lived always at the mercy of the theologian."

Anthony, Sister Geraldine. "Newman's Definition of Faith from the OXFORD UNIVERSITY SERMONS to the GRAMMAR OF ASSENT." CITHARA, 9 (1970), 47-63.

Baker, Joseph E. "Newman as Novelist." In his THE NOVEL AND THE OXFORD MOVEMENT. Princeton, N.J.: Princeton University Press, 1932.

> Criticizes the lack of plot in LOSS AND GAIN, but concludes that "besides esthetic and ethical interest, Newman's novels have unusual historical and biographical value."

Bankert, M.S. "Newman in the Shadow of BARCHESTER TOWERS." REN, 20 (1968), 153-61.

> Discusses Newman's attitude toward religious toleration in the Anglican Church, while BARCHESTER TOWERS is analyzed as "a study of the religious psychology of the nineteenth-century British churchman."

Barmann, Lawrence F. "The Notion of Personal Sin in Newman's Thought." DOR, 82 (1964), 209-21.

> Examines Newman's writings on theology and concludes that "his approach is almost never metaphysical, but nearly always psychological."

Barnes, Daniel R. "Brownson and Newman: The Controversy Re-examined." ESQ, 50 (1968), 9-20.

> A study of Brownson's influence on Newman "might open up whole new areas of investigation into Anglo-American philosophical relations."

Beer, John [B.]. "Newman and Romantic Sensibility." THE ENGLISH MIND: STUDIES IN THE ENGLISH MORALISTS PRESENTED TO BASIL WILLEY. Eds. H[ugh] S. Davies and George Watson. Cambridge: At the University Press, 1964.

> Contrasts Newman's romanticism to that of Blake, Wordsworth, Keats, and Coleridge. Concludes that "what is fascinating in Newman is the extent of his Romanticism, the degree of his acknowledgement."

Biemer, Gunter. NEWMAN ON TRADITION. Trans. Kevin Smyth. New York: Herder and Herder, 1967.

> Biemer's aim is to "give a clear and definite picture of Newman's notion of the tradition of revleation." He discusses the historical

development of Newman's views and his systematic structuring of doctrines.

Blehl, Vincent F. "The APOLOGIA: Reactions, 1864-1865." MONTH, 31 (1964), 267-77.

"A careful scrutiny of the 50 or 60 reviews of the APOLOGIA reveals that the reaction was not at all uniform but exceedingly complex, subtle, and nuanced."

_____. "Newman and the Missing Miter." THOUGHT, 35 (1960), 111-23.

Blehl analyzes the politics behind Newman's failure to be made a bishop while in Ireland.

_____. "Newman on Trial." MONTH, 27 (1962), 69-80.

Analyzes the Achilli libel suit of 1852.

_____. "Newman's Deletion: Some Hitherto Unpublished Letters." DUR, 234 (1960), 296-305.

Discusses Bishop Brown's charges of heresy against Newman in 1859.

_____. "Newman, the Bishops, and 'The Rambler.'" DOR, 90 (1972), 20-40.

Uses letters to "make clear the decisive role that Ullathorne and Wiseman played in the condemnation of 'The Rambler.' They also show how the uproar over Newman's article gave way to a more general opposition to 'The Rambler.'"

_____. "Newman, the Fathers, and Education." THOUGHT, 45 (1970), 196-212.

Discusses the influence of Origen and Clement on Newman's educational thought.

Blehl, Vincent F., and Francis X. Connolly, eds. NEWMAN'S APOLOGIA: A CLASSIC RECONSIDERED. New York: Harcourt, Brace, and World, 1964.

A collection of studies on the APOLOGIA: "Theological Implications in the APOLOGIA" by Hugo M. Achaval, "Early Criticism of the APOLOGIA" by Vincent Blehl, "The APOLOGIA and the Ultramontanes" by Edward Kelly, "The Rhetoric of Newman's APOLOGIA" by Mary B. Lenz, "Why Newman Wrote the APOLOGIA" by Martin Svaglic, "The APOLOGIA as Human Experience" by William [E.] Buckler, and "History, Rhetoric, and Literature" by Francis Connolly.

John Henry Newman

Bokenkotter, Thomas S. CARDINAL NEWMAN AS AN HISTORIAN. Louvain, Belgium: Neuwelaerts, 1959.

> Examines Newman's training in history and its influence on his religious development and prose style.

Bouyer, Louis. "Newman and English Platonism." MS, 1 (1963), 111-31.

> Studies Newman's world view and describes his "spiritual outlook" for similiarities with Wordsworth's "platonic" vision.

Brown, C.C. "Newman's Minor Critics." DOR, 89 (1971), 13-21.

> Brown reviews the critics of Newman's DEVELOPMENT OF CHRISTIAN DOCTRINE.

Buckley, Sister Mary Ancille. "Elements of Style in Newman's APOLOGIA." GREYFRIAR, 9 (1966), 19-30.

> "The kind of person Newman was decided the APOLOGIA's form, the whole of his mental and psychological make-up fashioned its structure; his personal history and habits bore intimately on his manner and method of expression."

Calkins, Arthur B. "J.H. Newman on Conscience and the Magisterium." DOR, 87 (1969), 358-69.

> Analyzes Newman's belief in the "primacy of conscience" as presented in Newman's LETTER TO THE DUKE OF NORFOLK.

Cameron, James M. JOHN HENRY NEWMAN. London: Longmans, Green, 1956; rev. ed. 1963.

> Surveys Newman's life and works and concludes that "whatever he writes--a sermon, an historical survey, discourse upon a theological mystery, a letter to a child--the whole man is there."

Capps, Donald. "A Biographical Footnote to Newman's 'Lead, Kindly Light.'" CH, 41 (1972), 480-86.

> Discusses the autobiographical elements, specifically, Newman's relationships with his sisters and grandmother, who function as "angels" in the hymn.

_____. "J.H. Newman: A Study of Vocational Identity." JSSR, 9 (1970), 33-51.

> Newman's "misgivings regarding the ministry are traced to his father's influence toward a 'secular' career and to the declining prestige of the ministry in early nineteenth-century England. His attraction to the ministry is traced to his grandmother."

Chadwick, Owen. FROM BOSSUET TO NEWMAN: THE IDEA OF DOCTRINAL DEVELOPMENT. Cambridge: At the University Press, 1957.

> Utilizes unpublished notes by Newman found at the Edgbaston Oratory and Scots' College, Rome, to trace the contradiction between Newman's theory of doctrinal growth and Bossuet's belief in unchanging tradition.

Clancey, Richard W. "Dublin Discourses: Rhetorical Method in Textual Revisions." REN, 20 (1968), 59-74.

> Discusses the "skillful audience awareness Newman employed to shape the rhetoric of these discourses in the series of revisions prior to their final form in the 1873 edition."

Cohen, Edward H. "Elements of Style in Newman's 'Implicit and Explicit Reason.'" AR, 2 (1971), 89-92.

> Newman's 'Implicit and Explicit Reason' "exemplifies a careful balancing of the diverse rhetorical techniques which Newman employed in his attempts to fulfill the purposes of Christian teaching. His prose style is thus an harmonious blending of scriptural allusion, methaphorical analogy, and analytic distinction."

Colby, Robert A. "Newman on Aristotle's POETICS." MLN, 71 (1956), 22-27.

> Colby discusses Newman's reading of Aristotle as it was filtered through critics like Bacon, Voltaire, and Johnson.

_____. "The Poetical Structure of Newman's APOLOGIA." JR, 33 (1953) 47-57.

> Analyzes Newman's use of devices usually employed by tragic or epic writers.

Coulson, John. "Belief and Imagination." DOR, 90 (1972), 1-14.

> "The publication of Newman's PHILOSOPHICAL NOTEBOOKS, [above], leads me to suggest that Newman's treatment of imagination and belief is subtler and much more tentative than is usually supposed."

_____. NEWMAN AND THE COMMON TRADITION: A STUDY IN THE LANGUAGE OF CHURCH AND SOCIETY. Oxford: Clarendon Press, 1970.

> Compares Newman with Coleridge and F.D. Maurice.

Coulson, John; A.M. Allchin; and Meriol Trevor. NEWMAN: A PORTRAIT RESTORED. London: Sheed and Ward, 1965.

This collection includes essays by Coulson on "The APOLOGIA Revalued" and "Newman's Own Guide to the Reading of His Works." Also includes "The Via Media" by Allchin and a "Biographical Summary" by Trevor.

Coulson, John, and A.M. Allchin, eds. THE REDISCOVERY OF NEWMAN: AN OXFORD SYMPOSIUM. London: Sheed and Ward, 1967.

Contains "The Evangelical Sources of Newman's Power" by David Newsome, "The Theological Vision of the Oxford Movement" by A.M. Allchin, "Newman and the Empiricist Tradition" by J[ames] M. Cameron, "A Note on Newman's Historical Method" by J.D. Holmes, and several essays on Newman's influence on others.

Cronin, John F. CARDINAL NEWMAN: HIS THEORY OF KNOWLEDGE. Washington, D.C.: Catholic University Press, 1935.

An examination of Newman's sources.

Culler, A. Dwight. THE IMPERIAL INTELLECT. New ed. New Haven, Conn.: Yale University Press, 1965.

Culler focuses on Newman's "work as an educator of others, and on his educational thought as expressed in THE IDEA OF A UNIVERSITY." Culler says that the "interaction between Newman's educational and his religious interests provide the central pattern of his entire life." Also see Townsend, below.

_____. "Newman on the Uses of Knowledge." JGE, 4 (1950), 269-79.

Newman's educational theory was not "practical or institutional--indeed, it was hardly even educational in the stricter sense."

Dale, P.A. "Newman's THE IDEA OF A UNIVERSITY: The Dangers of a University Education." VS, 16 (1972), 5-36.

Dale sees Newman's work as a defense of elitism and religious control of education.

Deen, Leonard W. "The Rhetoric of Newman's APOLOGIA." ELH, 29 (1962), 224-38.

Although the APOLOGIA emphasizes "personality and feeling, it nevertheless makes use of classical principles of rhetoric. The effectiveness of the APOLOGIA depends on Newman's using the basic principles of classical rhetoric in a way that virtually transformed them."

DeLaura, David J. "Matthew Arnold and J.H. Newman: The 'Oxford Sentiment' and the Religion of the Future." TSLL, 6 (1965), 571-602.

Stresses Arnold's great debt to Newman's critical writings.

_____. "Newman as Prophet." DUR, 241 (1967), 222-35.

John Henry Newman

Discusses the APOLOGIA as the culmination of Newman's many interests.

_____. "Pater and Newman: The Road to the 'Nineties." VS, 10 (1966), 39-69.

Explores Pater's reliance on Newman's writings to formulate his own aesthetic.

De Santis, Edward. "Newman's Concept of the Church in the World in His PAROCHIAL AND PLAIN SERMONS." ABR, 21 (1970), 268-82.

Contends that Newman's SERMONS were "his most valuable contribution to something very much like a revolutionary movement."

Dessain, Charles Stephen. "'Heart Speaks to Heart': Margaret Mary Hallahan and J.H. Newman." MONTH, 34 (1965), 360-67.

Includes letters between them.

_____. "Newman and Oxford." WR, 500 (1964), 295-302.

Examines Newman's long residence in Oxford and analyzes "how they reacted upon each other."

Eaker, J. Gordon. "J.H. Newman's Contribution to Belief." FH, 4 (1963), 22-25.

Sympathetically reviews Newman's religious writings: "Religion permeated his whole being, not only his intellect but his imagination, will, moral sense, and social sense."

Fremantle, Anne. "Newman and English Literature." A NEWMAN SYMPOSIUM. Ed. Victor R. Yanitelli. New York: Fordham University Press, 1952.

Discusses attitudes toward Newman by later nineteenth and twentieth-century writers.

Friedman, Norman. "Newman, Aristotle, and the New Criticism: On the Modern Element in Newman's Poetics." PMLA, 81 (1965), 261-71.

Friedman claims that Newman's "Poetry with Reference to Aristotle's POETICS" has much in common with the theories of modern critics like J.C. Ransom or E.M. Forster.

Gardner, W.H. "Hopkins and Newman." TLS, 15 September 1966, p. 868.

Gill, John M. "Newman's Dialectic in THE IDEA OF AN UNIVERSITY." QJS, 4 (1959), 415-18.

Discusses Newman's characteristic method of writing--employing thesis and antithesis.

Gordon, Jan B. "Wilde and Newman: The Confessional Mode." REN, 22 (1970), 183-91.

Gordon analyzes the influence of the APOLOGIA on DE PROFUNDIS.

Graef, Hilda C. GOD AND MYSELF: THE SPIRITUALITY OF J.H. NEWMAN. New York: Hawthorne, 1978.

A study of Newman's spiritual development that contrasts the sermons of the Anglican and Catholic periods.

Harrold, Charles F. JOHN HENRY NEWMAN: AN EXPOSITORY AND CRITICAL STUDY OF HIS MIND, THOUGHT, AND ART. London: Longmans, Green, 1945.

Harrold's study is generally considered one of the most valuable on Newman's thought. It is objective and informative on Newman's "literary method, his achievement as a poet, novelist, critic, rhetorician."

_____. "Newman and the Alexandrian Platonists." MP, 37 (1940), 279-91.

Explores the influence of Platonism and the Greek Church Fathers on Newman's thought.

Hogan, Jeremiah. "Newman and Literature." STUDIES, 42 (1953), 169-80.

Discusses Newman as a stylist and literary theorist.

Hollis, Christopher. NEWMAN AND THE MODERN WORLD. New York: Doubleday, 1968.

Hollis states he proposes to "discover what was the quality in Newman's teaching that makes it so especially pertinent to the modern world." Contains chapters on the APOLOGIA and the GRAMMAR OF ASSENT.

Holmes, J. Derek. "Cardinal Newman and the Affirmation Bill." HMPEC, 36 (1967), 87-97.

Examines Newman's attitude "as an example of a prominent Catholic who found himself at variance with other members of his Church over passing the Affirmation Bill."

_____. "Cardinal Newman and the Study of History." DUR, 239 (1965), 17-31.

Discusses Newman's critical attitude toward history, historical research, and his distinction between history and theology.

_____. "Gladstone and Newman." DUR, 241 (1967), 141-53.

> Uses unpublished letters from the Birmingham Oratory to discuss Gladstone's opinion of Newman.

_____. "J.H. Newman's Attitude toward History and Hagiography." DOR, 92 (1974), 248-64.

> "Newman did not confuse history and hagiography, nor approach hagiography in an uncritical way. On the whole, he adopted throughout his life, a balanced position on saints' lives, seeing them as didactic."

_____. "Newman and Modernism." BQ, 24 (1972), 335-42.

> Disagrees with Reardon's position, below, and concludes that "Newman's ultimate significance in the history of Modernism should probably be seen within the wider context of the significance of nineteenth-century Liberal Catholicism."

_____. "Newman and the Kensington Scheme." MONTH, 33 (1965), 12-23.

> Discusses Newman's silence during Manning's attempts to establish a Catholic University attached to London University.

_____. "Newman's Attitude Towards Historical Criticism and Biblical Inspiration." DOR, 89 (1971), 22-37.

> "Newman was strongly influenced by his appreciation of the results in understanding biblical inspiration, and to illustrate this, rather than attempt to reconstruct a synthesis of his writings on inspiration, is the purpose of the present article."

_____. "Newman's Reputation and THE LIVES OF THE ENGLISH SAINTS." CHR, 51 (1965), 528-38.

> "Examines Newman's connexion with the authors of these LIVES, and with James A. Froude in particular." Holmes asserts that there is a "definite need for a purely historical consideration of Newman's association with this series."

Holmes, J. Derek, Josef L[ewis] Altholz, et al. "Controversy: Newman, Christina Rossetti, Wilde." VS, 8 (1965), 271-81.

> A debate between Holmes and Altholz on Newman's historical approach. Holmes claims that Newman achieved a "balanced position which distinguished between theology and history," while Altholz asserts that "religion was the source of Newman's failure as an historian."

Houghton, Walter E. THE ART OF NEWMAN'S APOLOGIA. New Haven, Conn.: Yale University Press, 1945; rpt. New York: Archon Books, 1970.

Houghton analyzes Newman's "theory and practice of autobiography," his "Theories of Biography," and his "Analytic Method," and makes an overall evaluation of his work.

---------. "The Issue Between Kingsley and Newman." THEOLOGY TODAY, 4 (1947), 80-101.

Article explores that "Victorian Liberalism" Kingsley epitomized and Newman early recognized as his chief intellectual and spiritual antagonist.

Houppert, Joseph W., ed. JOHN HENRY NEWMAN. St. Louis, Mo.: Herder, 1968.

A collection of essays, including "Newman's Essay on Development in its Intellectual Milieu" by Walter Ong, "Newman's Idea of Literature: A Humanist's Spectrum" by Harold M. Petitpas, and "Newman the Poet" by John Pick.

JOHN HENRY NEWMAN: CENTENARY ESSAYS. London: Burns, Oates, and Washbourne, 1945.

A collection of essays, including "Newman and the Modern Age" by Douglas Woodruff, "Cardinal Newman and Dean Church" by Christopher Hollis, and "On Reading Newman" by Henry Tristram.

Jost, Edward F. "Newman and Liberalism: The Later Phase." VN, 24 (1963), 1-6.

"We will try to show that a clue to Newman's attitude toward Liberalism may be found in his relationship to Oxford, and that, in general, he tended to be more 'Liberal' after he became a Catholic in 1845."

Juergens, Sylvester. NEWMAN ON THE PSYCHOLOGY OF FAITH IN THE INDIVIDUAL. New York: Macmillan, 1928.

Discusses GRAMMAR OF ASSENT by analyzing Newman's sources.

Kelly, Edward E. "Newman's Catholic History as Background of the APOLOGIA." PERSON, 46 (1965), 382-88.

Discusses the controversy between Newman and Manning.

Lapati, Americo D. JOHN HENRY NEWMAN. New York: Twayne, 1972.

An introduction to the "whole" Newman--"writer, thinker, man."

Lawler, Justus G. "Newman's APOLOGIA and the Burthens of Editing." MLQ, 32 (1971), 291-304.

Criticizes all previous editors of the APOLOGIA.

Lawlis, Merritt E. "Newman on the Imagination." MLN, 68 (1953), 73-80.

Discusses how Newman's theory of the imagination is more eighteenth-century than romantic.

Levine, George [L.]. "Newman: Non-Fiction as Art." STYLE, 3 (1969), 209-25.

Levine analyzes Newman's use of parallelism, diction, and transitions as devices that amplify meaning.

_____. "Newman and the Threat of Experience." In his BOUNDARIES OF FICTION. Princeton, N.J.: Princeton University Press, 1968.

Discusses Newman's otherworldliness as an artistic restriction.

_____. "Newman's Fiction and the Failure of Reticence." TSLL, 8 (1966), 359-73.

Discusses Newman's failure to explain adequately the choice of celibacy by his fictional characters.

_____. "The Prose of the APOLOGIA." VN, 27 (1965), 5-8.

Analyzes four passages for their use of both particularized and generalized language.

MacDougall, Hugh A. THE ACTON-NEWMAN RELATIONS: THE DILEMMA OF CHRISTIAN LIBERALISM. New York: Fordham University Press, 1962.

Contrasts their educational, political, and religious views.

McElrath, Damian. "Richard Simpson and J.H. Newman: The RAMBLER, Laymen, and Theology." CHR, 52 (1966), 509-33.

A comparative analysis of the two writers' involvement with the Catholic journalism of their day.

McGrath, Fergal. THE CONSECRATION OF LEARNING: LECTURES ON NEWMAN'S IDEA OF A UNIVERSITY. New York: Fordham University Press, 1963.

An attempt to make Newman's writings relevant to current educational concerns.

_____. NEWMAN'S UNIVERSITY: IDEA AND REALITY. London: Longmans, Green, 1951.

A thorough analysis of the history of the Catholic University of Dublin.

John Henry Newman

Mendel, Sydney. "Metaphor and Rhetoric in Newman's APOLOGIA." EIC, 23 (1971), 357-71.

Reply by I.T. Ker, EIC, 24 (1974), 319-22.

Middleton, Robert D. NEWMAN AT OXFORD. London: Oxford, 1950.

A general study that centers on the development of Newman's religious thought. An appendix contains correspondence related to the publication of Tract No. 90.

Murray, Placid, ed. NEWMAN THE ORATORIAN: HIS UNPUBLISHED ORATORY PAPERS. Dublin: Gill, 1969.

Includes an introduction that emphasizes the continuity between Newman's Anglican and Catholic careers.

Nedoncelle, Maurice. "The Revival of Newman Studies--Some Reflections." DOR, 86 (1968), 385-94.

Reviews the importance of the Oxford Symposium's REDISCOVERY OF NEWMAN; see Coulson, above. Also comments on three French and three Italian studies.

Newman, Bertram. CARDINAL NEWMAN: A BIOGRAPHICAL AND LITERARY STUDY. London: Bell, 1925.

Intended for the general reader, this introductory study discusses Newman as preacher, writer, and "Man of Letters."

Newman, Jay. "Cardinal Newman's Phenomenology of Religious Belief." RS, 10 (1974), 129-40.

Analyzes Newman's distinction between "Real and Notional Assent in Religion" and Newman's idea of the "Illative Sense." Also concentrates on chapters 5-10 of GRAMMAR OF ASSENT as "the central part of Newman's philosophy of religion."

O'Faolain, Sean. NEWMAN'S WAY. London: Longmans, Green, 1952.

A study of the influences that led Newman to his decision to join the Catholic Church.

Pailin, David. THE WAY TO FAITH, AN EXAMINATION OF NEWMAN'S GRAMMAR OF ASSENT AS A RESPONSE TO THE SEARCH FOR CERTAINTY IN FAITH. London: Epworth, 1969.

Petitpas, Harold M. "Newman's Idea of Literature: A Humanist's Spectrum." REN, 17 (1965), 97-105.

Analyzes Newman's conception of the components of art criticism: "the artist, the work, the universe, and the audience."

_____. "Newman's Idea of Science." PERSON, 48 (1967), 297-316.

Discusses Newman's relation to the "tensions that were to develop between science and theology in nineteenth-century England" by analyzing THE IDEA OF A UNIVERSITY for its ambivalence toward the natural sciences.

_____. "Newman's Personalism: A Precursor to Existentialism." ABR, 16 (1965), 84-96.

Discusses Newman's "personal way of apprehending the truth," which links him with Coleridge: "Newman's Illative Sense appears not unrelated to the dynamic conception of the human mind advocated by Coleridge in the BIOGRAPHIA LITERARIA."

_____. "Newman's Universe of Knowledge: Science, Literature, and Theology." DR, 46 (1966), 494-507.

Describes Newman's three-level hierarchy which culminates in the study of God through theology.

Prickett, Stephen. ROMANTICISM AND RELIGION: THE TRADITION OF WORDSWORTH AND COLERIDGE IN THE VICTORIAN CHURCH. Cambridge: At the University Press, 1976.

Includes two essays on Newman: "Newman and Maurice: Development of Doctrine and the Growth of Mind," and "Newman: Imagination and Assent."

Reardon, B[ernard] M.G. "Newman and the Catholic Modernist Movement." CHQ, 4 (1971), 5-60.

Concludes that Newman anticipated an important and characteristic aspect of Modernism. See Holmes, above, for a critique of Reardon's position.

Reilly, Joseph J. NEWMAN AS A MAN OF LETTERS. New York: Macmillan, 1925.

The first study to treat Newman as a man of many letters: stylist, poet, preacher, novelist, historian, and controversial figure.

Reno, Stephen J. "Religious Belief: Continuities Between Newman and Cirne-Lima." NSC, 44 (1970), 489-514.

"By pointing out those elements in Newman's GRAMMAR which made it a 'turning point' I plan to show tendencies which suggest a kind of spiritual affinity with the participants in the current discussions of the question of religious belief."

Reynolds, Ernest E. THREE CARDINALS: NEWMAN, WISEMAN, MANNING. New ed. London: Burns and Oates, 1966.

Ribando, William. "Newman on the Prophetic and Pastoral World." ABR, 22 (1971), 381-86.

The later Newman in 1877 "accused the 'author' of the 'Via Media' lectures of having exaggerated the role of the prophetic office to the detriment of the other roles of the Church."

Robbins, William. THE NEWMAN BROTHERS: AN ESSAY IN COMPARATIVE INTELLECTUAL BIOGRAPHY. Cambridge, Mass.: Harvard University Press, 1966.

Robbins contrasts J.H. and F.W. Newman as representative of the split in Victorian society between conservative and liberal sentiments.

Robertson, T.L. "The Kingsley-Newman Controversy and the APOLOGIA." MLN, 69 (1954), 564-69.

Discusses Newman's motivations in publishing the Kingsley correspondence and thereby precipitating the events that led to the APOLOGIA.

Ryan, Alvan S. "The Development of Newman's Political Thought." RP, 7 (1945), 210-40.

Traces "the significant features of Newman's political thought, and shows that before his conversion in 1845 and afterward he was occupied with adjusting the respective claims of Church and State." Also traces a shift to "liberal" political beliefs.

──────. "Newman and T.S. Eliot." A NEWMAN SYMPOSIUM. Ed. Victor R. Yanitelli. New York: Fordham University Press, 1952.

Claims that Eliot was influenced more by Arnold than by Newman.

Ryan, John D. "Newman's Theory of Conscience." UDR, 7 (1970), 7-19.

Treats "certain aspects of Newman's psychological description of knowledge necessary for an understanding of this theory of conscience."

Ryan, John K., and E.D. Bernard, eds. AMERICAN ESSAYS FOR THE NEWMAN CENTENNIAL. Washington, D.C.: Catholic University Press, 1947.

This collection includes "Newman and Modern Educational Thought," "Newman and the Liberal Arts," and "The Psychology of a Conversion." Also includes a bibliography of other Newman centennial publications.

Sencourt, Robert. "Newman and Pusey." DUR, 217 (1945), 156-65.

Uses letters to examine their friendship and reciprocal influence, even after Newman's conversion.

Shook, Laurence K. "The Idea of Reform in Newman's Early Reviews." ESSAYS IN ENGLISH LITERATURE FROM THE RENAISSANCE TO THE VICTORIAN AGE. Eds. Millar MacLure and F.W. Watt. Toronto: University of Toronto Press, 1964.

Discusses seven "book reviews or 'critics' written by Newman for the BRITISH CRITIC," all of which "provide an insight into Newman's preoccupation with the idea of reform."

Smith, T.D. Wilson. "Newman and the Teaching of History." WR, 500 (1964), 147-56.

"In all his historical writings Newman is concerned with meaning. He is a historian of meaning because he seeks to experience the meaning of history."

Steele, Peter. "Newman and Arnold; Cadences of Belief." TWENTIETH CENTURY: AN AUSTRALIAN QUARTERLY, 24 (1969), 170-78.

"Newman has in even greater degree than Arnold that special gift of the imaginative rhetorician, the ability to sound as if what is said ought to be true even when it is not in fact true."

Stunt, T.C.F. "J.H. Newman and the Evangelicals." JEH, 21 (1970), 65-74.

Discusses Newman's split with the Church Missionary Society in 1826.

Svaglic, Martin J. "Newman and the Oriel Fellowship." PMLA, 70 (1955), 1014-32.

Svaglic reprints Newman's essay on diffidence and discusses his election to the Fellowship in 1822.

_____. "The Revision of Newman's APOLOGIA." MP, 50 (1952), 43-49.

Analyzes the revisions Newman made in the APOLOGIA in 1844 concerning his motivations for converting to Catholicism.

_____. "The Structure of Newman's APOLOGIA." PMLA, 66 (1951), 138-48.

> "Newman chose autobiography as his method because of his lifelong English preference of the concrete to the abstract, his vivid realization of the role in persuasion of personal influence."

Symondson, Anthony, ed. THE VICTORIAN CRISIS OF FAITH: SIX LECTURES. London: Society for Promoting Christian Knowledge (S.P.C.K.), 1971.

> Includes an essay on Newman.

Tillotson, Geoffrey. "Newman in his Letters." In his MID-VICTORIAN STUDIES. London: Athlone Press, 1965.

> Reviews Newman's letters as "the biography of their writer" and analyzes their style as "university slang."

──────. "Newman: The Writer." In his MID-VICTORIAN STUDIES. London: Athlone Press, 1965.

> "The case for regarding Newman as supremely literary as well as supremely 'ecclesiastical' is inescapable. One of the points I wish to make is that Newman is always literary, even when he is most narrowly ecclesiastical."

──────. "Newman: Thought and Action." In his MID-VICTORIAN STUDIES. London: Athlone Press, 1965.

> Discusses the Victorian split between meditation and action, which Newman reconciled in his educational writings: "Newman's writings are for most of us a world of experience."

──────. "Newman's Essay on Poetry." In his CRITICISM AND THE NINETEENTH CENTURY. London: Athlone Press, 1951.

> Praises Newman as a literary critic of Greek drama and claims that Newman "unconsciously applied to poetry his religious discoveries up to date."

Townsend, Francis G. "Newman and the Problem of Critical Prose." VN, 11 (1957), 22-25.

> A critique of Culler's method of analyzing Newman's prose in THE IMPERIAL INTELLECT, above.

Tristram, Henry. "Cardinal Newman and Baron von Hugel." DUR, 240 (1966), 295-302.

> Challenges and examines von Hugel's charges that Newman's preaching was "depressing."

Ulanov, Barry. "Newman and Dostoevsky: The Politics of Salvation." In his

SOURCES AND RESOURCES: THE LITERARY TRADITIONS OF CHRISTIAN HUMANISM. Westminster, Md.: Newman Press, 1960.

> Ulanov sees both writers as essentially conservative in their protective attitude toward the past.

Vargish, Thomas. NEWMAN: THE CONTEMPLATION OF MIND. Oxford: Clarendon Press, 1970.

> Discusses the influences of Evangelicalism and empiricism and analyzes the works that led to Newman's Catholic position.

Versfeld, Martin. "St. Thomas, Newman, and the Existence of God." NSC, 41 (1967), 3-30.

> Attempts to show "the common Christian mind of the two very different thinkers." Because their historical situations were so different, "Newman was driven back upon himself, by a culture which he felt to be inimical, to seek within himself the grounds for personal acceptance of the belief in God."

Vickers, Brian. "Hopkins and Newman." TLS, 3 March 1966, p. 178.

Walgrave, J.H. NEWMAN THE THEOLOGIAN. Trans. A.V. Littledale. New York: Sheed and Ward, 1960.

> A study of the "Nature of Belief and Doctrine" in Newman's works. Focuses on the development of Newman's "Psychology" and his conception of faith.

Watson, Edward A. "Newman and Aristotle's POETICS." REN, 20 (1968), 179-85.

> Watson argues that Newman viewed poetry as a means of expressing divine reality.

Weatherby, H.L. CARDINAL NEWMAN IN HIS AGE: HIS PLACE IN ENGLISH THEOLOGY AND LITERATURE. Nashville, Tenn.: Vanderbilt University Press, 1973.

> Weatherby focuses on "Newman's decision to accept the philosophical premises of modern thought as his own and to treat them as though they were capable of synthesis with Catholic dogma."

_____. "The Encircling Gloom: Newman's Departure from the Caroline Tradition." VS, 12 (1968), 57-82.

> "There are from the first elements in Newman's thought, certain basic philosophical assumptions, which are quite foreign to seventeenth-century High Churchmanship and which tend toward a dark

view of human nature and, in consequence, toward an authoritarian conception of the Church."

_____. "Newman and the Origins of a 'High Church' Left." MA, 12 (1968), 58-64.

Traces the origin of a "High Church Left" to Newman and the Oxford Movement.

_____. "Newman and Victorian Liberalism: A Study in the Failure of Influence." CRQ, 13 (1971), 205-13.

Asserts that modern Christian literature expresses more conservatism than do Newman's writings.

_____. "Newman Reconsidered: An Essay Review." SHR, 3 (1969), 186-92.

Reviews studies by Dessain, Coulson and Allchin, Hollis, and Graef, above, and concludes that "the real force of Newman has yet to strike American awareness. Perhaps one reason for this is the implicit criticism in Newman of so much of what might be considered typically American."

_____. "Newman's Critique of Popular Preaching." SAQ, 69 (1970), 108-17.

White discusses Newman's attempts to arrest the extreme enthusiasm for popular preaching.

Whyte, J.H. "Newman in Dublin: Fresh Light from the Archives of Propaganda." DUR, 234 (1960), 31-39.

Discusses Cardinal Cullen's opposition to Newman's advancement within the Catholic Church.

BIBLIOGRAPHIES

Dessain, Charles Stephen. "J.H. Newman: Newman's Philosophy and Theology." VICTORIAN PROSE: A GUIDE TO RESEARCH. Ed. David J. DeLaura. New York: MLA, 1973.

An extremely useful bibliographical essay that discusses the critical studies of Newman's philosophical prose.

Sloane, C.E. NEWMAN: AN ILLUSTRATED BROCHURE OF HIS FIRST EDITIONS. Worcester, Mass.: College of the Holy Cross Press, 1953.

Svaglic, Martin J. "J.H. Newman: Man and Humanist." VICTORIAN

PROSE: A GUIDE TO RESEARCH. Ed. David J. DeLaura. New York: MLA, 1973.

> A valuable bibliographical essay that surveys biographies and critical studies of Newman published through 1972.

EDWARD BOUVERIE PUSEY (1800-1882)

PRINCIPAL PROSE WORKS

TRACTS FOR THE TIMES, 1834-37. (Nos. 18, 66-70, 77, 81, and, perhaps, 76 are by Pusey).

A LETTER TO THE ARCHBISHOP OF CANTERBURY, 1842.

PAROCHIAL SERMONS. 3 vols. 1852-73.

THE DOCTRINE OF THE REAL PRESENCE, 1855.

THE REAL PRESENCE, 1857.

LENTEN SERMONS, 1858-74, 1874.

SERMONS PREACHED BEFORE THE UNIVERSITY OF OXFORD, 1859-1872, 1872.

THE MINOR PROPHETS, 1860.

WHAT IS OF FAITH AS TO EVERLASTING PUNISHMENT?, 1880.

PAROCHIAL AND CATHEDRAL SERMONS, 1883.

BIOGRAPHIES

Liddon, H.P. THE LIFE OF E.B. PUSEY, D.D. Eds. J.O. Johnston; R.J. Wilson; and W.E. Newbolt. 4 vols. London: Longmans, 1893-97.

Liddon's massive biography of Pusey also presents a full history of Church affairs in 1823-82. A complete bibliography of Pusey's writings compiled by F. Madan is given as appendix A in volume 4.

Prestige, Leonard. PUSEY. London: Allan, 1933.

Discusses Pusey as both an "outcast" and a "bridge-builder" in his involvement with the Oxford Movement.

Russell, George W.E. DR. PUSEY. London: Mowbray, 1907.

Includes chapters on THE TRACTS, Pusey's relationship with Wilberforce, and concludes that Pusey had "moral grandeur--an absolute and calculated devotion to a sacred cause."

Trench, M. THE STORY OF MR. PUSEY'S LIFE. London: Longmans, Green, 1900.

A chronological examination of Pusey's life. Includes chapters on THE TRACTS, "Tract No. 90," "The Sermon on the Eucharist," and "Pusey's Letters to Newman."

CRITICAL STUDIES

Clegg, Herbert. "Evangelicals and Tractarians." HMPEC, 36 (1967), 127-78.

Clegg discusses the striking similarities between the Evangelicals and the major figures of the Oxford Movement, particularly Pusey.

Grosskurth, Phyllis. "Pusey's Visit to Ireland in 1841." TLS, 3 December 1971, p. 1531.

Hugh, Father. NINETEENTH-CENTURY PAMPHLETS AT PUSEY HOUSE. London: Faith Press, 1961.

A discussion of the over 18,500 pamphlets related to the Oxford Movement in the Pusey House Library at Oxford.

WILLIAM WILBERFORCE (1759-1833)

PRINCIPAL PROSE WORKS

A PRACTICAL VIEW OF THE PREVAILING RELIGIOUS SYSTEMS OF PROFESSED CHRISTIANS, 1797.

SUBSTANCE OF THE SPEECHES OF WILLIAM WILBERFORCE, ESQ. ON THE CLAUSE IN THE EAST-INDIA BILL FOR PROMOTING THE RELIGIOUS INSTRUCTION AND MORAL IMPROVEMENT OF THE NATIVES OF THE BRITISH DOMINIONS IN INDIA ON 22ND JUNE AND 1ST AND 12TH OF JULY, 1813, 1814.

AN APPEAL TO THE RELIGION, JUSTICE, AND HUMANITY OF THE INHABITANTS OF THE BRITISH EMPIRE, IN BEHALF OF THE NEGRO SLAVES OF THE WEST INDIES, 1823.

BIOGRAPHIES

Brown, Ford K. FATHERS OF THE VICTORIANS. Cambridge: At the University Press, 1961.

> This important biography emphasizes Wilberforce's propagation of Evangelical doctrines. The thesis of the study is that all of Wilberforce's many interests, including abolition, were subservient to his Evangelicalism.

Danniell, George. BISHOP WILBERFORCE. London: Methuen, 1891.

> A survey of Wilberforce's life that stresses his position in the Church. Includes a chapter on "Wilberforce's Literary Influence and Personality," which praises him for possessing "a wonderful command of language, a great power of illustration and a singular clearness of thought."

Furneaux, Robin. WILLIAM WILBERFORCE. London: Hamilton, 1974.

> A full-length biography that discusses Wilberforce as a moral crusader, social conservative, and evangelical reformer.

Newsome, David. THE PARTING OF FRIENDS: THE WILBERFORCES AND HENRY MANNING. London: Murray, 1966.

> A composite biography of the Wilberforce family and their relationship with Cardinal Manning.

Warner, Oliver. WILLIAM WILBERFORCE AND HIS TIMES. London: Batsford, 1962.

> This biography stresses Wilberforce's vigorous campaigns for abolition.

Wilberforce, Robert, and Samuel Wilberforce. THE LIFE OF WILLIAM WILBERFORCE. 5 vols. London: Murray, 1838.

> Generally considered the standard biography. This massive study of Wilberforce's private and public life was written by his two sons, important religious figures in their own right.

CRITICAL STUDIES

Baker, William [J.]. "William Wilberforce on the Idea of Negro Inferiority." JHI, 31 (1970), 433-40.

> "In the course of his labors to abolish the slave trade, Wilberforce exposed the sham logic in the idea of Negro inferiority."

SCIENTIFIC

CHARLES DARWIN (1809-82)

PRINCIPAL PROSE WORKS

JOURNAL OF RESEARCHES INTO THE GEOLOGY AND NATURAL HISTORY OF THE VARIOUS COUNTRIES VISITED BY H.M.S. BEAGLE, 1839.

ON THE ORIGIN OF SPECIES BY NATURAL SELECTION, 1859.

THE DESCENT OF MAN, AND SELECTION IN RELATION TO SEX. 2 vols. 1871.

THE EXPRESSION OF THE EMOTIONS IN MAN AND ANIMALS, 1872.

THE LIFE OF ERASMUS DARWIN, 1879.

THE AUTOBIOGRAPHY OF CHARLES DARWIN, ed. F. Darwin, 1929; rpt. as THE AUTOBIOGRAPHY OF DARWIN: 1809-1882, ed. Nora Barlow, 1958.

COLLECTED WORKS

DARWIN FOR TODAY: THE ESSENCE OF HIS WORKS. Ed. Stanley E. Hyman. Cambridge, Mass.: Harvard University Press, 1963.

THE DARWIN READER. Eds. M. Bates and P.S. Humphrey. New York: Scribner's, 1957.

DARWIN'S EARLY AND UNPUBLISHED NOTEBOOKS. Ed. Paul H. Barrett. London: Wildwood, 1974.

THE LIVING THOUGHTS OF DARWIN. Eds. Julian Huxley and J. Fisher. London: Longmans, 1939.

Charles Darwin

LETTERS

THE LIFE AND LETTERS OF CHARLES DARWIN, INCLUDING AN AUTOBIOGRAPHICAL CHAPTER. Ed. F. Darwin. 3 vols. London: Murray, 1887; rpt. New York: Basic Books, 1959.

    The standard collection of Darwin correspondence.

MORE LETTERS OF CHARLES DARWIN. Eds. F. Darwin and A.C. Seward. 2 vols. London: Murray, 1903.

    Intended to supplement the LIFE AND LETTERS, above.

BIOGRAPHIES

Bettany, G.T. THE LIFE OF DARWIN. London: Scott, 1887.

    Includes a bibliography of Darwin's works compiled by J.P. Anderson.

Huxley, Leonard. CHARLES DARWIN. New York: Greenberg, 1927.

    A useful general introduction to Darwin's life, emphasizing his role within the scientific community.

West, Geoffrey [Geoffrey Wells]. CHARLES DARWIN: A PORTRAIT. New Haven, Conn.: Yale University Press, 1938.

    An attempt to "re-line Darwin's life imaginatively year by year, almost day by day, sharing his experience and displaying his ideas as growing out of it."

CRITICAL STUDIES

Appleman, Philip. DARWIN: TEXTS, BACKGROUND, CONTEMPORARY OPINION, CRITICAL ESSAYS. New York: Norton, 1970.

    Essays are arranged under the headings, "Scientific Opinion in the Early Nineteenth Century," "Darwin's Influence on Theological and Philosophical Thought," and "Darwin and the Literary Mind."

_____. "Darwin, Pater, and a Crisis in Criticism." In his 1859: ENTERING AN AGE OF CRISIS. Bloomington: Indiana University Press, 1959.

    "I shall attempt to establish that Darwin's influence on Pater was more significant than is usually assumed; that this influence led Pater's literary criticism toward two antithetical positions, the impressionistic and the historical."

Barnett, Samuel, ed. A CENTURY OF DARWIN. London: Heinemann, 1958.

> A valuable collection of essays about Darwin, including "Darwinism and Ethics" by D. Daiches Raphael, "Darwinism and the Social Sciences" by Donald MacRae, and several essays on Darwin's influence on biology.

Blau, Joseph L. "The Influence of Darwin on American Philosophy." BUR, 8 (1959), 141-53.

> Reviews Darwin's impact on American thinkers, particularly George Herbert Mead, James Edwin Creighton, and John Dewey.

Campbell, John A. "Darwin and the ORIGIN OF SPECIES: The Rhetorical Ancestry of an Idea." SM, 37 (1970), 1-14.

> Concludes that Darwin's enemies eventually discovered their best tactic against him was to accept the theory of evolution but deny his version of it.

――――. "Nature, Religion, and Emotional Response: A Reconsideration of Darwin's Affective Decline." VS, 18 (1974), 159-74.

> Disagrees with other biographers and asserts the "Darwin's affective responsiveness to nature did not undergo a decline at all comparable to his decline of interest in art."

Cannon, Walter F. "Darwin's Vision in ON THE ORIGIN OF SPECIES." THE ART OF VICTORIAN PROSE. Eds. George L. Levine and William A. Madden. New York: Oxford University Press, 1968.

> Cannon attempts to distinguish between Darwin's characteristic position and his "rhetoric, his theory, his overt philosophy, and the metaphors he inherited from his predecessors."

Centore, F.F. "Neo-Darwinian Reactions to the Social Consequences of Darwin's Nominalism." THOMIST, 25 (1971), 113-42.

> Reviews a "whole new perspective" on Darwin and outlines the "humanizing" efforts that mark the new interpretations.

Collins, James. "Darwin's Impact on Philosophy." THOUGHT, 34 (1959), 185-248.

> Concentrates on British thinkers (with the exception of Bergson) and agnosticism and idealism.

Colp, R. "Contacts between Karl Marx and Charles Darwin." JHI, 35 (1974), 329-38.

> Although the two thinkers never met, Colp finds that Darwin and Marx had many indirect and influential contacts.

Charles Darwin

Culler, A. Dwight. "The Darwinian Revolution and Literary Form." THE ART OF VICTORIAN PROSE. Eds. George L. Levine and William A. Madden. New York: Oxford University Press, 1968.

>Culler's purpose is to "inquire how the form of the Darwinian explanation has influenced, or is analogous to, forms of literary expression in the post-Darwinian world."

Darlington, Cyril D. DARWIN'S PLACE IN HISTORY. Oxford: Blackwell, 1959.

>Explores Darwin's ideas, "their origins before his time and their effects today. It is an account of a crisis in the history of science and indeed in the history of thought." Chapters on Darwin's relations with Butler, Huxley, and Chambers.

Dewey, John. THE INFLUENCE OF DARWIN ON PHILOSOPHY. New York: Holt, 1910.

>A seminal study that analyzes how Darwinian philosophy influenced American pragmatism.

Eiseley, Loren. "Darwin, Coleridge, and the Theory of Unconscious Creation." DAEDALUS, 94 (1965), 588-602.

>Finds that these two opposing intellectuals contributed early and significantly to a theory usually associated with the twentieth century.

_____. DARWIN'S CENTURY: EVOLUTION AND THE MEN WHO DISCOVERED IT. New York: Doubleday, 1958.

>An important intellectual history of the concept that culminated in Darwin's work.

Ellegård, Alvar. DARWIN AND THE GENERAL READER: THE RECEPTION OF DARWIN'S THEORY OF EVOLUTION IN THE BRITISH PERIODICAL PRESS, 1859-1872. Goteborg, Sweden: Almqvist and Wiksell, 1958.

>Discusses the reception of Darwin's theory by the general public as reflected in popular British journals. Also includes a chapter on the relation between the theory of evolution and nineteenth-century philosophers.

Farrington, Benjamin. WHAT DARWIN REALLY SAID. London: MacDonald, 1967.

>Farrington discusses "Darwin and the Poets," "Darwin and Christianity," and "Darwin's Place in the History of Thought."

Fitch, Robert E. "Darwinism and Christianity." ANTIOCH R, 19 (1959), 20-32.

Assesses the impact of Darwin's theory on religion, concluding that the triumph of relativism was its most important legacy.

Fleming, Donald. "The Centenary of the ORIGIN OF SPECIES." JHI, 20 (1959), 437-46.

"Now more than ever it is absurd to talk as if the discoverer of evolution through natural selection had not advanced beyond Lamarck and Chambers."

Gale, Barry G. "Darwin and the Concept of a Struggle for Existence: A Study in the Extrascientific Origins of Scientific Ideas." ISIS, 63 (1972), 321-44.

Believes that the intellectual roots of Darwin's theory of the struggle for existence lay in prevailing cultural norms, not in scientific thought.

George, P. Brandt. "Evolution and the 'Myth' of Darwin." FF, 4 (1971), 146-51.

"It is the purpose of this study to delve into certain popular conceptions concerning the nature of the role and importance of Charles Darwin in the development of biological and social evolutionary thought, with special reference to the British Anthropological School."

Ghiselin, Michael J. "The Individual in the Darwinian Revolution." NLH, 3 (1971), 113-34.

Finds the model of scientific revolution and its stress on social content inadequate to explain the role of the individual in Darwin's thought.

──────. THE TRIUMPH OF THE DARWINIAN METHOD. Berkeley and Los Angeles: University of California Press, 1969.

Ghiselin observes that Darwin's greatest achievement was his monumental synthesis, "a unitary system of interconnected ideas."

Girvetz, Harry K. "The Philosophical Implications of Darwinism." ANTIOCH R 19 (1959), 9-19.

Analyzes Darwin's theories in relation to several philosophical issues: being and becoming, teleology, and dualism.

Gray, Asa. DARWINIANA: ESSAYS AND REVIEWS PERTAINING TO DARWIN. New York: Appleton, 1876; rpt. Cambridge, Mass.: Harvard University Press, 1969.

> An important work that reveals the impact of Darwinism in America in the 1870s.

Greenacre, Phyllis. THE QUEST FOR THE FATHER: A STUDY OF THE DARWIN-BUTLER CONTROVERSY. New York: International Universities Press, 1963.

> Claims that her study is "an examination of the vicissitudes and struggles of the oedipal relationship in these two creative individuals."

Greene, John C. "Darwin and Religion." PAPS, 103 (1959), 716-25.

> Measures Darwin's impact on three religious and philosophical issues: revealed religion, natural religion, and the methods of natural science.

———. DARWIN AND THE MODERN WORLD VIEW. Baton Rouge: Louisiana State University Press, 1961.

> Explores "Darwin's influence on Christian thought, his role in modern social theory, especially the theory of social evolution." Concludes that, "although Darwin contributed powerfully toward shaping the dominant world view, he settled nothing in either philosophy or theology."

Gruber, Howard E. DARWIN ON MAN: A PSYCHOLOGICAL STUDY OF SCIENTIFIC CREATIVITY. New York: Dutton, 1974.

> Relies on early and unpublished notebooks to describe the whole range of Darwin's mind. Shows that he had an eclectic background in literature and philosophy, which he used in painstakingly constructing his theory.

Halliday, R.J. "Social Darwinism: A Definition." VS, 14 (1971), 389-405.

> Reviews several concepts associated with the term, but believes it refers properly only to eugenics.

Henkin, L.J. DARWINISM IN THE ENGLISH NOVEL, 1860-1910. New York: Corporate Press, 1940.

> Includes chapters on "Evolution and Darwinism from 1859," "Theology versus Evolution and Darwinism," and "Satires on Darwinism."

Himmelfarb, Gertrude. DARWIN AND THE DARWINIAN REVOLUTION. New York: Doubleday, 1959.

> An opinionated study that attempts to ascertain Darwin's own views in relation to prevailing opinions at the time and to discover what Darwin thought his theories meant and what they implied.

Hopkins, Vincent. "Darwinism and America." THOUGHT, 24 (1959), 259-68.

> The "survival of the fittest" theory made Darwinism highly congenial to the mood of late nineteenth-century America.

Hull, David L. DARWIN AND HIS CRITICS: THE RECEPTION OF DARWIN'S THEORY OF EVOLUTION IN THE SCIENTIFIC COMMUNITY. Cambridge, Mass.: Harvard University Press, 1973.

> Explores "the reception of Darwin's theory of evolution by the scientific community as reflected in the reviews written by competent scientists." Each review is introduced by a series of quotations from Darwin's correspondence, "the purpose of which is to provide some suggestion as to the value which Darwin and his correspondents placed on the review from both a scientific and a sociological point of view."

Huntley, William B. "David Hume and Charles Darwin." JHI, 33 (1972), 457-70.

> Raises the questionable thesis that Hume was an influence on Darwin.

Huxley, Julian, ed. A BOOK THAT SHOOK THE WORLD: ANNIVERSARY ESSAYS ON DARWIN'S ORIGIN OF SPECIES. Pittsburgh: University of Pittsburgh Press, 1958.

> Includes essays on Darwin by Reinhold Niebuhr, Oliver Reiser, Theo Dobzhansky, and Swami Nikhilananda.

Huxley, Julian, and H.B.D. Kettlewell. CHARLES DARWIN AND HIS WORLD. New York: Viking, 1965.

> A heavily illustrated volume intended for the general reader.

Hyman, Stanley E. "The ORIGIN as Scripture." VQR, 35 (1959), 540-52.

> Quotes heavily from the ORIGIN to display its "prophetic qualities."

Irvine, William. APES, ANGELS, AND VICTORIANS: DARWIN, HUXLEY, AND EVOLUTION. New York: McGraw-Hill; London: Weidenfeld and Nicolson, 1955.

> A composite study of both men and the scientific milieu of the later nineteenth century. See West, below.

_____. "The Influence of Darwin on Literature." PAPS, 103 (1959), 616-28.

> Discusses Darwin's impact on Saint-Beuve, Taine, Swinburne, Hardy, and Butler.

Lack, David. EVOLUTIONARY THEORY AND CHRISTIAN BELIEF: THE UN-RESOLVED CONFLICT. London: Methuen, 1957.

> Stresses the irreconcilability of the conflict between Darwin's theory and traditional Christian belief: "various writers, both Christian and agnostic, have claimed that the dispute is over, but this, I suggest, is because they have not accepted the full implications of evolution by natural selection or alternatively of Christianity."

Loewenberg, Bert J. "Darwin Scholarship of the Darwin Year." AQ, 11 (1959), 526-33.

> Reviews books and articles published in 1959.

_____. "The Mosaic of Darwinian Thought." VS, 3 (1959), 3-18.

> Emphasizes the "conceptual organization" of Darwin's writings and describes how his theological framework was the critical factor that distinguished him from all previous evolutionary theorists.

Lyon, John. "Immediate Reactions to Darwin: The English Catholic Press' First Reviews of the ORIGIN OF SPECIES." CH, 41 (1972), 78-93.

> Covers the major voices of Catholic opinions and summarizes their reaction to the Darwinian theory.

Macbeth, Norman. DARWIN RETRIED: AN APPEAL TO REASON. Boston: Gambit, 1971.

> "The mechanism of evolution suggested by Darwin has been found inadequate by the professional scientists and they have moved on to other views and problems. In brief, classical Darwinism is no longer considered valid by qualified biologists."

Marshall, Alan J. DARWIN AND HUXLEY IN AUSTRALIA. London: Hodder and Stoughton, 1970.

> Marshall discusses the influence of the voyages on the formation of the theory of evolution.

Mikulak, Maxim W. "Darwinism, Soviet Genetics, and Marxism-Leninism." JHI, 31 (1970), 359-76.

> Cites the persistence of Lamarckianism in Marxism and attributes it to the "near death" of genetics as a scholarly science in the Soviet Union.

Passmore, John. "Darwin's Impact on British Metaphysics." VS, 3 (1959), 41-54.

Covers a wide field, but gives particular attention to Herbert Spencer, Henry Mansel, James McCosh, C. Lloyd Morgan, and Edward Caird.

Peckham, Morse. "Darwinism and Darwinisticism." VS, 3 (1959), 19-40.

Peckham differentiates between the ORIGIN and the implications derived from it, and concludes that the two should not be confused.

Randall, John [H.]. "The Changing Impact of Darwin on Philosophy." JHI, 22 (1961), 435-62.

Views several aspects of Darwin's thought to demonstrate how "a fundamental intellectual revolution" emerged from others' interpretations of his theories.

Rogers, James A. "Darwinism and Social Darwinism." JHI, 33 (1972), 265-80.

Was Darwin a Social Darwinist? Roger's essay seeks definition and clarity in relating the thinker and the concept.

Russett, Cynthia E. DARWIN IN AMERICA: THE INTELLECTUAL RESPONSE, 1865-1912. San Francisco: Freeman, 1976.

Examines Darwin's influence on William James, Henry Adams, Thorstein Veblen, and others.

Sanford, William F. "Dana and Darwinism." JHI, 26 (1965), 531-46.

The Yale scientist was a late convert to Darwinism. Sanford explores Dana's movement away from catastrophism under the influence of Darwin's gradualist theory.

Scheick, William J. "Epic Traces in Darwin's ORIGIN OF SPECIES." SAQ, 72 (1973), 270-79.

An essay that attempts to interpret the ORIGIN as a literary, "artistic" work.

Sears, Paul. CHARLES DARWIN: THE NATURALIST AS A CULTURAL FORCE. New York: Scribner's, 1950.

Explores the influence of Darwin on philosophy, religion, and education.

Simpson, George E. "Darwin and 'Social Darwinism.'" ANTIOCH R, 19 (1959), 33-45.

An historical review of Social Darwinism, which finds the "nature red in tooth and claw" emphasis largely disappearing from the modern version of Social Darwinism.

Smith, Charles R. "Logical and Persuasive Structures in Darwin's Prose Style." L&S, 3 (1970), 243-73.

> Believes Darwin merits attention for "the integrated aesthetic aims" that give a distinct quality to his scientific prose writings.

Stevenson, Lionel. DARWIN AMONG THE POETS. Chicago: University of Chicago Press, 1932; rpt. New York: Russell and Russell, 1963.

> A study of Darwin's influence on the vision of nature in English poets.

Swisher, Charles N. "Charles Darwin on the Origins of Behavior." BHM, 41 (1967), 24-43.

> Delineates the various uses of Darwin's theory of the nervous system and believes that these theories constituted an important stage in medical history.

Thornburg, Thomas R. "Darwin and the Rhetorical Stance." BSUF, 12 (1971), 50-55.

> Reviews Darwin's writings to show that he utilized certain rhetorical devices tailored for his particular Victorian audience.

Vanderpool, Harold Y., ed. DARWIN AND DARWINISM: REVOLUTIONARY INSIGHTS CONCERNING MAN, NATURE, RELIGION, AND SOCIETY. Lexington, Mass.: Heath, 1975.

> Contains selections from religious and scientific writings grouped under the headings: "Before the ORIGIN OF SPECIES," "Evolution, Nature, and Religion," and "Evolution, Man and Society."

Vorzimmer, Peter. CHARLES DARWIN: THE YEARS OF CONTROVERSY: THE ORIGIN OF SPECIES AND ITS CRITICS, 1859-1882. Philadelphia: Temple University Press, 1970.

> An analysis of "Darwin's theory which treats it at the same time in its proper historical and scientific setting." Traces the changes in Darwin's thought in 1859-82 as it is reflected in the six editions of the ORIGIN prepared during his lifetime.

_____. "Charles Darwin, Malthus, and the Theory of Natural Selection." JHI, 30 (1969), 527-42.

> Grants a limited influence of Malthus on Darwin, modifying the larger claims made by others.

Ward, Henshaw. CHARLES DARWIN: THE MAN AND HIS WARFARE. Indianapolis: Bobbs-Merrill, 1927.

    A general study that examines the reception of the ORIGIN during 1859-70.

West, Anthony. "Darwin and Huxley." In his PRINCIPLES AND PERSUASIONS. New York: Harcourt, Brace and Co., 1951.

    Attacks the portraits of Darwin and Huxley presented by Irvine, above, as "grotesque, misleading, and denigrating."

Wichler, Gerhard. CHARLES DARWIN: THE FOUNDER OF THE THEORY OF EVOLUTION AND NATURAL SELECTION. New York: Pergamon, 1961.

    A three-part study that focuses on "the history of the theory of evolution," "the basis and development of theories of evolution by Darwin," and a biographical sketch stressing the major influences on Darwin--Huxley, Asa Gray, and Charles Lyell.

Willey, Basil. DARWIN AND BUTLER: TWO VERSIONS OF EVOLUTION. New York: Harcourt, Brace; London: Chatto and Windus, 1960.

    Contains two chapters on Darwin: "His Theory and Its Bearing Upon Religion" and "Evolution Before Darwin: Darwin Through Contemporary Eyes."

_____. "Darwin and Clerical Orthodoxy." 1859: ENTERING AN AGE OF CRISIS. Ed. Philip Appleman. Bloomington: Indiana University Press, 1959.

    Concludes that "it was not from Darwin, but from the theological liberals and from the Biblical criticism that the Scriptures suffered most."

Williams, Raymond. "Social Darwinism." LISTENER, 88 (1972), 696-700.

    Covers a wide range by brief reviews of those affected by Darwinian ideas--from Sumner to Rockefeller, Bagehot to Kidd, and Hardy to Ibsen.

Wilson, John F. "Darwin and the Transcendentalists." JHI, 26 (1965), 286-90.

    When Darwin's ORIGIN was originally published, several New England transcendentalists "rallied to Darwin's support." But a few years later, "the transcendentalists almost unanimously denounced Darwin as the 'latest opponent of idealism.'"

Wynne-Tyson, Esme. "Darwinism and Spiritual Evolution." CR, 196 (1959), 234-36.

    Contends that Darwin forced thinking Victorians to reexamine their faith and that a sounder Christian theism resulted.

Charles Darwin

Young, Robert. "Darwin's Metaphor: Does Nature Select." MONIST, 55 (1971), 442-503.

> Believes that Darwin's analogy between "natural" and "artificial" selection was the central factor in the scientific, philosophical, and theological controversies that ensued.

Zimmerman, Paul, ed. DARWIN, EVOLUTION, AND CREATION. St. Louis, Mo.: Concordia Press, 1959.

> A collection of critical essays, including "The Evidence for Creation" by Zimmerman, "Darwinism, Science, and the Bible" by Wilbert Rusch, and "The Influence of Darwinism" by Raymond F. Surburg.

BIBLIOGRAPHIES

Freeman, R.B. THE WORKS OF CHARLES DARWIN: AN ANNOTATED BIBLIOGRAPHICAL HANDLIST. London: Dawson's of Pall Mall, 1965.

HANDLIST OF DARWIN PAPERS AT THE UNIVERSITY LIBRARY, CAMBRIDGE. Cambridge: At the University Press, 1960.

Loewenberg, Bert J. "Darwin and Darwin Studies, 1959-63." HISTORY OF SCIENCE, 4 (1965), 15-54.

THOMAS HENRY HUXLEY (1825-95)

PRINCIPAL PROSE WORKS

ON RACES, SPECIES, AND THEIR ORIGIN, 1860.

EVIDENCE AS TO MAN'S PLACE IN NATURE, 1863.

LAY SERMONS, ADDRESSES AND REVIEWS, 1870.

CRITIQUES AND ADDRESSES, 1873.

AMERICAN ADDRESSES, 1877.

HUME, 1878.

SCIENCE AND CULTURE AND OTHER ESSAYS, 1881.

ESSAYS UPON SOME CONTROVERTED QUESTIONS, 1892.

EVOLUTION AND ETHICS, 1893.

COLLECTED WORKS

THE AUTOBIOGRAPHY OF T.H. HUXLEY AND ESSAYS. Ed. Brander Matthews. New York: Gregg, 1919.

COLLECTED ESSAYS OF T.H. HUXLEY. 9 vols. London: Macmillan, 1893-94; rpt. New York: Greenwood, 1968.

THE SCIENTIFIC MEMOIRS OF T.H. HUXLEY. 5 vols. Eds. Michael Foster

Thomas Henry Huxley

and E.R. Lankaster. NEW YORK Appleton, 1898-1903.

BIOGRAPHIES

Ainsworth-Davis, J.R. T.H. HUXLEY. London: Dent, 1907.

> Focuses on Huxley's works on embryology and comparative anatomy. Includes a bibliography.

Ayres, Clarence Edwin. HUXLEY. New York: Norton, 1932.

> A survey of Huxley's life that concludes with a chapter on "Huxley: Author of Darwinism," which states, "Huxley's interest from first to last was focused upon man, man's relation to the anthropoids and the significance of that relationship for the interpretation of all things human."

Clodd, Edward. T.H. Huxley. Edinburgh: Blackwood, 1902.

> A biography written by one of Huxley's students.

Huxley, Leonard. THE LIFE AND LETTERS OF T.H. HUXLEY. 2 vols. London: Macmillan, 1900; rpt. Westmead, Australia: Gregg, 1968.

> "I have endeavoured to give the public a picture of the man himself, of his aims in the many struggles in which he was engaged, of his character and temperament, and the circumstances under which his various works were begun and completed." Contains the only substantial collection of Huxley's letters. Also includes a valuable bibliography of Huxley's works.

──────. T.H. HUXLEY: A CHARACTER SKETCH. London: Watts, 1930; rpt. Freeport, N.Y.: Books for Libraries Press, 1969.

> "This little book is not a full-dress biography, it is designed to show not so much the work done by Huxley as what manner of man Huxley was, and the spirit in which he undertook that work."

MacBride, E.W. THOMAS H. HUXLEY. London: Duckworth, 1934.

> A survey of Huxley's life that concludes that his "definition of the agnostic position was a lasting contribution to clarity and honesty of thought, but his philosophy of materialism was radically unsound and has done enormous damage."

Mitchell, P. Chalmers. T.H. HUXLEY: A SKETCH OF HIS LIFE AND WORK. New York: Putnam's, 1900.

> Along with Leonard Huxley's biography, this study, though early, is generally considered one of the best biographies.

Peterson, Houston. HUXLEY: PROPHET OF SCIENCE. London: Longmans, Green, 1932.

> Peterson's biography concludes that Huxley is still a powerful force because "he happened to be a literary genius, as well as a biologist."

CRITICAL STUDIES

Armstrong, A. Mac. C. "Samuel Wilberforce vs. Huxley." QR, 296 (1958), 426-37.

> Discusses the pair's confrontation over Darwinian theories.

Ashford, Albert. T.H. HUXLEY. New York: Twayne, 1970.

> A useful general introduction to Huxley's relation to the "education, theology, philosophy, politics, morality, and art" of his age."

Bibby, Cyril. "Huxley and the Reception of the ORIGIN." VS, 3 (1959), 76-86.

> Discusses the role Huxley played in countering attacks made on Darwin's work.

――――. "The Prince of Controversialists." TC, 161 (1957), 268-76.

> Bibby praises Huxley's rhetorical ability.

――――. SCIENTIST EXTRAORDINARY: THE LIFE AND SCIENTIFIC WORKS OF T.H. HUXLEY, 1825-1895. New York: St. Martin's, 1972.

> Bibby observes that it is only "with the hindsight of a century [that] we can be startled by the astonishing modernity of some of his off-the-cuff comments about the deepest nature of the physical world."

――――. T.H. HUXLEY: SCIENTIST, HUMANIST, AND EDUCATOR. London: Watts, 1959.

> Focuses on Huxley's work as an educator.

――――. "T.H. Huxley and University Development." VS, 2 (1958), 97-116.

> Bibby discusses Huxley as a scientific humanist who promoted equal education for all.

Blinderman, Charles S. "Huxley and Kingsley." VN, 20 (1961), 25-28.

Thomas Henry Huxley

In spite of their friendship, the two men represented opposing views of life.

_____. "Semantic Aspects of T.H. Huxley's Literary Style." JC, 12 (1962), 171-78.

Blinderman analyzes Huxley's use of hyperbole and personification to make Darwin understandable to the layman.

_____. "T.H. Huxley: A Re-evaluation of His Philosophy." RATIONALIST ANNUAL, 40 (1966), 50-62.

"A reappraisal of Huxley's published and unpublished writings will shed light on the perennially perplexing and intriguing relationship between the two universal modes of philosophical thought: materialism and idealism."

_____. "T.H. Huxley's Theory of Aesthetics: Unity in Diversity." JAAC, 21 (1962), 49-55.

Discusses the form and structure of Huxley's philosophical works.

Burrow, John W. EVOLUTION AND SOCIETY: A STUDY IN VICTORIAN SOCIAL THEORY. London: Cambridge University Press, 1966.

Cherry, Douglas. "The Two Cultures of Matthew Arnold and T.H. Huxley." WAR, 1 (1966), 53-61.

Discusses Huxley in "Science and Culture" (1880) and Arnold in "Literature and Science" (1882) as the two spokesmen for the debate between what C.P. Snow has called the "two cultures of science and the humanities."

Chesterton, George K. "The Huxley Heritage." AMERICAN R, 8 (1937), 484-87.

Praises Huxley for his "strong English style and a stoical sincerity."

Clark, Ronald. THE HUXLEYS. London: Heinemann, 1968.

A study of the family that discusses T.H. Huxley's rhetorical style in the evolutionary writings.

Cockshut, A.O.J. "T.H. Huxley." In his THE UNBELIEVERS. New York: New York University Press, 1966.

Concludes that Huxley "was not a profound thinker or a great scientific innovator. Yet he imposes himself in the end, as Spencer does not, as a major figure of his age."

Dockrill, D.W. "The Origin and Development of Nineteenth-Century English Agnosticism." HIJ, 1 (1971), 3-31.

>Discusses Huxley's coining of the word "agnosticism" in 1869, the same year Huxley became a founding member of the Metaphysical Society.

──────. "T.H. Huxley and the Meaning of 'Agnosticism.'" THEOLOGY, 74 (1971), 461-77.

>Discusses the contradictions implicit in Huxley's use of the word "agnosticism."

Eisen, Sydney. "Huxley and the Positivists." VS, 7 (1964), 337-58.

>Discusses Huxley's reaction to attacks made against him by Frederic Harrison.

Foley, Louis. "The Huxley Tradition of Language Study." MLJ, 26 (1942), 14-22.

>An analysis of Huxley's educational theories.

Gardner, Joseph H. "A Huxley Essay as 'Poem.'" VS, 14 (1970), 177-91.

>Examining "On the Physical Basis of Life" reveals Huxley to be something of a poet, rather than solely a rhetorician.

Houghton, Walter E. "The Rhetoric of T.H. Huxley." UTQ, 18 (1949), 159-75.

>An important analysis of the rhetorical techniques used by a writer who claimed to be only a plainspeaker.

Huxley, Aldous. "T.H. Huxley as a Man of Letters." In his THE OLIVE TREE. New York: Harper's, 1937.

>A discussion by his grandson of Huxley's literary abilities.

Huxley, Julian. TOUCHSTONE FOR ETHICS. New York: Harper's, 1947.

>Examines T.H. Huxley's opposition to naturalistic in favor of evolutionary ethics.

Irvine, William. APES, ANGELS, AND VICTORIANS: DARWIN, HUXLEY, AND EVOLUTION. London: Weidenfeld and Nicolson, 1955.

>Irvine's composite biography compares Darwin to Huxley, and then focuses on the later life and writings of Huxley. See West, below.

Thomas Henry Huxley

_____. "Carlyle and T.H. Huxley." BOOKER MEMORIAL STUDIES. Ed. Hill Shine. Chapel Hill: University of North Carolina Press, 1950.

> Discusses Huxley's early perception of Carlyle as a precursor father-figure whose influence faded as Huxley matured.

_____. T.H. HUXLEY. London: Longmans, Green, 1960.

> A useful introduction to Huxley's life and works.

Jensen, J. Vernon. "The Rhetorical Influence of Huxley." WS, 31 (1967), 29-36.

> "Huxley seems to have made a meaningful rhetorical impact on the United States. He has been a symbol of courageous, free, responsible expression, and a leading stimulator of extemporaneous speaking."

_____. "The Rhetorical Strategy of T.H. Huxley and Robert G. Ingersoll: Agnostics and Roadblock Removers." SM, 32 (1965), 59-68.

> Claims that Huxley had seven rhetorical strategies in his battle against orthodox theology. These strategies basically consisted of "the active horizontal approach of removing a roadblock."

Marshall, Alan J. DARWIN AND HUXLEY IN AUSTRALIA. London: Hodder and Stoughton, 1970.

> Analyzes the influence of the voyages on the formation of the theory of evolution.

Minnick, Wayne C. "T.H. Huxley's American Lectures on Evolution." SSJ, 17 (1952), 225-34.

> Discusses and lists Huxley's lectures in America.

Noland, Richard W[ells]. "T.H. Huxley on Culture." PERSON, 45 (1964), 94-111.

> Compares Huxley's conception of morality with Freud's.

Osborn, Henry F. HUXLEY AND EDUCATION. New York: Scribner's, 1910.

> A general study of Huxley's educational theories, written by one of his students.

Randel, William P. "Huxley in America." PAPS, 14 (1970), 73-99.

> Analyzes Huxley's reception by scientists and fundamentalists during his seven-week visit to America in 1876.

Rose, Phyllis. "Huxley, Holmes, and the Scientist as Aesthete." VN, 38 (1970), 22-24.

> "Huxley reduces science to its lowest common denominator in order to give it what, as a kind of religion, it must have--the widest possible appeal. The adventures of Sherlock Holmes may be read as a corrective commentary on, perhaps, a parody of Huxley's oversimplification of science."

Stanley, Oma. "T.H. Huxley's Treatment of Nature." JHI, 18 (1957), 120-27.

> Stanley traces the evolution of Huxley's conception of Nature, which was originally romantic but became empirical after he read Mill's essay on "Nature."

West, Anthony. "Darwin and Huxley." In his PRINCIPLES AND PERSUASIONS. New York: Harcourt, Brace, 1958.

> Charges Irvine's portraits of Darwin and Huxley, above, are "grotesque, misleading, and denigrating."

BIBLIOGRAPHIES

Also see Minnick, p. 340.

Bicknell, John W. "The Unbelievers: T.H. Huxley." VICTORIAN PROSE: A GUIDE TO RESEARCH. Ed. David J. DeLaura. New York: MLA, 1973.

> A valuable bibliographical essay that surveys critical studies of Huxley.

Dawson, Warren R., ed. THE HUXLEY PAPERS: A DESCRIPTIVE CATALOGUE OF THE CORRESPONDENCE, MANUSCRIPTS, AND MISCELLANEOUS PAPERS. London: Imperial College of Science and Technology, 1946.

Pingree, Jeanne, ed. A LIST OF T.H. HUXLEY'S CORRESPONDENCE WITH HENRIETTA HEATHORN, 1847-54. London: Imperial College of Science and Technology, 1969.

> A listing of Huxley's letters to his future wife.

_____. T.H. HUXLEY: A LIST OF HIS SCIENTIFIC PAPERS. London: Imperial College of Science and Technology, 1968.

HERBERT SPENCER (1820-1903)

PRINCIPAL PROSE WORKS

ESSAYS SCIENTIFIC, POLITICAL, AND SPECULATIVE, Series 1-2. 1858-63.

A SYSTEM OF SYNTHETIC PHILOSOPHY. 10 vols. 1860-96.

EDUCATION: INTELLECTUAL, MORAL, AND PHYSICAL, 1861.

RECENT DISCUSSIONS IN SCIENCE, PHILOSOPHY, AND MORALS, 1871.

PHILOSOPHY OF STYLE, 1873.

THE MAN VERSUS THE STATE, 1884.

THE FACTORS OF ORGANIC EVOLUTION, 1887.

THE INADEQUACY OF NATURAL SELECTION, 1893.

THE AUTOBIOGRAPHY OF HERBERT SPENCER. 2 vols. 1904.

ESSAYS ON EDUCATION AND KINDRED SUBJECTS, 1904.

BIOGRAPHIES

Duncan, David. THE LIFE AND LETTERS OF HERBERT SPENCER. London: Methuen, 1908.
> The standard biography and major source of Spencer's correspondence.

CRITICAL STUDIES

Burrow, John W. "Herbert Spencer." In his EVOLUTION AND SOCIETY: A STUDY IN VICTORIAN SOCIAL THEORY. Cambridge: At the University Press, 1966.

> Discusses Spencer as "the symbol rather than the inspiration of evolutionary social theory." Concludes that "Spencer's sociology is a paradox. He is at once the most modern and the most dated of the Victorian social theorists."

_____. "Herbert Spencer, the Philosopher of Evolution." HT, 8 (1958), 676-83.

> Reviews Spencer's life and concludes that his "most useful and suggestive work was in Sociology. The SYNTHETIC PHILOSOPHY as a whole says nothing to us today; but it is an impressive monument in the history of thought."

Cockshut, A.O.J. "Spencer, the Scientific Sage." In his THE UNBELIEVERS. New York: New York University Press, 1966.

> Discusses Spencer as "the great system-maker of Victorian science. In him the characteristic agnostic search for certainty--a new certainty to replace the discarded certainty of religion--reached its apex."

Eisen, Sydney. "Frederic Harrison and Herbert Spencer: Embattled Unbelievers." VS, 12 (1968), 33-56.

> Examines the religious controversy between Harrison and Spencer and views them as they viewed themselves, "not merely as academic philosophers, but as crusaders and missionaries with philosophical systems designed to save mankind and set the world right."

_____. "Herbert Spencer and the Spectre of Comte." JBS, 7 (1967), 48-67.

> "The two major areas of direct conflict between Spencer and Positivism were the classification of the sciences and the religion of humanity. Only the former will be the concern of this paper."

Elliot, Hugh. HERBERT SPENCER. London: Constable, 1917; rpt. New York: Greenwood, 1970.

> A valuable study of the life and works.

Harrison, Frederic. ON HERBERT SPENCER. Oxford: Clarendon, 1905.

> An early study by a contemporary that focuses on Spencer's "agnostic metaphysics."

Herbert Spencer

Hearnshaw, Fossey J.C. "Spencer and Administrative Nihilism." In his SOME GREAT POLITICAL IDEALISTS OF THE CHRISTIAN ERA. London: Harrap, 1937; rpt. Freeport, N.Y.: Books for Libraries Press, 1970.

> Reviews Spencer's life and concludes that, "in spite of inconsistencies and confusions, Spencer was a great man and a notable thinker." Reprinted as "Spencer and the Individualists" in Hearnshaw's SOCIAL AND POLITICAL IDEAS OF SOME REPRESENTATIVE THINKERS OF THE VICTORIAN AGE (London: Harrap, 1933).

Hudson, William H. AN INTRODUCTION TO THE PHILOSOPHY OF HERBERT SPENCER. London: Chapman and Hall, 1897; rpt. New York: Haskell House, 1974.

> Includes a biographical sketch and analyzes the SYNTHETIC PHILOSOPHY, "Spencerian Sociology," and the "Religious Aspects of Spencer's Philosophy."

MacPherson, Hector. SPENCER AND SPENCERISM. New York: Doubleday, 1900.

> Presents an analysis of "Spencerism"--the fundamental idea behind the SYNTHETIC PHILOSOPHY.

Munro, Thomas. "Evolution and Progress in the Arts: A Reappraisal of Spencer's Theory." JAAC, 18 (1960), 294-315.

> Claims that Spencer believed "the Darwinian processes of variation and environmental selection were operative in the cultural realm as well as the organic."

_____. EVOLUTION IN THE ARTS AND OTHER THEORIES OF CULTURE HISTORY. Cleveland: Western Reserve University Press, 1964.

> Discusses "the 'Synthetic Philosophy' as a merging of previous lines of evolutionary thought." Also analyzes the "weak points in Spencer's theory" and explains "the attacks and excessive antagonism toward Spencer in recent years."

Peel, John D. HERBERT SPENCER, THE EVOLUTION OF A SOCIOLOGIST. London: Heinemann, 1971.

> Peel sets Spencer's philosophy into the social context: his relation to predecessors and his influence on Marx, Kuhn, Dahrendorf, Weber, and Durkenheim.

Schneider, H.W. "The Influence of Darwin and Spencer on American Philosophical Theology." JHI, 6 (1945), 3-18.

> Discusses the adaptation of Spencer by such theologians as Brownson, Hodge, and McCosh.

Simon, Walter M. "Spencer and the 'Social Organism.'" JHI, 21 (1960), 294-99.

> Analyzes the political and philosophical implications of Spencer's use of biological analogy to describe society.

Taylor, Arthur J. "The Originality of Spencer." UTSE, 34 (1955), 101-06.

> "Spencer patently resented the insinuation [made by Elie Halévy] that the development of his ideas owed anything to his journalistic association with Thomas Hodgskin."

TRAVEL

GEORGE BORROW (1803-81)

PRINCIPAL PROSE WORKS

THE ZINCALI: OR AN ACCOUNT OF THE GYPSIES OF SPAIN. 2 vols. 1841.

THE BIBLE IN SPAIN. 3 vols. 1843.

LAVENGRO: THE SCHOLAR, THE GYPSY, THE PRIEST. 3 vols. 1851.

THE ROMANY RYE: A SEQUEL TO LAVENGRO. 2 vols. 1857.

WILD WALES. 3 vols. 1862.

ROMANO LAVO-LIL: A WORD BOOK OF THE ROMANY, OR ENGLISH GYPSY LANGUAGE, 1874.

COLLECTED WORKS

THE WORKS OF GEORGE BORROW. Ed. Grant Richards. 4 vols. London: Oxford University Press, 1900-1902.

THE WORKS OF GEORGE BORROW. Ed. Clement Shorter. 16 vols. London: Constable, 1923-24.
    The definitive collection known as the "Norwich Edition."

THE WORKS OF GEORGE BORROW. Ed. H.G. Wright. 5 vols. London: Routledge, 1906.

George Borrow

LETTERS

Also see Knapp's biography, below.

THE LETTERS OF GEORGE BORROW TO HIS MOTHER ANN BORROW, AND TO OTHER CORRESPONDENTS. Ed. T.H. Darlow. London: Private circulation, 1913.

THE LETTERS OF GEORGE BORROW TO HIS WIFE MARY BORROW. Ed. T.H. Darlow. London: Private circulation, 1913.

THE LETTERS OF GEORGE BORROW TO THE BRITISH AND FOREIGN BIBLE SOCIETY. Ed. T.H. Darlow. London: Hodder and Stoughton, 1911.

BIOGRAPHIES

Elam, Samuel. GEORGE BORROW. New York: Knopf, 1929.

> Elam concludes that Borrow was not a "gypsy," only a "true vagabond"; not a "scholar," only a "capable linguist"; not a "priest," but a "consistent deist."

Hopkins, R. Thurston. GEORGE BORROW: LORD OF THE OPEN ROAD. London: Jarrolds, 1922.

> An appreciation of Borrow's travelling exploits and his physical prowess.

Jenkins, Herbert. THE LIFE OF GEORGE BORROW, COMPILED FROM UNPUBLISHED OFFICIAL DOCUMENTS, HIS WORKS, CORRESPONDENCE, ETC. New York: Putnam's 1912.

> Supplements Knapp's biography, below, with new letters and information.

Knapp, W.I. THE LIFE, WRITINGS, AND CORRESPONDENCE OF GEORGE BORROW; DERIVED FROM OFFICIAL AND OTHER AUTHENTIC SOURCES. 2 vols. New York: Putnam's, 1899; rpt. Detroit: Gale, 1967.

> The standard biography, containing over 1,000 letters and the single largest source of information about Borrow's life.

Shorter, Clement. THE LIFE OF GEORGE BORROW. London: Dent, 1920.

> A biography that relies heavily on letters and private documents. An expanded version of his GEORGE BORROW AND HIS CIRCLE, 1913.

Thomas, Edward. GEORGE BORROW: THE MAN AND HIS BOOKS. London: Chapman and Hall, 1912.

    Relies heavily on Knapp's life of Borrow, above, but also includes chapters on the major writings. Concludes that "Borrow's principal study was himself, and in all his best books he is the chief subject and the chief object."

CRITICAL STUDIES

Adams, Morley. IN THE FOOTSTEPS OF BORROW AND FITZGERALD. London: Jarrolds, 1914.

    Adams attempts to interpret the novels as autobiography.

Armstrong, Martin. GEORGE BORROW. London: Claves, 1950.

    Armstrong observes that Borrow's novels of travel have "no shape." He also accuses Borrow of egotism and instability and notes that we appreciate his novels "not as works of art, but as psychological documents."

Bartle, G.E. "Borrow's Old Radical." N&Q, 10 (1963), 242-47.

    Examines Borrow's motivations for viciously attacking Sir John Bowring and his family in LAVENGRO and ROMANY RYE.

Cross, A.G. "George Borrow and Russia." MLR, 64 (1969), 363-71.

    Discusses Borrow's translation of published Russian folktales.

Dearden, Seton. THE GYPSY GENTLEMAN. London: Murray, 1939.

    A popularized and appreciative study.

Fraser, Angus. "The Diaries of George Borrow's Walking Tours." JGLS, 49 (1970), 25-34; 97-110.

    A discussion of tours around the British Isles, 1853-67.

_____. "George Borrow and 'The Painter of the Heroic.'" N&Q, 18 (1971), 380-86.

    Claims that Borrow's depiction of Benjamin Haydon as a painter in LAVENGRO is "a coherent caricature of the original."

_____. "George Borrow's Birthplace and 'Gypsy' Ancestry." JGLS, 51 (1972), 60-81.

    A critique of Borrow's claims to gypsy origins.

Herbert, Lucille. "George Borrow and the Forms of Self-Reflection." UTQ, 40 (1971), 152-67.

> Herbert claims that Borrow's prose technique is a form of subjective narrative that reveals the process of its own creation as it is being read.

Hustvedt, S.B. "George Borrow and His Danish Ballads." JEGP, 22 (1923), 262-70.

> Discusses Borrow's translations of Danish poems and concludes that Borrow was not a scholar, but a poet who wrote in prose.

Maxwell, Ian R. "'But the Fight! With Respect to the Fight, What Shall I Say?'" AUMLA, 37 (1972), 18-36.

> An analysis of coherence in Borrow's prose narrations.

Meyer, Robert. GEORGE BORROW. New York: Twayne, 1966.

> A valuable introduction to the life and works. Meyer observes that Borrow's appeal is due to his use of the "travel motif, his extensive moralizing, and the pervading impression of a flamboyant and unique personality."

More, Paul Elmer. "George Borrow." In his THE DEMON OF THE ABSOLUTE. Princeton, N.J.: Princeton University Press, 1928.

> Concludes that Borrow was "essentially a picaresque character to whom life was an adventure on which the conscience and heart had no concern."

Pearsall, Ronald. "A Corner in Gipsies." QR, 305 (1967), 189-95.

> Discusses Borrow's life and work, specifically focusing on Theodore Watts-Dunton's portrait of Borrow in the ENCYCLOPAEDIA BRITANNICA as "the father of the Gipsie Movement."

Sampson, John. "An Englishman in Wales." JGLS, 51 (1972), 82-91.

> Sketches Borrow's life, dwelling on his tours of Wales, and concluding that "Borrow was perhaps the only Englishman who really understood all that is implied by the name Wales."

Speck, William A. "Borrow and Goethe's Faust." PMLA, 41 (1926), 167-78.

> Disagrees with Shorter's claim, in his biography, that Borrow used a French text in order to translate the German work.

Stephen, G.A. BORROW HOUSE MUSEUM: A BRIEF ACCOUNT OF THE

LIFE OF BORROW AND HIS NORWICH HOME. Norwich, Conn.: Norwich Public Library, 1927.

> Contains a valuable bibliography of Borrow's writings.

Tilford, John E. "The Critical Approach to LAVENGRO-ROMANY RYE." PMLA, 64 (1949), 369-84.

> Tilford disagrees with critics who charge Borrow with chaotic, episodic writing. He contends that Borrow's works do have "action, structure, themes, purposes" that lead to "artistic form."

―――. "A Note on Borrow's Bookish Dialogue." STUDIES FOR STURGIS E. LEAVITT. Eds. T.B. Stroup and S.A. Stoudemire. Washington, D.C.: Scarecrow Press, 1953.

> "Bookish" refers to "occasional disconcerting lapses in the speech of his uneducated characters" or "the slightly elevated tone of his Gypsies' speech."

Vesey-Fitzgerald, B. GYPSY BORROW. London: Dobson, 1953.

> An attempt to explain Borrow's eccentricities as caused by his Gypsy and Cornish ancestry.

Wade, R.A. "A Gypsy's View on LAVENGRO." JGLS, 45 (1966), 147.

Walling, Robert A. GEORGE BORROW: THE MAN AND HIS WORK. New York: Cassell, 1908.

> Focuses on Borrow's Celtic origins.

BIBLIOGRAPHIES

Also see Stephen's study, p. 352.

Wise, Thomas G. A BIBLIOGRAPHY OF THE WRITINGS IN PROSE AND VERSE OF GEORGE BORROW. London: Clay and Son, 1914; rpt. London: Dawson's of Pall Mall, 1966.

> The standard bibliography of Borrow's work.

RICHARD BURTON (1821-90)

PRINCIPAL PROSE WORKS

A PERSONAL NARRATIVE OF A PILGRIMAGE TO EL-MEDINAH AND MECCAH. 3 vols. 1855-56.

FIRST FOOTSTEPS IN EAST AFRICA, 1856.

THE LAKE REGIONS OF CENTRAL AFRICA, A PICTURE OF EXPLORATION. 2 vols. 1860.

THE CITY OF THE SAINTS AND ACROSS THE ROCKY MOUNTAINS TO CALIFORNIA, 1861.

WANDERINGS IN WEST AFRICA FROM LIVERPOOL TO FERNANDO PO. 2 vols. 1863.

EXPLORATIONS OF THE HIGHLANDS OF THE BRAZIL. 2 vols. 1869.

ZANZIBAR. 2 vols. 1872.

ULTIMA THULE: A SUMMER IN ICELAND. 2 vols. 1875.

TWO TRIPS TO GORILLA LAND AND THE CATARACTS OF THE CONGO. 2 vols. 1876.

THE BOOK OF THE THOUSAND NIGHTS AND A NIGHT. Trans. Richard Burton. 16 vols. 1885-88.

COLLECTED WORKS

THE MEMORIAL EDITION OF THE WORKS OF CAPTAIN SIR RICHARD BUR-

TON. Eds. Isabel Lady Burton and Leonard Smithers. 7 vols. London: Tylston and Edwards, 1893-94.

SELECTED PAPERS ON ANTHROPOLOGY, TRAVEL, AND EXPLORATION BY RICHARD BURTON. Ed. Norman [M.] Penzer. London: Philpot, 1924.

BIOGRAPHIES

Brodie, Fawn M. THE DEVIL DRIVES: A LIFE OF SIR RICHARD BURTON. New York: Norton, 1967.

> Brodie's biography contains new material and emphasizes the importance of Burton's wife. It also contains an appendix on the "Burton-Payne Controversy."

Burton, Lady Isabel. THE LIFE OF CAPTAIN SIR RICHARD BURTON. 2 vols. London: Chapman and Hall, 1893.

> Less a biography than a eulogistic, memorial compilation of papers relating to Burton.

Dearden, Seton. THE ARABIAN KNIGHT: A STUDY OF SIR RICHARD BURTON. London: Barker, 1953.

> Surveys Burton's life and works, concluding that "this failure to understand character, this indifference to the feelings and opinions in others, are the chief defects in Burton's character and writing."

―――. BURTON OF ARABIA: THE LIFE STORY OF SIR RICHARD BURTON. New York: National Travel, 1937.

> Dearden focuses on the three events he considers most important in Burton's life--the pilgrimage to Mecca, the ride to Harar, and the discovery of Tanganyika.

Edwardes, Allen. DEATH RIDES A CAMEL: A BIOGRAPHY OF SIR RICHARD BURTON. New York: Julian, 1963.

> Edwardes' study is a "romantic biography" that claims to be an exposé.

Farwell, Byron. BURTON: A BIOGRAPHY OF SIR RICHARD BURTON. New York: Holt, Rinehart, and Winston, 1963.

> Farwell treats Burton as a paradoxical character "who was both a man of action and a scholar, who made significant contributions to the world in both science and literature."

Leigh, Edward, ed. SIR RICHARD BURTON: THE EROTIC TRAVELER. New York: Putnam's, 1967.

Emphasizes Burton's writings on sexual customs, and concludes that "when the hundreds of thousands of words he wrote about countries in which he travelled gather dust upon library shelves, his name will still be remembered as the translator of ARABIAN NIGHTS."

Schonfield, Hugh J. RICHARD BURTON, EXPLORER. London: Joseph, 1936.

Attempts to present an "unbiased portrait" of Burton by relying heavily on his letters. Depicts Burton as "a baffling mixture of qualities, so unusual and contradictory, that it is difficult to form a just estimate of his character."

Stisted, Georgianna M. THE TRUE LIFE OF CAPTAIN SIR RICHARD BURTON. London: Nichols, 1896.

Stisted's biography is a popular study.

Wilson, Sir Arnold. RICHARD BURTON. London: Oxford University Press, 1937.

A brief biographical account that emphasizes the importance of Burton's "translations of Oriental erotica." This pamphlet is part of the Burton Memorial Lectures (the rest of the series can be found in the JOURNAL OF ROYAL ASIATIC SOCIETY, 1925-35).

Wright, Thomas. THE LIFE OF SIR RICHARD BURTON. London: Everett, 1906; rpt. New York: Franklin, 1968.

Wright's study is an attempt to reinforce Isabel Burton's glowing portrait of her husband. He praises Burton as "one of the greatest, noblest, and most fearless of Englishmen."

CRITICAL STUDIES

Assad, Thomas J. THE VICTORIAN TRAVELLERS. London: Routledge and Kegan Paul, 1964.

Compares Burton to Blunt and Doughty.

Bishop, Jonathan. "The Identities of Sir Richard Burton: The Explorer as Actor." VS, 1 (1957), 119-35.

Bishop concludes that "to press any distance into the personality Burton displays to the world is to discover uncertainty, failure, perhaps shoddiness."

BIBLIOGRAPHIES

Penzer, Norman M. AN ANNOTATED BIBLIOGRAPHY OF SIR RICHARD BUR-

TON. London: Philpot, 1923; rpt. London: Dawson's of Pall Mall, 1967. The standard bibliography of Burton's works.

4. NINETEENTH-CENTURY PERIODICALS: GUIDES AND STUDIES

Altholz, Josef L[ewis]. THE LIBERAL CATHOLIC MOVEMENT IN ENGLAND: THE RAMBLER AND ITS CONTRIBUTORS, 1848-1864. London: Burns and Oates, 1962.

Includes chapters on Newman, above, but also examines "the development of a catholic periodical press," which began in 1848 with the founding of "The Rambler" by John Moore Capes.

Altick, Richard D. THE ENGLISH COMMON READER: A SOCIAL HISTORY OF THE MASS READING PUBLIC, 1800-1900. Chicago: University of Chicago Press, 1957.

An important study of the development of a mass reading public. Also includes a listing of best sellers and of periodical circulations.

_____. "English Publishing and the Mass Audience in 1852." SB, 6 (1954), 3-24.

An exploration of "the true nature of the Victorian reading public" and "the average publisher's conception of it and the degree to which that conception influenced his editorial decisions."

_____. "Nineteenth-Century English Periodicals." NLB, 9 (1952), 255-64.

A survey of the periodicals that Altick concludes were "the nineteenth century's most characteristic products; they constitute a comprehensive symbol of the age."

_____. "The Sociology of Authorship: The Social Origins, Education, and Occupations of 1,100 British Writers, 1800-1935." BNYPL, 66 (1962), 389-404.

Aspinall, Arthur. "The Social Status of Journalists at the Beginning of the Nineteenth Century." RES, 2 (1945), 216-32.

Discusses the low repute of journalists until 1820.

Nineteenth-Century Periodicals

Bauer, Josephine. THE LONDON MAGAZINE, 1820-29. Copenhagen: Rosenkilde and Baggar, 1953.

> Discusses the major periodicals and then "analyzes the contents of the 'London Magazine' as it struck its contemporaries." Chapters include "Politics Under Scott's Leadership" and "Criticism of Contemporary Literature under Scott's Editorship," with sections on Hazlitt, Lamb, and Godwin.

Behrman, Cynthia F. "The Creation of Social Myth: Journalism and the Empire." VPN, 11 (1971), 9-13.

> Explores the role newspapers played in supporting imperialism.

Bevington, Merle M. THE SATURDAY REVIEW, 1855-1868: REPRESENTATIVE EDUCATED OPINION IN VICTORIAN ENGLAND. New York: Columbia University Press, 1941.

> Includes chapters on SATURDAY REVIEW articles on "Religion, Morals, Manners, and Social Subjects," "Novels and Light Literature," and "General Literature." Discusses the periodical as "both an index of leading critical opinion and an influence on literary taste." An appendix discusses "Authorship of Articles."

Bourne, H.R. Fox. ENGLISH NEWSPAPERS: CHAPTERS IN THE HISTORY OF JOURNALISM. 2 vols. London: Chatto and Windus, 1887.

> A standard work that surveys the material available on this topic.

Casford, E.L. THE MAGAZINES OF THE 1890'S. Eugene: University of Oregon Press, 1929.

> The emphasis is on the ALBEMARLE, THE YELLOW BOOK, and THE SAVOY.

Clive, John. SCOTCH REVIEWERS: THE EDINBURGH REVIEW, 1802-1824. Cambridge, Mass.: Harvard University Press, 1969.

> A valuable survey of the EDINBURGH REVIEW, the major voice of Whig social and literary opinion.

Cox, Reginald G. "The Great Reviews." SCRUTINY, 6 (1937), 2-20.

> Emphasizes the importance of the EDINBURGH REVIEW, the QUARTERLY, and BLACKWOOD'S.

----------. "The Reviews and Magazines." FROM DICKENS TO HARDY. Ed. Boris Ford. Middlesex, Engl.: Pelican, 1958.

> "The periodicals ministered vitally to the maintenance of a healthy

culture, and they cannot be ignored in any balanced account of Victorian literature."

Ellegård, Alvar. THE READERSHIP OF THE PERIODICAL PRESS IN MID-VICTORIAN BRITAIN. Goteborg, Sweden: Almqvist and Wiksell, 1957.

> A valuable intellectual history that traces the growth of a mass reading public.

Everett, Edwin. THE PARTY OF HUMANITY: THE FORTNIGHTLY REVIEW AND ITS CONTRIBUTORS. Chapel Hill: University of North Carolina Press, 1939.

> A study of the periodical "gives on an intimate acquaintance with Mid-Victorian radicalism." Also discusses the contributors--"Millite Utilitarians, Comtean Positivists, and Darwinian Evolutionists."

Graham, Walter. ENGLISH LITERARY PERIODICALS. New York: Nelson, 1930; rpt. New York: Octagon, 1966.

> A standard source that surveys the evolution of periodicals, "the authors associated with them, their influence upon each other and upon English literature since 1665." Chapters 8 and 9 deal with the EDINBURGH REVIEW, the QUARTERLY REVIEW, THE FORTNIGHTLY REVIEW, and the WESTMINSTER REVIEW. Chapter 10 is devoted to "Literary Magazines Since 1800."

──────. TORY CRITICISM IN THE QUARTERLY REVIEW, 1809-1853. New York: Columbia University Press, 1921.

> A "detailed explanation of the criticism in the 'Quarterly' and an analysis of its long-standing duel with the 'Edinburgh Review.'" Also shows how "political and social predilections" caused reviewers to display animosity toward certain poets.

Hayden, John O. THE ROMANTIC REVIEWERS, 1802-1824. Chicago: University of Chicago Press, 1969.

> Includes discussions of Coleridge, Hazlitt, and Lamb, besides presenting a detailed study of some sixty periodicals.

Hollis, Patricia. THE PAUPER PRESS: A STUDY IN WORKING-CLASS RADICALISM OF THE 1830'S. London: Oxford University Press, 1970.

> An attempt to study the Unstamped Press, "its sales, its profits, its readers, and its vendors." Concludes by discussing the importance of the campaign in the repeal of stamp duties on newspapers during 1830-36.

Houghton, Esther R. "The BRITISH COMIC and the Oxford Movement." SB, 16 (1963), 119-37.

Nineteenth-Century Periodicals

Based on research done at Pusey House, this article shows the relation between the Tractarians and the COMIC.

Houghton, Walter E. "British Periodicals of the Victorian Age: Bibliographies and Indexes." LIBRARY TRENDS, 7 (1959), 554-65.

Stresses the importance of periodicals in understanding the age. Also focuses on "bibliographical indexes: what is now available? what additional aids are needed?"

_____. "Reflections on Indexing Victorian Periodicals." VS, 7 (1963), 192-96.

Discusses the decisions behind beginning THE WELLESLEY INDEX, below: "we saw an opportunity to further the Victorian 'revival' by opening up a new area for the study of men and ideas."

_____. "Victorian Periodicals." TLS, 3 September 1971, p. 1057.

Houghton, Walter E., et al., eds. THE WELLESLEY INDEX TO VICTORIAN PERIODICALS, 1824-1900. Projected 4 volumes. Toronto: University of Toronto Press, 1966-- .

The major source in the field and one of great imporance. Houghton observes that understanding the periodicals is "indispensable for the study of opinion at a given moment." Each volume of the index--1 (1966) and 2 (1972) have been issued at present--contains a subject list, a book review index, and an author identification and checklist of writings--signed, anonymous, or pseudonymous-- in the periodicals indexed.

Landon, Philip J. "Research in Victorian Periodicals: A Checklist of Doctoral Dissertations in the United States, 1921-1967." VPN, 2 (1969), 33-44.

Lockhead, Marion. "Lockhart, the 'Quarterly,' and the Tractarians." QR, 291 (1953), 196-209.

Discusses the alternate attitudes held by the "Quarterly" toward the Oxford Movement.

Lysiak, Arthur. "Victorian Periodicals and Newspapers in Microfilm." VPN, 5 (1972), 29-46.

A checklist.

McCready, Herbert W. "Toward a Checklist of MS. Resources for Victorian Periodicals." VPN, 7 (1974), 22-39.

An author index that lists the locations of collections of papers in libraries and private hands.

Madden, Lionel, and Diana Dixon, eds. "The Nineteenth-Century Periodical Press in Britain: A Bibliography of Modern Studies, 1901-1971." VPN, 5 (1975), 3-76.

>The first complete bibliography on this subject, and a basic resource.

Marchand, Leslie A. THE ATHENAEUM: A MIRROR OF VICTORIAN CULTURE. Chapel Hill: University of North Carolina Press, 1941.

>Draws on editor Sir Charles W. Dilke's memoirs for a discussion of the periodical. Presents "something like a rounded image of the ATHENAEUM, with particular attention to its fight for independent literary criticism and its reflection of the current tastes."

Maurer, Oscar. "Anonymity versus Signature in Victorian Reviewing." UTSE, 27 (1948), 1-27.

>A discussion based on primary sources that explores the difficulty of identifying the authors of Victorian reviews. See also the introduction to THE WELLESLEY INDEX, edited by Houghton, above.

_____. "'My Squeamish Public': Some Problems of Victorian Magazine Publishers and Editors." SB, 12 (1959), 21-40.

>Editors and publishers "in warning and censoring contributors, implied a double standard of judgment in protecting the reader under a complex of influences: economic pressures, literary conscience, social, political, religious influences."

Mineka, Francis E. THE DISSIDENCE OF DISSENT: THE MONTHLY REPOSITORY, 1808-1838. Chapel Hill: University of North Carolina Press, 1944.

>Surveys English religious periodicals from 1700 to 1825, and then examines the REPOSITORY under W.J. Fox's editorship, 1827-38. Observes that "usually of little importance as literature, these publications are often of genuine significance as a record of both the clerical and the lay mind."

Morgan, Peter F. "Problems in Examining Periodical Criticism." VPN, 2 (1969), 9-11.

>In reading Victorian reviews, one feels "he was moving through an unpathed wasteland of pseudo-criticism." Morgan proposes to "consider the criticism of the periodicals stylistically."

Morris, R.J. "The Unitarian View of Fifteen Periodicals in 1834." VPN, 5 (1972), 31-32.

>Uses THE CHRISTIAN REFORMER's list of "critical notices of periodicals," in which fifteen major periodicals are discussed: "The

list is a guide to the fine distinctions within the established
Church."

Morrison, John L. "The Oxford Movement and the British Periodicals." CHR,
45 (1959), 137-60.

> Discusses reactions to the Oxford Movement by the WESTMINSTER
> REVIEW, EDINBURGH REVIEW, QUARTERLY, and BLACKWOOD'S.

Nesbitt, George Lyman. BENTHAMITE REVIEWING: THE FIRST TWELVE
YEARS OF THE WESTMINSTER REVIEW, 1824-36. New York: Columbia University Press, 1934.

> Discusses Bentham and Utilitarian journalism during this period.

Palmegiano, E.M., ed. "Women and British Periodicals, 1832-1867." VPN,
9 (1976), 3-36.

> "This bibliography is intended to give readers some sense of the
> violence and scope that the "Woman Question" occupied in the
> nineteenth-century journals, and to provide an additional guide to
> the material itself."

Poole, William F., ed. POOLE'S INDEX TO PERIODICAL LITERATURE. 6
vols. Boston: Houghton, 1887-1906; rpt. Gloucester, Mass.: Smith, 1963.

> A subject index to ninety British periodicals, 1802-1900. Best
> used in conjunction with M.V. Bell and J.C. Bacon, eds.,
> POOLE'S INDEX: DATE AND VOLUME KEY (Chicago: College
> and Reference Library, 1957).

Redpath, Theodore. THE YOUNG ROMANTICS AND CRITICAL OPINION,
1807-1824. London: Harrap, 1973.

> Includes lengthy discussions of the major literary periodicals as reviewers of the major romantic poets. Also includes several excerpts by the major periodicals arranged according to their commentaries on Byron, Keats, and Shelley.

Richardson, E.C., ed. PERIODICAL ARTICLES ON RELIGION: AN ALPHABETICAL SUBJECT INDEX AND INDEX ENCYCLOPEDIA TO PERIODICAL
ARTICLES ON RELIGION, 1890-1899. 2 vols. New York: Scribner's, 1907-11.

> Indexes close to 58,000 articles published in 600 periodicals.

Roberts, Helene E. "British Art Periodicals of the Eighteenth and Nineteenth
Centuries." VPN, 3 (1970), 2-56.

> A checklist of 317 periodicals published during 1774-1899.

Rosenberg, Henry, and Sheila Rosenberg. "Bibliography of Writings on Nineteenth-Century Periodicals." VPN, 3 (1970), 11-13.

"Our present aim is to produce a listing, annotated when necessary, which will reflect, as the New CBEL does, the technical problems and achievements of the press; biographies and memoirs of those connected with it; and a general history of the press."

Scott, John W.R. THE STORY OF THE PALL MALL GAZETTE, OF ITS FIRST EDITOR FREDERICK GREENWOOD, AND OF ITS FOUNDER GEORGE MURRY SMITH. London: Oxford University Press, 1934.

A survey of "The Old Journalism," the "Cornhill," and the most famous contributors to the "Pall Mall"--Leslie Stephen, Matthew Arnold, and John Ruskin.

Shepard, Douglas H. "Some Early Lists of Victorian Periodicals." VPN, 3 (1970), 9-11.

Discusses two heretofore unknown bibliographical resources: A CATALOGUE OF LONDON PERIODICALS, 1847-49; 1850-86.

Shine, Hill, and Helen Chadwick Shine. THE QUARTERLY REVIEW UNDER GIFFORD: IDENTIFICATION OF CONTRIBUTORS, 1809-1824. Chapel Hill: University of North Carolina Press, 1949.

"Of the 733 articles published under Gifford, 616 are identified; 60 are tentatively identified; and 57 are totally unidentified." The introduction discusses the QUARTERLY's contents and contributors in general.

Soldon, Norbert C. "Individualist Periodicals: The Crisis of Late Victorian Liberalism." VPN, 6 (1973), 17-26.

Describes "the attitudes and backgrounds of the editors and publishers of some individualist-oriented periodicals between 1870-1914."

Stratman, Carl J. BRITAIN'S THEATRICAL PERIODICALS, 1720-1967: A BIBLIOGRAPHY. New York: New York Public Library, 1972.

Lists over 505 periodicals published from 1820 to 1900.

Sussman, Herbert [L.]. "The Language of Criticism and the Language of Art: The Response of Victorian Periodicals to the Pre-Raphaelite Brotherhood." VPN, 6 (1973), 21-29.

Demonstrates how Victorian periodicals are "an invaluable resource for charting with great accuracy the pattern of shock and modification which by the later nineteenth century had become the process by which the avant-garde alters culture."

Nineteenth-Century Periodicals

Thomas, William Beach. THE STORY OF THE SPECTATOR, 1828-1928. London: Methuen, 1928.

> A commemorative history with sections on Cobbett, "Carlyle's Demands for Ireland," Arnold, and "Leigh Hunt's 'Occasional.'"

Thompson, Denys. "A Hundred Years of the Higher Journalism." SCRUTINY, 4 (1935), 25-34.

> Generally considered on the the best critical essays on the public importance of Victorian periodicals.

Thrall, Miriam. REBELLIOUS FRASER'S: YORKE'S MAGAZINE IN THE DAYS OF MAGINN, THACKERAY, AND CARLYLE. New York: Columbia University Press, 1934.

> Presents a bibliography of contributions to FRASER'S, among them Carlyle's and Thackeray's.

Van Arsdel, Rosemary. "The WESTMINSTER REVIEW: Change of Editorship, 1840." SB, 25 (1972), 191-204.

> Discusses the transfer of editorship from J.S. Mill to William Hickson.

Vann, J. Don, and Kenneth Mews, eds. "Victorian Periodicals, 1973: A Checklist of Scholarship and Criticism." VPN, 7 (1974), 34-38.

> "This checklist covers articles and books. The indexes include a Name, Named Periodical, and Subject listing."

VICTORIAN PERIODICAL NEWSLETTER. Bloomington: Indiana University, 1968-- .

> The major publication devoted exclusively to the study of Victorian periodicals.

Wallins, Roger P. "Victorian Periodicals and the Emerging Social Conscience." VPN, 8 (1975), 47-59.

> Discusses how Dickens, Disraeli, and Charles Kingsley were influenced by the periodicals.

Ward, William S. "Periodical Literature." SOME BRITISH ROMANTICS. Eds. James V. Logan et al. Columbus: Ohio State University Press, 1966.

> Discusses the major periodicals in order to "understand the place of the 'vast abyss' in literary history."

Weintraub, Sidney, ed. THE SAVOY: NINETIES EXPERIMENT. University Park: Pennsylvania State University Press, 1966.

This collection includes selections by Yeats, Shaw, Beardsley, Dowson, and Symons. The introduction discusses the evolution and demise of the periodical.

White, Robert B., Jr. THE ENGLISH LITERARY JOURNAL TO 1900. Detroit: Gale, 1977.

This recent guide aims at making available the critical commentary since 1890 on the genre of the literary journal in Britain. Chapters on bibliographical aids and general studies of the subject and on periodicals, persons, and places are alphabetically listed; four indexes.

Wolff, Michael. "Charting the Golden Stream: Thoughts on a Dictionary of Victorian Periodicals." EDITING NINETEENTH-CENTURY TEXTS. Ed. John M. Robson. Toronto: University of Toronto Press, 1967.

Wolff explores the tremendous difficulties facing scholars who attempt to use the thousands of these serials.

_____. "Victorian Reviewers and Cultural Responsibility." 1859: ENTERING AN AGE OF CRISIS. Ed. Philip Appleman. Bloomington: Indiana University Press, 1959.

Discusses the EDINBURGH REVIEW, the QUARTERLY, and BLACKWOOD'S as the major means whereby the society at large "ensured itself a prompt opportunity of using an idea, a poem, or a discovery."

Zeitlin, Jacob. "The Editor of the LONDON MAGAZINE." JEGP, 20 (1921), 328-54.

Discusses the political opinions and literary judgments of John Scott.

AUTHOR INDEX

This index includes authors, editors, compilers, and translators cited in this text. For further references to specific authors, see subject index. This index is alphabetized letter by letter.

A

Abbott, Edwin A. 296
Abrams, Meyer H. 6, 13, 16, 116, 118
Achaval, Hugo M. 299
Adams, Henry 331
Adams, Maurianne S. 116, 137
Adams, Morley 351
Ades, J.I. 173
Ainsworth-Davis, J.R. 336
Alaya, Flavia M. 42
Albee, Ernest 74, 188
Albrecht, William P. 148, 156-57
Aldington, Richard 223, 234
Alexander, Edward 43, 91, 187, 188-89, 248-49
Alkon, Paul K. 117
Allan, Sir William 161
Allchin, A.M. 301-02
Allentuck, Marcia 74, 148
Alley, Alvin D. 117
Allott, Kenneth 7, 10, 40, 43
Allott, Miriam 7
Altholz, Josef Lewis 1, 24, 297, 305, 359
Altick, Richard D. 1, 7, 24, 359
Ames, Robert J. 67
Anderson, J.P. 324
Anderson, Warren D. 13, 43

Angelo, Giovanni 82
Angus-Butterworth, L.M. 263
Annan, Noel 18, 29, 189, 217
Anschutz, Richard 189
Anthony, Sister Geraldine 298
Antippas, Andy 208
Appleman, Philip 24, 195, 234, 324, 333, 367
Appleyard, J.A. 117, 119
Aristotle 129, 301
Armato, Philip 87
Armstrong, A. Mac. C. 337
Armstrong, Martin 351
Armytage, Walter H.G. 41
Arnold, Matthew 39-42, 62-63
Arnold, Frederick 265
Arnot, Robert Page 206, 208
Arvidson, K.O. 249
Ashford, Albert 337
Ashton, Thomas S. 24
Aspinall, Arthur 25, 359
Assad, Thomas J. 356
Atkinson, C.M. 84
Atwood, E.B. 212
Auden, W.H. 279, 281
August, Eugene R. 75, 91, 189
Augustine, Saint 129
Austin, Mrs. 280
Ausubel, Herman 110
Axelrod, Rice B. 189

Author Index

Ayres, Clarence Edwin 336

B

Babson, J.E. 171
Bachem-Alent, Rose 43
Backes, James G. 189
Bacon, J.C. 364
Badawi, Muhammed M. 117
Badger, K. 263
Bagehot, Walter 64–66, 68
Bailey, Richard W. 92
Baird, John D. 75, 120
Baker, D.A. 28
Baker, Herschal 155
Baker, James V. 117
Baker, Joseph E. 13, 298
Baker, William J. 189, 289, 319
Bald, R.C. 83, 100, 174, 249, 276
Balfour, Graham 223
Ball, A.H.R. 206
Ball, Patricia M. 13–14, 117
Bankert, M.S. 298
Bantock, Geoffrey H. 44
Barfield, Owen 117–18
Barlow, Nora 323
Barmann, Lawrence F. 298
Barnes, Daniel R. 298
Barnes, Warner 164
Barnet, Sylvan 156, 174
Barnett, George L. 172, 174, 179
Barnett, Samuel 325
Barrett, Paul H. 323
Barrington, Mrs. Russell 65, 66
Barry, William 296
Barth, J. Robert 118
Bartholomew, A.T. 81, 82
Bartle, G.E. 351
Barton, Mary N. 138
Barzun, Jacques 67
Bate, Walter J. 24, 115
Bates, M. 323
Bateson, Frederick W. 1, 40
Batho, Edith C. 2, 7
Battiscombe, Georgina 291
Bauer, Josephine 360
Baugh, Albert C. 7
Baumgardt, David 75
Baumgarten, Murray 91

Baylen, Joseph O. 41
Beatty, J.M. 276
Beatty, Richard Croom 265
Becker, George J. 182
Beek, Willem J. 292
Beer, John B. 118, 298
Beer, Max 25
Beers, Henry A. 7
Behrman, Cynthia F. 360
Bekker, Willem G. 82
Bell, Alan 280
Bell, M.V. 364
Bell, Quentin 218, 247
Benjamin, Lewis S. 109
Benn, Alfred W. 25
Bennett, R.M. 262
Benson, Arthur 234
Bentley, Eric 91
Berger, Harold L. 91
Bernard, E.D. 310
Bernbaum, Ernest 14
Besterman, Theodore 2
Bettany, G.T. 324
Bevington, Merle M. 360
Bibby, Cyril 337
Bicknell, John W. 218, 220, 341
Biemer, Gunter 298
Billings, John R. 190
Bilsland, John W. 141
Bingham, P. 73
Birrell, Augustine 67
Birrell, T.A. 111
Bisanz, Adam 83
Bishop, Jonathan 356
Bissell, Claude T. 83
Bizot, Richard 234–35
Blau, Joseph L. 325
Blehl, Vincent F. 295, 299
Blinderman, Charles S. 337–38
Bloom, Harold 9, 234, 235, 246
Bloomfield, Paul 206
Blount, Paul G. 44
Blunden, Edmund 118, 164–65, 172–73
Blythe, Ronald 155
Boas, Frederick S. 16
Boas, George 235
Bokenkotter, Thomas S. 300
Bonner, W.H. 140
Booth, Bradford A. 222

Author Index

Booth, Charles 25
Borchard, Ruth 187
Bostetter, Edward E. 2, 118
Boulger, James 119
Bourne, H.R. Fox 360
Bouyer, Louis 296, 300
Bowen, Marjorie 109
Bowra, Maurice 235
Bowring, John 73, 74
Bowyer, John W. 7
Brack, O.M. 165
Bradley, John Lewis 247, 249
Braendel, Doris 179
Brailsford, Henry N. 148
Bremond, Henri 296
Brendan, Piers 289
Brett, Raymond L. 119
Brewer, Luther A. 169
Brier, Peter 174, 179
Briggs, Asa 25, 67, 109
Briggs, John 25
Brinkley, R. Florence 119, 137
Brinton, Crane 25, 67, 149
Britton, Karl 190
Brockriede, Wayne E. 75
Brodie, Fawn M. 355
Broers, B.C. 208
Bromwich, Rachel 44
Brookes, Gerry H. 91
Brooks, Cleanth 12
Brooks, John L. 7
Brooks, Roger L. 41, 44
Brosskurth, Phyllis 218
Brown, Alan W. 26
Brown, C.C. 300
Brown, Donald G. 190
Brown, Edward K. 44
Brown, Ford K. 148, 318
Brown, George A. 225
Brownell, William C. 14
Bruns, Gerald L. 14
Bryant, Sir Arthur 26, 265
Bryce, James 217
Buchan, Alastair 66, 67
Buchdahl, Gerd 190
Buckler, William E. 7, 41, 44, 299
Buckley, Jerome 2, 13, 14, 18, 24, 106, 235
Buckley, Sister Mary Ancille 300
Buckley, Vincent 45

Bufano, Randolph J. 92, 272
Bullett, Gerald 280
Bullitt, John M. 157
Burd, Van Akin 247, 249
Burdett, Osbert 280
Burgess, Anthony 68
Burgum, Edwin B. 45
Burn, William L. 26
Burns, James H. 73, 75, 78
Burrell, Sidney A. 218
Burrow, John W. 338, 343
Burton, Lady Isabel 355
Burton, Richard 354-55
Burwick, Frederick L. 92, 140, 141
Bury, John B. 26
Bush, Douglas 45
Butts, Denis 45, 225
Buyniak, Victor O. 45
Byatt, A.S. 119
Byrns, Richard H. 141

C

Cabell, Joseph Carrington 148
Caird, Edward 331
Calder, Grace 92
Caldwell, Elsie 223
Calkins, Arthur B. 300
Calleo, David P. 119
Cameron, James M. 68, 300, 302
Cameron, Kenneth W. 92, 149
Campbell, Ian 92-93, 104
Campbell, John A. 325
Canby, Henry S. 83
Cannon, Gilbert 83
Cannon, Walter F. 325
Capps, Donald 300
Carey, Glenn O. 83
Carey, George W. 194
Carlyle, Alexander 90
Carlyle, E.I. 109
Carlyle, Thomas 91
Carnall, Geoffrey 45
Carver, P.L. 157
Cary, Elizabeth L. 207
Casford, E.L. 360
Castan, C. 93
Castle, Barbara 208
Cate, George A. 89

Author Index

Cazamian, Louis 9
Cech, Svatopluk 211
Cecil, David 157, 235
Centore, F.F. 325
Chadwick, Owen 7, 26, 292, 301
Chambers, Edmund K. 42, 115, 182
Chandler, Alice 15
Chandler, Edmund 235
Chandler, Zilpha E. 157, 236
Chapman, Raymond W. 26, 68
Charlesworth, Barbara 15
Charpentier, John 115
Cheney, David 165
Cherry, Douglas 45, 338
Chester, John 126
Chesterton, George K. 15, 338
Chesterton, Gilbert K. 110, 223
Cheuse, Alan 121
Chew, Samuel C. 7
Chilcott, Tim 141
Child, Ruth C. 236
Christensen, Allan 93
Christensen, Merton A. 119
Christie, Ian R. 74
Church, Richard W. 26
Churchill, Reginald 8
Clancey, Richard W. 301
Clareson, T.D. 13
Clark, G. Kitson 18, 27
Clark, Harry H. 266
Clark, Sir Kenneth M. 27, 246
Clark, Peter 265
Clark, Ronald 338
Clegg, Herbert 290, 317
Clive, John 264, 266, 272, 360
Clodd, Edward 336
Clubbe, John 93
Cobban, Alfred 149
Coburn, Kathleen 114-15, 119, 157
Cockburn, Henry T. 275
Cockshut, A.O.J. 10, 15, 27, 46, 48, 83, 190, 338, 343
Cohen, Edward H. 301
Cohen, I. Bernard 9
Colburn, William E. 249
Colby, Robert A. 301
Cole, George D.H. 27, 81, 83-84, 109, 110, 206, 208
Coleridge, H.N. 114

Coleridge, Mrs. H.N. 114
Coleridge, John T. 292
Collier, John P. 121
Collins, James 325
Collins, John 208
Collis, John 90
Colmer, John 115, 120, 149
Colp, R. 325
Colvin, Sidney 181, 222, 223
Conarroe, Joel O. 174
Confer, David 93
Connell, William F. 46
Connolly, Francis X. 299
Connolly, Terence L. 23
Cook, Sir Edward T. 246
Cook, John D. 8
Cooke, M.G. 120
Cooney, Seamus 190
Cooper, James Fenimore 160
Cooper, Lettice 223
Cordasco, Francesco 153
Corner, Martin 46
Corrance, H.C. 296
Coulling, Sidney M.B. 46-47, 93
Coulson, John 301-02
Coupet, Armel J. 295
Court, Franklin E. 236
Court, W.H.B. 27
Cowling, Maurice 187, 191
Cox, Catherine 236
Cox, Reginald G. 47, 360
Craig, Hardin 8
Crane, Ronald S. 2
Cranston, Maurice 188
Crawford, Walter B. 137
Creighton, James Edwin 325
Crews, Frederick C. 242
Crinkley, Richmond 236
Cronin, John F. 302
Cross, A.G. 351
Cross, Frank L. 297
Crossman, R.H.S. 68, 93
Cruse, Amy 15
Crutwell, Patrick 149
Culler, A. Dwight 15, 41, 47, 48, 302, 326
Cunningham, Donald H. 272
Curtin, Frank D. 249-50
Cutts, Elmer 266

Author Index

D

Dahl, Curtis 266
Daiches, David 8, 15, 93, 223, 225-26
Dale, P.A. 302
Dalglish, Doris N. 226
Damon, Philip 43
Daniel, Robert 276
Daniels, R. Balfour 84
Danniell, George 318
Darbishire, Helen 139
Dark, Sidney 224
Darlington, Cyril D. 326
Darlow, T.H. 350
Darvall, Frank O. 27
Darwin, F. 323, 324
Das Gupta, R.K. 266
David, James Atterbury 165
Davidson, Angus 21
Davidson, William L. 27
Davies, Godfrey 266
Davies, H.S. 58, 124, 142, 175, 189, 298
Davis, Arthur Kyle 62
Davis, Herbert 83, 100, 249
Davis, W. Eugene 4
Dawson, Christopher 27
Dawson, Warren R. 341
Day, John P. 191
Day, Paul W. 47
Dearden, James S. 250
Dearden, Seton 351, 355
De Beer, Esmond S. 267
Deen, Floyd 149
Deen, Leonard W. 94, 302
Deily, Robert H. 3, 62, 215, 228
De La Mare, Walter 16
DeLaura, David J. 3, 15, 47, 62, 84, 94, 107, 120, 158, 204, 236-37, 244, 246, 257, 272, 302-03, 314, 315, 341
Dellamora, Richard J. 250
DeLuca, Vincent A. 142
Demetz, Peter 128
Deneau, Daniel P. 94
De Quincey, Thomas 139-40
De Santis, Edward 303
Dessain, Charles Stephen 296, 297, 303, 314

DeVane, William C. 83, 100, 249
Dewey, John 326
Dibble, J.A. 94
Dickens, Charles 190
Dilke, Sir Charles W. 363
Dilthey, Wilhelm 94
Dilworth, Ernest 182, 280
DiPasquale, P. 120
Dixon, Diana 363
Dobrée, Bonamy 7, 11, 158
Dobzhansky, Theo 329
Dockrill, D.W. 339
Dolezel, Lubomir 92
Dollarhide, Louis E. 250
Dollerup, Cay 84
Donagan, Alan 191
Donovan, Robert A. 48
Dopland, R.A. 84
Daughtery, Charles T. 250
Doughty, Oswald 121
Downer, Robert S. 28
Downes, David A. 237
Drinkwater, John 16
Driver, Cecil H. 68, 149
Duff, Gerald A. 109, 111
Duffy, John J. 237
Dumas, Donald G. 149
Dunlap, Joseph 208
Dunn, Richard J. 94, 104
Dunn, Waldo H. 95, 262, 263
Dunseath, Thomas 126
Dupee, F.W. 84
Durham, Weldon B. 142
Dwyer, J. Thomas 278
Dyer, Isaac W. 106
Dyke, C. 191
Dyson, A.E. 84

E

Eaker, J. Gordon 303
Eaton, Horace A. 139, 140
Ebel, Henry 95, 191
Edgeworth, Maria 251
Edwardes, Allen 355
Eells, John S., Jr. 49
Egan, Joseph J. 226
Ehrsam, Theodore G. 3, 62, 215, 228

Author Index

Eigner, Edwin 226
Eiseley, Loren 326
Eisen, Sydney 339, 343
Elam, Samuel 350
Eliot, T.S. 16, 24, 48, 49
Elkin, Felice 182
Elkins, A.C. 3
Elledge, W. Paul 93, 131, 167
Ellegård, Alvar 326, 361
Ellery, John 191
Elliot, Hugh 343
Ellis, T.F. 264
Ellison, Joseph 224
Ellmann, Richard 243
Elton, Oliver 8
Elwin, Malcolm 115, 140, 181, 227
Emmet, Dorothy M. 119
Engelberg, Edward 49
Engels, Friedrich 30
Erdman, David V. 115, 121
Evans, B. Ifor 209
Evans, Edward W. 181
Evans, Frank B. 150
Evans, Joan 246
Evans, John 247
Evans, Lawrence 234, 244
Evanson, Elizabeth Moss 29
Everett, Charles W. 75, 79
Everett, Edwin 361

F

Faber, Geoffrey 27
Fain, John T. 250
Fairchild, Hoxie N. 292
Fairlie, Henry 68
Fairweather, Eugene R. 8
Farrell, John P. 49
Farrington, Benjamin 326
Farwell, Byron 355
Faulkner, Peter 89, 209
Fausset, Hugh l'Anson 116
Faverty, Frederic E. 49, 62, 215
Feltes, Norman N. 50, 191, 250
Fenner, Theodore 165-66
Ferguson, DeLancey 222
Ferguson, William 95
Ferrier, James 283
Fetter, Frank W. 69
Field, J.T. 140

Fielding, K.J. 166
Firth, Sir Charles 267
Fisher, J. 323
Fisher, Walter 166
Fishman, Solomon 250
Fitch, Robert E. 326
Fleay, F.G. 87
Fleece, Jeffrey 166
Fleisher, David 150
Fleishman, Avrom 267
Fleming, Donald 327
Fleming, Gordon H. 251
Fletcher, Angus 121
Fletcher, Ian 238
Foakes, Reginald A. 121
Fogle, Richard H. 4, 119, 121
Fogle, Stephen F. 166
Foley, Louis 339
Fong, David 267
Fontaney, Pierre 251
Ford, Boris 8, 99, 253
Ford, George H. 7, 209
Forman, H. Buxton 215
Forster, E.M. 86, 303
Forster, John 180, 181
Forstner, L.J. 3
Foster, Michael 335
Foulk, Gary J. 192
Fowler, J.H. 142
Fraser, Angus 351
Fraser, George S. 238, 267
Frazier, Sloane 238
Fredeman, William E. 3, 215
Freedman, Ralph 121
Freeman, R.B. 334
Fremantle, Anne 303
French, Walter H. 264
Friedman, Martin B. 158
Friedman, Norman 303
Friedman, Richard B. 192
Friguglietti, James 29
Froude, James A. 90
Froude, John A. 88
Fruman, Norman 122
Frye, Northrop 16, 250
Fukuda, Tsutomu 175
Fulford, Roger 251
Fuller, Roy 50
Fulweiler, Howard W. 16
Furbank, P.N. 82, 150

Author Index

Furnas, J.C. 224
Furneaux, Robin 319

G

Gaines, Pierce U. 111, 113
Gale, Barry G. 327
Gardner, Joseph H. 339
Gardner, W.H. 303
Garrett, Clarke 122
Garrod, H.W. 158
Gascoyne, David 95
Gates, Lewis E. 276
Gates, Payson G. 166
Gaunt, William 16
Gay, Peter 267
Geckle, George 122
George, P. Brandt 327
Gerber, H.E. 87
Geyl, Pieter 267
Ghiselin, Michael J. 327
Gilbert, Elliot L. 95
Gill, John M. 303
Gillispie, Charles C. 28
Gilpin, George H. 122
Girvetz, Harry K. 327
Glasier, Bruce 209
Glover, A. 155
Godwin, William 148, 149, 150, 151, 152, 153
Goff, Penrith 238
Gohdes, Clarence 95
Goldberg, James F. 50
Goldberg, Maxwell H. 96
Goldberg, Michael 76, 96
Goldman, Albert 142
Goldsworth, Amnon 76
Gooch, George P. 17, 28, 267
Goode, John 50, 209-10
Goodheart, Eugene 96
Goodstein, Jack D. 50
Gordon, G.S. 171
Gordon, Jan B. 50, 210, 238, 304
Gordon, Mary 283
Gordon, Walter R. 210
Gossman, Anne 182
Gottfried, Leon 50
Graef, Hilda C. 304
Graff, J.A. 192

Graham, Walter 18, 361
Grant, Allen 122
Grant, Douglas 143
Granville-Barker, Harley 16
Grave, S.A. 76
Gravely, William H. 283
Gray, Asa 327
Gray, Donald J. 11
Grayburn, William F. 145
Green, David B. 3, 166, 172
Green, F.E. 110
Green, John A. 146
Greenacre, Phyllis 84, 328
Greenberg, Robert A. 69, 251
Greene, David 84
Greene, John C. 328
Greene, Thomas 128
Gregor, Ian 51
Greig, James A. 276
Grennan, Margaret 207
Grierson, Herbert J. 96
Griffin, John R. 268
Griggs, Earl L. 115, 118, 158
Griggs, Edward H. 118
Grob, Alan 150
Gross, Beverly 238
Gross, John 17
Grosskurth, Phyllis 317
Grube, John 192
Gruber, Howard E. 328
Grylls, Rosalie 150
Guiney, Louise I. 290
Guyer, Byron 276

H

Haight, Gordon S. 8
Hainds, John R. 192, 203
Halévy, Elie 18, 28, 76, 79, 345
Hall, Roland 122, 192
Hall, Thomas 137
Halladay, Jean 257
Halliday, R.J. 328
Halpern, Sheldon 282
Halsted, John Burt 69
Haltresht, Michael 143
Hamburger, Joseph 193
Hamilton, G. Rostrevor 182
Hammond, Barbara 28

Author Index

Hammond, J.L. 28
Haney, James E. 51
Haney, John Louis 137
Hannah, Barbara 227
Hanson, Lawrence 116
Harding, F.J.W. 51
Harkness, Stanley B. 87
Harnshaw, Fossey J. 28
Harper, Gordon H. 290, 296
Harris, Alan 51
Harris, John 122
Harris, Ronald W. 28
Harris, S. Dale 210
Harris, Wendell V. 51, 122, 193, 238, 251
Harrison, Frederic 339, 343
Harrison, John S. 239
Harrold, Charles F. 4, 9, 13, 96, 304
Hart, H.L.A. 73, 76, 77, 198
Hart, James 221
Hartley, Ladwick 268
Hartman, Geoffrey H. 17, 121
Harvey, J.W. 30
Hascall, Dudley 203
Hassler, Donald M. 123
Hatch, Ronald B. 277
Haven, Josephine 137
Haven, Richard 116, 123, 137, 175
Haworth, Helen E. 51
Hayden, John O. 123, 158, 361
Hayek, Frederick A. von 187, 188, 193
Hayman, John 251
Hayter, Althea 123, 143
Hazlitt, W.C. 155
Hazlitt, William 48, 163
Hearnshaw, Fossey J.C. 68, 149, 344
Heath, William 124
Heertje, Arnold 193
Heffernan, James A. 239
Hellman, George 224
Helpern, Sheldon 281
Henderson, Arnold 175
Henderson, Philip 82, 206, 207, 210
Henderson, Thomas F. 265
Henderson, W.B.D. 183

Henkin, L.J. 328
Hennessy, James P. 224
Herbert, C. 143
Herbert, Lucille 352
Herbert, Robert 246
Heseltine, G.C. 279, 280
Hidden, Norman 239
Hill, A.A. 212
Hill, Brian 81
Hill, Charles G. 239
Hill, Donald L. 239
Hilles, Frederick W. 96
Himmelfarb, Gertrude 28, 69, 76, 193, 218, 328
Hinkley, Laura 224
Hipple, Walter J. 51
Hirst, Francis W. 68
Hiton, Timothy 251
Hoare, Dorothy 210
Hobson, J.A. 257
Hoctor, Sister T.M. 40
Hoffman, Daniel 9
Hoffman, Richard L. 93, 131, 167
Hogan, Jeremiah 304
Hogg, James 141
Holland, Norman 17, 124
Holland, Lady Sara 280
Hollander, John 9
Hollis, Christopher 304, 306
Hollis, Patricia 361
Hollow, John W. 210
Holloway, John 17, 51, 69
Holmes, J. Derek 302, 304-05
Holt, Lee Elbert 85
Holthoon, F.L. von 193
Honan, Park 51
Hopkins, R. Thurston 350
Hopkins, Robert 143
Hopkins, Vincent 329
Hoppé, A.J. 87
Hopwood, Alison 96
Horn, Robert D. 268
Houck, James A. 158
Hough, Graham 17, 124
Houghton, Esther R. 361
Houghton, Walter E. 28, 52, 162, 175, 272, 278, 282, 285, 305-06, 339, 362
Houppert, Joseph W. 306
House, Humphry 116

Author Index

Houston, Robert 124
Houtchens, Carolyn W. 4, 107, 146, 162, 164, 169, 179, 185
Houtchens, Lawrence H. 4, 107, 146, 162, 164, 169, 179
Howard, Daniel F. 81
Howard-Hill, Trevor H. 4
Howe, P.P. 155
Howe, Will 173
Hudson, William H. 344
Hugh, Father 317
Hughes, Arthur M.D. 89
Hughes, Merritt Y. 277
Hughes, William H. 194
Hull, David L. 329
Hulse, James W. 211
Hultin, Neil C. 111
Hume, Robert D. 124
Humphrey, P.S. 323
Hunt, Bishop C., Jr. 124
Hunt, Everett Lee 52
Hunt, Leigh 154, 163-64, 165, 166, 167, 168, 169
Hunt, Robert 165
Hunt, Thornton 164
Huntley, William B. 329
Hustvedt, S.B. 352
Hutchings, Patrick 124
Hutchinson, T. 171
Hutton, Richard H. 65, 66, 97
Huxley, Aldous 339
Huxley, Julian 323, 329, 339
Huxley, Leonard 324, 336
Hyman, Stanley E. 18, 323, 329
Hynes, Samuel 9

I

Ikeler, A. Abbott 97
Inge, Dean 257
Ingram, Archibald Kenneth 292
Inman, Billie A. 239
Ireland, Alexander 162, 170
Irvine, A.L. 211
Irvine, Helen Douglas 9
Irvine, William 29, 66, 329, 339-40
Iseman, Joseph S. 175

J

Jack, Ian 11, 143

Jackson, Holbrook 18, 205, 207
Jackson, James R. de J. 125
Jackson, Reginald 194
James, David G. 52, 125
James, Sir William J. 247
Jamison, William A. 52
Japp, A.H. 139, 140
Jefferson, D.W. 117
Jeffrey, Francis 275, 277
Jenkins, Herbert 350
Jensen, J. Vernon 340
Jensen, Jay 111
Jerrold, Walter 158, 173
Jessop, T.E. 30
Jessup, Bertram 175
Joad, C.E.M. 85
Johnson, Edith 175
Johnson, Fridolf 211
Johnson, Lionel 15
Johnson, R.B. 164
Johnson, Robert V. 175, 239-40
Johnson, Wendell Stacy 252
Johnston, J.O. 316
Jones, Henry F. 81, 82
Jones, Howard Mumford 9, 215
Jones, Iva G. 97
Jones, Joseph 85, 97
Jones, Stanley 111, 158-59
Jordan, Frank, Jr. 138
Jordan, John E. 143-44, 146
Jordan, R. Furneaux 211
Joseph, Robert J. 252
Josephs, Lois 125
Jost, Edward F. 306
Joyce, James 85
Juergens, Sylvester 306
Jump, John D. 40, 52-53, 252

K

Kauvar, Gerald B. 9, 125
Keating, P.J. 40
Keble, John 289
Kegel, Charles H. 97, 112
Kelly, Edward E. 299, 306
Kelly, Marshall 262
Kelly, Michael 125, 176
Kelvin, Norman 206
Kendall, Kenneth E. 167
Kendall, Willmoore 192, 194, 198

Author Index

Kennedy, Arthur G. 4
Kennedy, Virginia W. 138
Kennedy, Wilma L. 126
Kenner, Hugh 85
Kenney, Blair G. 97
Keppel-Jones, David 126
Ker, I.T. 308
Kermode, John Frank 9
Kettlewell, H.B.D. 329
Keynes, Geoffrey 81, 162
Keynes, John Maynard 86
Kiely, Robert 227
Kingsley, Charles 295
Kissane, James 18
Kitson, Michael 252
Klingender, Francis D. 29
Klingopulos, G.D. 159
Knapp, W.I. 350
Knickerbocker, William S. 53
Knoepflmacher, Ulrich C. 29, 85, 126, 240
Knowles, D. David 268
Knox, Bishop E.A. 29
Kobayashi, Shozo 144
Kocmanova, Jesse 211
Koffler, Richard 121
Kogan, Pauline 53
Kohli, Devindra 126
Kohn, Hans 69
Korshin, Paul J. 76
Krieger, Murray 53
Kroeber, Karl 18
Kubitz, Oskar 194
Kumar, Shiv K. 18
Kusch, Robert W. 97-98

L

Lack, David 330
Ladd, Henry 252
Lamb, Charles 175, 176, 177, 178
Land, Stephen 126
Landon, Philip J. 362
Landor, Walter Savage 180-81, 183, 184
Landow, George P. 252-53
Landré, Louis 167
Lang, Berel 194
Langbaum, Robert 18
Lange, Petronella J. de 85

Lankaster, E.R. 335
Lapati, Americo D. 306
Larrabee, H.A. 74
Lauterbach, Edward S. 4, 137
La Valley, Albert J. 98
Law, Marie H. 159, 167, 176
Lawler, Justus G. 306
Lawlis, Merritt E. 307
Lawrence, Barta 126
Lea, Frank A. 98
Leary, Lewis 4, 167
Leavis, Frank R. 53, 77, 128, 183
Leavis, Queenie D. 218
Lee, Robert A. 53
Lefebvre, Georges 29
Legouis, Emile 9
Lehman, B.H. 98
Leicester, H.M. 98
Leigh, Edward 355
LeMire, Eugene D. 85, 206
Lenz, Mary B. 299
Leon, Derrick 248
Lerner, Max 187
LeRoy, Gaylord C. 53
Letwin, Shirley R. 76-77
Levi, Albert W. 194, 198
Levine, George L. 9, 17, 18-19, 20, 22, 59, 98, 191, 238, 254, 268, 271, 307, 325, 326
Levine, Richard A. 29
Levy, Robert H. 167
Lewis, Clive S. 212
Lewisohn, David H. 195
Lichtman, R. 195
Liddon, H.P. 316
Lieb, Michael 176
Lindberg, John 98
Lindley, Dwight N. 187, 195
Lindsay, Jack 211
Lippincott, Benjamin E. 29
Litzenberg, Karl 211
Lock, Walter 292
Lockhart, John G. 101
Lockhead, Marion 362
Lodge, Sir Oliver 16
Loewenberg, Bert J. 330, 334
Logan, James V. 143, 166, 178, 183, 366
Lomer, Gerhard R. 77

Author Index

Lovejoy, Arthur O. 19
Lovett, Robert M. 10
Lowes, John 126
Lowry, Howard F. 41, 53
Lubell, Albert J. 53
Lucas, Edward V. 171, 172, 173
Lucas, F.L. 24
Lucas, John 50, 54, 210, 253
Lund, Mary G. 150
Lutyens, Mary 247, 253
Lyell, Charles 333
Lyon, John 330
Lyon, Judson 144
Lyons, David 77
Lyons, Richard S. 240
Lysiak, Arthur 362

M

McAleer, John J. 159
McAlindon, T. 211
Macaulay, Thomas Babington 264-65, 266, 267, 268, 269, 270
Macbeth, Norman 330
MacBride, E.W. 336
McCallum, Robert B. 195
McCarthy, Patrick J. 54
McCartney, Hunter 167
McCelvey, G. 150
McCloskey, H.J. 195
McCosh, James 331
McCracken, David 151
McCraw, Harry W. 263
McCready, Herbert W. 362
McCrimmon, James 203
McDonald, William 171
MacDougall, Hugh A. 307
McDowell, Frederick P. 127
McElrath, Damian 307
McFarland, Thomas 118, 127
McGrath, Fergal 307
Mack, Mary P. 73, 74
Mackail, John W. 207
McKay, George L. 228
MacKay, H.F.B. 290
McKenzie, Gordon 127, 240
McKenzie, Robert 69
Mackerness, E.D. 99, 253
MacKinnon, D.M. 118
Maclean, Catherine M. 156

McLean, Robert S. 253, 281
Macleod, Robert D. 207
MacLure, Millar 16, 78, 199, 255, 311
McMaster, Rowland D. 99
MacMinn, Ney 203
McNamee, Laurence F. 5
McNeisch, James 85
MacPherson, Harriet 227
MacPherson, Hector 344
MacRae, Donald 325
Madan, F. 317
Madden, Lionel 5, 363
Madden, William A. 17, 19, 20, 22, 48, 54, 59, 191, 238, 254, 268, 271, 325, 326
Magoun, Francis P. 268
Mahan, Charles 54
Mainwaring, Marion 62
Maitland, Frederic W. 217
Major, John Campbell 54
Makail, John W. 212
Malin, James C. 99
Man, K.S. 195
Mandelbaum, Maurice 196
Mann, Peter 115
Manning, David J. 77
Mansel, Henry 331
Marchand, Leslie A. 363
Marcus, Steven 29
Margoliouth, H.M. 116
Margolis, John D. 159
Mariani, John F. 181
Marken, Jack W. 147, 151
Marriott, Sir. J.A.R. 69
Marrs, Edwin W. 90, 99, 172
Marshall, Alan J. 330, 340
Marshall, William 167
Martin, E.W. 112
Martin, Peter 99
Martin, Rex 196
Martin, Richard T. 127
Martin, Robert B. 30
Martindale, Father 16
Masefield, John 257
Mason, Mary G. 240
Massingham, Harold J. 19
Massingham, Hugh 19
Masson, David 139
Masterman, C.F.G. 257

Author Index

Mather, Marshall 248
Mathewson, George 54
Matthews, Brander 335
Matthews, Charles 196
Matthews, William R. 1
Maurer, Oscar 212, 218, 263, 363
Maurice, F.D. 31, 131, 218
Maxwell, Ian R. 352
Mayhew, Henry 30
Mazlish, Bruce 196
Mead, George Herbert 325
Megill, A.D. 196
Mehrotra, R.R. 128
Melville, Herman 176
Melville, Lewis [pseud.]. See Benjamin, Lewis S.
Mendel, Sydney 99, 308
Mercier, Vivian 183
Merritt, Travis R. 19
Merz, John T. 30
Metcalf, John 141
Metz, Rudolph 30
Metzger, Lore 99
Mews, Kenneth 366
Meyer, Robert 352
Meyers, Terry L. 54
Middleton, Robert D. 308
Mikulak, Maxim W. 330
Miles, Josephine 20
Mill, Anna J. 99, 196-97
Mill, John Stuart 20, 73, 77, 128, 186-87, 189, 192, 193, 194, 195, 198, 199, 200, 201, 202, 203
Miller, J. Hillis 20
Millett, Kate 254
Millgate, Jane 268-69
Millhauser, Milton 240
Mills, Howard 159, 167-68
Milne, Alexander T. 79, 269
Milne, Fred 128
Milner, Perry L. 159
Mineka, Francis E. 187, 197, 363
Minnick, Wayne C. 340
Misenheimer, James B. 168
Mitchell, Alexander 170
Mitchell, P. Chalmers 336
Mitford, Nancy 100
Miwa, Akira 224
Miyoshi, Masao 197, 227
Monro, David H. 151

Monsman, Gerald 240-41
Moody, William V. 10
Moore, Carlisle 100, 106
Moore, Doris L. 168
Moore, E.H. 140
Moorman, John R. 30
More, Paul Elmer 20, 352
Morgan, C. Lloyd 331
Morgan, Forrest 66
Morgan, H.A. 269
Morgan, Peter F. 100, 269, 277, 363
Morley, F.V. 176
Morley, John 24
Morpurgo, J.E. 163
Morris, Bertram 254
Morris, John N. 20
Morris, Mary 76, 79
Morris, May 205
Morris, R.J. 363
Morris, William 205-06, 207, 210, 211, 212, 214
Morrison, John L. 364
Morse, Samuel 241
Morton, A.L. 206
Moyer, Charles R. 55
Mozley, Anne 296
Mozley, Dorothea 296
Mozley, J.B. 289
Mueller, Iris W. 197
Muggeridge, Malcolm 82
Muirhead, Arnold M. 79, 113
Muirhead, John H. 30, 128, 227
Mulcahy, David J. 176
Mumford, Lewis 213
Munby, Alan N.L. 269-70
Munby, Lionel 213
Munro, Hector 128
Munro, Thomas 344
Murphy, James 281
Murray, James G. 144, 197
Murray, Placid 308
Murry, John Middleton 20, 55, 85, 151, 213
Murti, K.V.S. 176
Myers, C.J. 197

N

Nabholtz, John R. 10, 155, 176

Author Index

Nagel, Ernest 197
Nakajima, Atsushi 224
Nedoncelle, Maurice 308
Neff, Emery E. 13, 20, 90, 100, 198
Neiman, Fraser 40, 55, 62
Nelson, Lowry 128
Nesbitt, George Lyman 364
Nethery, Wallace 176-77
Newbolt, W.E. 316
Newman, Bertram 308
Newman, Jay 309
Newman, John Henry 289, 294-96, 298, 299, 300, 301, 303, 304, 305, 306, 307, 308, 309, 310, 311, 312
Newsome, David 302, 319
Newton, J.M. 55
Nickerson, Charles C. 86
Niebuhr, Reinhold 329
Nikhilananda, Swami 329
Noland, Richard Wells 55, 340
Norton, C.E. 89
Nowell-Smith, Simon 168
Noxon, James 159
Noyes, Russell 277

O

Obertello, Alfredo 100
O'Brien, Conor Cruise 121
O'Connor, Peter 262
O'Connor, William Van 86
Oddie, William 100
O'Faolain, Sean 308
Ogden, C.K. 77
O'Halloran, Bernard C. 290
O'Hara, James D. 157, 159-60
Ohmann, Richard 20, 55
Ong, Walter 206
Orage, A.R. 177
Orel, Harold 70, 156
Orrick, James Bentley 55
Orsini, G.N.G. 128
Osborn, Henry F. 340
Osborne, John W. 109, 112
Osbourn, R.V. 55
Osbourne, Lloyd 225
Otten, Terry 270
Owen, Huw Parry 129

Owen, W.J.B. 277

P

Packe, Michael St. J. 188
Paden, William D. 70
Pailin, David 308
Palmegiano, E.M. 364
Palmer, Chris 112
Pankhurst, Richard K.P. 101, 198
Pappe, H.O. 198
Parekh, Bhikhie 77
Park, Roy 78, 129, 160
Parker, Reeve 129
Parrish, Stephen M. 129
Parrott, T.M. 30
Passmore, John 330
Pater, Walter 175, 177, 233-34, 235, 236, 237, 238, 239, 240, 241, 242
Patmore, D. 233
Patterson, Charles I. 144, 160, 177
Patterson, Margaret 5
Patton, Lewis 115
Paul, Charles K. 148
Paul, Herbert W. 42, 217, 262
Paul-Emile, Barbara T. 129
Pearl, M.L. 113
Pearsall, Ronald 352
Pearson, Hesketh 281
Pearson, J.G. 70
Peckham, Morse 21, 331
Peel, John D. 344
Pemberton, William Baring 110
Penzer, Norman M. 355, 356
Perrine, Laurence 183
Peters, John U. 278
Peters, Robert L. 21
Peterson, Houston 337
Peterson, William S. 56, 198
Petitpas, Harold M. 306, 308-09
Pevsner, Sir Nicholous 254
Philips, Cyril 266
Pick, John 306
Pickering, Leslie P. 168
Pictet, Marc Auguste 92
Pierle, Robert C. 241
Pilcher, Donald 30
Pingree, Jeanne 341
Pinney, Thomas 264, 265, 270, 272

Author Index

Plumb, John H. 217, 270
Pocock, Guy 172
Pollard, Arthur 10
Pollin, Burton R. 147, 151-52, 153
Poole, Tom 126
Poole, William F. 364
Potter, George R. 270
Potter, J. 112
Potter, Stephen 116
Powell, Grosvenor 129
Pradhan, S.V. 130
Prasher, A. LaVonne 183
Praz, Mario 21
Prestige, Leonard 317
Preu, James 152
Preyer, Robert O. 10, 78, 119
Prickett, Stephen 56, 130, 293, 309
Prideaux, W.F. 228
Priestley, F.E.L. 152, 186
Priestley, John B. 160
Pritchett, Victor S. 86
Proctor, Sigmund 144
Proudfit, Charles L. 183, 184
Purves, J. 275
Pusey, Edward Bouverie 291, 316, 317

Q

Quennell, Peter 246, 248, 254

R

Raben, Joseph 134
Radcliffe, Peter 198
Rahme, Mary 130
Raleigh, John Henry 56
Randall, John H. 198, 331
Randel, Fred V. 177
Randel, William P. 340
Ransom, J.C. 303
Raphael, D. Daiches 325
Rathburn, Robert C. 86
Rauber, D.F. 130
Rawlinson, H.G. 233, 262
Razzell, P.E. 30
Rea, E.E. 42
Read, Sir Herbert 70, 119, 130, 177, 241

Reardon, Bernard M.G. 30, 130, 309
Redpath, Theodore 364
Reed, John R. 31
Reed, Mark 177
Reed, Walter L. 101
Rees, John C. 198-99
Reeves, Paschal 56
Reid, S.W. 130-31
Reid, Stuart J. 281
Reilly, Joseph J. 309
Reiman, Donald H. 149, 177
Reiser, Oliver 329
Reitzel, William 109
Remnant, Peter 199
Reno, Stephen J. 309
Renwick, W.L. 11
Revor, Meriol 297, 301
Reynolds, B. 163
Reynolds, Ernest E. 310
Rhys, Ernest 65
Ribando, William 310
Rice, E.E. 225
Richards, Grant 349
Richards, I.A. 131
Richardson, E.C. 364
Richardson, Joanna 281
Rickaby, J. 295
Ricks, Christopher 56
Robbins, Larry M. 199
Robbins, Lionel 78
Robbins, William 56, 310
Roberts, Helene E. 364
Roberts, John K. 56
Roberts, Mark 101
Roberts, Michael 168
Robertson, John M. 22
Robertson, T.L. 310
Robinson, Charles E. 131
Robinson, David M. 183
Robson, John M. 56, 78, 103, 186-87, 199-200, 203, 204, 367
Rockmore, Tom 200
Rodman, Barbee-Sue 78
Rodway, A.E. 152
Roe, Frederick William 10, 101
Roellinger, Francis X. 101, 241, 254
Rogers, James A. 331
Rogers, William Hudson 101, 270
Rollins, C. 208

Author Index

Rollins, Hyder E. 263
Ronson, R.H. 57
Rooke, Barbara 115
Rose, Phyllis 341
Rosen, Frederick 152
Rosenberg, Henry 365
Rosenberg, John D. 246, 248, 254
Rosenberg, Philip 101
Rosenberg, Sheila 365
Rosenblatt, Louise 242
Ross, Donald 102
Ross, Malcolm Mackenzie 255
Rossi, Alice S. 187, 200
Rothstein, Eric 126
Rouff, A. LaVonne 181, 183-84
Routh, H.V. 10
Rudman, Harry W. 70
Rusch, Wilbert 334
Ruskin, John 245-47, 248, 249, 251, 253, 254, 255, 256, 257
Russell, George W.E. 41, 42, 281, 317
Russett, Cynthia E. 331
Rutherford, Andrew 102
Ryals, Clyde de L. 48, 57, 102, 126
Ryan, Alan 200
Ryan, Alvan S. 102, 310
Ryan, John D. 310
Ryan, John K. 310

S

Sackville-West, Edward 141
St. Aubyn, Giles 265
St. John-Stevas, Norman 65, 67, 70, 71, 72
Saintsbury, George 11, 22, 284
Sallé, J.C. 160
Salt, H.S. 145
Sambrook, J. 110
Sampson, John 352
Sanders, Charles R. 89, 102, 131, 164, 218
Sanders, Gerald D. 264
Sanderson, David R. 131, 200
Sands, Donald B. 4
Sanford, William F. 331
San Juan, Epifanio 57, 255
Saposnik, Irving 227-28

Saunders, Beatrice 168
Saurat, Denis 177
Sawin, Lewis 5
Scanlon, James P. 200
Scheick, William J. 331
Schickel, Richard 57
Schilling, Bernard N. 22
Schneewind, Jerome 31, 187, 201
Schneider, Duane B. 172, 280, 282
Schneider, Elizabeth W. 160, 162
Schneider, H.W. 344
Schoen, Max 242
Schonfield, Hugh J. 356
Schoorl, Evert 193
Schuetz, Lawrence F. 242
Schulz, Max F. 131
Schumaker, Wayne 57
Schuyler, Robert L. 270
Schwartz, Lewis M. 178
Schwartz, Pedro 201
Scoggins, James 178
Scott, John W.R. 365
Scott, P.G. 57
Scott, Temple 215
Sears, Paul 331
Seigel, Jules Paul 103
Selincourt, Ernest de 184
Sellers, Ian 25
Sencourt, Robert 311
Senghor, Leopold 209
Seton-Watson, R.W. 31
Severn, Arthur 250
Severn, Derek 168
Seward, A.C. 324
Sewell, Elizabeth 127, 132
Shackleton, Robert 78
Shaffer, Elinor 132
Shapiro, Harold I. 247, 255
Sharma, Govind Narain 86
Sharples, Edward 57
Sharpless, Francis P. 187, 201
Sharrock, Roger 103
Sheen, Edwin 219
Shelley, Percy Bysshe 134
Shelston, Alan 89
Shepard, Douglas H. 365
Sheppard, R. 57
Sherburn, George 152
Sherburne, James C. 255
Sherman, Stuart P. 57

Author Index

Shine, Helen Chadwick 365
Shine, Hill 14, 103, 192, 201, 365
Shipley, John B. 90
Shmiefsky, Marvel 242
Shoenberg, Robert E. 86
Shook, Laurence K. 311
Short, Clarice 213
Shorter, Clement 349, 350
Shuter, William F. 242
Sigman, Joseph 103
Sikes, Herschel M. 155
Sillem, Edward J. 295
Silver, Arnold 81
Simms, William 149
Simon, Walter M. 345
Simpson, George E. 331
Simpson, J. 58
Sinclair, Nora Rea 133
Singer, Charles 31
Sirkin, Gerald 270
Sirkin, Natalie R. 270
Sisson, Charles H. 71
Slack, Robert C. 2, 6
Slater, Joseph H. 89, 228
Sloane, C.E. 314
Small, I.C. 242
Smart, J.P. 257
Smart, Thomas Burnett 63
Smeed, J.W. 104
Smith, Adam 65
Smith, Adrian 71
Smith, Charles R. 332
Smith, Edward 110
Smith, Elton E. 153
Smith, Esther G. 153
Smith, Jack 213
Smith, Janet A. 222, 225
Smith, Nichol 275
Smith, Sheila M. 104
Smith, Sydney 279-80
Smith, T.D. Wilson 311
Smithers, Leonard 355
Snow, C.P. 209
Snyder, Alice D. 133, 228
Soldon, Norbert C. 365
Somerville, D.C. 18, 31
Sonstroem, David 255
Sorenson, G. 9

Sorley, William R. 31
Sparing, Henry H. 213
Spark, Muriel 296
Sparrow, John 282
Speck, William A. 352
Spence, Margaret 246, 247
Spencer, Herbert 342, 344
Sprigge, Timothy L. 74
Stachey, Lytton 86
Stahl, Gary 194
Standley, Fred L. 198
Stanford, Derek 71, 296
Stang, Richard 71
Stange, George Robert 22
Stanley, Oma 341
Stanonik, Janez 255
Stapleton, Laurence 145, 161
Stark, William 74, 78
Starzyk, Lawrence 58
Steegman, John 31
Steele, E.D. 201
Steele, Peter 58, 311
Stein, Richard L. 242
Stein, Roger B. 255
Steinmann, Martin 86
Steintrager, James 79
Stempel, Daniel 133
Stephen, G.A. 352
Stephen, Leslie 22, 71, 79, 202, 216-17, 218, 219, 225
Stephens, Fran 133
Stephenson, Anthony 31
Sterling, John 102
Stern, Gladys B. 228
Steuart, J.A. 225
Stevens, L. Robert 256
Stevenson, Lionel 4, 8, 213, 332
Stevenson, Robert Louis 221-23, 225, 226, 227
Stewart, John Hall 29
Stillinger, Jack 202
Stillman, Clara G. 86
Stisted, Georgianna M. 356
Stocker, Michael 202
Stokes, Eric 271
Stonehill, Charles A. 244
Story, Patrick L. 161
Stouck, David 161
Stoudemire, S.A. 353
Stout, George D. 168-69

Author Index

Strachey, Lytton 263
Straka, Gerald M. 104
Stratman, Carl J. 365
Straumann, Heinrich 58
Streatfeild, R.A. 80, 81
Stroup, T.B. 353
Stroupe, John H. 256
Strout, Alan L. 284-85
Stunt, T.C.F. 311
Sturt, Henry 30
Sullivan, Harry R. 71
Sullivan, John P. 282
Sullivan, William H. 243
Sultana, Donald 133
Sundell, Michael G. 58
Super, Robert H. 40, 58-59, 181, 182, 184-85
Surburg, Raymond F. 334
Surtees, Virginia 247
Sussman, Herbert L. 22, 256, 365
Sutherland, James R. 23
Sutton, Max K. 104
Svaglic, Martin J. 271, 299, 311, 314
Swann, E. 283
Swannell, J.N. 213
Swanson, Donald R. 104, 256
Swinnerton, Frank Arthur 225
Swisher, Charles N. 332
Symondson, Anthony 312
Symons, Arthur 243
Symons, Julian 89, 90
Szenczi, Nicholas J. 133

T

Tagliacozzo, Giorgio 132
Taine, Hippolyte 11
Talbot, Norman C. 214
Tarr, Rodger L. 90, 104, 107
Tatalovich, Anne 202
Tatchall, Molly 169
Tave, Stuart M. 140, 179
Taylor, Arthur J. 345
Taylor, Harriet 187
Teich, Nathaniel 134
Temple, Ruth Z. 243
Templeman, William D. 2, 6, 9
Ten, C.L. 202
Tener, Robert H. 71-72

Tennyson, Alfred 70
Tennyson, George B. 11, 88, 105, 107
Thackeray, William 267
Thomas, Edward 351
Thomas, William Beach 366
Thomas, William E. 202
Thompson, Denys 366
Thompson, Edward P. 31, 112, 208
Thompson, Francis 23
Thompson, Paul R. 214
Thomson, D. Cleghorn 278
Thomson, Joseph C. 179
Thomson, Mark A. 271
Thornburg, Thomas R. 332
Thorpe, Clarence D. 144, 161, 164
Thorpe, Michael 59
Thrall, Miriam 366
Thurman, William R. 105
Tilford, John E. 353
Tillotson, Geoffrey 23, 59, 178, 214, 243, 312
Tillotson, Kathleen 23, 60
Tillyard, E.M.W. 171
Timko, Michael 60
Tinker, C.B. 208
Todd, Ruthven 134
Tollers, Vincent L. 63
Tompkins, J.M.S. 214
Torossian, Aram 228
Townsend, Francis G. 60, 256, 257, 312
Townsend, Robert C. 60
Toynbee, Philip 86
Traill, Henry D. 32, 89
Trench, M. 317
Trevelyan, Lady 265
Trevelyan, George O. 32, 266, 271
Trevor, Meriol 301
Trevor-Roper, Hugh 271
Trilling, Lionel 9, 16, 41, 42
Tristam, Henry 295, 306, 312
Trowbridge, Ronald L. 105
Tulloch, John 32
Turner, Frank Miller 32, 105

U

Uglow, Jennifer 233

Author Index

Ulanov, Barry 312-13
Ullman, Samson O.A. 60, 217, 219 220
Unrau, John 256
Uttrachi, Patricia 112

V

Valenti, Jack 271
Van Arsdel, Rosemary 366
Vance, William S. 105
Vanderpool, Harold Y. 332
Vanech, William 121
Van Laun, H. 11
Vann, J. Don 366
Van Thal, Herbert 182
Vargish, Thomas 313
Vaughan, C.E. 215
Veblen, Thorstein 331
Versey-Fitzgerald, B. 353
Versfeld, Martin 313
Vicinus, Martha 254
Vickers, Brian 313
Vidler, Alec R. 32
Viljoen, Helen Gill 246, 248, 262
Viner, Jacob 202
Vogeler, Martha S. 60, 219
Vorzimmer, Peter 332

W

Wade, R.A. 353
Wahl, John R. 214
Wain, John 72, 278, 285
Waingrow, Marshall 222
Wainwright, Alexander 229
Wainwright, R.W. 30
Walcott, Fred G. 60
Walgrave, J.H. 313
Walker, Hugh 11, 23
Wall, Bernard 214
Waller, Alfred R. 11, 155
Waller, John O. 256
Walling, Robert A. 353
Wallins, Roger P. 366
Wallis, Graham 79
Walsh, William 134
Ward, Adolphus W. 11
Ward, Anthony 243
Ward, Henshaw 333

Ward, Maisie 297
Ward, Wilfrid 297
Ward, William R. 32
Ward, William S. 366
Wardle, Ralph M. 148, 156, 161
Warner, Oliver 319
Warren, Leland E. 145
Watkins, E.I. 28
Watson, D.R. 203
Watson, Edward A. 313
Watson, Francis 256
Watson, George 6, 58, 60-61, 134, 145, 161, 178, 298
Watson, J. Steven 32
Watson, Melvin R. 169, 178
Watt, F.W. 16, 78, 199, 255, 311
Watters, Reginald 134
Wearmouth, Robert F. 32
Weather, Winston 134
Weatherby, H.L. 313-14
Webb, Alice 178
Webb, Timothy 134
Weber, Ronald 271
Webster, David H. 72
Wedderburn, Alexander D.O. 246
Weiner, M.J. 112
Weintraub, Sidney 366
Welby, T. Earle 180, 214
Welch, Jack 169
Wellek, René 16, 19, 21, 23, 105-06, 121, 135, 138, 145, 162, 169, 203, 219, 243, 257, 271, 278
Wells, Geoffrey [pseud.]. See West, Geoffrey
Wells, John E. 145
Welty, Gordon A. 203
Werkmeister, Lucyle 135, 153
Wertz, S.K. 203
Wesling, Donald 257
West, Alick 244
West, Anthony 333, 341
West, Geoffrey [Geoffrey Wells] 324
West, Henry R. 203
West, Paul 106, 244
Whalley, George 119, 135-36, 178
Wheeler, Charles B. 136
Wheeler, D.H. 261
Wheeler, Stephen 180-81, 185

Author Index

White, Hayden 132
White, Reginald J. 32, 115
White, Robert B., Jr. 367
Whitehill, Joseph 136
Whitehouse, John Howard 246, 257
Whitley, William T. 33
Whyte, J.H. 314
Wichler, Gerhard 333
Wilberforce, Robert 8, 319
Wilberforce, Samuel 319
Wilberforce, William 27
Wilcox, Stewart 162
Wilding, M. 86
Wilenski, Reginald 248
Wiley, Paul L. 87
Wilkinson, D.R.M. 61, 106
Willey, Basil 24, 33, 87, 119, 136, 178, 333
Williams, Raymond 18, 33, 333
Williams, Stanley T. 24, 184, 282
Williams, T.L. 61
Williamson, Eugene 42, 61
Willson, Robert 136
Wilson, Sir Arnold 356
Wilson, David Alec 91, 263
Wilson, Douglas B. 136
Wilson, F.P. 11
Wilson, John Dover 28, 219
Wilson, John F. 333
Wilson, John R. 106
Wilson, R.F. 291
Wilson, R.J. 316
Wimsatt, William K. 12
Winthrop, H. 244
Wise, Thomas G. 353
Wise, Thomas J. 138, 185, 257
Witte, William 106
Wojcik, Manfred 136-37
Wolff, Michael 367

Wood, Anthony 33
Wood, Edward F.L. 292
Wood, Margaret 272
Woodcock, George 148
Woodring, Carl R. 12, 164
Woodrow, H. 264
Woodruff, Douglas 306
Woods, Thomas 203
Woodward, Sir E. Llewellyn 33
Woolf, Leonard 86
Woolf, Virginia 145, 218, 219
Wordsworth, Dorothy 124
Wordsworth, William 142, 161
Worth, George J. 70, 156, 157
Wright, Austin 6, 24
Wright, Brooks 146
Wright, Charles D. 61-62
Wright, H.G. 349
Wright, Raymond 12
Wright, Samuel 241, 244
Wright, Thomas 234, 356
Wright, William C. 162, 257
Wynne-Tyson, Esme 333

Y

Yanitelli, Victor R. 303, 310
Yoder, Edwin M. 272
Young, George M. 18, 33-34, 72, 264
Young, Helen H. 244
Young, Louise 106
Young, Robert 334

Z

Zall, Paul M. 137, 138
Zeitlin, Jacob 162, 367
Zimmerman, Paul 334
Zink, David D. 219

TITLE INDEX

This index contains titles of books and plays cited in this text. It does not include titles of periodicals or articles within periodicals. It is alphabetized letter by letter.

A

Abstracts of English Studies 5
Across the Plains, with Other Memories and Essays, 1892 221
Acton-Newman Relations, The 307
Addresses Commemorating the One-Hundredth Anniversary of the Birth of William Morris 208
Advice to Young Men 109
Aesthetic Adventure, The 16
Aesthetic and Critical Theories of John Ruskin, The 252
Aesthetic of Walter Pater, The 236
Aesthetics of Hazlitt, The 160
Age of Equipoise, The 26
Age of Reform, 1815-1870, The 33
Agnostic's Apology, and Other Essays, 1893, An 216
Aids to Reflection 129
Albemarle 360
Alexander Pope, 1880 216
Alps and Sanctuaries, 1882 80
American Addresses, 1877 335
American Essays for the Newman Centennial 310
Analysis and Synopsis of the Stylistic Technique of Addison, Johnson, Hazlitt, and Pater, An 157, 236
Anglican Career of Cardinal Newman, The 296

Annotated Bibliography of Sir Richard Burton, An 356-57
Annual Bibliography of English Language and Literature 1
Apes, Angels, and Victorians 29, 329, 339
Apologia Pro Vita Sua 295, 303, 304, 307
Appeal to the Religion, Justice, and Humanity of the Inhabitants of the British Empire, in Behalf of the Negro Slaves of the West Indies, 1823, An 318
Appreciations, with an Essay on Style 175, 233
Arabian Knight, The 355
Archetype and the Psyche, The 134
Arnold and Celtic Literature 44
Arnold and the Romantics 52
Arnold and the Three Classes 54
Arnold's Response to German Culture 61
Art and Industrial Revolution 29
Art Criticism of John Ruskin, The 246
Art in England: 1800-1820 33
Art in England: 1821-1837 33
Artist, Writer, Socialist 205
Art of Newman's APOLOGIA, The 305

Title Index

Art of Victorian Prose, The   19
Aspects of Literature   85
Athenaeum, The   363
Auguste Comte and Positivism   186
Authoress of the Odyssey, The   80
Autobiographical Writings of J.H. Newman   295
Autobiography   186, 197, 199, 202
Autobiography and other Writings   202
Autobiography of Charles Darwin, The   323
Autobiography of Herbert Spencer, The   342
Autobiography of Leigh Hunt, The   163
Autobiography of T.H. Huxley and Essays, The   335
Autobiography of William Cobbett, The   108

B

Backgrounds of English Victorian Literature   31
Backgrounds to Victorian Literature   29
Background to English Romantic Literature   18
Bagehot's Historical Essays   65
Bagehot's Literary Studies   65
Barchester Towers   298
Bartleby   174
Bentham, Coleridge, and the Science of History   78
Bentham and the Ethics of Today   75
Bentham Collection, A   79
Bentham in the Twentieth Century   78
Benthamite Reviewing   364
Bentham Reader, A   73
Bentham's Theory of Fiction   77
Bernard Shaw and William Morris   208
Best of Hazlitt, The   155
Between Science and Religion   32
Beyond the Tragic Vision   21
Bible in Spain, The   349
Bibliographies of Studies in Victorian Literature for the Ten Years 1955-1964   2
Bibliographies of Studies in Victorian Literature for the Ten Years 1945-1954   2

Bibliographies of Studies in Victorian Literature for the Thirteen Years 1932-1944   2
Bibliographies of Twelve Victorian Authors   3, 62
Bibliography of British Literary Bibliographies   4
Bibliography of Hazlitt   162
Bibliography of Matthew Arnold   63
Bibliography of Matthew Arnold, 1932-1970, A   63
Bibliography of Robert Louis Stevenson, A   228
Bibliography of Samuel Taylor Coleridge, A   137
Bibliography of the Published Writings of J.S. Mill, The   203
Bibliography of the Works of Morris   215
Bibliography of the Works of Robert Louis Stevenson, A   228
Bibliography of the Writings in Prose and Verse of George Borrow, A   353
Bibliography of the Writings in Prose and Verse of Samuel Taylor Coleridge   138
Bibliography of the Writings in Prose and Verse of Walter Savage Landor, A   185
Bibliography of the Writings of Butler and of Writings about Him, A   87
Bibliography of the Writings of Charles and Mary Lamb, A   179
Bibliography of the Writings of Walter H. Pater, A   244
Bibliography of Thomas Carlyle's Writings, A   106
Billy Budd   176
Biographia Literaria, or Biographical Sketches of My Literary Life and Opinions   114, 121, 123, 125, 126, 129, 134, 136
Biographical Studies by the Late Walter Bagehot   65, 66
Biographies by Lord Macaulay Contributed to the ENCYCLOPAEDIA BRITANNICA   264
Bishop Wilberforce   318
Booker Memorial Studies   14
Book of Fallacies   73

Title Index

Book of R.L.S., A 225
Book of the Thousand Nights and a Night, The 354
Books of William Morris 215
Book That Never Was, The 208
Book That Shook the World, A 329
Born under Saturn 156
Borrow House Museum 352
Boundaries of Fiction, The 18
Brantwood Diary of John Ruskin, The 246
Britain in Europe, 1789-1914 31
Britain's Theatrical Periodicals, 1720-1967 365
British Victorian Literature 18
Bunyan 261
Burton: A Biography of Sir Richard Burton 355
Burton of Arabia 355
Butler: A Mid-Victorian Modern 86
Butler: Critic and Philosopher 85
Butleriana 81
Butler's Notebooks 81
Byron, Shelley, Hunt, and the LIBERAL 167

C

Caleb Williams 148
Cambridge Bibliography of English Literature, The 1
Cambridge History of English Literature, The 11
Captain's Death Bed and other Essays, The 219
Cardinal Newman: A Biographical and Literary Study 308
Cardinal Newman: His Theory of Knowledge 302
Cardinal Newman and William Froude, F.R.S., a Correspondence 296
Cardinal Newman as an Historian 300
Cardinal Newman in His Age 313
Cardinal Newman's Best Plain Sermons 295
Cardinal Newman's Works 295
Career of Samuel Butler, 1835-1903, The 87
Carlyle 90
Carlyle: Prophet of Today 98

Carlyle and Dickens 96
Carlyle and German Thought, 1819-1834 96
Carlyle and Mill: An Introduction to Victorian Thought 20, 100, 198
Carlyle and Mill: Two Scottish University Rectors 99, 196
Carlyle and the American Transcendentalists 105
Carlyle and the Idea of the Modern 98
Carlyle and the Saint-Simonians 103
Carlyle and the Victorian Dilemma 93
Carlyle as Historian 95
Carlyle Reader, A 88
Carlyles: A Biography of Thomas and Jane Carlyle, The 90
Carlyle's Critical Theories 100
Carlyle's Early Readings to 1834 103
Carlyle's Fusion of Poetry, History, and Religion by 1834 103
Carlyle's Life 91
Carlyle's Theory of the Hero 98
Case of Catholic Subscription to the XXXIX Articles, The 291
Case of Walter Bagehot, The 71
Catalogue of the Manuscripts of Jeremy Bentham in the Library of University College, London 79
Cat's Pilgrimage, The 261
Central Self, The 13
Century of Darwin, A 325
Century of Hero-Worship, A 91
Characters of Shakespear's Plays 154
Charles Darwin 324
Charles Darwin: A Portrait 324
Charles Darwin: The Founder of the Theory of Evolution and Natural Selection 333
Charles Darwin: The Man and His Warfare 333
Charles Darwin: The Naturalist as a Cultural Force 331
Charles Darwin: The Years of Controversy 332
Charles Darwin and His World 329
Charles Lamb (Blunden) 172

Title Index

Charles Lamb (Jerrold) 173
Charles Lamb: His Life Recorded by His Contemporaries 173
Charles Lamb: The Evolution of ELIA 174
Charles Lamb and His Contemporaries 173
Charles Lamb and His Friends 173
Charles Lamb in America to 1848 176
Check-List of Twentieth-Century English Language Articles on Thomas Carlyle, 1900-1965 107
Christabel 123, 158
Christianity Past and Present 33
Christian Year, The 291
Christopher North 283
Christopher North: A Memoir of John Wilson, Compiled from Family Papers and Other Sources 283
Churches in the Nineteenth Century, The 24
Church in an Age of Revolution, The 32
Church of the Fathers, The 294
City of the Saints and Across the Rocky Mountains to California, The 354
Civilization in the United States 40
Civil Law 73
Cobbett: A Bibliographical Account of His Life and Times 113
Cobbett: A Study of His Life as Shown in His Writings 109
Cobbett's Poor Man's Friend 108
Cobbett's Sermons 108
Cobbett's Two-Penny Trash 108
Coleridge (Bate) 115
Coleridge (House) 116
Coleridge (Watters) 134
Coleridge: A Collection of Critical Essays 119
Coleridge: Critic of Shakespeare 117
Coleridge: Critic of Society 120
Coleridge: Studies by Several Hands 118
Coleridge: The Critical Heritage 125
Coleridge: The Damaged Archangel 122
Coleridge, the Sublime Somnambulist 115
Coleridge: The Works and the Relevance 134
Coleridge and Christian Doctrine 118
Coleridge and German Idealism 128
Coleridge and Imagination 131
Coleridge and S.T.C. 116
Coleridge and the Broad Church Movement 131
Coleridge and the Idea of the Modern State 119
Coleridge and the Pantheist Tradition 127
Coleridge and Wordsworth in Somerset 126
Coleridge as a Religious Thinker 119
Coleridge as Critic 130
Coleridge as Philosopher 128
Coleridge on Logic and Learning 133
Coleridge on Shakespeare 121
Coleridge on the Seventeenth Century 119
Coleridge's Meditative Art 129
Coleridge's Philosophy of Literature 117
Coleridge's Variety 118
Coleridge the Visionary 118
Collected Essays, Literary and Critical 217
Collected Essays and Addresses 67
Collected Essays of T.H. Huxley 335
Collected Letters of Coleridge, The 115
Collected Letters of Thomas and Jane Welsh Carlyle, The 89
Collected Works of John Stuart Mill, The 186
Collected Works of Samuel Taylor Coleridge, The 114, 135
Collected Works of Walter Bagehot, The 65, 66
Collected Works of William Hazlitt, The 155, 157
Collected Works of William Morris, The 205
Collected Writings of Thomas De Quincey, The 139
Commentary on Macaulay's HISTORY OF ENGLAND 267
Common Reader, The 145
Companion to Victorian Literature 30

Title Index

Complete Bibliography of the Writings in Prose and Verse of John Ruskin, A 257
Complete Prose Works of Matthew Arnold, The 40
Complete Works of Walter Savage Landor, The 180
Complete Works of William Hazlitt, The 155
Concise Bibliography for Students of English, A 4
Concise Cambridge Bibliography of English Literature, 600-1950 6
Concise Economic History of Britain from 1750 to Recent Times, A 27
Condition of the Working Class in England in 1844, The 30
Confessions of an English Opium Eater 139, 141, 143
Confessions of an Inquiring Spirit 114
Consecration of Learning, The 307
Considerations on Representative Government 186
Consort of Taste, The 31
Constitutional Law 73
Contemporary Literary Scholarship 4
Contemporary Reviews of Romantic Poetry 278, 285
Contributions to the EDINBURGH REVIEW 275, 277
Correspondence 73
Correspondence between Goethe and Carlyle, The 89
Correspondence of Butler with His Sister May 81
Correspondence of Emerson and Carlyle, The 89
Correspondence of J.H. Newman and John Keble and Others, 1839-45, The 296
Correspondence of Jeremy Bentham 74
Correspondence of Leigh Hunt, The 164
Count Your Enemies and Economise Your Expenditure 64
Cradle of Erewhon, The 85
Crazy Fabric, The 84
Critical and Historical Essays, Contributed to the EDINBURGH REVIEW 264
Critical and Miscellaneous Essays 88
Critical Essays on the Performers of the London Theatres 163
Critical History of English Literature, A 8
Criticism and the Nineteenth Century 23
Criticism on Contemporary Thought and Thinkers 97
Critiques and Addresses 335
Crown of Wild Olive, The 245
Cult of the Ego in Modern Literature, The 96
Culture and Anarchy 39, 40, 45, 53, 60, 200
Culture and Society, 1780-1950 33

D

Darkening Glass, The 248
Dark Passages 15
Darwin, Evolution, and Creation 334
Darwin: Texts, Background, Contemporary Opinion, Critical Essays 324
Darwin among the Poets 332
Darwin and Butler 87, 333
Darwin and Darwinism 332
Darwin and His Critics 329
Darwin and Huxley in Australia 330, 340
Darwin and the Darwinian Revolution 328
Darwin and the General Reader 326
Darwin and the Modern World View 328
Darwin for Today 323
Darwiniana 327
Darwin in America 331
Darwinism in the English Novel, 1860-1910 328
Darwin on Man 328
Darwin Reader, The 323
Darwin Retried 330
Darwin's Century 326
Darwin's Early and Unpublished Notebooks 323
Darwin's Place in History 326
Dean and the Anarchist, The 152

Title Index

Dearest Mama Talbot 246
Death Rides a Camel 355
Decorative Arts, Their Relation to Modern Life and Progress, The 205
Democratic Education 40
De Profundis 304
De Quincey (Elwin) 140
De Quincey (Salt) 145
De Quincey: A Portrait 141
De Quincey and His Friends 141
De Quincey and Wordsworth 143
De Quincey as Literary Critic 142
De Quincey at Work 140
De Quincey Memorials 130
De Quincey's Literary Criticism 139
Descent of Man, and Selection in Relation to Sex, The 323
Development of Christian Doctrine 300
Development of J.S. Mill's System of Logic, The 194
Devil Drives, The 355
Diaries of John Ruskin, 1835–1889, The 246
Diary of Thomas De Quincy for 1803, A 139
Dickens and Carlyle: The Question of Influence 100
Dictionary of National Biography 216
Disappearance of God, The 20
Discourses in America 40
Discourses on the Scope and Nature of University Education, Addressed to the Catholics of Dublin 294
Dissent and Dogma 40
Dissertations in English and American Literature 5
Dissidence of Dissent, The 363
Dr. Pusey 317
Doctrine of the Real Presence, The 316
Dreamers of Dreams 18
Dream of John Ball and a King's Lesson, A 205, 207, 211
Dream of Order, A 15
Drift of Romanticism, The 20
Dumphries and Galloway Courier 92

E

Earlier Letters, The 187
Earlier Letters of John Stuart Mill, The 187
Early Kings of Norway 92
Early Victorian England, 1830–1865 33
Earnest Atheist: A Study of Butler, The 82
Economic Essays 65
Economics and Society 73
Economic Studies by the Later Walter Bagehot 65, 66
Economist, 1843–1943 68
Economist, Physics and Politics 66
Edmund Burke and the Revolt against the Eighteenth Century 149
Education: Intellectual, Moral, and Physical 342
Educational Thought and Influence of Matthew Arnold, The 46
Education and Enlightenment in the Works of William Godwin 151
Education of Bentham, The 75
Eighteen-Eighties, The 16
1859: Entering an Age of Crisis 24
Eighteen-Nineties, The 18
Eighteen-Seventies, The 16
Eighteen-Sixties, The 16
Eighteenth-Century Background, The 33
Elementary Sketches 280
Elementary Sketches of Moral Philosophy 279
Elia 171
Eliana 171
Eliana Americana 177
Emergence of Victorian Consciousness, The 9
Emerson 40
Engels, Manchester, and the Working Class 29
England and Ireland 201
England and the Italian Question 39
English Common Reader, The 359
English Constitution, The 64, 66, 68, 71

Title Index

English Familiar Essay in the Early Nineteenth Century, The 159, 167, 176
English Heritage of Coleridge of Bristol, The 126
English in Ireland in the Eighteenth Century, The 261
English in the West Indies 262
English Literary Criticism 9
English Literature, 1815-1832 11
English Literature, 1789-1815 11
English Literature and Irish Politics 40
English Literature and Society in the Eighteenth Century 217
English Literature of the Nineteenth Century 8
English Literature of the Victorian Period 8
English Literature 1660-1800 2
English Mail-Coach, The 143
English Newspapers 360
English Political Thought in the Nineteenth Century 25, 67
English Prose of the Victorian Era 9
English Romantic Poets and Essayists 4
English Thought in the Nineteenth Century 31
English Utilitarians, The 79, 202, 216
English Utilitarians and India, The 271
Enquirer, The 147
Enquiry Concerning the Principles of Political Justice, and Its Influence on General Virtue and Happiness, An 147
Erewhon 80, 82, 83, 85
Erewhon Revisited 80
Ernest Pontifex or the Way of All Flesh 81
Essay in Aid of a Grammer of Assent, An 295
Essay in Faith 129
Essay on Beauty 275, 276
Essay on the Development of Christian Doctrine, An 294
Essays, Critical and Historical 295
Essays, 1802-27 279
Essays, Letters, and Reviews by Matthew Arnold 40
Essays Critical and Imaginative 283
Essays in Criticism 39, 43, 47
Essays in Criticism, First Series 40
Essays in English Literature, 1780-1860 22, 284
Essays in the History of Ideas 19
Essays on Economics and Society 187
Essays on Education and Kindred Subjects 342
Essays on English Literature 40
Essays on Ethics, Religion, and Society 187
Essays on Free Thinking and Plain Speaking 216
Essays on His Times 115
Essays on Life, Art and Science 80
Essays on Literature and Art 233
Essays Religious and Mixed 40
Essays Scientific, Political, and Speculative 342
Essays Social and Political, 1802-1825 279
Essays upon Some Controverted Questions 335
Essential Butler, The 81
Essential Newman, The 295
Essential Works of John Stuart Mill, The 187
Estimates of Some Englishmen and Scotchmen 64
Estimations in Criticism 65
Ethical Idealism of Matthew Arnold, The 56
Evidence as to Man's Place in Nature 335
Evidence for the Resurrection of Jesus Christ, The 80
Evolution, Old and New 80
Evolution and Ethics 335
Evolution and Society 338
Evolutionary Theory and Christian Belief 330
Evolution in the Arts and other Theories of Culture History 344
Examination of Sir William Hamilton's Philosophy 186
Examination of the Deductive Logic of J.S. Mill, An 194
Excursion 277

Title Index

Explorations of the Highlands of the Brazil 354
Expression of the Emotions in Man and Animals, The 323

F

Factors of Organic Evolution, The 342
Fair Haven, The 80, 82, 83
Faith and Revolt 26
Fall of Robespierre, The 125
Familiar Studies of Men and Books 221
Family Letters of Butler, 1841-86, The 81
Fathers of the Victorians 318
First Footsteps in East Africa 354
First Romantics, The 115
First Year in Canterbury Settlement, A 80
Five Uncollected Essays of Matthew Arnold 40
Flame in Sunlight, A 141
Fleetwood 147
Fors Clavigera 245
Fragment on Government, A 73
Francis Jeffrey of the EDINBURGH REVIEW 276
French Revolution, The (Carlyle) 88, 97, 98, 103
French Revolution, The (Lefebvre) 29
Friend, The 114, 115, 123
Friendship's Garland 39
From Bossuet to Newman 301
From Coleridge to Gore 130
From the Battle of Waterloo to the General Election of 1885 32
Froude and Carlyle 95, 263
Froude Family in the Oxford Movement, The 290
Froude-Ruskin Friendship as Represented through Letters, The 262
Froude's Remains: Part 1 289
Froude's Remains: Part 2 289
Further Extracts from the Note-Books 81

G

Genesis and Geology 28

Genius of John Ruskin, The 246
George Borrow (Armstrong) 351
George Borrow (Elam) 350
George Borrow (Meyer) 352
George Borrow: Lord of the Open Road 350
George Borrow: The Man and His Books 351
George Borrow: The Man and His Work 353
George Borrow and His Circle 350
George Eliot 217
German Influence on Thomas Carlyle 104
Giotto and His Works in Padua 245
Girl's Journey and the Lad's Quest, The 214
God and Myself 304
God and the Bible 39, 40
God the Known and God the Unknown 81
Godwin and Mary 148
Godwin and the Age of Transition 152
Godwin Criticism 153
Godwin's Moral Philosophy 151
Godwin's Novels 150
Gothic Architecture 205
Gothic Revival, The 27
Grammar of Assent 304, 306, 308, 309
Grammar of the English Language, A 108
Great Victorians, The 19
Greek Studies 233
Growth of Philosophic Radicalism, The 76, 79
Guide through the Romantic Movement 14
Guide to Doctoral Dissertations in Victorian Literature, 1886-1958 1
Guide to English Literature, A 1
Guide to the Year's Work in Victorian Poetry and Prose 4
Gulliver's Travels 85, 152
Gypsy Borrow 353
Gypsy Gentleman, The 351

H

Handbook of Political Fallacies 74

Title Index

Handlist of Darwin Papers at the University Library, Cambridge 334
Hazlitt 156
Hazlitt and the Creative Imagination 156
Hazlitt and the Spirit of the Age 160
Hazlitt in the Workshop 162
Hazlitt on English Literature 162
Hebrew and Hellene in Victorian England 15
Heinrich Heine 39
Hellenics of Walter Savage Landor, The 180
Henry James and Robert Louis Stevenson 222
Herbert Spencer 343
Herbert Spencer, the Evolution of a Sociologist 344
Historical and Critical Review of Samuel Butler's Literary Works, An 83
Historical and Other Sketches 261
Historical Essays 65
Historical Novel, The 267
Historical Sketches 295
History and Historians in the Nineteenth Century 17
History of British Philosophy to 1900, A 31
History of British Socialism, A 25
History of England from the Accession of James II, The 264
History of England from the Fall of Wolsey to the Death of Elizabeth, The 261
History of English Criticism, A 11
History of English Literature, A (Craig) 8
History of English Literature, A (Legouis and Cazamian) 9
History of English Literature, A (Moody and Lovett) 10
History of English Literature, A (Taine) 11
History of English Prose Rhythm, A 11
History of English Romanticism in the Nineteenth Century, A 7
History of English Thought in the Eighteenth Century 216, 218
History of English Utilitarianism, A 74, 188
History of European Thought in the Nineteenth Century, A 30
History of Freethought in the Nineteenth Century, A 22
History of Friedrich II of Prussia, Called Frederick the Great, The 88
History of Modern Criticism, 1750-1950, A 23, 278
History of Nineteenth-Century Literature, 1780-1895, A 11, 284
History of Technology, A 31
History of the Church in England, A 30
History of the Commonwealth of England from Its Commencement to the Restoration of Charles the Second 147
History of the English People in the Nineteenth Century, A 28
History of the Regency and Reign of King George the Fourth 108
History of the Renaissance 235
History of the Unreformed Parliament and Its Lessons 64
Hopes and Fears for Art 205
Hours in a Library 216, 217
How to Find Out about the Victorian Period 5
Human Dignity and the Great Victorians 22
Hume 335
Hurrell Froude: Memoranda and Comments 290
Hurrell Froude and the Oxford Movement 289
Huxley 336
Huxley: Prophet of Science 337
Huxley and Education 340
Huxley Papers, The 341

I

Idea of a University, The 309
Idea of Coleridge's Criticism, The 121
Idea of Progress, The 26
Illustrated English Social History 32

Title Index

Image and Experience 17
Imaginary Conversations 183, 184
Imaginary Conversations of Greeks and Romans 180
Imaginary Conversations of Literary Men and Statesmen 180
Imaginary Portrait [the Child in the House], An 233
Imaginary Portraits 233
Imagination and Fancy 163, 166
Immanuel Kant in England 135
Imperial Intellect, The 302, 312
Improvement of Mankind, The 199
Inadequacy of Natural Selection, The 342
Independent Essays 282
Indian Education Minutes of Lord Macaulay, The 264
Industrial Revolution, 1760-1830, The 24
Influence of Darwin on Philosophy, The 326
Inland Voyage, An 221
Intellectual Milieu of Lord Macaulay, The 268
Intellectuals in Politics 193
Interpretation of Art 250
In the Footsteps of Borrow and Fitzgerald 351
In the Interests of the Governed 77
Intimate Portrait of Robert Louis Stevenson, An 225
Introduction to a Bibliography of Cobbett, An 113
Introduction to Ruskin, An 249
Introduction to the Philosophy of Herbert Spencer, An 344
Introduction to the Principles of Morals and Legislation, An 73
Irish Essays and Others 40
Italian Letters 147

J

J.A. Froude 262
J.A. Froude's Works 262
James and J.S. Mill: Father and Son in the Nineteenth Century 196
James Anthony Froude, a Biography 262

Jeffrey's Literary Criticism 275
Jeremy Bentham (Atkinson) 74
Jeremy Bentham (Everett) 75
Jeremy Bentham: An Odyssey of Ideas 74
Jeremy Bentham: Ten Critical Essays 77
Jeremy Bentham and University College 75
Jeremy Bentham's Economic Writings 74
John Henry Newman (Cameron) 300
John Henry Newman (Cross) 297
John Henry Newman (Dessain) 297
John Henry Newman (Houppert) 306
John Henry Newman (Lapati) 306
John Henry Newman: An Expository and Critical Study of His Mind, Thought and Art 304
John Henry Newman: Centenary Essays 306
John Keble (Ingram) 292
John Keble (Wood) 292
John Keble: A Biography 292
John Keble: A Study in Limitations 291
John Keble's Literary and Religious Contribution to the Oxford Movement 292
John Ruskin (Bell) 247
John Ruskin (Evans) 247
John Ruskin (Quennell) 254
John Ruskin: An Introduction to Further Study of His Life and Work 248
John Ruskin: His Life and Teaching 248
John Ruskin: The Portrait of a Prophet 248
John Ruskin and Aesthetic Thought in America, 1840-1900 255
John Ruskin and Effie Gray 246
John Ruskin or the Ambiguities of Abundance 255
John Stuart Mill (Britton) 190
John Stuart Mill (Cranston) 188
John Stuart Mill (Ellery) 191
John Stuart Mill (Ryan) 200
John Stuart Mill: A Critical Study 195

Title Index

John Stuart Mill: Literary Essays 187
John Stuart Mill, the Man 187
John Stuart Mill and French Thought 197
John Stuart Mill and Harriet Taylor 188
John Stuart Mill and Harriet Taylor Mill 187
Jonathan Swift 275
Journal of Researches into the Geology and Natural History of the Various Countries Visited by H.M.S. Beagle 323
Journey to Upolu 225
Judicial Procedures 73

K

Keats, Shelley, Byron, Hunt and Their Circles 3
Keats and the Victorians 209
Kelmscott Press and William Morris, Master Craftsman, The 213
Kidnapped 221

L

Lake Regions of Central Africa, a Picture of Exploration, The 354
Lamb: Prose and Poetry 171
Lamb Always Elia 175
Lamb and Hazlitt 155
Lamb before Elia 176
Lamb's Criticism 171
Lamp of Beauty, The 246
Landor 181
Landor: A Biographical Anthology 182
Landor: A Biography (Evans) 181
Landor: A Biography (Forster) 181
Landor Library, A 185
Landor's Studies of Italian Life and Literature 182
Last Essays of Elia, The 171
Last Essays on Church and Religion 39
Last Fruit Off an Old Tree, The 180
Last Romantics, The 17
Last Witness for Robert Louis Stevenson 223

Later Letters of John Stuart Mill, The 187
Later Nineteenth Century, The 22
Latter-Day Pamphlets 88, 92
Lavengro 349, 351
Lay Sermons 115
Lay Sermons, Addresses and Reviews 335
Lectures and Essays in Criticism 40
Lectures and Essays on University Subjects 295
Lectures Chiefly on the Dramatic Literature of the Age of Elizabeth 154
Lectures on Certain Difficulties Felt by Anglicans in Submitting to the Catholic Church 294
Lectures on Justification 294
Lectures on the English Comic Writers 154
Lectures on the English Poets 154
Lectures on the History of Literature 88
Lectures on the Present Position of Catholics in England 294
Lectures 1795 115
Leigh Hunt: A Biography 164
Leigh Hunt and His Circle 164
Leigh Hunt and Opera Criticism, 1808-1821 165
Leigh Hunt's Dramatic Criticism, 1808-1831 164
Leigh Hunt's EXAMINER Examined 165
Leigh Hunt's Literary Criticism 164
Leigh Hunt's Political and Occasional Essays 164
Leigh Hunt's Prefaces, Mainly to His Periodicals 164
Leigh Hunt's REFLECTOR 167
Lenten Sermons, 1858-74 316
Leslie Stephen (Grosskurth) 218
Leslie Stephen (Zink) 219
Leslie Stephen: His Thought and Character in Relation to His Times 217
Leslie Stephen and Matthew Arnold as Critics of Wordsworth 219
Letters, 1826-1836 89
Letters and Correspondence of J.H.

Title Index

Newman during His Life in the English Church 296
Letters and Diaries of J.H. Newman, The 296
Letters and Miscellany 65
Letters between Butler and Miss E.M.A. Savage 81
Letters from William Cobbett to Edward Thornton, 1797-1800 109
Letters of a Conservative 180
Letters of Carlyle to John Stuart Mill, John Sterling, and Robert Browning 90
Letters of Charles and Mary Ann Lamb, The 172
Letters of Charles Lamb, The 172
Letters of Charles Lamb, to Which Are Added Those of His Sister, Mary Lamb, The 172
Letters of George Borrow to His Mother Ann Borrow, and to Other Correspondents, The 350
Letters of George Borrow to His Wife Mary Borrow, The 350
Letters of George Borrow to the British and Foreign Bible Society, The 350
Letters of J.H. Newman, The 296
Letters of Jeffrey to Ugo Foscolo, The 275
Letters of John Ruskin to Lord and Lady Mount-Temple, The 247
Letters of Matthew Arnold, 1848-1888 41
Letters of Matthew Arnold to Arthur Henry Clough 41
Letters of Morris to His Family and Friends, The 206
Letters of Spiritual Counsel and Guidance 291
Letters of Stevenson to His Family and Friends, Selected, The 222
Letters of Sydney Smith, The 280
Letters of T.B. Macaulay, The 265
Letters of Thomas Carlyle to His Brother Alexander, With Related Family Letters 90
Letters of Walter Pater, The 234
Letters of Walter Savage Landor Private and Public, The 180
Letters of William Cobbett 109

Letters on the French Coup D'Etat 66
Letters on the Subject of the Catholics, to My Brother Abraham, Who Lives in the Country 279
Letter to the Archbishop of Canterbury, A 316
Letter to the Duke of Norfolk 300
Liberal Catholic Movement in England, The 297, 359
Liberalism of Thomas Arnold, The 61
Liber Amoris 154, 158
Life, Writings, and Correspondence of George Borrow, The 350
Life and Adventures of Peter Porcupine, The 108
Life and Habit 80
Life and Labour of the People of London 25
Life and Letters of Charles Darwin, Including an Autobiographical Chapter, The 324
Life and Letters of Erasmus 262
Life and Letters of Herbert Spencer, The 342
Life and Letters of Leslie Stephen, The 217
Life and Letters of Lord Macaulay 266
Life and Letters of T.H. Huxley, The 336
Life and Letters of William Cobbett, The 110
Life and Work of Morris, The 206
Life of Burns 101
Life of Captain Sir Richard Burton, The 355
Life of Darwin, The 324
Life of E.B. Pusey, D.D., The 316
Life of Erasmus Darwin, The 323
Life of George Borrow, The 350
Life of George Borrow, Compiled from Unpublished Official Documents, His Works, Correspondence, Etc., The 350
Life of Hurrell Froude, The 290
Life of J.A. Froude, The 262
Life of Jeffrey, The 275
Life of John Henry Cardinal Newman Based on His Private Journals and

Title Index

Correspondence 297
Life of John Sterling 88
Life of John Stuart Mill, The 188
Life of Lamb, The 173
Life of Napoleon Buonaparte, The 154
Life of Robert Louis Stevenson, The 223
Life of Samuel Taylor Coleridge, The 116
Life of Schiller 92
Life of Sir Richard Burton, The 356
Life of Walter Bagehot 66
Life of Walter Pater, The 234
Life of William Cobbett, The 110
Life of William Godwin, The 148
Life of William Hazlitt, The 155
Life of William Morris, The 207
Life of William Wilberforce 319
Light, Wind, and Dreams 224
Limits of Liberty 198
List of T.H. Huxley's Correspondence with Henrietta Heathorn, 1847-54, A 341
List of the Writings of William Hazlitt and Leigh Hunt, A 162, 170
Literary Character of Walter Pater, The 240
Literary Criticism 12
Literary Criticism of John Ruskin, The 246
Literary Criticism of John Stuart Mill, The 187, 201
Literary Criticisms 23
Literary Essays 65
Literary History of England, A 7
Literary Remains of Samuel Taylor Coleridge, The 114
Literary Remains of the Late William Hazlitt 155
Literary Research Guide 5
Literary Studies 65, 66
Literary Studies, Religious and Metaphysical Essays 66
Literature and Dogma 39, 56
Literature English and American 2
Literature of the Victorian Era, The 11, 23
Living Thoughts of Darwin, The 323

Logic of Political Economy, The 139
Lombard Street 64, 66
London Labour and the London Poor 30
Lord Beaconsfield 262
Lord Byron, Leigh Hunt, and the LIBERAL 168
Lord Byron and Some of His Contemporaries 163
Lord Macaulay, 1800-1859 268
Lord Macaulay: Victorian Liberal 265
Loss and Gain 294, 298
Love Letters of Thomas Carlyle and Jane Welsh, The 90
Love-Letters of Walter Bagehot and Eliza Wilson Written from 10 November 1857 to 23 April 1858, The 66
Luck, or Cunning as the Main Means of Organic Modification 80
Luther: A Short Biography 261

M

Macaulay (Bryant) 265
Macaulay (Millgate) 269
Macaulay (Potter) 270
Macaulay (St. Aubyn) 265
Macaulay (Thomson) 271
Macaulay: Prose and Poetry 264
Macaulay: The Shaping of the Historian 266
Macaulay's Library 270
Magazines of the 1890's, The 360
Making of the English Working Class, The 31, 112
Making of Victorian England 27
Mandeville 147, 152
Man Versus the State, The 342
Marius the Epicurean 233, 239
Master of Ballantrae, The 221
Matthew Arnold (Allott) 43
Matthew Arnold (Jump) 52
Matthew Arnold (Neiman) 55
Matthew Arnold (Paul) 42
Matthew Arnold (Russell) 42
Matthew Arnold (Trilling) 42
Matthew Arnold: A Collection of Critical Essays 48

Title Index

Matthew Arnold: A Study 42
Matthew Arnold: A Study in Conflict 44
Matthew Arnold: A Study of the Aesthetic Temperament in Victorian England 54
Matthew Arnold: A Survey of His Poetry and Prose 45
Matthew Arnold: How to Know Him 57
Matthew Arnold, John Ruskin and the Modern Temper 43
Matthew Arnold: Selected Prose 40
Matthew Arnold: The Critic and France 51
Matthew Arnold, the Ethnologist 49
Matthew Arnold and American Culture 56
Matthew Arnold and His Critics 46
Matthew Arnold and John Stuart Mill 43, 188
Matthew Arnold and the Classical Tradition 43
Matthew Arnold and the Modern Spirit 53
Matthew Arnold and the Philosophy of Vico 47
Matthew Arnold and the Romantics 50
Matthew Arnold Prose Selection, A 40
Matthew Arnold's Books 44
Matthew Arnold's Letters 62
Medieval Vision of William Morris, The 211
Meditations and Devotions 295
Memoir of Sydney Smith by His Daughter 280
Memoir of the Rev. John Keble, A 292
Memoir of the Right Honorable John Wilson 64
Memoirs of Hazlitt, with Portions of His Correspondence 155
Memorial Edition of the Works of Captain Sir Richard Burton 354-55
Memories and Portraits 221
Men, Books, and Mountains 217, 220
Men, Women and Books 163
Metaphysical Society, The 26
Method and Imagination in Coleridge's Criticism 125
Mid-Victorian Studies 23
Milk of Paradise, The 13
Mill: A Collection of Critical Essays 201
Millais and the Ruskins 247
Mill and His Early Critics 198
Mill and Liberalism 191
Mill and the Harriet Taylor Myth 198
Mill on Bentham and Coleridge 77, 128
Mill's Essays on Literature and Society 187
Milton to Ouida 158
Mind and the Mint, The 142
Mind of Jeremy Bentham, The 77
Mind of the Oxford Movement, The 7
Minor Prophets, The 316
Mirror and the Lamp, The 13
Miscellaneous Writings of Lord Macaulay, The 264
Mixed Essays 40
MLA Abstracts of Articles in Scholarly Journals 5
MLA International Bibliography of Books and Articles on the Modern Languages and Literatures 5
Modern Humanists 22
Modern Painters 245
More Letters of Charles Darwin 324
More Nineteenth-Century Studies 24
Morris: Medievalist and Revolutionary 207
Morris: Poet, Craftsman, Socialist 207
Morris: Romantic to Revolutionary 208
Morris: The Critical Heritage 209
Morris: The Man and the Myth 206
Morris without Mackail 207
Movements of Religious Thought in Britain during the Nineteenth Century 32
Mr. Froude and Carlyle 263
Munera Pulveris 245
Musical Evenings 165
My Leigh Hunt Library 169
My Relations with Carlyle, Together

Title Index

with a Letter from the Late Sir James Stephen 261
Mystery of Newman, The 296

N

National Apostasy Considered in a Sermon 291
Natural Supernaturalism 13
Nemesis of Faith, The 261
New Arabian Nights 221
New Cambridge Bibliography of English Literature, The 6
New Essays by De Quincey 140
New Letters of Thomas Carlyle 90
Newman 296
Newman: An Illustrated Brochure of His First Editions 314
Newman: A Portrait Restored 301
Newman: His Life and Spirituality 296
Newman: Light in Winter 297
Newman: The Contemplation of Mind 313
Newman: The Pillar of the Cloud 297
Newman and the Common Tradition 301
Newman and the Modern World 304
Newman as a Man of Letters 309
Newman at Oxford 308
Newman Brothers, The 310
Newman Companion to the Gospels, A 295
Newman Family Letters 296
Newman on the Psychology of Faith in the Individual 306
Newman on Tradition 298
Newman's APOLOGIA 299
Newman's University 307
Newman's Way 308
Newman the Oratorian 308
Newman the Theologian 313
New Political Economy of J.S. Mill, The 201
News from Nowhere, or an Epoch of Rest 205, 210
Nightmare Abbey 149
Nineteenth-Century Britain 33
Nineteenth-Century English Prose 10

Nineteenth-Century Pamphlets at Pusey House 317
Nineteenth-Century Studies 24
NOCTES AMBROSIANAE of BLACKWOOD'S, The 283
Norton Anthology of English Literature, The 6
Notebooks of Matthew Arnold, The 41
Notebooks of Samuel Butler, The 81
Notebooks of Samuel Taylor Coleridge, The 115
Notes and Lectures upon Shakespeare and Some of the Old Poets and Dramatists 114

O

Occasional Papers and Reviews 291
Oceana 261
Of Population 147
Old Gods Falling 227
Old School Ties 31
On Art and Socialism 205
On English Prose 23
On Eucharistical Adoration 291
On Herbert Spencer 343
On Heroes, Hero-Worship, and the Heroic in History 88
On Liberty 186, 199, 200
On Liberty and Liberalism 193
On Races, Species, and Their Origin 335
On the Classical Tradition 40
On the Constitution and State 115
On the Constitution of the Church and State 114
On the Origin of Species by Natural Selection 323
On the Principles of Human Action 157
On the Prometheus of Aeschylus 114
On the Subject of Women 186
On the Trapenese Origin of the Odyssey 80
On Translating Homer 39
Opium and the Romantic Imagination 123, 143
Organic Unity in Coleridge 127
Origins of CULTURE AND ANARCHY, The 60

Title Index

Other Victorians, The 30
Oxford Anthology of English Literature, The 9
Oxford Apostles 27
Oxford History of English Literature 11
Oxford Movement, The 8
Oxford Movement: Twelve Years, 1833-1845, The 26

P

Parliamentary Reform 64
Parochial and Cathedral Sermons 316
Parochial Sermons (Newman) 294
Parochial Sermons (Pusey) 316
Parting of Friends, The 319
Party of Humanity, The 361
Passages from the Prose Writings of Matthew Arnold Selected by the Author 41
Past and Present 88, 93, 98
Pater on Style 235
Pater's Portraits 241
Patterns of Consciousness 123
Pauper Press, The 361
Peacock: His Circle and His Age 159, 167
Pelican Guide to English Literature, The 8
Penology and Criminal Law 73
Perfect Sympathy, A 175
Periodical Articles on Religion 364
Personal Narrative of a Pilgrimage to El-Medinah and Meccah, A 354
Peter Porcupine: A Study of William Cobbett 109
Phantasies 56
Philistinism in England and America 40
Philosophical Notebook of J.H. Newman, The 295
Philosophical Notebooks 301
Philosophy and Education 73
Philosophy of John Stuart Mill, The 189
Philosophy of Style 342
Physics and Politics, or Thoughts on the Application of the Principles of Natural Selection and Inheritance to Political Society 64, 70

Plain Sermons by Contributors to the TRACTS FOR THE TIMES 294
Plain Speaker, The 154
Plato and Platonism 233, 234
Plea for the Constitution, A 73
Plough-Boy to a Seat in Parliament 109
Poet as Critic, The 127
Poetical Works 125
Poetry and Morality 45
Poetry and Philosophy 203
Poetry of History, The 20
Political Economy of Art, The 245
Political Essays 65
Political Essays, with Sketches of Public Characters 154
Political History of Hunt's EXAMINER, The 169
Political Ideas of the English Romantics 149
Political Justice 148, 149
Political Thought in England 27
Political Writings 73
Political Writings of William Morris, The 206
Politics and the Press, 1780-1850 25
Poole's Index to Periodical Literature 364
Popular Disturbances and Public Order in Regency England 27
Porcupine, The 108
Porcupine's Gazette 108
Porcupine's Works 109
Portable Matthew Arnold, The 41
Portable Victorian Reader, The 8
Portrait of a Rebel 223
Portraits of Genius 168
Posthumous Works of De Quincey 140
Postulates of English Political Economy, The 65
Practical Plan for Assimilating the English and American Money 64
Practical View of the Prevailing Religious Systems of Professed Christians, A 318
Praeterita 246, 248
Preface to Coleridge, A 122
Pre-Raphaelite Dream, The 17
Pre-Raphaelite Poets, The 213
Pre-Raphaelites, The 251

Title Index

Pre-Raphaelite Tragedy, The 16
Pre-Raphaelitism 245
Pre-Raphaelitism: A Bibliocritical Study 3
Presbyterian Pirate 226
Primitive Tradition Recognized in Holy Scripture 291
Principles of Political Economy 186, 187
Prose of the British Romantic Movement 10
Prose of the Romantic Period 12
Prose of the Romantic Period, 1780-1830 12
Prose of the Victorian Period 7
Publication of Landor's Works, The 184
Public Life of Lord Macaulay, The 265
Puritan Temper and the Transcendental Faith 97
Pursuit of Certainty, The 77
Pusey 317

Q

Quest for the Father, The 84, 328

R

Rationale of Evidence, The 73
Readership of the Periodical Press in Mid-Victorian Britain, The 361
Reader's Macaulay 264
Realizations 295
Real Presence, The 316
Reason, the Understanding and Time, The 19
Rebellious FRASER'S 366
Recent Discussions in Science, Philosophy, and Morals 342
Recollections of Christ's Hospital 171
Recreation 285
Recreations of Christopher North, The 283
Rediscovery of Newman, The 302
Reflections on Modern History 69
Regency Style, 1800-1830, The 30
Reign of George III, 1760-1815, The 32
Reinterpretation of Victorian Literature, The 13

Religion and Society in England, 1790-1850 32
Religion and the Church 73
Religion of the Heart, The 163
Religious Controversies of the Nineteenth Century 27
Religious Humanism and the Victorian Novel 29
Religious Thought in the Nineteenth Century 30
Reminiscences 88
Reverend Smith, The 280
Revolutionists in London 211
Rhetorical Form of Carlyle's SARTOR RESARTUS, The 91
Rhythm in the Prose of Thomas De Quincey 144
Richard Burton 356
Richard Burton, Explorer 356
Ringers in the Tower, The 235
Rise and Fall of the Man of Letters, The 17
RLS: From Scotland to Silverado 221
RLS: Stevenson's Letters to Charles Baxter 222
Road to Utopia, The 193
Road to Xanadu, The 126
Robert Louis Stevenson (Butts) 225
Robert Louis Stevenson (Chesterton) 223
Robert Louis Stevenson (Cooper) 223
Robert Louis Stevenson (Daiches) 225
Robert Louis Stevenson (Dark) 224
Robert Louis Stevenson (Hennessy) 224
Robert Louis Stevenson (Saposnik) 227
Robert Louis Stevenson (Smith) 225
Robert Louis Stevenson (Stephen) 217
Robert Louis Stevenson (Stern) 228
Robert Louis Stevenson: A Catalogue of the Gertsley Stevenson Collection, the Stevenson Section of the Parrish Collection of Victorian Novelists, and Items from Other Collections of the Princeton Univ. Library 229
Robert Louis Stevenson: A Critical Study 225
Robert Louis Stevenson: A Study in French Influence 227
Robert Louis Stevenson and His World 223

Title Index

Robert Louis Stevenson and Romantic Tradition 226
Romano Lavo-Lil 349
Romantic Agony, The 21
Romantic Bards and British Reviewers 123
Romantic Comedy, The 125
Romanticism 21
Romanticism and Religion 56, 130, 293, 309
Romanticism and the Social Order 28
Romanticism Reconsidered 16
Romantic Movement and the Study of History, The 271
Romantic Movement Bibliography, 1936-1970, The 3
Romantic Poets and Prose Writers 3
Romany Rye, The 349, 351
Romola 237
Round Table, The 154, 163
Rural Rides, Life and Adventures of Peter Porcupine 109
Rural Rides in the Counties of Surrey, Kent, Sussex, . . . with Economical and Political Observations 108
Ruskin: The Great Victorian 248
Ruskin and the Economists 250
Ruskin and the Landscape Feeling 256
Ruskin and Viollet-Le-Duc 254
Ruskin Family Letters, The 247
Ruskin in Italy 247
Ruskins and the Grays, The 253
Ruskin's Letters from Venice, 1851-1852 247
Ruskin's Scottish Heritage 248
Ruskin the Prophet and Other Centenary Studies 257
Ruskin Today 246

S

Sacred River, The 117
St. Leon 147
St. Paul and Protestantism 39
Saint-Simonianism in the Radicalism of Thomas Carlyle 93
Saint-Simonians, The 101, 198
Samuel Butler (Cole) 83
Samuel Butler (Furbank) 82
Samuel Butler (Joad) 85
Samuel Butler: A Critical Study 83
Samuel Butler: A Memoir 82
Samuel Butler: The Incarnate Bachelor 82
Samuel Johnson 216
Samuel Richardson 275
Samuel Taylor Coleridge (Brett) 119
Samuel Taylor Coleridge (Chambers) 115
Samuel Taylor Coleridge (Fausset) 116
Samuel Taylor Coleridge (Willey) 136
Samuel Taylor Coleridge: An Annotated Bibliography of Criticism and Scholarship 137
Samuel Taylor Coleridge: A Selected Bibliography 138
Samuel Taylor Coleridge in Malta and Italy 133
SARTOR Called RESARTUS 105
Sartor Resartus 88, 92, 98
Savage Landor 181
Schools and Universities on the Continent 39, 40, 58
Science and Culture and Other Essays 335
Science before Darwin 9
Science of Aspects, The 14
Science of Ethics 216, 217
Scientific Memoirs of T.H. Huxley, The 335
Scientist Extraordinary 337
Scotch Reviewers 360
Selected Essays 81
Selected Essays of Hazlitt 155
Selected Essays of J.A. Froude 262
Selected Essays of Walter Pater 233
Selected Essays on Rhetoric by Thomas De Quincey 140
Selected Papers on Anthropology, Travel, and Exploration by Richard Burton 355
Selected Prose of Walter Pater 233
Selected Works, Reminiscences, and Letters by Thomas Carlyle 89
Selected Works of Walter Pater 234
Selected Writings of Hazlitt 155
Selected Writings of John Ruskin 246
Selected Writings of John Stuart Mill 187

Title Index

Selected Writings of Sydney Smith, The 279
Selected Writings of Walter Pater 234
Selections 89
Selections from the Note-Books of Samuel Butler 81
Selections from the Prose Works of William Morris 206
Selections from the Writings of Sydney Smith 279
Selections Grave and Gay, from Writings, Published and Unpublished, of Thomas De Quincey 139, 143
Self-Conscious Imagination, The 120
Sense of Glory 70
Sermons, Academical and Occasional 291
Sermons, Chiefly on the Theory of Religious Belief 294
Sermons, Occasional and Parochial 291
Sermons Bearing on Subjects of the Day 294
Sermons for the Christian Year 291
Sermons Preached at St. Paul's 279
Sermons Preached before the University of Oxford, 1859-1872 316
Sesame and Lilies 245
Seven Lamps of Architecture, The 245
Seven Lectures on Shakespeare and Milton 121
Seventh Hero, The 101
Shelley, Godwin and Their Circle 148
Shelley and His Circle 1773-1822 149
Short History of the British Working Class, 1789-1947, A 27
Short Studies on Great Subjects 261
Shrewsbury Edition of the Works, The 81, 82
Signs of Change 205
Silverado Squatters, The 221
Sir Richard Burton: The Erotic Traveler 355
Six Sermons 279
Sketches and Essays 155
Sketch of the Life and Times of Sydney Smith, A 281
Smith of Smiths, The 281
Social and Political Ideas of Some Representative Thinkers of the Victorian Age, The 28, 344
Social England, a Record of the Progress in Religion, Laws, Learning, Arts, Industry, Commerce, Science, Literature, and Manners 32
Social Philosophy of Carlyle and Ruskin 101
Social Rights and Duties 216
Some Articles on the Depreciation of Silver and on Topics Connected with It 64
Some Late Victorian Attitudes 15
Some Working Class Movements of the Nineteenth Century 32
Spanish Story of the Armada and Other Essays, The 262
Spare Chancellor, The 66
Specimens of the British Critics 283
Specimens of the Table-Talk of the Late Samuel Taylor Coleridge 114
Spencer and Spencerism 344
Spirit of the Age, The 154, 158, 161
Spirit of the Oxford Movement, The 27
Statesman's Manual, The 114
Stevenson: His Work and Personality 223
Stevenson: Man and Writer 225
Stevenson and the Fiction of Adventure 227
Stevenson Library, A 228
Stevensons, The 224
Stones of Venice, The 245, 249
Story of Mr. Pusey's Life, The 317
Story of the PALL MALL GAZETTE, of Its First Editor Frederick Greenwood, and of Its Founder George Murry Smith, The 365
Story of the SPECTATOR, 1828-1928, The 366
Strange Case of Dr. Jekyll and Mr. Hyde, The 221
Strange Case of Robert Louis Stevenson, The 227
Striving Towards Wholeness 227
Studies in the History of the Renaissance 233, 237, 240, 243
Studies in the Text of Matthew

Title Index

Arnold's Prose Works 44
Studies in Victorian Literature 24
Studies of a Biographer 22, 71, 216, 217
Study in the Social Philosophy of John Stuart Mill, A 194
Study of Lamb's ESSAYS OF ELIA, A 175
Study of Walter Pater, A 243
Style and Proportion 20
Style in History 267
Subjection of Women 254
Sublime and Instructive 247
Substance of the Speeches of William Wilberforce, Esq. on the Clause in the East-India Bill for Promoting the Religious Instruction and Moral Improvement of the Natives of the British Dominions in India on 22nd June and 1st and 12th of July, 1813 318
Surplus Population 111
Survey of English Literature, A 8
Swift 216
Swinburne and Landor 183
Sydney Smith (Halpern) 281
Sydney Smith (Russell) 281
Sydney Smith: A Biography and a Selection 280
Sydney Smith, Rector of Foston, 1806-29 280
Synthetic Philosophy 343, 344
System of Logic, Ratiocinative and Inductive, A 186, 194, 198, 202
System of Synthetic Philosophy, A 342

T

Tables Turned, or Nupkins Awakened, The 205
Table Talk 163
Table Talk; or, Original Essays 154
Tangled Bank, The 18
Temper of Victorian Belief, The 237
Ten Master Historians 263
That Ne'er Shall Meet Again 251
Theory of the Novel in England, The 71
T.H. Huxley (Ainsworth-Davis) 336

T.H. Huxley (Ashford) 337
T.H. Huxley: A Character Sketch 336
T.H. Huxley: A List of His Scientific Papers 341
T.H. Huxley: A Sketch of His Life and Work 336
T.H. Huxley: Scientist, Humanist, and Educator 337
Things As They Are 147
Thomas B. Macaulay: Selected Writings 264
Thomas Carlyle (Campbell) 93
Thomas Carlyle (Gascoyne) 95
Thomas Carlyle: A History of His Life in London, 1834-1881 90, 261
Thomas Carlyle: A History of the First Forty Years of His Life, 1795-1835 90, 261
Thomas Carlyle: Selected Writings 89
Thomas Carlyle: The Critical Heritage 103
Thomas Carlyle: The Life and Ideas of a Prophet 90
Thomas Carlyle: The Nigger Question 91
Thomas Carlyle and the Art of History 106
Thomas Carlyle as a Critic of Literature 101
Thomas De Quincey (Davies) 142
Thomas De Quincey (Lyon) 144
Thomas De Quincey: A Bibliography 146
Thomas De Quincey: A Biography 140
Thomas De Quincey: His Life and Work 141
Thomas De Quincey, Literary Critic 144
Thomas De Quincey's Theory of Literature 144
Thomas De Quincey's Writings 140
Thomas H. Huxley 336
Thoughts on Parliamentary Reform 186
Three Cardinals 310
Three Essays on Religion 186
Three Studies in Literature 276

Title Index

Time-Spirit of Matthew Arnold, The 58
To the Lighthouse 218
Touchstone for Ethics 339
Touchstones of Matthew Arnold, The 49
Towards the Twentieth Century 10
Town Labourer, 1760-1832, The 28
Tractarian Movement, The 29
Tracts, Theological and Ecclesiastical 295
Tracts for the Times, 1834-41 291
Tracts for the Times, 1834-37 316, 317
Tracts for the Times, 1833-35 289
Transitional Age, The 4
Travels with a Donkey 221
Treasure Island 221
Triumph of Romanticism 21
Triumph of the Darwinian Method, The 327
Triumph of Time, The 14
True Life of Captain Sir Richard Burton, The 356
True Stevenson, The 224
Tusitala of the South Seas 224
Two Note-Books of Thomas Carlyle, from 23 March 1822 to 16 May 1832 89
Two Trips to Gorilla Land and the Cataracts of the Congo 354

U

Ultima Thule 354
Unbelievers, The 15
Unconscious Memory 80
Unpublished Lectures of William Morris, The 206
Unpublished Letters of Morris, The 206
Unto This Last 245
Utilitarianism 186, 203

V

Vailima Letters 222
Versions of the Self 20
Victorian Age: Essays in History and in Social and Literary Criticism, The 18

Victorian Age: Prose, Poetry, and Drama, The 7
Victorian Age in Literature, The 15
Victorian Church, The 26
Victorian Crisis of Faith 312
Victorian Critics of Democracy 29
Victorian Debate, The 26
Victorian England 34
Victorian England, 1837-1901 1
Victorian Essays 13
Victorian Frame of Mind, 1830-1870, The 28
Victorian Literature: Modern Essays in Criticism 24
Victorian Literature: Prose 11
Victorian Literature: Selected Essays 10
Victorian Mind, The 9
Victorian Minds 28
Victorian Morality of Art, The 252
Victorian Nonconformity 25
Victorian People 25
Victorian People and Ideas 24
Victorian Poets and Prose Writers 2
Victorian Portraits 237
Victorian Prose 10
Victorian Prose: A Guide to Research 3
Victorian Prose, 1830-1880 7
Victorian Prose Masters 14
Victorian Revolutionaries 21
Victorian Romantics, The 214
Victorians, The 10
Victorian Sage, The 17
Victorians and after, 1830-1914, The 7
Victorians and their Reading, The 15
Victorians and the Machine 22
Victorians on Literature and Art 21
Victorian Taste 31
Victorian Temper, The 14
Victorian Travellers, The 356
View of the English Stage, A 154
Village Labourer, The 28
Village Sermons on the Baptismal Service 291
Virginibus Puerisque 221
Voyage in Vain, A 123
Voyage to Windward 224

Title Index

W

Walter Bagehot (Irvine) 66
Walter Bagehot (St. John-Stevas) 70
Walter Bagehot (Sullivan) 71
Walter Bagehot: A Study of His Life and Thought, together with a Selection from His Political Writings, A 67
Walter Pater (Benson) 234
Walter Pater (Fletcher) 238
Walter Pater: A Study of His Critical Outlook and Achievement 240
Walter Pater: Humanist 236
Walter Pater: The Idea in Nature 243
Walter Savage Landor (Dilworth) 182
Walter Savage Landor (Hamilton) 182
Walter Savage Landor: A Biography 182
Wanderings in West Africa from Liverpool to Fernando Po 354
Watchman, The 114, 115
Waterloo to Peterloo 32
Way of All Flesh, The 80, 82, 83, 86, 87
Way to Faith, an Examination of Newman's GRAMMAR OF ASSENT as a Response to the Search for Certainty in Faith, The 308
Well at the World's End, The 205
Wellesley Index to Victorian Periodicals, The 162, 272, 278, 282, 285
What Coleridge Thought 117
What Darwin Really Said 326
What Is Materialism? 216
What Is of Faith as to Everlasting Punishment? 316
Wild Wales 349
William Cobbett (Briggs) 109
William Cobbett (Chesterton) 110
William Cobbett (Pemberton) 110
William Cobbett (Sambrook) 110
William Cobbett: A Biography 110
William Cobbett: His Thought and His Times 112
William Cobbett and the Politics of Earth 111
William Cobbett and the United States, 1792-1835 113
William Godwin (Paul) 148
William Godwin (Smith) 153
William Godwin: A Biographical Study 148
William Godwin: A Handlist of Critical Notices and Studies 153
William Godwin: A Study in Liberalism 150
William Godwin and His World 150
William Godwin's Uncollected Writings (1785-1822) 147
William Hazlitt (Baker) 155
William Hazlitt (Priestley) 160
William Morris 210
William Morris: Craftsman, Socialist 207
William Morris: His Life, Work, and Friends 207
William Morris, Writer 212
William Morris: Stories in Prose, Stories in Verse, Shorter Poems, Lectures, and Essays 206
William Morris and His Circle 212
William Morris and Old Norse Literature 213
William Morris and the Early Days of the Socialist Movement 209
William Morris as a Socialist 208
William Morris as Seen by His Contemporaries 207
William Wilberforce 319
William Wilberforce and His Times 319
Winnington Letters, The 247
Wit and Wisdom of Smith, The 280
Word of Elia, The 177
Wordsworth and Coleridge 124
Wordsworth and Coleridge, 1795-1834 116
Wordsworth and Coleridge in Their Time 119
Wordsworth and Jeffrey in Controversy 277
Works and Life of Landor, The 180
Works and Life of Walter Bagehot, The 65
Works in Prose and Verse of Charles Lamb and Mary Lamb, The 171
Works of Bentham, The 74

Title Index

Works of Charles and Mary Lamb, The 171
Works of Charles Darwin, The 334
Works of Charles Lamb, The 171
Works of George Borrow, The (Richards) 349
Works of George Borrow, The (Shorter) 349
Works of George Borrow, The (Wright) 349
Works of Jeremy Bentham, The 74
Works of John Ruskin, The 246
Works of Lord Macaulay, The (Henderson) 265
Works of Lord Macaulay, The (Trevelyan) 265
Works of Morris and Yeats in Relation to Early Saga Literature 210
Works of Peter Porcupine, The 109
Works of Professor Wilson of the University of Edinburgh, The 283
Works of Robert Louis Stevenson, The (Colvin) 222
Works of Robert Louis Stevenson, The (South Seas Edition) 222
Works of Robert Louis Stevenson, The (Tusitala Edition) 222
Works of Robert Louis Stevenson, The (Vailima Edition) 222
Works of Sydney Smith, The (1839-40) 280
Works of Sydney Smith, The (1844) 280
Works of Thomas Carlyle, The 89
Works of Thomas De Quincey, The 140
Works of Walter Bagehot with Memoirs by R.H. Hutton, The 66
Works of Walter Pater, The 234
Work of William Morris, The 214
Writings of Walter Pater, The 244

Y

Years of Endurance, 1873-1902, The 26
Years of Victory, 1802-1812, The 26
Year's Residence in the United States of America, A 108, 109
Year's Work in English Studies, The 6
Yellow Book, The 360
Young Mr. Newman 297
Young Mrs. Ruskin in Venice 247
Young Romantics and Critical Opinion, 1807-1824, The 364

Z

Zanzibar 354
Zincali, The 349

SUBJECT INDEX

This index is alphabetized letter by letter. Underlined numbers refer to main areas in the subject.

A

Abolitionism. See Racial theories and problems
Abstraction, Hazlitt's theory of 159, 160
Action
 in Borrow's writings 353
 Carlyle's concern with 93
Acton, John, Newman compared to 307
Actors
 Hunt on 163
 Lamb on 174
 See also Theater
Adams, Henry, Darwin's influence on 331
Addison, Joseph 117
 Arnold's criticism of 59
 literary style of 157
 relationship with Hunt 169
Aeschylus
 Coleridge on 115, 130
 Landor's knowledge of 183
Aesthetics 3, 11, 13, 16, 17, 18, 19, 21, 231-57
 of Arnold 48, 54, 58, 60
 of Carlyle 98
 of Coleridge 122, 130, 132, 133, 135, 136, 137
 of Hazlitt 159, 160-61
 of Huxley 338

 of Keble 293
 of Lamb 173, 175-76
 of Mill 201
 of Morris 210, 211
 of Pater 233-44, 303
 of Ruskin 235, 245-57
 of Stephen 219
Affirmation Bill, Newman on 304
Africa, Burton on 354, 355
Agnosticism 15
 Darwin's impact on 325
 of Huxley 336, 339, 340
 of Spencer 343
 of Stephen 216
 See also Free thought
ALBERMARLE (periodical) 360
Alison, Archibald, influence on Jeffrey 276, 277
Allan, William, Hazlitt and 161
Allegory
 Coleridge's use of 127
 Mill's use of 196
Allusion
 Carlyle's use of 105
 Hazlitt's use of 160
 Mill's use of 189
 Newman's use of 301
Altruism, of Ruskin 253
America. See United States
Analogism, as a stage in Romanticism 21

Subject Index

Anarchy
  Arnold on 39, 50
  Godwin on 28, 152, 153
  Mill on 200
Angelico, Giovanni (Fra), Ruskin on 250
Anglicanism. See Church of England
Anthropomorphism
  Arnold's rejection of 61
  in Butler's humor 84
Anxiety in literature 15
  as expressed by Coleridge 118
Apostasy, Keble on 291
Architecture
  critics of 31
  Ruskin on 245, 254, 255
Aristocracy 27
Aristotle
  Coleridge on 129
  Newman on 301, 313
Arnold, Matthew 3, 8, 9, 10, 12, 13, 14, 15, 16, 17, 18, 19, 20, 22, 23, 24, 26, 28, 30, 31, 33, 39-63, 70, 94, 106, 120, 124, 158, 160, 188, 200, 217, 218, 219, 237, 238, 242, 243, 266, 268, 302, 310, 311, 338, 365, 366
Arnold, Thomas 55, 61, 131
  Coleridge's influence on 124
Art 9, 10, 33, 34
  bibliography of periodicals concerning 364
  critics of 31
  Hazlitt on 162, 257
  Morris on 205, 207, 208, 211, 212, 214
  Newman on 309
  Pater on 235, 236, 238, 240, 241, 242, 250
  Ruskin on 245, 246, 248, 249, 250, 252, 253, 254, 255, 256, 257
  See also Architecture
Associationalism
  Hazlitt's connection with 160
  influence of on Coleridge 117
Atheism, of Butler 83
ATHENAEUM (periodical) 363
  Ruskin reviewed in 252
Atkinson, Blanche, correspondence with Ruskin 247
Austen, Jane, Smith and 282
Authority 16
  Arnold and Mill on 56
Autobiography
  as literary art 20
  Newman's theory of 306, 312
  See also Biography

B

Bacon, Francis
  Coleridge compared to 132
  influence on Newman 301
Bagehot, Walter 10, 22, 25, 28, 50, 64-72, 333
Bailey, Philip James, Bagehot as a reviewer of 72
Baldwin, James 53
Balfour, Arthur James, Bagehot compared to 68
Balzac, Honore de, influence on Stevenson 227
Baptism, Keble on 291
Baudelaire, Charles Pierre, Ruskin compared to 252
Baxter, Charles, correspondence with Stevenson 222
Beardsley, Aubrey Vincent 15
  the SAVOY and 367
Beauty
  Jeffrey on 276
  Ruskin's conception of 251, 253
Beerbohm, Max, influence of Pater on 238
Belief and doubt, Newman's treatment of 301, 303, 308, 309-10, 313
Bell, Clive, art criticism of 250
Bell, Margaret Alexis, correspondence with Ruskin 247
Bensley, Robert, Lamb on 174
Bentham, Jeremy 2, 25, 28, 33, 73-79, 128, 160, 188, 189, 191, 193, 195, 199-200, 201, 202, 203, 364
Berkeley, George, influence on Coleridge 126

Subject Index

Arnold on 39
Newman on 305
Biography 11, 22, 23
Newman's theory of 306
See also Autobiography
Biology, Darwin's influence on 325
Birmingham, Engl. 25
Birth control, Mill's concern with 197
BLACKWOOD'S (periodical) 360, 364, 367
Wilson's contributions to 283, 285
Blake, William 8
Carlyle compared to 98
characterized by Lamb 177
Newman compared to 298
Blunden, Anna, correspondence with Ruskin 247
Blunt, . . . , Burton compared to 356
Boehme, Jakob, Coleridge's relation to 127
Bolingbroke, Henry St. John, Bagehot on 65
Book reviewers
Carlyle and Macaulay as 101, 270
identification of in periodical literature 363
politics and 360, 361
treatment of Coleridge by 123, 125
Borrow, George 22, 56, 349-53
Borrow, Mary, correspondence with her husband 350
Boswell, James, Macaulay on 268, 269
Botticelli, Sandro, Pater on 243
Bossuet, Jacques, Newman compared to 301
Bowles, William L. 7
Bowring, John, Borrow's attack upon 351
Bradley, F.H., Mill compared to 191
Brazil, Burton on 354
Brick, William, correspondence with Landor 181
BRITISH COMIC (periodical) 361-62
BRITISH QUARTERLY REVIEW 55
Brougham, Henry, Bagehot on 65
Brown, Bishop, charges Newman with heresy 299

Browne, Thomas, Lamb and 175
Browning, Robert 184
Carlyle and 90, 105
influence on T.S. Eliot 84
Mill's influence on 197, 198
Ruskin and 246, 249, 251
Brownson, Orestes Augustus
Newman's influence on 298
Spencer's influence on 344
Bunyan, John, Froude on 261
Buonaparte, Napoleon, Hazlitt's biography of 154, 157. See also Napoleonic Wars
Burke, Edmund 149
Bentham compared to 76
Butler compared to 86
influence on Coleridge 132
influence on Godwin 151
Mill compared to 193
Burkhardt, Jacob, Macaulay compared to 267
Burne-Jones, Edward Coley, Morris and 208-09, 214
Burton, Richard 354-57
Business, Ruskin on 256. See also Commerce; Industrialization
Butler, Samuel 4, 8, 15, 16, 19, 23, 32, 80-87, 238, 292, 326, 328, 329, 333
Byron, George Gordon 3, 8
Carlyle compared to 102
Hazlitt on 161
Hunt and 163, 165, 167, 168
Jeffrey and 278
reviews of 123, 364
Byzantium, the idea of in Morris' writing 212

C

Cabell, Joseph Carrington, relationship with Godwin 148
Caird, Edward, Darwin's influence on 331
Calvinism, of Carlyle 103
Cambridge critics 218
Cambridge University. Library, Darwin papers at 334
Carlyle, Alexander, correspondence with Thomas Carlyle 90

Subject Index

Carlyle, Jane Welsh 89, 90
Carlyle, Thomas 3, 4, 8, 9, 10,
  14, 16, 17, 18-19, 20, 21,
  22, 23, 24, 25, 26, 28,
  29, 30, 33, 47, 55, 58,
  60, 61, 88-107, 131, 164,
  188, 196, 198, 199, 251,
  253, 256, 261, 263, 269,
  270, 271, 277, 340, 366
Catholic Church
  Froude and 289
  Keble on 291, 292
  liberal movement in 359
  Newman and 294, 297, 305, 307,
    308, 309, 311, 313, 314
  reaction to Darwin's theories 330
  See also Modernism, of Newman
Catholic Emancipation Bill, Smith
  on 281
Catholic University (Dublin) 307
Celtic literature, Arnold on the study
  of 39, 44, 49-50
Censorship
  of Landor's writings 183
  in literary periodicals 363
  of Stevenson's writings 227
Chambers, Robert, Darwin and 326,
  327
Characterization
  in Lamb's writing 174, 176, 178
  in Newman's fiction 307
  in Pater's fiction 241
Chartism, Carlyle on 88
Chester, John 126
Children, Pater's idealization of 243
Christianity. See Religion
CHRISTIAN REFORMER (periodical)
  363
Church, Dean, Newman and 306
Church Missionary Society, Newman
  and 311
Church of England
  Arnold on 39
  Landor on 180
  Newman and 294, 297, 298,
    308, 314
  view of history possessed by 78
Cirne-Lima, Newman compared to
  309
Civil law. See Law

Civil liberty. See Liberty
Clarke, Samuel, Godwin and 152
Classical literature, Landor's
  knowledge of 183
Classicism, literary 29
  of Arnold 52, 57
  of Jeffrey 276
  of Macaulay 271
  of Pater 234, 239
Claude, Mary, Arnold's relationship
  with 43, 51
Clemenceau, Georges Eugene
  Benjamin, Mill's influence
  on 203
Clement, influence on Newman 299
Clough, Arthur Hugh 10, 24, 41,
  48, 51, 53, 60, 65, 93
Cobbett, William 2, 25, 31, 33,
  108-13, 158-59, 284, 366
Cole, Henry, relationship with Mill
  197
Coleridge, Samuel Taylor 7, 10,
  11, 12, 13, 14, 19, 22,
  24, 25, 27, 28, 31, 33,
  48, 52, 65, 77, 78, 114-38,
  143, 145, 147, 153, 158,
  168, 173, 175, 178, 181,
  191, 195, 199, 218, 276,
  293, 298, 301, 309, 326,
  361
Colonization, Froude on 261, 262.
  See also Imperialism
Colvin, Sidney, correspondence with
  Stevenson 223
Comedy
  Hazlitt on 154, 156, 161
  Lamb on Restoration 175
  See also Wit and humor
Commerce 29, 32. See also Business,
  Ruskin on; Industrialization
Communication
  Coleridge's theory of 136
  Ruskin's awareness of the arts in
    255
Comte, Auguste 27
  Mill and 186, 195, 199
  Spencer compared to 343
Conrad, Joseph
  Carlyle compared to 96-97
  influence on T.S. Eliot 84

Subject Index

Conscience, Newman on 310
Conservatism
  of Butler 86
  Coleridge on 28
  of De Quincey 143
  of Jeffrey 277
  of Newman 310, 313
  of Pater 243
  of Ruskin 253
  of Wilberforce 319
Constitutionalism 25
  Bagehot on 64, 66, 67, 68, 71
  Bentham on 73
  Coleridge on 114, 115, 119
Cooper, James Fenimore, Hazlitt on 160
Copyright. See Literary piracy
CORNHILL MAGAZINE
  Arnold and 60
  Stephen and 218
Cowper, William, Bagehot on 65
Crabbe, George
  Jeffrey on 277
  opium use by 13
Creativeness, of Coleridge 136. See also Imagination
Creighton, James Edwin, Darwin's influence on 325
Crime, in London 30
Criminal law. See Law
Croker, John Wilson, Macaulay's hatred of 267
Cromwell, Oliver, Carlyle as editor of his letters 102
Crystal Palace 25
Cudworth, Ralph, Godwin and 152
Cullen, Bishop, on Newman 314
Culture
  as a background for literary study 24-34
  in literature 8
  Mill on 189, 200
Customs. See Manners and customs

D

Dahrendorf, Spencer's influence on 344
Dana, Richard H., Darwin's influence on 331
Dante Alighieri
  nineteenth century revival of 7
  Pater's quotation of 241
Darwin, Charles 18, 19, 21, 83, 84, 87, 190, 234, 323-34, 336, 337, 339, 340, 341.
  See also Evolution; Social Darwinism
Darwin, Erasmus 323
  Coleridge's attitude toward 123
da Vinci, Leonardo, Pater on 243
Death
  De Quincey on 143
  Landor on 182
  Pater on 236, 240
Decadence in literature 14, 15
Defoe, Daniel, Lamb's reading of 177
Deism, of Borrow 350
Democracy 24, 33
  Bagehot on 69
  Carlyle and 97, 98
  Coleridge and 117
  English opposition to 29
  Mill on 189, 201, 203
  See also Liberty
De Quincey, Thomas 4, 10, 12, 13, 14, 20, 139-46, 161, 178, 197
Descartes, Rene, Coleridge's relation to 127
Determinism. See Free will and determinism
de Tocqueville, Alexis. See Tocqueville, Alexis de, influence on Mill
Dewey, John, Darwin's influence on 325
d'Holbach, Baron, influence on Godwin 153
Dialectic
  of Carlyle 98
  of Coleridge 133
  of De Quincey 145
  of Newman 303
  of Ruskin 250
Dialogue, in Borrow's writings 353
Dickens, Charles 8, 189

Subject Index

Arnold compared to 54
Bagehot on 65
Bentham's influence on 76
Carlyle and 94, 96, 97, 100, 104
correspondence with Jeffrey 278
De Quincey's influence on 143
influence on Smith 281
Mill compared to 188
periodical influence on 366
satirical attack of on Hunt 166
Diction
De Quincey on poetic 144
Mill's use of 192
Newman's use of 307
Pater's use of 236
Wordsworth-Coleridge controversy on 129
Didactic literature, Carlyle's writings as 104, 105
Dilke, Charles W., the ATHENAEUM and 363
Disraeli, Benjamin
Bagehot on 65
Coleridge's influence on 124
periodical influences on 366
Divine immanence. See Immanence of God, Arnold's rejection of
Divorce, Mill on 187
Dostoevsky, Feodor Mikhailovich, Newman compared to 312-13
Doughty, Charles, Burton compared to 356
Dowson, Ernest, the SAVOY and 367
Drama. See English drama, nineteenth century
Dreams
Coleridge's concern with 117, 125-26
De Quincey's use of 141, 143
Morris' use of 211-12
Dualism, Darwinism and 327
DuBos, Charles, Pater's influence on 239
Dumas, Alexandre, influence on Stevenson 227
Durkheim, Emile, Spencer's influence on 344
Duty, concept of 19

E

Economics
background material on 7, 20, 30
influence on censorship practices 363
major writers on
Bagehot 64, 65, 66, 67, 69
Bentham 73, 74, 77, 78, 79
Cobbett 108
Mill 186, 187, 193, 201, 202
Morris 209
Ruskin 245, 248, 250, 255, 257
Edgeworth, Maria, Ruskin compared to 251
EDINBURGH EVENING POST, De Quincey's contributions to 140
EDINBURGH MAGAZINE, Hazlitt's contributions to 158
EDINBURGH REVIEW 360, 361, 364, 367
Carlyle's contributions to 269, 277
Cobbett's relationship with 111, 158-59
Hazlitt's contributions to 157
Jeffrey and 275, 276, 277, 278
Macaulay's contributions to 264, 268-69, 270
Smith's contributions to 279, 281, 282
EDINBURGH SATURDAY POST, De Quincey's contributions to 140
Edinburgh University, influence on Carlyle 93
Educational thought
background material on 16, 25, 28, 32, 33
Darwin's influence on 331
major writers on 9
Arnold 39, 40, 42, 44, 46, 58, 60, 63
Bentham 75, 77
Butler 83
Carlyle 99, 196

418

Subject Index

Cobbett 111
Coleridge 120, 122, 133, 134
Godwin 147, 151
Huxley 337, 339, 340
Macaulay 264, 266, 270-71
Mill 99, 196, 202, 254
Newman 294, 299, 302, 303, 305, 307, 309, 311, 312
Ruskin 254
Smith 281, 282
Spencer 342
See also Public schools in literature
Eliot, George, Stephen on 217
Eliot, T.S. 45
  Arnold compared to 51, 53, 310
  Butler's influence on 84
  Coleridge compared to 120
  Mill compared to 199
  Newman's influence on 310
  Pater and 84, 236-37, 239
Elitism
  of Mill 194
  of Newman 302
Emerson, Ralph Waldo
  Arnold on 40
  Carlyle and 89, 91, 92, 95-96, 105
  style of 102
Emotionalist trend in literature, De Quincey and 145
Emotions, in Ruskin's idea of art 253
Empiricism
  of De Quincey 145, 152
  of Mill 198
  of Newman 302, 313
  See also Realism
ENCYCLOPAEDIA BRITANNICA, Macaulay's contributions to 264
Engels, Friedrich 29-30
English drama, nineteenth century 7
  criticism of 127, 154, 175
  Romanticism in 13
English fiction, nineteenth century 29
  criticism of 165
  De Quincey's conception of 144, 151
  development of criteria for writing 71
  historical accuracy and 210

psychoanalytic 86
theory of 77
English literature, nineteenth century
  basic surveys and reference works 1-12
  cultural backgrounds of 24-34
  influence on the tastes of the period 14
  literary backgrounds of 13-24
  relationship to poetry 22
  See also names of nineteenth century writers
English periodicals, nineteenth century 18, 33
  acceptance of evolution in 326
  bibliography 5
  cataloging of the information in 219
  development of 11
  guides to and studies of 359-67
English poetry, nineteenth century 12
  bibliography 2-3, 4
  criticism of 47, 49, 50, 141, 154
  Darwin's influence on 332
  influence on philosophy 203
  relationship to prose 22
  theory of 51, 53, 56, 62, 125, 127, 131, 134, 203, 214
Enlightenment, influence on Romanticism 21
Epicureanism
  of Arnold 43
  of Pater 241
Epistomology, of Godwin 153
Erasmus, Desiderius, Froude on 262
Escapism
  in Lamb's writing 176
  in Macaulay's history 268
  in Morris' poetry 212-13
Ethics. See Morality and ethics
Eucharist. See Lord's Supper
Evangelicalism 24, 29
  Newman and 290, 311, 313
  Pusey and 317, 318
  of Wilberforce 319
Evil. See Good and evil
Evolution 325, 326, 327, 329, 330, 332, 333, 334
  Butler on 80, 82, 83, 84, 85, 86, 87

Subject Index

in fiction 328
in the FORTNIGHTLY REVIEW 361
Huxley on 335, 338, 339, 340
relationship to theology 28
Spencer on 342, 343, 344
See also Darwin, Charles; Social Darwinism
EXAMINER (periodical)
Hunt's contributions to 164, 165, 168, 169
Landor's contributions to 181
Mill's contributions to 192
Existentialism, of Coleridge 117

F

Faith. See Belief and doubt, Newman's treatment of
Fame, Landor on 182
Family, Cobbett's concern for 110
Feurback, Ludwig 27
Fichte, Johann Gottlieb 240
influence on Coleridge 133
Fiction. See English fiction, nineteenth century
Fielding, Henry
Hazlitt on 160
Lamb as a reader of 177
Fine arts. See Art
Flaubert, Gustave, influence on Stevenson 227
Fleay, F.G., correspondence with Butler 87
Formalism
Arnold on 48
of Coleridge 137
Forman, Harry Buxton, Morris and 208
Form in art 211
Form in literature 94, 130
Forster, E.M.
Butler's influence on 86
Newman compared to 303
Forster, John, relationship with Hunt 165
FORTNIGHTLY REVIEW 361
Foscolo, Ugo, correspondence with Jeffrey 275
Fox, William Johnson
editorship of the MONTHLY REVIEW 363
influence on Mill 201

Fra Angelico. See Angelico, Giovanni (Fra)
France
Arnold on 51
influence on Mill 197
influence on Stevenson 227
Franchise
Harriet Taylor Mill on 187
John Stuart Mill on 189, 195, 202
FRASER'S MAGAZINE 366
Froude's editorship of 263
Frazer, James George 18
Frederick the Great, Carlyle on 88, 100
Freedom. See Liberty
Free thought 22
Stephen on 216, 217
See also Agnosticism
Free will and determinism
Carlyle and 103
Coleridge and 125
French Revolution
Carlyle on 88, 95, 96, 97, 98, 103, 104, 191
Coleridge on 116
Godwin and 149
Hazlitt on 156
influence on England 29
Mill on 95, 191
Freud, Sigmund 18, 196
Coleridge and 126, 128
Huxley compared to 340
Froude, James Anthony 9, 10, 22, 24, 28, 93, 95, 261-63, 269, 305
Froude, Richard Hurrell 26, 28, 289-90, 292
Froude, William, Newman's relations with 290, 296
Fry, Roger 17
art criticism of 250
Frye, Northrop 53

G

Gardens, as symbols in Ruskin's writings 250
Gautier, Theophile, Pater and 235, 241

Subject Index

Gentry. See Aristocracy
George IV, Cobbett on 108
Gerard, Alexander, influence on Jeffrey 277
Germany
  Arnold's response to 61
  influence on Carlyle 93, 96, 100, 101, 104, 105, 106
  influence on Coleridge 121, 128
Gibbon, Edward
  Bagehot on 65
  Macaulay compared to 267
Gibson, George Stacey, correspondence with Arnold 42
Gide, Andre, Pater's influence on 239
Gifford, William, QUARTERLY REVIEW under 365
Giotto de Bondone, Ruskin on 245
Gissing, George, Morris compared to 209-10
Gladstone, William Ewart
  Bagehot on 65
  on Newman 305
God. See Immanence of God, Arnold's rejection of; Religion
Godwin, William 2, 22, 28, 33, 135, 147-53, 360
Goethe, Johann Wolfgang
  Arnold and 42, 43, 54, 55, 58, 61-62
  Borrow's translation of 352
  Carlyle and 89, 96, 99
Goldsmith, Oliver, Lamb's reading of 177
Good and evil
  Coleridge on 132
  Stevenson on 226
Gothic
  elements of in Coleridge 119
  fiction 144
  Ruskin's interest in the 251, 252, 254, 256
Government. See Politics and government
Gray, Asa, influence on Darwin 333
Gray, Effie, correspondence with Ruskin 246-47
Gray family, Ruskin's relations with 253
Grotesque in literature, Carlyle's use of 96
Grub Street writers 17
Guilt, as a theme in De Quincey's writings 143
Gypsies, Borrow on 349, 351

H

Hagiography. See Saints, Newman's writings on
Halévy, Elie, on Spencer 345
Hallahan, Margaret Mary, correspondence with Newman 303
Hallam, Henry, correspondence with Macaulay 265
Hamilton, William, Mill on 186, 194
Happiness
  Godwin on 147
  Mill on 203
Hardenberg, Friedrich von
  Coleridge compared to 121
  influence on Carlyle 96
Harding, J.D., influence on Ruskin 252
Hardy, Thomas 8, 17
  Darwin's influence on 329, 333
Harrison, Frederic
  Arnold on 60
  attack of on Huxley 339
  relationship with Spencer 343
Hartley, David 123
  Godwin as a disciple of 149
Hawkesworth, John, Coleridge compared to 125
Hawthorne, Nathaniel, Coleridge's influence on 121
Haydon, Benjamin
  Borrow on 351
  Keats's attitude toward 159
Hazlitt, William 4, 9, 10, 12, 14, 48, 78, 111, 126, 145, 154-62, 170, 178, 257, 360, 361
Heathorn, Henrietta, correspondence with Huxley 341
Heaton, Ellen, correspondence with Ruskin 247

Subject Index

Hedonism
  of Mill 196, 203
  of Pater 239
Hegel, George Wilhelm Friedrich
  influence on Pater 242
  Mill compared to 191
Heine, Heinrich 239
  Arnold on 39, 62
Helvetius, Claude Adrien, Godwin compared to 152, 153
Henley, William Ernest 224
Herder, Johann Gottfried von, influence on Carlyle 103
Heresy, Newman charged with 299
Heroes and hero worship
  Carlyle on 88, 91, 93, 94, 95, 98
  in Pater's writings 236, 238, 241
Hickson, William, editorship of the WESTMINSTER REVIEW 366
History
  influence on Bentham 78
  major writers of 11, 14, 16, 17, 259-72
    Arnold 42, 54, 55, 59
    Bagehot 65
    Carlyle 83, 95, 100, 103, 105-06, 271
    Cobbett 110, 111
    Coleridge 118, 119
    Froude 261-63
    Godwin 147
    Macaulay 264-72
    Newman 297-98, 300, 302, 304, 305, 309, 311
    Pater 59, 242
    Stephen 218
  relationship to literature 7, 14, 18, 20
  See also names of historical events (e.g. French Revolution)
Hobbes, Thomas, Godwin compared to 152
Hodge, Charles, Spencer's influence on 344
Hodgskin, Thomas, influence on Spencer 345
Hofmannsthal, Hugo von, Pater's influence on 238

Hogg, James, Wilson on 284
Holcroft, Thomas, relationship with Godwin 152
Holism 57
Homer
  Arnold on translating 39
  Butler's version of 85
  Macaulay's similarity to 268
Hooker, Richard 255
Hopkins, Gerard Manley 14
  Newman and 303, 313
  Pater compared to 237, 240-41
Horace, Landor on 184
Horne, Richard 158
Hugel, Friedrich von, influence on Newman 312
Humanism 18, 20, 22, 29, 33
  of Arnold 43, 45, 50, 51, 56, 57, 237
  of Coleridge 119
  of Jeffrey 277
  of Mill 43
  of Newman 306, 308
  of Pater 236, 237
Humanitarianism, of Coleridge 131
Humboldt, Wilhelm von, Arnold compared to 57
Hume, David 77
  Huxley on 335
  influence on Carlyle 95
  influence on Coleridge 133
  influence on Darwin 329
  influence on Jeffrey 277
  influence on Shelley 150
Humor. See Comedy; Wit and humor
Hunt, Leigh 3, 4, 7, 10, 12, 14, 158, 163-70, 251, 256, 276, 366
Hunt, Robert 165
Hunt, Thornton 169
Huntington Library, San Marino, Calif.
  Coleridge collection of 137, 138
  Lamb collection of 179
Hutchinson sisters, relationships with Coleridge 124, 126
Huxley, Thomas Henry 15, 22, 24, 30, 33, 41, 45, 326, 329, 330, 333, 335-41
Hyperbole, in Huxley's writings 338

Subject Index

I

Ibsen, Henrik, Darwin's influence on 333
Iceland, Burton on 354
Idealism 18
  of Arnold 53
  of Coleridge 124, 128, 131, 132
  Darwin's influence on 325, 333
  in historical interpretation 78
  of Hunt 167
  of Landor 184
  of Mill 194
  of Pater 236, 241, 243
  of Ruskin 250, 253
Illusion, Lamb's theory of dramatic 174
Imagery
  Carlyle's use of 105
  Lamb's use of 177
  Mill's use of 189, 196
  Morris' use of 213
  Ruskin's use of 248, 251
Imagination 18, 23
  Carlyle's use of 92
  Coleridge's theory and use of 116, 117, 118, 119, 121, 123, 124, 125, 126, 127, 129-30, 131, 133, 137
  De Quincey's capacity for 143
  Froude's use of 263
  Hazlitt's theory and use of 156, 157, 160
  Hunt's theory and use of 163, 166, 169
  Lamb's use of 173, 176
  Macaulay's theory and use of 266, 267, 270, 271
  Mill's use of 195-96
  Newman's theory and use of 301, 307, 309, 311
  Ruskin's theory of 249, 250
Immanence of God, Arnold's rejection of 61
Immortality, Landor on 183
Imperialism
  of Mill 201
  newspaper support of 360
  See also Colonization, Froude on
Impressionism, in Pater's criticism 234, 236, 237, 239, 240

India
  Macaulay on 264, 266, 270-71
  Wilberforce on 318
Industrialization 24-25, 27, 30, 31, 33
  influence on art 208
  literature and 10, 18, 29
  See also Business, Ruskin on; Commerce; Technology
Ingersoll, Robert G. 340
Inspiration, Newman on 305
Intellectual life and thought
  background material on 7, 15, 18, 31
  bibliography 1
Intuition, Coleridge on 133
Irish Question
  Froude on 261
  Macaulay on 269
  Mill on 201
Irony
  of Butler 84
  of Lamb 176
  See also Satire
Irving, Edward, Carlyle and 93
Italian literature, Hunt's appreciation of 169
Italian Question, Arnold on 39
Italy
  importance of in Landor's development 182
  Ruskin in 250

J

James, David, reaction to Arnold's theories 49
James, Henry, correspondence with Stevens 222
James, William, Darwin's influence on 331
Jeffrey, Francis 10, 22, 23, 72, 92, 96, 102, 158, <u>275-78</u>, 284, 285
Jerrold, Douglas, satirical attack upon Hazlitt by 158
Johnson, Samuel
  friendship with Bentham 76
  influence on Newman 301

Subject Index

literary style of 157
Macaulay on 267, 268
Johnson, Lionel 15
Johnson, Samuel, Stephen on 216
Journalistic writings 273-85, 359, 360
  of Arnold 59
  of Cobbett 111
  of Hazlitt 157
  of Hunt 163, 167, 168
  of Jeffrey 275-78
  of Smith 279-82
  in support of imperialism 360
  of Wilson 283-85
Joyce, James, Butler's influence on 85
Justice, Smith on 281
Justification, Newman on 294

K

Kant, Immanuel 19
  Coleridge and 118, 122, 124, 127, 128, 129, 132, 133, 135
  influence on Carlyle 96
  Mill compared to 191
Keats, John 3, 7, 126
  Arnold on 51
  Hazlitt and 157, 159, 161
  Jeffrey on 278
  Morris' interest in 209, 213
  Newman compared to 298
  relationship with Hunt 166, 169
  reviews of 123, 364
Keble, John 7, 8, 25, 26, 28, 289, 290, 291-93, 296
Kelmscott Press 213
Kendall, Willmoore, on Mill 192
Keynes, John Maynard, Butler's influence on 86
Kidd, Benjamin, Darwin's influence on 333
Kierkegaard, Soren Aabye, Carlyle compared to 106
Kingsley, Charles 14
  Huxley and 337-38
  Newman and 295, 306, 310
  periodical influence on 366
Kipling, Rudyard, Carlyle and 102

Kuhn, Spencer's influence on 344

L

Labor and laboring classes 27, 28, 30, 31, 32
  Cobbett as a supporter of 108, 110, 111, 112
  in London 25, 30
  Ruskin on 245
  See also Luddites
Lamarck, Jean Baptiste
  impact on Marxism 330
  relationship to Darwin 327
Lamb, Charles 4, 10, 12, 14, 145, 150, 155, 161, 165, 167, 171-79, 233, 360, 361
Lamb, Mary 171, 172, 173
Landor, Walter Savage 4, 10, 12, 23, 180-85
Language
  Coleridge's use of 131
  Hazlitt's use of 158, 161-62
  Jeffrey's use of 277
  Landor's use of 183
  Newman's use of 307
  Pater's use of 241
  Wilberforce's use of 318
  See also Dialogue, in Borrow's writings; Diction; Metaphor; Narrative technique; Rhetoric; Style, literary; Syntax
LaTouche, Rose, correspondence with Ruskin 248, 253
Law
  background material on 25, 26, 32, 33
  Bentham on 73, 77, 78
  Macaulay on 266
Lawrence, D.H.
  Carlyle compared to 91
  Ruskin's influence on 256
Leavis, F.R. 45, 209
Leeds, Engl. 25
Leibniz, Gottfried Wilhelm von, Coleridge's relation to 127
Libel and slander
  Hunt's trial for 167
  Newman's trial for 299

Subject Index

LIBERAL (periodical) 165, 167, 168
Liberalism
  of Arnold 43, 61
  of the Catholic Church 359
  of Coleridge 131
  of Godwin 150
  of Macaulay 265
  of Mill 43, 191, 192, 193, 194, 202, 203
  of Newman 306, 310, 314
Liberty
  Carlyle's opposition to 96
  Cobbett's concern with 110
  Mill on 186, 190, 191, 192, 193, 195, 196, 197, 198, 199, 200, 203
  See also Democracy
Linguistic theory, Coleridge as an antecedent to 136
Literary piracy
  of Arnold's works 58
  of Hunt's works 167
Literature, English. See English literature, nineteenth century
Locke, John, Godwin as a disciple of 149, 153
Lockhart, John Gibson
  Carlyle as a reviewer of 101
  QUARTERLY REVIEW and 362
Logic
  Coleridge on 128, 133
  Mill on 144, 186, 189, 190, 194, 195, 198, 199, 200, 202, 203
  See also Dialectic
London 25
  life and labor in 25, 30
LONDON MAGAZINE 360
  De Quincey and 141-42
  Lamb's contributions to 171
  Scott and 367
London TIMES. See TIMES (London), Arnold on
Lord's Supper, Keble on 291
Louisa (Marchioness of Waterford), correspondence with Ruskin 247
Love, Landor on 182
Loyalty, Mill on 202
Luddites 27

Lyell, Charles, influence on Darwin 333
Lyricism, in Stevenson's essays 226, 228

M

Macaulay, Thomas Babington 3, 8, 9, 10, 17, 18-19, 24, 65, 100, 101, <u>264-72</u>
McCormac, Henry, correspondence with Carlyle 90
McCosh, James
  Darwin's influence on 331
  Spencer's influence on 344
MacDonald, George, Arnold compared to 56
MacKenzie, Henry, influence on Jeffrey 277
Mallock, William Hurrell 243
Malraux, Andre, Pater compared to 244
Malthus, Thomas Robert
  Bagehot on 65
  Cobbett's denunciation of 110-11, 112
  Godwin on 147, 148, 152
  influence on Darwin 332
  See also Neo-Malthusianism, Mill and
Manchester, Engl. 25
Mann, Thomas, Pater compared to 236
Manners and customs 32
  Godwin on 147
  Hazlitt on 154
Manning, Henry Edward 16
  Newman and 306, 310
  Wilberforce and 319
Mansel, Henry, Darwin's influence on 331
"Marguerite." See Claude, Mary, Arnold's relationship with
Marguerite (Countess of Blessington), correspondence with Landor 181
Marriage, Mill on 187
Marx, Karl 18
  Carlyle compared to 98
  Darwin and 325

425

Subject Index

Morris compared to 211, 214
Spencer's influence on 344
Marxism, Lamarckianism in 330
Marxist literary criticism
  of Arnold's prose 53
  of Pater's social writings 244
Masochism in literature. See
  Sadomasochism in literature
Materialism
  Carlyle as a crusader against 101
  of Coleridge 131
  of Huxley 336
  Stephen on 216
Maurice, F.D. 31, 131
  Newman compared to 301, 309
  Stephen's attitude toward 218
Mead, George Herbert, influence of
  Darwin on 325
Medicine
  Coleridge's knowledge of 122
  Darwin's influence on 332
Medieval ideals
  in Morris' world view 211, 212
  in nineteenth century literature 15
Melville, Herman, Lamb's influence
  on 174, 176
Memory, as a theme in De Quincey's
  writings 143
Metaphor 17
  Butler's use of 84
  Carlyle's use of 97
  Coleridge's use of 121
  Darwin's use of 334
  Mill's use of 189, 196, 200
  Morris' use of 211
  Newman's use of 301, 308
  Pater's use of 242
  Ruskin's use of 250
Metaphysics
  of Coleridge 117, 118, 124,
    125, 132
  Darwin's impact on 330
  of Mill 191, 195
  of Morris 211
  of Ruskin 251
  of Spencer 343
Middle class 9
  education for 42
  secularism of 16
Mill, Harriet Taylor 187, 188, 197,
  198, 199, 200
Mill, James 196, 200
  Bentham's influence on 78
Mill, John Stuart 3, 8, 9, 10,
  15, 16, 17, 19, 20, 22,
  25, 28, 30, 31, 33, 42,
  50, 56, 69, 75, 77, 78,
  79, 90, 91, 95, 99, 100,
  101, 144, 160, 186-204,
  211, 341, 366
Millais, John Everett, Ruskin and
  247, 251, 253
Milton, John
  Bagehot on 65
  Coleridge on 123, 125, 126
Modernism, of Newman 305, 309
Monarchy
  Bagehot's defense of 71
  Morris on 212
Monetary reform, Bagehot on 64
Montagu, Basil, correspondence with
  Lamb 172
Montaigne, Michel Eyquem, influence
  on Stevenson 227
Montesquieu, Charles Louis
  Godwin's debt to 151
  Mill compared to 193
MONTHLY REPOSITORY (periodical)
  363
Morality and ethics
  of Arnold 50, 58, 60
  of Bentham 73, 75
  of Borrow 352
  of Carlyle 94, 95, 101, 104,
    105
  of Coleridge 132, 133
  Darwinism and 325
  of Godwin 151
  of Hazlitt 159, 161
  of Huxley 335, 339, 340
  of Mill 187, 190, 191, 194,
    195, 197, 198, 199, 200,
    203
  of Morris 207, 209
  of Pater 236, 238, 240, 242,
    243
  of Ruskin 252, 256, 257
  of Smith 279
  of Spencer 342
  of Stephen 216, 217, 219

Subject Index

of Stevenson 226, 227, 228
of Wilberforce 319
Morgan, C. Lloyd, Darwin's
   influence on 331
Morley, John 24
Morris, William 3, 8, 16, 17,
   18, 19, 22, 23, 30, 33,
   205-15, 243
Mothers, Pater's idealization of 243
Mount-Temple (Lord and Lady),
   correspondence with Ruskin
   247
Moxon, William, correspondence
   with Hunt 167
Music
   Hunt's appreciation and criticism
      of 165, 166
   Mill's interest in 192
   Pater on 242
Mysticism
   of Coleridge 118, 123
   of De Quincey 139, 145
   language of 7
Myth in literature 18, 23
   Coleridge and 116, 121, 127
   De Quincey and 146
   Pater and 238, 240, 242

N

Napoleonic Wars 26
   De Quincey on 143
   See also Buonaparte, Napoleon,
      Hazlitt's biography of
Narrative technique
   of Borrow 352
   of Butler 85
   of Macaulay 268, 269
NATIONAL REVIEW, Bagehot as a
   reviewer for 70
Naturalism
   of Arnold 45, 53
   of Carlyle 105
   of Godwin 153
   of Mill 194
   of Ruskin 256
Nature 17, 23, 33
   Coleridge's conception of 123
   Darwin's influence on poetry of
      332

Hazlitt on 156, 159
Huxley's conception of 341
Mill on 254
Ruskin on 254
Necessity, doctrine of 150
Negro question. See Racial theories
   and problems
Neo-Malthusianism, Mill and 197
Newman, F.W. 24, 310
Newman, John Henry 3, 7, 8, 9,
   10, 16, 17, 18-19, 23,
   24, 25, 27, 28, 30, 31,
   33, 45, 48, 58, 124, 125,
   237, 289, 290, 292, 294-
   315, 359
Newspapers. See English periodicals,
   nineteenth century; Journalistic
   writings
Nietzsche, Friedrich Wilhelm,
   Carlyle compared to 91, 98
Nihilism
   Morris' borrowings from 211
   of Spencer 344
Nobility. See Aristocracy
Nominalism, of Darwin 325
Nonconformity 25, 61
   of Hazlitt 156
North, Christopher. See Wilson,
   John
Norton, Charles Eliot, the Froude-
   Carlyle controversy and 263
Novalis. See Hardenberg, Friedrich
   von

O

Objectism, as a stage in Romanticism
   21
Old Norse literature, influence on
   Morris 213
Opium
   Coleridge's use of 123, 128
   De Quincey's use of 141, 143
   effect upon writers 13
Order, Carlyle's concern with 93
Organicism
   Coleridge's views of 128, 133
   of Ruskin 257
Oriel Fellowship, Newman and the
   311

Subject Index

Origen, influence on Newman 299
OXFORD AND CAMBRIDGE
  MAGAZINE, Morris and 210
Oxford Movement 3, 7, 8, 13, 16,
  26, 27-28, 29, 289, 290,
  292, 298, 302, 314, 317
  periodical press and 361-62, 364
Oxford University
  Arnold and 48, 53
  Morris and 212
  Newman and 297, 306, 308
  Pater and 240

P

PALL MALL GAZETTE 365
  Arnold and 41
Pantheism, Coleridge and the
  tradition of 127, 129
Parliament
  Bagehot on 64, 65
  Cobbett on 109, 110
  Mill on 186
Pater, Walter Horatio 3, 8, 9, 11,
  15, 16, 17, 18, 19, 22,
  23, 24, 48, 49, 51, 59,
  84, 157, 175, 233-44, 303,
  324
Pathetic fallacy 254, 255
Payne, controversy with Burton 355
Peacock, Thomas Love
  Godwin's influence on 149
  Hazlitt compared to 159
  Hunt compared to 167-68
  irony of 84
Peel, Robert, Bagehot on 65
Penology, Bentham on 73, 78
Perfection, Arnold on 43
Periodicals, English. See English
  periodicals, nineteenth century;
  names of periodicals
Personification, in Huxley's writings
  338
Pessimism in literature 15, 18
Philosophy 11
  Darwin's impact on 324, 325,
    326, 327, 328, 331
  history of 30, 31
  influence of poetry on 203

of major writers
  Arnold 42, 63
  Bentham 202
  Butler 85, 86
  Carlyle 91, 94, 98, 99, 101,
    104, 105-06
  Coleridge 115, 117, 118, 119,
    122, 124, 128, 130, 131,
    132-33, 134, 135, 138
  Darwin 325, 328
  De Quincey 144
  Godwin 150
  Hazlitt 159, 160, 161
  Huxley 338
  Jeffrey 276-77
  Landor 181
  Mill 189, 190, 193, 194, 195,
    200, 202
  Morris 210
  Newman 295, 313, 314
  Pater 240, 244
  Smith 279, 280
  Spencer 342, 343, 344, 345
  Stevenson 277
  relationship to literature 4
  of Romantic literature 23
  See also Empiricism; Holism;
    Materialism; Metaphysics;
    Morality and ethics; Plato and
    Platonism; Pragmatism, Darwin's
    influence on; Rationalism;
    Realism; Relativism; Utilitarian-
    ism
Pictet, Marc Auguste, influence on
  Carlyle 92, 96
Picturesque
  Mill's interest in the 196-97
  in Morris' writings 209
Pindar, Landor's knowledge of 183
Piracy, literary. See Literary piracy
Pitt, William, Bagehot on 65
Plagiarism, of Smith 281
Plato and Platonism
  Coleridge and 119, 124, 127,
    129, 137
  Godwin and 152
  Jeffrey and 277
  Newman and 300, 304
  Pater on 233, 234, 242
  Ruskin and 257

Subject Index

Pleasure, Coleridge's use of the word and concept of 122, 123
Plot, in Pater's fiction 236
Plotinus, Coleridge's relation to 127
Poe, Edgar Allan, Wilson's influence on 284
Poetry. See English poetry, nineteenth century; names of poets (e.g. Matthew Arnold)
Politics and government
  background material on 8, 20, 25, 27, 28, 30, 31, 32, 34
  influence on censorship practices 363
  in the LONDON MAGAZINE 360, 367
  major writers on
    Arnold 39, 42, 61
    Bagehot 64, 65, 66, 67, 68, 69, 70
    Bentham 73, 74, 77, 78, 79, 202
    Carlyle 91, 93-94
    Cobbett 108, 109, 111
    Coleridge 115, 119, 120, 122
    De Quincey 145
    Godwin 147, 148, 149, 150, 151, 152, 153
    Hazlitt 154, 156
    Hunt 164, 165, 168, 169
    Landor 181, 182
    Macaulay 265, 266, 267, 271, 272
    Mill 186, 187, 188, 191, 193, 194, 195, 196, 197, 199, 200, 201, 202
    Morris 206, 211, 213, 214
    Newman 307, 310
    Ruskin 245, 248, 257
    Smith 279, 281
    Spencer 342, 345
    Stevenson 226
  in the QUARTERLY REVIEW 361
  See also Authority; Constitutionalism; Democracy; Franchise; Parliament; Reform Act of 1867, Bagehot and Mill on; Representative government, Mill on; Republicanism, of Godwin;
Sovereignty, Bentham on; Utilitarianism
Poole, Tom 126
Pope, Alexander
  Arnold on 59
  Hunt on 163
  Stephen on 216
Pope controversy 7
Population, Godwin on 147, 148, 152
Pornography 30
Positivism
  in the FORTNIGHTLY REVIEW 361
  Mill on 186
  Spencer's conflict with 343
Poverty, in London 30
Powell, Thomas 166
Pragmatism, Darwin's influence on 326
Preaching, Newman on 314. See also Sermons
Pre-Raphaelite Brotherhood 31, 365
Pre-Raphaelites 3, 16-17, 18, 213, 235, 252
  bibliography 215
  Ruskin on 245
Press, politics and 25. See also English periodicals, nineteenth century; Journalistic writings; Kelmscott Press; Publishers and publishing
Princeton University. Library, Stevenson collections of 229
Printing, of Morris 213. See also Publishers and publishing
Progress 14, 26
Property, right of, Mill on 194
Prophecy, Newman on 310
Protestantism
  Arnold on 39
  Godwin's radical 153
  See also Calvinism, of Carlyle; Catholic Church; Church of England; Puritanism; Reformation, Froude on; Unitarianism
Proust, Marcel, Ruskin's influence on 248
Psychological interpretations of literature 17
  of Newman's writings 300

Subject Index

of Pater's writings 243, 251
of Stevenson's writings 227
using Lamb's letters 177
Psychological studies
  of Darwin 328
  of James and J.S. Mill 196
  of Ruskin 252, 256
Psychology
  Bentham on linguistic 77
  Coleridge's preoccupation with
    118, 122, 123, 124, 126,
    128
  De Quincey's literary expressions of
    theories of 145
  use of in Godwin's fiction 149
Public schools in literature 31. See
  also Educational thought
Publishers and publishing 359
  Morris and 213, 215
Pugin, Augustus Welby Northmore,
  influence on Ruskin 251, 256
Puritanism
  Arnold on 39
  Bagehot as representative of 67
  Carlyle's 97
Pusey, Edward Bouverie 7, 8, 25,
  26, 28, 311, 316-17

Q

QUARTERLY REVIEW 360, 361,
  362, 364, 365, 367

R

Racial theories and problems
  Arnold on 50
  Carlyle on 91, 92, 97, 104
  Coleridge on 129
  Mill on 91, 97
  Wilberforce on 318, 319
Radicalism
  Bentham's philosophic 76, 79
  of Carlyle 93, 101, 104
  of Cobbett 109, 110, 112
  Mill's philosophic 193
  press and 361
  See also Anarchy; Revolution and
    rebellion
RAMBLER (periodical) 359

Ransom, J.C., Newman compared to
  303
Rationalism 14, 25
  Carlyle and 105
  Coleridge and 132, 133
  Godwin and 152
  Mill and 191
  Stephen and 218
Read, Herbert, art criticism of 251
Realism
  of Bagehot 70
  of Mill 194
  See also Empiricism
Reality
  Arnold on 58
  Coleridge's inability to cope with
    116
  in De Quincey's writings 146
Reason
  Coleridge on 118, 126, 129
  Godwin on 150, 151
  Macaulay on 267, 270, 271
Rebellion. See Revolution and
  rebellion
Redwood, Charles, correspondence
  with Carlyle 89
REFLECTOR (periodical)
  Hunt's connection with 167, 169
  Lamb's connection with 167, 178
Reform Act of 1867, Bagehot and
  Mill on 69
Reformation, Froude on 289
Relativism
  Darwin's influence on 327
  of Pater 242
Religion
  background material on 15, 17,
    18, 20, 22, 24, 26, 27,
    28, 29, 30-31, 32, 33, 34
  bibliography 1, 3, 4, 5
  the function of art in · 58
  influence of Darwin on 324, 326-
    27, 328, 330, 331, 333
  influence on censorship practices
    363
  major writers on 9, 10, 11,
    287-319
  Arnold 39, 40, 42, 45, 46,
    50, 55, 56, 57, 58, 61,
    63, 219

Subject Index

Bagehot 66, 67, 71
Bentham 73, 79
Butler 80, 81, 83, 84, 86, 87
Carlyle 91, 93, 94, 97, 98, 101, 103, 104
Cobbett 111
Coleridge 114, 115, 116, 118, 119, 120, 122, 125, 129, 130, 131, 132
Froude, J.A. 263
Froude, R.H. 289-90
Keble 291-93
Landor 181
Macaulay 266
Mill 186, 187, 188, 190, 191, 193, 195, 196
Morris 210-11, 213
Newman 294-315
Pater 241
Pusey 316-17
Ruskin 254, 255, 256
Smith 281
Spencer 343, 344
Stephen 219
Stevenson 223
Wilberforce 318-19
See also Agnosticism; Atheism, of Butler; Belief and doubt, Newman's treatment of; Bible; Calvinism, of Carlyle; Catholic Church; Church of England; Deism, of Borrow; Evangelicalism; Immanence of God, Arnold's rejection of; Nonconformity; Oxford Movement; Pantheism, Coleridge and the tradition of; Protestantism; Puritanism; Reformation, Froude on; Revelation, Newman on; Ultramontanism, Newman on; Unitarianism
Renaissance
   Pater and 233, 236, 238, 239, 240, 241, 242-43
   Ruskin and 250, 251
Renan, Ernest
   Arnold compared to 42, 43-44, 47
   Bagehot compared to 72
   influence on Pater 242

Representative government, Mill on 186
Republicanism, of Godwin 153
Revelation, Newman on 298
Revolution and rebellion
   Coleridge on 132
   De Quincey on 142
   Mill on 188
   Morris on 206, 207, 210, 211
   See also French Revolution
Reynolds, Joshua, influence on Coleridge 126
Rhetoric
   Bentham's philosophic 75
   Carlyle's use of 101
   Darwin's use of 325, 332
   De Quincey's use of 142
   Hazlitt's use of 162
   Huxley's use of 337, 338, 339, 340
   Lamb's use of 176
   Macaulay's use of 271
   Mill's use of 196
   Newman's use of 299, 301, 302, 304, 308, 311
   Ruskin's use of 251
   use of during Hunt's trial 167
   See also Language; Metaphor; Style, literary
Rhone River, Ruskin's description of 251
Rhythm, in De Quincey's prose 144
Ricardo, David, Bagehot on 65
Richards, I.A. 53
Richardson, Samuel, Jeffrey on 275
Richter, Jean Paul Friedrich, influence on De Quincey 141
Robertson, William, influence on Carlyle 95
Rockefeller, John D., Darwin's influence on 333
Romanticism
   anthologies and histories 7, 8, 9, 10, 11
   bibliography 1, 2, 3, 4, 5, 146
   cultural background 28, 33
   literary background 13, 14, 16, 17, 18, 19, 20, 21, 23
   major writers and 361, 366

Subject Index

Arnold 50, 52, 56, 63
Carlyle 101, 104, 106
Coleridge 115-16, 118, 119, 121, 123, 125, 130, 132, 133
De Quincey 139, 141, 142, 143
Godwin 149
Hazlitt 157, 159
Hunt 166, 167, 168, 169
Jeffrey 276, 277, 278
Lamb 173, 175, 178
Macaulay 268, 271
Mill 191
Morris 209, 211, 214-15
Newman 298, 309
Pater 235, 239-40
Ruskin 252, 257
Stevenson 224, 226
Wilson 285
poetry of 3, 47
Rosenbach Foundation, Lamb collection of 179
Rossetti, Christina 305
Rossetti, Dante Gabriel 15, 208, 249
Morris and 212, 214
Ruskin and 251
Rousseau, Jean Jacques
influence on Godwin 153
Mill compared to 191
Royal Society of Literature, Coleridge in the 135
Rural life, Cobbett's descriptions of 108, 109, 110, 111, 112
Ruskin, John 3, 8, 9, 14, 16, 17, 18, 19, 21, 22, 23, 24, 29, 30, 31, 33, 43, 56, 89, 97, 99, 101, 104, 105, 162, 245-57, 262, 365
Ruskin, John (Mrs.) 247
Russell, G.W.E. 56
Russia, acceptance of Darwinism in 330

S

Sadomasochism in literature 21
Saint-Beuve, Charles Augustin
Darwin's influence on 329
relationship with Arnold 58
St. Paul, Arnold on 39
Saints, Newman's writings on 305
Saintsbury, George Edward Bateman, Pater's influence on 238
Saint-Simonianism
influence on Carlyle 93, 101, 103, 198
influence on Mill 101, 192, 195, 198, 199, 201
St. Thomas, Newman compared to 313
Sappho, Landor's knowledge of 183
Sartre, Jean Paul, Carlyle compared to 99
Satanic School, Landor and 184
Satire
Butler's use of 83, 85, 86
Carlyle's distrust of 93
Cobbett's use of 111
on Darwinism 328
Dickens' use of to attack Hunt 166
Jerrold's use of to attack Hazlitt 158
Smith's use of 281
See also Irony
SATURDAY REVIEW 360
hostility of toward Arnold 52
Ruskin reviewed in 252
Savage, Eliza
correspondence with Butler 81
relationship with Butler 82
SAVOY (periodical) 360, 366-67
Say, Jean-Baptiste, influence on Mill 193
Schelling, Friedrich Wilhelm Joseph von, influence on Coleridge 128, 132, 133
Scherer, Edmond, Arnold compared to 44
Schiller, Johann Christoph Friedrich von, influence on Carlyle 95, 96
Schlegel, A.W., influence on Coleridge 128
Scientific thought 8, 9, 16, 22, 29, 31, 32, 33
composite biography concerning 29
major writers on 321-45

Subject Index

Bagehot 71
Butler 83
Carlyle 105
Coleridge 118
Darwin 323-34
Huxley 335-41
Landor 181
Mill 190, 194
Newman 309
Ruskin 248
Spencer 342-45
See also Industrialization; Technology
Scientism, in Stephen's writings 219
Scott, Walter
  Bagehot on 65
  influence on Carlyle 95
  influence on Macaulay 271
Scott, John, LONDON MAGAZINE under 360, 367
Scott, William Bell 249
Secularism, Tractarian movement as a reaction to 16
Security, Pater's search for 243
Senghor, Leopold, Morris compared to 209
Sermons
  of Keble 291
  of Newman 294, 295, 298, 303, 304
  of Pusey 316, 317
  of Smith 279
  See also Preaching, Newman on
Severn, Arthur, on Ruskin in Italy 250
Sex
  Burton on 356
  Coleridge's attitudes toward 122
  Stevenson and 224
Shakespeare, William
  Arnold on 48
  Bagehot on 65
  Coleridge on 114, 117, 120, 121, 122, 125, 126, 132, 136
  De Quincey on 144
  Hazlitt on 154, 159
  Hunt on 166, 169
  Lamb on 173
  Wilson on 284

Sharp, F.J. 249
Shaw, George Bernard
  Morris' influence on 208
  the SAVOY and 367
Shelley, Mary, Godwin's relationship with 150
Shelley, Percy Bysshe 3
  Arnold on 47, 54
  Bagehot on 65
  Coleridge and 128, 131, 134
  Godwin and 148-49, 150, 151-52
  Hunt and 166, 167, 168, 169
  reviews of 123, 364
Simpson, Richard, Newman compared to 307
Sin, Newman on 298
Slavery. See Racial theories and problems
Smith, Adam, Bagehot on 65
Smith, Sydney 22, <u>279-82</u>, 284
Smollett, Tobias George
  Hazlitt on 160
  Lamb's reading of 177
Snow, C.P. 209
Social Darwinism 28, 325, 327, 328, 329, 331-32, 333
Socialism
  development of in Great Britain 25
  Mill on 194
  Morris and 205, 206, 207, 208, 209, 211, 212, 213, 214
Socialist League 206
Social science
  Mill's methodology in 195
  Ruskin's teachings about 248
Society and social thought 7, 8, 9, 10
  background material on 13, 15, 17, 18, 19, 22, 24, 26, 28, 29-30, 31, 32, 33
  bibliography 1, 4
  influence on censorship practices 363
  major writers on 366
    Arnold 39, 43, 45, 47, 50, 51, 52, 53, 54, 55, 60
    Bagehot 69, 71
    Carlyle 93-94, 101
    Cobbett 109, 110, 111, 112

Subject Index

Coleridge 119, 120
De Quincey 149
Hazlitt 157, 161
Hunt 165, 168
Huxley 338
Mill 69, 187, 191, 193-94, 199, 200, 201
Morris 209, 210, 212, 213
Pater 244
Ruskin 43, 249, 253, 254, 255, 256, 257
Smith 279, 281
Spencer 343, 344, 345
Stephen 216, 217
Stevenson 227
Wilberforce 319
Socrates, Mill's use of 194
Solomon, Simeon, Morris and 214
Southey, Robert
  correspondence with Landor 182
  Jeffrey's attack on 276
  relationship with Coleridge 116, 134
Sovereignty, Bentham on 77
Spain, Borrow on 349
Spanish Armada, Froude on 262
SPECTATOR (periodical) 178, 366
  Arnold's relations with 52
  Bagehot as a reviewer for 70
  Ruskin reviewed in 252
Spencer, Herbert 15, 22, 25
  Darwin's influence on 331
Spinoza, Baruch, Coleridge's relation to 127
Stachey, Lytton, Butler's influence on 86
Stamp duties, effect on newspaper publishing 361
Stanley, Arthur, relationship with Arnold 61
Steele, Richard, relationship with Hunt 169
Stephen, James 261
Stephen, Leslie 15, 23, 28, 33, 216-20, 365
Sterling, John, Carlyle and 88, 90, 102
Sterne, Laurence
  Bagehot on 65
  Hazlitt on 160

influence on Carlyle 105
Stevenson, Fanny 224, 225, 227
Stevenson, Robert Louis 3, 4, 22, 217, 221-29
Stoicism, of Arnold 43
Strauss, David Friedrich 27
Style, literary 11, 19-20, 23
  Arnold's 54, 55, 60
  Carlyle's 92, 94, 96, 98, 101, 102, 105, 106
  Cobbett's 111
  Coleridge's 129, 134
  Darwin's 332
  Hazlitt's 157, 162, 236
  Huxley's 338
  Jeffrey's 276
  Lamb's 175
  Landor's 182
  Macaulay's 266, 267, 268, 269
  Mill's 191, 196, 200
  Newman's 300, 301, 304, 307, 309, 312
  Pater's 233, 235-36, 237, 238, 239, 241
  Ruskin's 250, 254-55
  Smith's 280
  Stevenson's 223, 225, 226
  See also Dialogue, in Borrow's writings; Diction; Metaphor; Narrative technique; Symbolism
Stylism, as a stage in Romanticism 21
Subconscious, Coleridge's treatment of 128, 133
Sublime, The
  Coleridge's conception of 123, 132
  Hazlitt's definition of 157
Suffering in literature 21
  De Quincey's use of 143
Suffrage. See Franchise
Sumner, William G., Darwin's influence on 333
Super, Robert H. 51
Swedenborg, Emanuel
  Carlyle compared to 99
  Coleridge's relation to 127
Swift, Jonathan
  Arnold on 59
  Godwin compared to 152

Subject Index

Hunt on 163
influence on Carlyle 93, 105
Jeffrey on 275
Stephen on 216
Swinburne, Algernon Charles 208, 235
  Bagehot as a reviewer of 70
  Darwin's influence on 329
  Landor's influence on 183, 184
  literary relationship with Arnold 47, 54
  Macaulay's influence on 266
  Morris' influence on 215
Symbolism 13, 23
  Carlyle's use of 98, 99
  Coleridge's use of 118, 122, 129, 130, 136
  De Quincey's use of 139, 146
  Pater's use of 240
  Ruskin's use of 250
  Stevenson's use of 226, 227
Symons, Arthur, the SAVOY and 367
Syntax
  Lamb's use of 176
  Morris' use of 211
  Pater's use of 236

T

Taine, Hippolyte Adolphe, Darwin's influence on 329
Talbot, Fanny, correspondence with Ruskin 246
TATLER (periodical), Hunt's contributions to 164
Taylor, Harriet. See Mill, Harriet Taylor
Taylor, Henry 266
Taylor, John, correspondence with Godwin 152
Technology
  history of 31
  Morris on 214
  Victorian attitudes toward 22-23
  See also Industrialization; Scientific thought
Teleology, Darwinism and 327
Tennyson, Alfred
  Bagehot as a reviewer of 70, 71
  Carlyle and 102

Wilson on 284
Thackeray, William Makepeace
  Bagehot on 65
  FRASER'S MAGAZINE and 366
  irony in the writings of 84
  Macaulay compared to 267
  relationship with Carlyle 102
Theater
  bibliography of periodicals concerning 365
  Mill's interest in 192
  See also Actors
Theme 14, 16
  in Borrow's writings 353
  Carlyle's use of 105
  in Lamb's writings 173, 177, 178
  in Pater's writings 242-43
  similarity between De Quincey's and Dickens' 143
  in Stevenson's writings 226
  See also specific themes (e.g. Death; Fame; Love)
Thomas, . . . , relationship with Arnold 53
Thompson, Francis, opium use by 13
Thoreau, Henry David, style of 102
Thorton, Edward, correspondence with Cobbett 109
Time, concept of in literature 13, 14, 20
TIMES (London), Arnold on 61
Tocqueville, Alexis de, influence on Mill 193, 198, 199
Toleration
  Bagehot on 69
  Mill on 192
  Newman on 298
  Smith on 281
Tolstoy, Leo, Arnold's resemblance to 45
Tractarianism. See Oxford Movement
Tragedy
  Arnold's idea of 49
  Coleridge's idea of 132
  Hazlitt's preference for 156, 157
Transcendentalism
  Carlyle's relationship to American 105
  Darwinism and 333
  influence of on Coleridge 117, 137

Subject Index

as a stage in Romanticism 21
Travel literature 347-57
  background material on 33
  of Borrow 349-53
  of Burton 354-57
Trollope, Anthony 25
  Bagehot compared to 67
  racial ideas of 97
Truth
  Arnold on 58
  Coleridge on 153
  Godwin on 153
  Hazlitt on 161
  Lamb on 176
  Mill on 144
  Stephen on 219
Turner, John, Ruskin on 249
Tytler, John, correspondence with Macaulay 271

U

Ullathorne, William, on Newman 299
Ultramontanism, Newman on 299
Union of Soviet Socialist Republics. See Russia, acceptance of Darwinism in
Unitarianism 363-64
  of Coleridge 121
United States
  Arnold on 40, 56
  Burton on 354
  Carlyle's reputation in 92
  Cobbett in 108, 112, 113
  Huxley's reputation in 340
  impact of Darwinism on 328, 329, 331
  Lamb's reputation in 176-77
  Macaulay's reputation in 266
  Smith's reputation in 282
  Stevenson on 222
University College (London), Bentham manuscripts of 79
Utilitarianism 27
  of Bentham 74, 76, 77, 78, 79
  in the FORTNIGHTLY REVIEW 361
  of Hazlitt 78, 160
  journalism of 364
  of Macaulay 271
  of Mill 186, 188, 194, 196, 199, 200, 202, 203

Stephen on 216
Utopias, of Morris 208, 213

V

Values. See Morality and ethics
Veblen, Thorstein, Darwin's influence on 331
Vico, Giambattista
  Arnold's reliance upon 47
  Coleridge compared to 132, 135
Victorian literature. See English literature, nineteenth century; Romanticism
Virtue
  Godwin on 147
  Pater on 236
Vogeler, Martha S. 251
Voltaire, Francois Marie Arouet, influence on Newman 301
von Hardenberg, Friedrich. See Hardenberg, Friedrich von
von Herder, Johann Gottfried. See Herder, Johann Gottfried von, influence on Carlyle
von Hofmannsthal, Hugo. See Hofmannsthal, Hugo von, Pater's influence on
von Hugel, Friedrich. See Hugel, Friedrich von, influence on Newman
von Humboldt, Wilhelm. See Humboldt, Wilhelm von, Arnold compared to
von Leibniz, Gottfried Wilhelm. See Leibniz, Gottfried Wilhelm von, Coleridge's relation to
von Schelling, Friedrich Wilhelm Joseph. See Schelling, Friedrich Wilhelm Joseph von, influence on Coleridge

W

Wales, Borrow on 349, 352
Walpole, Robert, Macaulay on 268
War, Ruskin on 245. See also French Revoltuion; Napoleonic Wars
Webb, Beatrice 77

Subject Index

Weber, Max, Spencer's influence on 344
Welsh, Jane. See Carlyle, Jane Welsh
West Indies
  Froude on 262
  Wilberforce on 318
WESTMINSTER REVIEW 361, 364, 366
WESTMORELAND GAZETTE, De Quincey as editor of 145
Whewell, William, Mill compared to 190
White, William Hale, Froude compared to 263
Whitman, Walt, his opinion of Carlyle 97
Wilberforce, Robert 8
Wilberforce, Samuel, Darwinism and 337
Wilberforce, William 27, 317, 318-19
Wilde, Oscar 51, 239, 305
  Arnold's influence on 50
  irony in the writings of 84
  Newman's influence on 304
  Pater and 241, 242, 244
Wilson, Eliza, Bagehot's love letters to 66
Wilson, John 10, 22, 64, 276, 283-85
Winckelmann, Johann Joachim, Pater on 241, 243
Wiseman, Nicholas Patrick Stephen, Newman and 299, 310
Wit and humor
  of Butler 84
  of Carlyle 94-95, 104, 105
  of Lamb 174, 177
  of Smith 280
  of Wilson 284
  See also Comedy
Wollstonecraft, Mary, correspondence with Godwin 148
Women
  Mill on 186, 187, 189, 200, 202, 254
  Morris on 214
  in periodical literature 364
  Ruskin on 250, 254
  See also Mothers, Pater's idealization of
Woolf, Virginia and Leonard 218
  Butler's influence on 86
Wordsworth, William 12, 159, 184, 203, 237
  Arnold on 44, 48, 60, 219
  Bagehot on 65
  correspondence with Landor 181
  De Quincey and 140, 142, 143-44
  Godwin and 150
  Hazlitt and 156, 158, 161
  Hunt on 168
  influence on Keble 292, 293
  Jeffrey and 276, 277, 278
  Lamb and 177
  Newman and 298, 300, 309
  Pater and 48, 240
  politics of 145
  recent works on 136
  relationship with Coleridge 116, 119, 122, 123, 124, 125, 126, 127, 129, 133, 134
  reviews of 123
  Stephen on 219
  Wilson on 285

Y

Yeats, William Butler
  Morris compared to 209, 210, 212
  the SAVOY and 367
YELLOW BOOK 360